# HEAVEN ON EARTH

*Also by Michael D' Antonio*

Fall from Grace: the Failed Crusade
of the Christian Right

# HEAVEN ON EARTH

## MICHAEL D'ANTONIO

CROWN PUBLISHERS, INC.
NEW YORK

Published by Crown Publishers, Inc., 201 East 50th Street, New York, New York 10022. Member of the Crown Publishing Group.

CROWN is a trademark of Crown Publishers, Inc.

Manufactured in the United States of America

Book Design by Shari deMiskey

Library of Congress Cataloging-in-Publication Data

D'Antonio, Michael.
    Heaven on earth. dispatches from America's spiritual frontier / by Michael D'Antonio.—1st ed.
        1. New Age movement—United States. 2. United States—Religion—1960– 3. D'Antonio, Michael. I. Title.
    PB605.N48D36   1992
    299'.93—dc20                                                    91-24873
                                                                        CIP

ISBN 0-517-57802-6

10  9  8  7  6  5  4  3  2  1

First Edition

For Elizabeth and Amy

# Contents

# CONTENTS

# Acknowledgments

My wife, Toni, shared all of the labor
pains that accompanied the birth of
this book. And like my gifted editor,
David Groff, she has been a
continual source of encouragement,
wisdom, and invaluable criticism.
Both of them deserve substantial credit
for whatever is good in this book, but
none of the responsibility for its flaws.

# PROLOGUE

## Shaman of the Suburbs

THE FIRST FULL MOON OF SPRING, BRIGHT AND PERFECT, rose over Long Island and cast its pale light on a quiet subdivision of whirring sprinklers and razor-trim hedges. Neighborhood boys took advantage of the moonlight, extending the baseball game they played in the street past eight o'clock. If they could hear the sound of drums, emanating like a heartbeat from the little house on the corner, they didn't peek inside to see the three-foot flames in the fireplace or the shadows dancing on the living-room wall. Gathered in a standard, three-bedroom suburban home, eighteen adults were chanting for a new-moon ritual conducted by a shaman who had been trained by Peruvian Indians.

**Nichi tai tai**
**En You I**
**Ora nikka, ora nikka**
**Hey, hey**
**Hey, hey**
**Oh-oh, I**

1

Inside the house a petite thirty-year-old woman with short brown hair and wide dark eyes stood in front of a fireplace that was filled with flames. Dressed in a long blue sweater and dark wool leggings, she held a six-foot wooden staff, decorated with crudely carved figures of a woman, a cat, a snake, a jaguar, and the sun, moon, and stars. Tied around the staff was a huge rattle made of hundreds of llama-toe nails strung together like dusty gray arrowheads. She shook it in time with the chant. Behind her, polished quartz crystals, feathers, and several pieces of jewelry were piled on the hearth, to be used as offerings. On the floor in front of her, thirteen women and four men sat in a circle. Their eyes were closed and they joined in the chant, repeating it over and over until the smoke and the song made them hoarse. Several of them beat small drums. Others shook rattles made of hollow gourds.

**Nichi tai tai**
**En You I**
**Ora nikka, ora nikka**
**Hey, hey**
**Hey, hey**
**Oh-oh, I**

Earlier in the evening, shaman Irene Siegel had prayed, summoning various animal spirits: the serpent of the South, the jaguar of the West, the horse of the North, and the eagle of the West. "Come to us, come to us with your powers," she said. The serpent symbolized spiritual renewal. The jaguar represented mortality, she explained. The horse traveled to the crystal caves where the masters dwell, and the eagle brought visionary insights.

I had taken a place in the circle. Amid the beating drums I closed my eyes and meditated with the believers, breathing deeply on the shaman's command and calling silently to the animal spirits of the four winds. I tried, as Siegel asked, to let myself be stalked by my "personal power animal." According to the shamans of South America, and to Irene Siegel, every person is spiritually connected to an animal from a mysterious nether-realm. This power animal can provide comfort, wisdom, and mystical insights to its partner in the natural world. During meditations, shamans make journeys with their power animals, exploring an unseen world inhabited by other animals and humanoid spirit masters.

The smoky air and the urgent chanting made me feel vaguely numb, light-headed, and relaxed. I fought my first impulses—the desire to laugh, to observe, to judge. I had come to experience something strange and spiritual in the middle of the great blandness of suburbia, so I coaxed my mind to produce scenes of the jungle, forest, desert, and shore, and I populated them with great cats, deer, lizards, and birds. Gradually the drums sounded, to me, as if they were speaking the word "wolf, wolf, wolf," and I saw in my mind a gray and white wolf in a snowy wood. It had blue eyes.

After we called our power animals, the chanting ceased. Irene Siegel's husband, John, filled a brass infuser with burning sage and swung it on a chain in circles over us, using the smoke to "cleanse" our spiritual "auras." A small, lithe man clad entirely in white, John was serious and purposeful, moving slowly as he completed his part of the ritual. Then Irene, turning to face the four directions of the compass, clanged together two dome-shaped brass Tibetan chimes. She poured oils on the fire, making the flames grow higher, and then resumed the chanting:

**Nichi tai tai**
**En You I**
**Ora nikka, ora nikka**
**Hey, hey**
**Hey, hey**
**Oh-oh, I**

I joined, reciting the verse steadily and rhythmically. Feeding on the oil, the flames of the fire grew higher. Siegel motioned to a thin, plain-looking woman of about forty, with long brown hair. She solemnly went to the hearth and knelt. The fire illuminated her pale, sober face. She pushed up the sleeves of her shirt and calmly plunged her hands deep into the flames. She waved her hands gracefully from side to side and then slowly withdrew them, pressing her fingertips against her abdomen. She then put her hands in the flames a second time, and drew them back to her heart. She went to the flames a third time, then brought her hands back to her forehead, completing the process of drawing spirit power to her body, heart, and mind. She then placed a small twig on top of the burning logs and sat back on her haunches, watching as the offering was overcome by the flames. She heaved a long, loud sigh, stood, and returned to the circle.

The shaman looked at me and nodded. I rose, grateful that at least I wasn't the first, and tried to imitate what I had seen. I proceeded to the fire, moving slowly to signify my respect for the ritual. The believers had welcomed me, indulging the intrusion of a writer embarked on an exploration of an unusual spiritual movement. I owed them as much sincerity as I could muster. I knelt, put my hands in the flames, then quickly pulled them out and touched my stomach. I felt nothing more than a little warmth, as if I had passed my hand over a burner on a stove. Relieved, I made the second pass, plunging my hands more deeply into the fire and waving them more slowly. I stared at the fire, studying the rhythm of the yellow flames. The light was bright in my eyes. The combustion roared in my ears. But again I was not burned. On the third try I reached even further into the fire. This time I didn't rush. I slowly waved my hands through the flames and then brought them back and pressed my palms against my forehead. They were hot, but not burned. I felt both relieved and brave. (At home that night I would notice that the hair on my hands had been singed off.)

Siegel had told me to bring an offering—something symbolic but burnable. I settled for a piece of paper and a pencil—emblems of my vocation—sealed in an envelope. I placed them in the fire and watched them blaze. Then I returned to the circle.

As I sat and watched the others go to the fire, I was reminded of the program called Outward Bound, in which people develop self-esteem by overcoming obstacles in the wilderness. Outward Bound confronts you with physical challenges that are daunting but not overwhelming. The program works because it uncovers the individual's hidden strengths, dissolves fear, and teaches trust. I had had a similar experience in my moment before the fire.

Over the next hour, many more offerings were made. Some people returned to the fire a second time, to request blessings for a family member or friend. The rite ended with a final offering to the flame, a twig, which John passed among all the members of the group so it could be blessed. Siegel explained that this stick would carry the positive energy of each person who had held it, and that it would help heal the sorely polluted Earth.

During this closing gesture John did a curious thing, which broke the feeling of accomplishment I had earned before the fire. He denied me the Earth stick. He gave it to the woman on my right, who closed her eyes to bless it and then handed it back to him. Then he moved past me, to the woman on my left and then to the rest of the people in the circle.

When John at last placed the Earth stick in the fire, the ceremony was complete. Siegel rested her staff against a wooden bookcase, which was laden with stereo equipment, then walked to the back of the room and clicked on a light. Suddenly, the room was no longer a sanctuary for ritual. It was an ordinary living room—beige carpets and sofas, a TV, and an easy chair. And Siegel wasn't a shaman, but a hostess, scurrying into the kitchen to make coffee and put out plates of fresh-baked oatmeal cookies. For several minutes her guests stayed in the living room, watching the flames flicker and die. It seemed now to me like the aftermath of a Long Island cocktail party. Close friends lingered, others moved to leave. After five or ten minutes a few people got up and retrieved the crystals, feathers, and other symbolic treasures they had placed before the fire. The woman on my left, whose long black hair was threaded through little turquoise beads, touched my arm.

"John didn't hand you the Earth stick. I hope you didn't think I grabbed it ahead of you."

"No, of course not. I don't know if he passed over me deliberately or if it was an oversight. But it's okay."

She was a public-school teacher, and she had recently begun attending the full-moon ceremonies with her husband, also a teacher. "I get a very good feeling from this," she told me. I feel very connected to the Earth, to my spiritual self. It's very real to me."

While some people went to the kitchen for coffee and cookies, others stayed in the living room and talked to me about the ceremony. They were all college-educated people who had been raised as Christians or Jews but had found traditional religion confining or sterile. The shamanic ceremonies provided them spiritual expression, a community of belief, and a connection with supernatural powers.

I had meditated with the group and I had placed an offering in the fire. I had even seen the image of a wolf in my mind. But that was as close as I got to a spiritual experience that night. The others reassured me that, since this was my first encounter with shamanism, I couldn't expect much more.

As the other guests left the house, I stayed behind to thank Irene Siegel for letting me attend. I had contacted her the week before, after seeing a bulletin board announcement in a nearby delicatessen for one of her public lectures on shamanism. It was posted between a notice for a yard sale and an advertisement for a high-school play. She had invited me to her home for coffee and cookies and we had talked for hours about her growing up, her job as a social worker for a state psychiatric hospital, and her discovery of shamanism.

* * *

"My family always said I was a little strange," she had said that day. As a girl growing up in a nominally religious Jewish family in New York City, Siegel had been fascinated by spiritual ideas. She was an intelligent, curious, intuitive child and would entertain her mother and her sister by guessing their thoughts. They loved to play games such as Twenty Questions. Irene invariably won.

Siegel went through public school, studied psychology in college, and went on for her masters degree in social work. It was not until she was working in the hospital that she began to consider her intuition a psychic ability. On several occasions she was able to describe, sight unseen, deceased relatives of her friends and coworkers. Once she even told a female friend that her dead father was grateful for the daisies that had been placed on his grave the week before. "I don't know how I know these things," Siegel said. "They just come to me, and I know."

While she was slowly coming to believe that she possessed special intuitive powers, Siegel signed up for a seminar offered at a retreat center called the Omega Institute in upstate New York. Omega holds conferences on a wide range of esoteric subjects, from spirituality to nutrition to experimental psychology. When Siegel went there, one of the guest speakers was Albert Villoldo, a University of California psychology professor who had studied shamanism in South America. Villoldo's lecture included a group meditation on power animals, during which Siegel vividly saw the images of several creatures. She was thrilled. Villoldo encouraged her to study shamanism further.

Over the next three years Siegel attended several workshops on shamanism, run by Villoldo and others, where she learned the chants, rites, and meditations that shamans use to promote physical and spiritual healing. She also learned of the growing interest in shamanism in the United States, where it is being promoted as a new religion and an adjunct to the ecology movement. Finally, in 1985, she took a rigorous two-week course in Peru, where she visited sacred sites and participated in many different rituals, leading up to her initiation as a shaman.

Peru is a spiritual hot spot for modern religious seekers, thousands of whom travel there every year, to be led by shamans—and drugs—into the world of spirits and ancient wisdom. Following both American and Peruvian teachers, the pilgrims trek across the countryside to participate in fire ceremonies and other rites at various ancient Indian monuments. They try the homemade hallucinogens, which the Indians have used for centuries to help them conjure the spirits. The lucky few are asked to join the shamanic fraternity.

Siegel recorded her experiences in Peru in a manuscript, titled *Eyes of the Jaguar*. The dramatic high point of the book is a midnight ritual where she is required to drink, through her nose, a concoction of perfume and drugs. She then sees visions of the power animals and is healed of her nausea by a local shaman and restaurateur named don Eduardo Calderon. At the end of her trip, don Eduardo invites her to become a shaman. The story is remarkable for two things, its sincerity and Siegel's lack of skepticism. She seems to have an overwhelming need to discover something magical, something powerful, to help her combat a world of danger and evil. She writes that she is motivated by fears of nuclear war and pollution and her own struggle with issues of mortality. And she concludes that she returned to "ordinary reality" with magical powers to heal people and the planet.

Considering her story, I had to wonder if there wasn't an even more personal demon she was trying to exorcise, something so terrible that she needed magic on her side. But there was no clue about this in her manuscript, no hint in any of our conversations. Indeed, Siegel spoke as if spiritual forces, not her own free will, drew her to shamanism. "Some of the shamans of South America have decided that the new shamans will have to be from the developed countries because that's where it's needed," she said during our long afternoon talk. "They feel there's an urgent need now. That's why I became a shaman, to help bring about a healing of people and a healing of the Earth, on a much bigger scale."

Siegel spoke with the conviction of any religious convert, like a Catholic who had returned to the Church, or a sinner who has been "born again." It was familiar. What was not familiar was the content of her faith—power animals, magic staffs, rattles, drums, hallucinogens, the spirit realm—in the context of impeccable, homemade cookie, suburban ordinariness.

Still, shamanism had given Siegel ways of interpreting life's events and making sense of the world. The power animals filled her with a sense of control, which, she admitted, had been missing from her life. She had reached her mid-thirties single, unhappy at work, and unhappy in her personal relationships. She had been frustrated by patients who were difficult to cure and by colleagues who placed social workers at the bottom of the hospital pecking order. "We do all the work, get little of the credit and even less pay," she told me.

Since becoming a shaman, though, she had met and married John and begun using shamanism in her psychotherapy practice. In most cases, she supplements the standard therapy techniques with her own meditations, done without the patient's knowledge. After entering a trance, Siegel solicits the spirits' help for her clients, even those who would consider her beliefs nonsense. She goes much further with those few patients who are also spiritual seekers, teaching them to use their own meditations, to discover their power animals, and to journey to mystical realms. The process is similar to the fire ceremony, only it is repeated over and over again. In this way, the shaman/therapist gives her patients both psychological and spiritual tools to help them cope with life's problems.

This is unusual psychotherapy, to say the least. It is also

evidence of the frustration and sense of powerlessness many therapists must feel. But Siegel said it worked and, for those who believe, it probably does. Faith is a powerful thing. It instills a feeling of control where none exists, of power where all seems lost. Siegel had come to regard her faith this way, believing in her power animals and the shaman's gifts, and they made her feel powerful and in control.

My own lack of faith at the fire ceremony might explain why my experience fell short of mystical bliss. I was, perhaps, too much an observer, too much interested in learning about what was going on around me. At least that's what John said later that night when I asked him why he had passed over me during the blessing of the Earth stick.

"There was something wrong with your energy in the beginning," he said. "Maybe it was fear. You didn't seem very committed."

"I was probably thinking about putting my hands in the flames," I told him. "I hadn't done that before."

"I didn't want your energy going into the offering," he added, more bluntly. "It was inappropriate."

Irene offered a more kindly assessment. "You looked afraid the first time you came to the fire, but on the second time you were better." She said she would have given me the Earth stick. "But that was John's choice to make."

Then she too became serious, touching my shoulder and lowering her voice. "I hope you are taking this seriously, Michael, because I don't think you are writing this book by accident. There is a purpose behind this. Your power animal is stalking you."

For a moment, I was irritated by Irene's hard-sell warning. I felt as though I had been trapped by one of those tract-wielding evangelists you see in airports. She might enjoy thinking of herself as a pawn in a game played by magical powers who rule the universe. I did not. And besides, she seemed to be saying that she and the gods shared the same view. This was too certain for my taste.

But then I remembered that I had asked her to let me into her circle of faith. She had been generous with her time and her stories. She could be forgiven a little zeal. I thanked her again, accepted some cookies she offered for me to take home, and turned to leave.

"Don't deny the power that's stalking you," she warned me again as I headed to the door. "Denying it could have very serious consequences. Shamanism is something powerful. You will see. Many, many more people are going to become part of it."

Siegel, the people at her home, and those who attended other full-moon ceremonies, which I knew took place that same night in neighboring suburbs, were already part of a large, social and spiritual phenomenon. It includes shamanism and crystals worship, ecologists and psychics, holistic healers and spirit channelers. It is called the New Age.

Growing out of the counterculture of the 1960s, the New Age has slowly evolved into a complex American subculture that includes hundreds of churchlike congregations and dozens of institutes, radio stations, magazines, publishing houses, and businesses. New Age resorts and hotels can be found on both coasts and New Age healing centers offer "holistic" health care in big and small communities. There are New Age restaurants in most major cities, New Age shops in most large towns, and a New Age music industry, which has grown so big that *Billboard* magazine tracks its recordings with a separate Top Twenty score card. There are even New Age towns—Sedona, Arizona; Mt. Shasta, California; Carbondale, Illinois; and Vail, Boulder, and Crestone, Colorado—where so many believers have settled that they dominate local business, politics, and culture.

By now most Americans are at least generally aware of the New Age, but what they know of it makes many of them leery. Early in 1990, a New Age group called the Church Universal and Triumphant made nationwide headlines and endured a great deal of derision when it established a community of bomb shelters in Montana's isolated Paradise Valley. The church is led by a former New Jersey homemaker named Elizabeth Clare Prophet, who is known to believers as Guru Ma. She rules according to the instructions she claims to receive psychically from beings she calls the Ascended Masters of the Great White Brotherhood. In March of 1990, more than two thousand of Guru Ma's followers left their homes and jobs and moved to Montana, where they hoped to survive a Soviet nuclear attack, which she prophesied.

For several weeks the bomb shelter village provided a font of material for comedians and bemused journalists. But while they were depicted as strange, Prophet's followers couldn't have been more all-American. They were simply the latest in a line of spiritually inspired groups who would await the end of the Earth while snuggled in a utopian community. Early Americans, who believed they were founding a "New Zion," held a such view. So have hundreds of other groups who have tried to create heaven-on-Earth in America. All have been inspired, either directly or indirectly, by Bible prophesy and the dream of a perfect community in the New World. The settlers of Paradise Valley had simply made the New Age movement's contribution to this long American tradition. This didn't mean, however, that they weren't an embarrassment to many New Agers who considered the Church Universal a cult that damaged the reputation of the larger movement.

Though it has many spiritual or religious aspects, the New Age is not a distinct religion in the traditional sense. Indeed, a huge survey of American religious attitudes published by City University of New York found that few Americans cite New Age as their primary religious affiliation. As the author of the study told me, this is because the New Age is made up of millions who also consider themselves Christian, Jewish, Muslim, atheist, etc. Typically, people hold to much of their old religious identity while adopting any number of New Age ideas about health, politics, psychology, or spirituality. In this way, the New Age movement, in its broadest sense, is an attempt to discover ideas and practices that might be added to mainstream culture in order to make modern life richer and more satisfying. The vast majority of New Agers pick up an idea or practice from the movement and add it to their mix of beliefs. They become New Age Catholics who wear crystals, or New Age Jews who consult psychics.

Of course, it is the more extreme and flamboyant New Agers who tend to capture the public's attention. Thus, no one was more associated with the movement than Shirley MacLaine, who authored a series of books about her own explorations in the New Age. With titles such as *Dancing in the Light* and *Out on a Limb*, MacLaine's books have introduced many millions to psychics and channelers, healers and spirit guides. MacLaine extols the healing powers of crystals—such as quartz and amethyst—and even promotes the frequently debunked practice of "psychic surgery." (Widely known to be a sleight of hand, psychic surgery usually involves the palming of animal organs, which are then "removed" from folded skin.) MacLaine describes herself as miraculously transformed by her New Age journeys, which have filled her with insight and special powers. Like an old-fashioned tent preacher, she urges her readers to get the same kind of religion.

Those who do soon discover that the New Age is large and complex and filled with millions of fellow seekers. Indeed, sociologists at the University of California at Santa Barbara estimate that as many as 12 million Americans could be considered active participants and another 30 million are avidly interested. If they were somehow brought together in a churchlike organization, these serious and almost-serious New Agers would constitute the third largest religious denomination in America.

More important than the number of New Agers, though, is their wealth and influence. A 1988 article in *American Demographics* magazine looked at the profile of subscribers to *New Age Journal,* which saw a nine-fold increase in readership during the 1980s. The demographers discovered that more than 90 percent of the New Age magazine's subscribers are college graduates, compared with less than half the general population. They are three times more likely than others to travel abroad and four times more likely to be active in politics or community affairs. (Many of the most prominent New Agers are famous figures from the television and movie industries. Among them are actresses Sharon Gless, Marsha Mason, and Linda Evans, actor Michael York, and TV mogul Ted Turner. Their fame makes the New Age movement even more influential.) New Agers, concluded the magazine, "tend to be educated, affluent and successful people. They are hungry for something mainstream society has not given them. . . . They don't care for existing religions, so they've come out with a new kind of religion."

Education level is perhaps the most important of the traits discovered by *American Demographics.* New Agers seemed to be those whose education—and experience with the 1960s-style counterculture—has drawn them away from traditional religion. Though certainly there are many highly educated people in churches and synagogues, the tendency for college-educated people to drift away from religion is well-documented. Higher education tends to foster deep religious doubts. In recent decades it has also become synonymous with both the rejection of traditional values and the exaltation of individualism. The sense of independence and regard for rationality acquired at the university tend to drive a person away from traditional, spiritual, and religious life.

The New Age arose, in part, because those who leave the structure of mainstream religion nonetheless retain the basic human need for community, ritual, and spiritual expression. New Agers have not stopped considering the spiritual questions that, as psychiatrist Robert Coles has shown, first visit us in childhood. They wonder: Why are we here?

Where we are going? Why do we suffer? These are universal concerns and, as such, deserve as much respect and serious consideration as the motivations of other, more conventional spiritual pilgrims. Indeed, because they are willing to try the unconventional, to risk looking foolish or strange, the New Agers seem to me to be particularly worthy of respect. They are the experimenters, the theorizers, the explorers who will defy convention and chart their own routes to fulfillment. Despite what the many critics of the New Age may say, in limited ways the movement does offer spiritual succor and moral leadership.

These were in great demand in the 1980s. There was hardly a social observer who didn't agree that the Eighties was a repugnantly materialistic decade, not unlike the years that preceded the Great Depression. It was a time when American credit-card debt tripled and the average age of a first-time fur-coat-buyer dropped from fifty to twenty-six. It was also a time when individuals seemed to grow more isolated, even more lonely. By the end of the decade, half of all married couples had been split by divorce and 40 percent of American adults lived alone. In cities like New York, there were three single women to every one unmarried man. At the same time, families struggled with momentous changes as feminism and the demands of the economy pushed millions of women into the workplace. For the first time in modern history, a majority of mothers held full-time jobs and their children were entrusted to day care or baby-sitters. Without their traditional roles, men and women were forced to chart their lives without familiar landmarks.

These changes left millions of Americans feeling unsure of their identity. The widespread uneasiness was documented in a thoughtful study published by one of America's most prominent sociologists, Robert Bellah. Bellah's best-selling book, *Habits of the Heart,* declared that the nation suffered from a "damaged social ecology" that had left many feeling beleaguered, confused, insecure, and spiritually empty. The book follows middle-class Americans in their pursuit of happiness and finds that they must struggle against powerful feelings of isolation and confusion. "Our problems today are not just political," Bellah writes. "They are moral and have to do with the meaning of life."

The New Age movement is one way in which many struggle to repair the damaged social ecology described in *Habits of the Heart*. The term "New Age" comes from the belief that mankind is about to create an extraordinary era—a New Age—that will yield tremendous advances in human development and social organization. The movement's writers and prophets differ greatly in their descriptions of the New Age. Some envision a time when wisdom and love prevail, ending war, hunger, and confusion. With the guidance of philosophical and spiritual leaders, we will learn to live in harmony with nature. Others have a more fantastic view. They prophesy a utopian society in which all people have extraordinary psychic abilities. In this more magical New Age, we will communicate through mental telepathy, travel via astral protection, and heal ourselves by psychic means. In this version of the New Age, creatures from outer space, souls from eons gone by, and modern man live together in glory.

To reach the New Age, the different leaders of the movement promote a wide variety of ideas, all of which have their own specific language, literature, institutes, practitioners, and promoters. Some emphasize spiritual healing, suggesting that the proper metaphysical approach could help any person reconcile with death and even, perhaps, produce an outright miracle. Other New Agers are among the most ardent environmentalists. They consider the planet Earth a single organism, even a kind of god, and they approach ecological activism as a religious calling. Another large group is immersed in the study of so-called "paranormal" phenomena, exploring everything from extrasensory perception to spirit channeling to Unidentified Flying Objects. Finally there are the mystics of the movement, whose beliefs include ideas drawn from every religious tradition. Through meditation and other practices, these serious spiritual seekers try to reach a state of consciousness where they hope to gain insights into personal problems, past lives, and future destinies.

As the amazing variety shows, the New Age is a very flexible, amorphous, spontaneous movement. There is no national organization, no hierarchy, no clearinghouse for information. People became part of the movement by studying books, visiting small institutes, joining study groups, attending seminars, and working with the thousands of New Age therapists, teachers, healers, and gurus scattered around the country. A typical believer draws on these different interests to create his own, personal way of thinking about himself and the world around him.

This informality, and the splintered nature of the New Age community, obscure its size and its impact on the larger society. It is easy for the uninformed to turn the New Age label into a pejorative and relegate its concepts to the intellectual and religious fringe. Many writers and social critics have dismissed the New Age in this way. But such a negative assessment ignores the ways that the movement has come to influence mainstream culture. New Age ideas—meditation, mind-body theories, staunch environmentalism, visualization—can be found in public schools, hospitals, corporate offices, and the popular media. It is not uncommon for schoolteachers to have their students pause to calm themselves, and visualize writing correct answers, before taking an exam. Athletes use visualization to improve their performance, and oncologists routinely advise patients to visualize their bodies healing from cancer. (This practice was popularized by Yale surgeon Bernie S. Siegel, M.D., whose books *Love, Medicine, and Miracles* and *Peace, Love, and Healing* have sold millions of copies.) Many medical schools offer courses on the interaction of the mind and mood with the body's immune system. Indeed, one of the fastest-growing specialities in medicine is psychoneuroim-

munology, the study of mind-body interactions. New Age
ideas have even infiltrated big business. It is not unusual
for a Wall Street trader to consult a channeler or a psychic,
and dozens of Fortune 500 companies have hired New Age
advisers to make their firms more humane and productive.

While all of this evidence suggests that the New Age
movement is a significant social development, my curiosity
has also been piqued by the instances when I have encountered the movement in the course of my own life. There is
my neighbor Fred, who has studied both Native American
religion and the concept of reincarnation. He is convinced
that he was an Indian in a past life. A builder by trade,
Fred now devotes several weeks each summer to building
housing for the poor on an Indian reservation. Then there
is my sister, who once worked with a New Age–style peace
group that involved her directly in an antinuclear weapons
campaign. Her volunteer work gave her the sense that she
could actually do something, no matter how small, to solve
a problem that seems unsolvable.

Of course, not all of my personal encounters with the
New Age have been positive. A journalist I know became
so obsessed with New Age pursuits that he eventually quit
his job and abandoned his wife and child, "dropping out"
to take up a new life in a New Age community. Then there
is the successful young New York lawyer I know who spends
hundreds of dollars for consultations with psychics and seers
who are obviously crooks preying on her insecurities.

Like so many movements, the New Age has its charlatans,
and under intense scrutiny much of it falters. But these
failings are not peculiar to the New Age. After all, born-
again Christianity has its scandal-smeared TV evangelists
and Catholicism endures despite the occasional corrupt or
perverted clergyman. In the end, what is fascinating about
the New Age is not its failures but its effect on the American scene. The impact of the New Age is real. Today it is
hard to imagine that anyone wouldn't know about past lives,
karma, channeling, and crystal healing. These terms were

not part of the American vernacular before the New Age. Today, in almost any suburb, city, or small town, a seeker can find a swami, a psychic, or a practicing shaman who performs monthly new-moon rituals. Repeated polls have found that a majority of Americans believe they have had psychic experiences, one-quarter believe in reincarnation, and more than 10 percent believe in channeling.

The sudden appearance of a strange religious or social movement and its infiltration of the larger culture is not unprecedented. America's history is marked by the successive rise of many utopian or mystical movements that seemed extreme at their beginning but eventually found a niche in the national culture. The Mormons are one such group. The Jehovah's Witnesses are another. As America approached the millennium, the New Age arose as the utopian movement of the moment.

This book, a one-year journey through the New Age, documents the breadth and influence of a movement that is flourishing among ordinary Americans. Since it is a grassroots phenomenon, I have concentrated primarily on the everyday, rank-and-file participants. But along the way I encountered some of the glittering stars of the New Age: Lazaris the channeled spirit, faith healer Louise Hay, psychiatrist M. Scott Peck, surgeon Bernie Siegel. These and other prominent New Age leaders are in these pages, but most of the people you will meet here are the seekers, the people who attend the seminars and retreats, and pay for the crystals, books, tapes, and holistic treatments.

As an outsider, I have asked the questions any outsider might ask: What is the New Age? Who are the New Age believers? What motivates them? What is their goal? Does the New Age movement have something of value to offer? What does the rise of the New Age say about present-day America?

And yet the New Age is a participatory movement, open to all. Indeed, it is as much about experience as anything else, and as I traveled inside the New Age, I was welcomed with few reservations. I often joined in the rituals, classes, seminars, and meditations, choosing to be a participant as well as an observer, to put my hands in the fire whenever I could. What follows is an account of what I saw, experienced, and came to understand in my travels in New Age America.

# 1 · SEDONA

## Among the Vortex Pilgrims

GEOLOGISTS ESTIMATE THAT IT TOOK TWO BILLION YEARS for wind and water to create Bell Rock, Courthouse Butte, Cathedral Rock, and the other mesas and canyons of Sedona, Arizona. Millimeter by millimeter, the red stone that had been left by a Precambrian sea was carved into sandcastle spires hundreds of feet high, sheer cliffs, and huge domes. Yucca, wild flowers, juniper, and pear cactus filled the dry meadows between these formations. Towering ponderosa pines, straight as schooner masts, crowded the cool banks of Oak Creek, the rushing stream that cut many of the red-rock formations.

No matter where you stand in this little town, you cannot escape the vistas of looming red rock. In the evening, as the sky turns pink and then purple, Sedona looks like those NASA pictures of another planet—Mars or perhaps Venus. The Anasazi (ancient ones) Indians, ancestors of today's Apaches, were so awed by the scenery that they decided it must have been the site of creation. It was here, they determined, that Changing Woman, the first being to emerge from the underworld, settled and birthed the human race.

Recently Sedona has acquired a new legend, one that has transformed it from an isolated mountain town into a jumble of crystal shops, souvenir stands, overbooked motels, and trendy restaurants. It all began with a book published by a psychic named Page Bryant, which declared that Sedona was the site of the most powerful collection of natural "vortexes" on Earth. Word of the vortexes spread quickly in the New Age community. Millions made pilgrimages to Sedona, certain that the red rocks had supernatural power. They believed that the buttes and canyons are actually "vortexes" of psychic energy, places where all kinds of paranormal phenomena—spirit channeling, healing, extrasensory perception—are dramatically enhanced.

The promoters who picked up on Bryant's idea turned Sedona into a New Age bazaar jammed with psychics, channelers, healers, teachers, and vendors. The literature I received from the Sedona Center for the New Age, a kind of chamber of commerce for psychics, offered a stunning array of services. I could learn to be a psychic, be healed, plumb past lives, maybe even contact UFOs, all in a long weekend. The flyers proclaimed Sedona the capital city of the New Age. It was a natural starting point for my exploration of this American subculture.

Most New Age pilgrims fly into Phoenix and then drive Interstate 17 northward, as I did, through a vast white-sand desert of stately saguaro cactus and sagebrush, into Verde Valley and finally to Sedona. Two things strike a traveler who gets off the highway and follows the state road into town—the towering red-rock formations and the vortex hype. Nowhere in the world is the word *vortex* used more often. The streets of Sedona are jammed with jeeps and vans, all plastered with signs that advertise "vortex tours." Sedona has a gift shop called Eye of the Vortex and a trade school called Vortex Computer Training. Vortex maps are given out by the chamber of commerce, and people on the street wear vortex T-shirts. There were even little vortex guidebooks for sale at the gas station where I stopped for directions to the Center for the New Age.

Located in a shopping strip on the west side of town, the center is New Age headquarters, where tourists can hear lectures, attend social functions, and pick up information on everything from vortex tours to sweat lodge ceremonies. Half of the front room is given over to shelves filled with advertisements and books. On the day I arrived, the new book *You Are Psychic* was prominently displayed along with flyers advertising vortex tours conducted by the author, local "MIT-trained scientist" Pete Sanders. As I walked past the display, a little white-haired woman who twinkled with crystal jewelry came out from behind a counter and scurried over to give me a hug.

"This is the Sedona greeting," she said before letting me go and stepping back to focus her green-blue eyes on me. Georgia Gandalf was volunteer-of-the-day at the center, and she considered it her responsibility to guide every visitor through the many delights offered in the hundreds of brochures. She walked me through the stacks, filling my arms with the pamphlets she plucked from the shelves.

I was dumbfounded. There were so many possibilities: acupressurists and acupuncturists, vortex tours, psychic teachers, UFO hunters, health spas. Who could choose? And this woman—Georgia—wasn't anything like what I expected. At least fifty years old, she wasn't a Sixties-generation holdover. She was more like a grandmother in crystals. Given all the hype surrounding Sedona, I had come prepared to meet a hard-selling young promoter, someone I would resist. Instead I met Georgia Gandalf, and I liked her.

As I explained that I had come as a writer, Georgia insisted, like Irene Siegel, that I must also be on a personal, spiritual guest. As far as she was concerned, the spirit is involved in everything.

"We'll help you find the teacher you might be looking for or the experience that's looking for you, whether you know it or not," she said, taking me by the arm. I pocketed a brochure describing Pete Sanders's vortex tour and another that promised "You Can Communicate with Dolphins!" I also chose a flyer that advertised "The Healing Center of Sedona," a "unique healing vortex" offering everything from acupressure to an Indian sweat lodge. And I inquired about Page Bryant. Georgia said Bryant was lecturing in England. "And besides, from what I hear, she doesn't give interviews," she added. We then sat down in some folding chairs that were arranged near the counter, and she told me about her pilgrimage to Sedona, a journey she said began on the day she was born.

Born in 1937 and raised in Milwaukee, Georgia Gandalf is the daughter of Lutheran parents who sent her to church and Sunday school and taught her to live by the Golden rule. "Back then everyone had their own religion, their own beliefs," she said, "and they stayed in their little cages and never met other people."

As a child, Georgia found the church stern and confining, and as an adult, she broke away. But the guilt and sense of sinfulness she had learned in church stayed with her. "I had left the church, but I still had to get rid of the feeling that I was no good, that I was dumb."

As she spoke, Georgia stared directly into my eyes with a look that seemed to beg for agreement. She would stop when she said something that mattered—about feeling "no good," for example—and wait for me to confirm that I understood what she meant. I would nod, or say, "I understand." Only then would she continue.

Georgia said little about her marriage, only that it had produced five children and ended in divorce in 1974. An artist, she went to work in advertising in Milwaukee, eventually becoming an executive for a prominent local agency.

"I was pretty contented then," she told me, "but life was cold there. And I don't mean the weather. I mean the whole thing. Life is very cold in big cities. It's not like it used to be, with people in neighborhoods looking out for each other. People are pretty estranged from each other now. I worked and had a few friends, but that was it."

This sense of isolation even affected the way Georgia regarded politics. "After Nixon and the Vietnam War, I felt like I didn't know this country," she said. She decided voting was futile. She stopped reading the newspaper, even stopped driving her car. She turned inward, determined to rid herself of the feeling that she was "dumb" and "no good."

"The church teaches intolerance and judgment, and it didn't hold much of a place for women, so that was out. But I needed something to explain my life, and the world, the way it was," she said. Quite by accident she stumbled upon some books on metaphysics. She was hooked. She consumed volumes on astrology, numerology, reincarnation, Tarot, and ESP. These books gave her the sense that life had some preordained order and purpose and that the afterlife was real, a wondrous place where we exist as immortal creatures of the soul, endowed with the power to cross space and time in an instant, to know all there is to know, to understand everything that is a mystery in man's world.

Gradually, Gandalf developed a tailor-made, New Age faith that was as strong as any possessed by a typical American churchwoman. It was tested in 1989 when her twenty-four-year-old son, Kevin, was killed in a hit-and-run auto accident. He had been walking along a roadway that had been closed for spectators watching a fireworks display. The young driver of the car that hit him was traveling at high speed on the wrong side of the road.

Georgia spoke more slowly as she told this part of her story. It had been less than a year since her son's death. Still, she didn't cry and her voice remained steady. She said that a psychic had made contact with heavenly creatures where Kevin was existing, quite happily. "He's in the light now, and I know it," she said, smiling gently. "I've had friends help me go into a state of mind where I can see him all in the light."

After the accident and a ceremony in which Kevin's ashes were scattered on Lake Michigan, Georgia took a trip to Las Vegas to visit a sister. She carried along some paintings, mostly pictures of angels ("Angels are what come to me when I paint"), and she sold a few to dealers in Las Vegas. Georgia had heard of Sedona and convinced her sister to make the one-hundred-and-fifty-mile drive south with her. The day was a milestone in her life.

"It was October 17, 1989, the day after the San Francisco earthquake," Georgia recalled. "We came down the canyon road and I knew immediately that I wanted to live here. It was a spiritual thing, a force I felt. The first thing I did was start looking for a place to stay. In three hours I found a trailer."

Georgia returned to Milwaukee, immediately quit her job, took whatever possessions she could, and left. "I realized I had been living estranged from other people, from nature, from myself. Here you don't feel that way."

In her New Age studies Georgia had come to believe that she could use mystical means to influence events. Her main tools were "affirmations," phrases she recited as a kind of blessing on the future. She settled in Sedona, using these affirmations: "The universe will provide for me here" and "I am safe and happy."

So far, the universe had provided for Georgia and she was safe and, by all appearances, happy. A local New Age gallery sold her paintings on consignment and Georgia opened a little business as a spiritual adviser. She lived on the money from the paintings, her counseling service, and her savings. In her free time she studied with psychics and New Age spiritual experts. She had even participated in a fire-walking workshop where she learned to over-come her fears by crossing a bed of hot coals. "That took the word *fear* right out of my life," she said, throwing her hands up in the air, as if she was heaving her fear out the window. Comfortable in her new small-town home, Georgia had gotten a new driver's license and even registered to vote.

Georgia Gandalf's sudden move to Sedona and her embrace of the New Age community was remarkable but not unique. Since 1980, several thousand visitors have been so impressed by Sedona that they have returned to settle, eventually doubling the town's population to more than thirteen thousand. The New Age settlers filled the local schools with children, pushed up real-estate prices, and transformed Sedona from an ordinary tourist town into a metaphysical mecca. When I visited, the town's superintendent of schools had recently resigned, in part because he had tired of fighting with those who wanted more New Age ideas put to use in the classrooms.

"We in the New Age, especially in Sedona, are actually going back to older teachings, older ways of living," Georgia Gandalf said as she described her utopia. "We have trust in each other. We live like they say Christians are supposed to live. We help each other. I found life here in a kind of time warp," she said. "People here are close. The town is small, so you feel like you have an impact."

I said good-bye to Georgia—she kissed me this time—and then I drove back, through the center of town, past the ice cream parlors and motels and about a dozen bright pink jeeps operated by a company called Pink Jeep Tours. I set off to find the aggressively promoted Pete Sanders, the "MIT-trained scientist" who, for fifty dollars, would take me on a tour of the vortexes. Sanders lived five miles north of the center of town. His home, a dark brown two-story house perched on a hillside, overlooked a lush forest and the steep red-rock sides of Oak Creek Canyon.

A tall, bearded man with bushy hair and glasses, Pete Sanders was a competitive swimmer in high school and college, and at age thirty-nine he retained the broad, muscled shoulders he had developed doing thousands of laps. His house was a monument to psychic abilities, he said as we sat down. It had belonged to a builder who had shown Sanders other homes. "But I said to him psychically, 'Let me know when you want to sell us *your* house.' " A few days later, the story goes, the man called to offer to sell Sanders his home.

To Pete Sanders, this was scientific proof of his psychic powers of telepathy and precognition. He had devoted almost twenty years to cataloging his experiences with such psychic phenomena, building anecdote upon anecdote, a mountain of stories to support his faith in the existence of spiritual beings and paranormal phenomena. But, he admitted, they were only stories, not hard evidence. No one has been able to actually record or measure psychic energy. But that wasn't a serious problem for Sanders. He was certain that science just hadn't caught up with his beliefs.

Clearly, science meant a great deal to Sanders. His brochures and his book refer repeatedly to his work at MIT and note that when he graduated, in 1974, he was accepted by Harvard Medical School. Did he intend the Harvard and MIT labels to lend credibility? "It has helped me, I admit," he said. "I think it has opened doors—to getting my book published, for example—that otherwise might have been closed.

"MIT was a great nerd school, very, very much oriented toward hard science. But they aren't very open minded to anything new and they train you to be the same," he recalled. None of the MIT nerds could have deterred him from plunging into his study of the paranormal. An only child whose father died when he was just three years old, Sanders had been raised in New York City by a mother who was a lifelong spiritual seeker. He was her constant companion at spiritual lectures, psychic meetings, and séances. Sanders's earliest memory is of accompanying her to a class on Zen Buddhism at New York University. He was five years old.

When he was an adolescent, Sanders and his mother

moved to the San Fernando Valley, in California, where he went to high school. Always there were spiritual pursuits—channelers and psychics to visit, classes to attend. "My mom was pretty discerning," he told me. "She showed me how to separate the phonies from the genuine ones." Sanders described himself as a detached teenager, a serious, lonely student.

At college, searching through volumes of scientific reports, Sanders became convinced that he had found proof of the existence of one paranormal phenomenon, no matter what his hard-science colleagues would claim. The evidence was in a little-known study of monkeys whose spinal nerves had been severed. The monkeys apparently surprised the researchers when they regained some use of their muscles. While other researchers may have searched for a more mundane explanation, Sanders theorized that the animals had tapped the power of their psychic auras, an energy field that supposedly surrounds the body. "I had to be careful, though, because the professors control the grades and none of them accepted what I was finding," he recalled. "It was a very difficult time."

As Sanders finished explaining his scientific breakthrough, his two sons, four-year-old Michael and five-year-old Brian, came spilling out onto the deck. They had just returned from school with their mother, Debbie Sanders, who is a special-education teacher for the local school district. The boys dashed onto the porch brandishing sticks as if they were rapiers.

"Ah-ha! This is my power sword!" cried Brian as he lunged at his brother.

"So what!" answered Michael as he held up his own stick. "This is my crystal sword!"

The boys clambered, like a single eight-legged creature, out to the backyard while Debbie, a thin woman with straight black hair, came out to say hello. "I can see Pete is into it," she said, wagging her head knowingly. "I'll just leave you alone."

Pete was indeed "into it." He was adamant about his beliefs, so adamant that I decided not to question him aggressively. I framed my questions carefully, inquiring rather than challenging. I asked him why he chose to forego medical school. "Somebody else, anybody else, might have gone on to medical school," he said. "I didn't have patience for that. I preferred to get out and teach what people wanted to learn rather than butt heads within the scientific community."

We were again interrupted by the boys. They brought over a green-shelled snail, which they had found and confined to a plastic cup. Their hands shook with excitement as they showed us their catch.

"Look, look, he's coming out!" said Michael.

"He's . . . he's . . . he's suction-cupping up the side of the cup!"

Brian giggled.

Sanders told the boys they could keep the snail for a while, but that they must eventually return it to the yard. Before he left, Brian lingered to join the adults' conversation.

"Daddy, I can do something you can't do. I can take energy from the sun."

"That's great, Brian," said Sanders. "Now run along.

"I teach them about using their energy and the energy of the Earth," Sanders explained to me as his sons toddled off. During walks in the woods, he teaches his sons how to "sit down when they are tired and take in energy from the rocks." He had also begun to teach them about psychic spirit guides, whom he called "Super Boys." Brian and Michael already knew how to meditate in order to contact the Super Boys for guidance. "They are lucky," said their father. "It gives them something other kids don't have." (The Super Boy idea sounded strange to me. I wondered if it could distort a child's sense of reality. Then I recalled the guardian angels placed on my boyhood shoulders by Catholic nuns. They didn't hurt me. Why should the Super Boys hurt Brian and Michael?)

Returning to our discussion of his work, Sanders said he had looked for other evidence, besides the monkey experiments, to explain what he had experienced as a child with psychics, mediums, and channels, as well as in his own meditative trances. Some of his favorite proofs were drawn from various theories of physics developed in the last fifty years. These theories—aspects of quantum mechanics—show that there is much about matter, energy, and the structure of the universe that science does not yet understand. Sanders believed that these gaps in our understanding could be filled by the human soul and psychic phenomena. "There are physicists who say there are many more dimensions of reality than we understand," said Sanders. "Maybe that's where psychic abilities lie." His was a faith-based kind of logic that went something like this: Science cannot explain all of creation, so therefore psychic phenomena such as vortexes could be real and may be proven real as science advances.

To promote his teachings, connecting science with psychic powers, Sanders founded an organization called Free Soul. Something like a psychic self-help group, Free Soul trains teachers who then show clients how to tap their "innate psychic abilities." Sanders said that his book, *You Are Psychic,* had sold twenty-five thousand copies, bringing hundreds of new believers to Free Soul and creating a growing demand for him to lecture on his special blend of mysticism and science.

At home in Sedona, Sanders offered vortex tours to those who wanted to discover and develop their psychic abilities. Vortexes could be found all over the world, on mountain peaks and in beautiful valleys, but Sedona was blessed with many different vortexes where even a novice could experience remarkable things, he said.

"Come out with us tomorrow," said Sanders as I got up to leave. "Listen. Judge for yourself."

The boys had resumed their duel on the deck. Suddenly Brian took a spill, banging his elbow. He came into the house rubbing it and crying loudly.

"It hurts, it hurts!" he howled.

His father ran to him, plucked him up, and sat him down in a big, stuffed chair.

"Here, put some energy into it, some healing energy," he said, placing his son's hand on the elbow.

Brian closed his eyes, placed his hand on his elbow, and stopped crying. In a few minutes he hopped down from the chair and went back to play.

The next morning I met four New Age tourists in the lobby of Sedona's largest and poshest hotel, a resort called Las Abrigadas. There was an athletic-looking young couple from California, Rory Freeman and his wife, Cindy. He was a veterinarian. She ran a small stable. The other couple was Jack and Kaye Finch, who were in their late fifties and came from Tulsa. Tall and fit, Jack had recently ended a thirty-year career in the oil and gas business. Kaye had always been a homemaker. We sat together on a pair of sofas near a bubbling fountain in the hotel lobby, waiting for Pete Sanders and a semi-private vortex tour.

Sanders arrived at eight-thirty, looking a bit like Crocodile Dundee. He carried a curved walking stick, which he said he had acquired when he climbed Mount Fuji, one of the places where he had tested his psychic ability while in the Navy in the 1970s. We piled into a van and headed for a vortex spot called "Airport Mesa," which was on federal park land near the Sedona airport. On the way over, Sanders asked why the couples had signed up for the tour.

"Stress reduction," Jack said, rather loudly.

Kaye explained, matter-of-factly, that one of their two daughters had died in a drug-related accident ten years before. Their second daughter was a recovering addict and the single mother of a five-year-old daughter. They had recently moved in with the Finches.

"I feel a lot of early-morning anxiety now," Jack added. "It all adds up, over the years."

"You know, we wake up the way that we go to sleep,"

Pete Sanders said sympathetically. "If you could find a way to let go of these worries, release them before you sleep, you'd be all right. We'll try to help you with that today."

When we arrived at the mesa, there were already two jeeps and a van—operated by other tour guides—parked in a small dirt lot. Smoke and the scent of burning sage hung in the air. About a dozen people were picking their way up the steep incline, inching their way to the mesa top.

Sedona is overrun with tour guides and spiritual questers, so many that the local office of the U.S. Forest Service was beginning to regulate them more strictly. Most of the vortexes are located on federal parklands, and park rangers were concerned that the tours were hastening the erosion of the red-rock buttes and cliffs. They had placed a twelve-person-per-tour limit on the guides and had begun requiring special insurance for tour operators. More regulations were being considered, but local opposition to the Forest Service plan was growing. A flyer I had noticed at the Center for the New Age warned that the Forest Service had begun issuing citations to unlicensed guides and advised large groups of vortex visitors to pose as individuals "who just happen to be there at the same time."

Following the two other groups, we picked our way up the mesa, which was a large mound of red rock about as far across as a football field and perhaps ten stories high. The top was relatively flat, red rock. "Healing sites often have red rock, which is rich in iron and other heavy elements," Sanders said as we climbed. "The rocks are condensed energy. They store more energy than silica. You can literally draw energy from them."

The view from the mesa top included other vortex sites— Bell Rock, Cathedral Rock, Boynton Canyon, and Long Canyon—as well as most of the city of Sedona. It was a peaceful setting, except for the buzz of the airplanes at the nearby airport and the rasp of someone operating a chainsaw nearby.

As we sat on the boulders, Sanders explained that the

mesa was an "upflow vortex," a place where energy flowed upward and created a sense of metaphysical expansion. It is a good place to try to psychically project yourself over time or space, or to try out-of-body traveling, he said. "Upflow vortexes are masculine," said Sanders. Inflow vortexes, where the Earth receives energy from the beyond, were feminine, he said, completing the anatomical metaphor. They were good sites for introspection.

Although we were all psychic novices, Sanders said everyone possesses one or more specific psychic abilities—psychic hearing, psychic vision, intuition, or psychic feeling. Each of these gifts could be tapped by turning one's attention to the area of the body where these abilities reside. The ears represent hearing. The top of the head is the focal point for intuition. The forehead is where psychic vision is centered. Psychic feeling is located in the abdomen. "The whole body is a psychic antenna," Sanders explained. Our job was to tune our antennae properly.

While Sanders walked softly among us, calmly offering instructions, I sat on the rock with the others, crossed my legs, and closed my eyes to meditate and fine-tune my psychic vision. Following Sanders's directions, I relaxed my body, trying to loosen the tension in my feet, ankles, calves, all the way up to my head. I then tried to project my consciousness into the sky and across the valley or canyons. To do this, Sanders said, we must imagine our souls hovering about our heads, in a space that might be best described as an invisible chef's hat, or perhaps a halo.

It was, at first, a restful experience, broken only by the noise of a garbage truck climbing Airport Mesa Road. I could imagine myself flying high above the mesa, looking out across a landscape that looked much like what one sees from the window of an airplane on a transcontinental flight. I imagined that I then soared northward, to the Grand Canyon, stopping to hover like one of the helicopters that tourists can hire. I felt as though I could see Los Angeles and the Pacific to the west and the Great Plains to the north.

Soon, though, my meditation took on the character of the famous *New Yorker* magazine drawing that shows a New Yorker's view of the nation, with Manhattan in detail and the rest of the country a brief swatch of green interrupted only by Chicago, the Mississippi River, and a patch of Los Angeles smog. It was then that I opened my eyes.

Sanders then instructed us to tune our psychic intuition receptor, which is located in the top of the head. Psychic intuition allows one to sense future events. It was here that I hit a definite block. My eyes felt strained; they even hurt a bit.

"Be careful as you do this," Sanders said quietly. "Don't roll your eyes up and back into your head as you try to lift your consciousness up. A lot of people do that and it doesn't feel good. Don't try too hard. Just relax."

I pulled my eyes back down, took a deep breath, and relaxed. The pressure in my head subsided. But nothing else happened. No visions, no sounds, no psychic feelings, at least as far as I could tell. After a few moments, Sanders told us to open our eyes. Jack, Kaye, Cindy, and Rory all took deep breaths and looked about. No one said anything about having had an extraordinary psychic experience, but we agreed that the view was inspiring and the brief period of meditation had been restful.

We went back to the van and drove to a second vortex site, Long Canyon, much of which, according to Sanders, had been purchased by a New Age benefactor and is being preserved as a sacred place. The Long Canyon vortex is actually centered on a hill. The geological combination of a deep canyon and this promontory makes it a rare kind of vortex, with both upflow and inflow energy, Sanders said.

It was near noon by the time we walked from a main road through fields of juniper to the canyon vortex. It was apparently peak tour time. Dozens of people littered the site. Most were gathered around a tour guide who sat in the middle of a circle of rocks, about thirty feet in diameter.

It was a replica of an Indian medicine wheel. As we passed by, the man in the center of the circle was preaching loudly to those on its perimeter.

"You are like the God spirit. You are the center of your own universe, your own medicine wheel."

We stopped about one hundred yards away and Sanders shook his head at what we had just heard. "Indians never used the medicine wheel that way," he whispered. "They used it to help a person with a problem. The troubled person would be inside the wheel and those outside would be his advisers. You would never see someone inside the wheel preaching to people sitting around it. That's a sacrilege." Sanders's criticism illustrated the free-lance nature of the New Age. With no organization and no standards, most everything seemed open to interpretation. It all depended on which tour guide you hired.

At another makeshift medicine wheel—there were dozens in the canyon—Sanders stopped to explain inflow vortexes. "They are a place to go for introspection, even to confront your dark side." He quoted a scene from a *Star Wars* film in which the hero, Luke Skywalker, is advised by his teacher, a creature named Yoda, to discover his true self.

"He told Luke Skywalker to go into the cave where the dark side of The Force was very powerful. Yoda said, 'Find yourself, you will.' Luke does. He finds Darth Vader, rips off his mask, and sees his own face underneath. That's the kind of experience people have in an inflow vortex. You have to be prepared for that."

Sanders said that the Anasazi used the Sedona vortexes to discover their "true selves." He pointed out various locations around the canyon where he was certain that braves had spent sleepless days and nights on "vision quests," fasting until they had a spiritual experience that would suggest the vocation they should follow, a name they should adopt, or a lesson they must learn. Vision quests are a romantic ideal among many New Agers, who equate them with ancient wisdom and noble aspirations.

As we walked around the mesa and looked out over fields of scrub oak and juniper, Sanders repeatedly referred to the inherent, spiritual power of the canyon. On one side of the canyon stood the wooden frames of several half-built houses, which had been started and then abandoned. "Many developers have tried to build here and failed," Sanders explained. He offered those failures as proof that "this is a sacred place where only sacred uses will be successful."

It seemed as though every rock of any size was occupied by a meditating man or woman, so it took several minutes for Sanders to find a small area, near the edge of a cliff, for our group. "Take a spot nearer the edge, but then move back two or three feet. I don't want to lose anyone." Sanders told us to be still, to receive the energy that was all around us. "Here you practice how to live life as a soul, to be in the world but not of it."

Seated on a ledge between Kaye and Rory, I closed my eyes and tried to experience the inflow vortex, life as a soul. But when I closed my eyes, I immediately became worried about falling off the cliff. I opened my eyes and stared at the canyon. Visibility in the dry Sedona climate often exceeds fifty miles. The vast landscape, the vaulting red-rock walls, the hawk that circled in the updrafts of the canyon—it all made me feel serene and small. It was easy, sitting before so much natural grandeur, to feel peaceful and untroubled, like a free soul. The utter silence and the vast expanse quieted my mind until it was almost as still, almost as silent, as the canyon.

In a few moments Sanders announced that our time was up. I hadn't encountered my Darth Vader in the vortex, and by the look of my companions, none of them had either. But we had, in a way, worshipped together there in a red-rock cathedral. I felt closer to my fellow pilgrims as we walked out, following Sanders, who talked on and on about the vortexes until we reached the van. He said we had all lived "a mountaintop existence" in a previous lifetime. That explained why being in the mountains felt so good.

"I have memories of a lot of my past lifetimes," he told us. "It's no big deal. I've gotten a glimpse of a Tibetan lifetime I had. It was easy to be on that mountaintop back then, with no mortgage, no job or kids. That's why we get that incredible peaceful feeling on mountaintops. We're remembering past experiences."

"Is your past-life recall limited to this galaxy?" asked Jack Finch.

"Oh, no," answered Sanders, "absolutely not. We are all star children."

It was after noon when we got into the van and headed back to the hotel. It would have taken several days to explore all of Sedona's vortexes, but we had sampled two of the most famous. Sanders reminded us that any high place could be an upflow vortex—even the Empire State Building—and that any calm, low-lying place, like the ocean, could be an inflow site. The methods for using the vortexes to tune your psychic abilities were detailed in his book, he reminded us. "The bottom line is, find your own vortexes—and practice."

Back in the hotel lobby, Kaye and Jack Finch and Cindy Freeman sat with me for a while to review our experience. No one revealed a psychic breakthrough, but they all said that they had enjoyed the tour, that it was probably worth the fifty dollars.

The Finches said that they had taken a course in transcendental meditation in the late 1970s, as part of their effort to cope with their youngest daughter's drug abuse. Ever since then, they have been exploring spiritual ideas, from traditional Christianity to New Age notions of past lives and psychic power.

"I would have to say that yes, we've been searching," said Kaye. "It's bewildering, when you are June and Ward Cleaver, to find you have a daughter with chemical dependence."

When their twenty-one-year-old daughter drowned while

taking drugs, Kaye and her husband could no longer believe they were the Cleavers, living in American perfection.
Similarly, she said, as she moved from a small town in Okla-
homa to the East Coast and then back west, her old way of
looking at the world was challenged. "It is very difficult
when you have your reality changed, but I think it's all for
the better," said Kaye. "We've grown and broadened our
outlook. But it's still bewildering. Everybody feels it, feels
the fear and the loneliness. It's not just me. Why do you
think that TV show 'America's Funniest Home Videos' is
so popular? It's a replacement for real family life," she said.
"Don't you see? We're all living through the TV."

Just before their trip to Sedona, the Finches had visited
their other daughter at a rehabilitation center where, in a
gesture of support, they had given up their social drinking.
"We have tried a lot of things," Jack interjected. "We did
meditation the first time because we were really scared and
we were trying anything we could to break the drug syn-
drome in our family. It helped with stress, but after our
first daughter died, every time I tried it, I found myself
imagining how she died."

Jack gave up meditating and immersed himself in his
work. But the 1980s were a turbulent time of mergers and
takeovers in the oil and gas business, and his firm was
bought and sold several times. Each time he had to adjust
to new bosses, new goals, and new corporate structures.
Each time his work grew more difficult. Eventually he took
early retirement, at age fifty-five, and began to accompany
Kaye on her spiritual quest.

"If there's one thing I've learned," said Jack, "it's that
you have to change, adjust, explore. Life throws a lot at
you. You have to adjust."

With that Jack departed for a round of golf. Cindy and
Kaye left for lunch and some time by the pool. I walked to
my car, thinking about the Finches and their struggle to
adjust to a life that had been filled with crisis and a world
that was filled with change.

Like Georgia Gandalf, the Finches spoke longingly of life

in a simpler time, when children rebelled by smoking ciga-
rettes and businesses were stable, predictable places. Kaye
and Jack had said that they still went to church. Traditional
religion offered some comfort. But it didn't help them resolve the conflict they felt as they considered life as it
"should be" and life as it is. So they were looking for answers and tools—meditation, psychic powers—anything to
help them feel better.

"We're not any different than anyone else," Kaye Finch
said during our post-vortex-tour chat. "We're not strange,
way-out people. If you ask me, it's the world that's crazy.
We're just doing our best to figure things out."

There were still many other New Age phenomena to explore in Sedona. There was the woman who advertised that
"You Can Communicate with Dolphins" and a channel who
was said to receive the spirit of a nineteenth-century French
nun. There was also Page Bryant, the woman who started
the whole vortex craze.

But I was interested in finding someone with a different
point of view, an outsider who could tell me whether there
was anything to the vortex idea and what Pete Sanders had
said about the red rocks filled with heavy metals.

Some of the nation's top geologists work at Northern Arizona University, a school that turns out many of the engi-
neers and scientists who work in oil and mining in the
Southwest. From a pay phone in Sedona I called the school,
eventually reaching the chairman of the geology department, an Englishman named Paul Morgan. Morgan said he
would be delighted to talk about the special geology of the
region; it was why he had settled in Flagstaff, the site of
the university, in the first place. We made an appointment
to meet that afternoon. I had just enough time to stop by
one of the other major attractions of Sedona—the health
spa called the Healing Center of Arizona.

The healing center was a collection of five domed buildings on a hillside on the north side of town, near Oak Creek
and the national forest. According to the flyer I had picked

up, all of the domes had been built by the center's director, a former nurse and practicing acupressurist named John Paul Weber. The center was like a retreat house, with half a dozen private rooms, and it offered everything from sauna and steam baths to crystal healing, herbal medicine, and, of course, vortex tours. The brochure said that Weber also had an Indian sweat lodge and facilities for medicine wheel ceremonies.

I found John Paul Weber in the central dome, a three-story tower. He was bustling from one guest room to another arranging for various therapies for a dozen or so women who were there on a retreat. A bald, pudgy man with a bushy red beard, Weber was red-faced and sweating. He had just returned from the golf course. "My [spirit] guides recommended I play golf because my eyes were going bad," he said. "It works. I don't need glasses."

While Weber tended his flock, I followed a spiral staircase up to the second-floor conference room. I could hear some women laughing as I approached. One of them called down as she heard the stairs squeak.

"If you're a man, come up slowly. We're still getting dressed."

The room was filled with giggles. It was as if I had stumbled into a summer camp or a college dorm.

The upstairs meeting room was a white, domed expanse that was fifty feet across and lined with bookshelves. Against the wall were Weber's golf clubs. At a table by one of the windows, three middle-aged women were talking and sipping drinks. Their spirits were high. I sat down with them, and they agreed to answer a few questions.

"What do we do here? It's all very simple," said Barbara Schierman, a sixty-one-year-old grandmother with a distinct Mississippi drawl. "New Age is finding yourself, whether it's religion or Buddha or whatever. I have had a hard time with my feelings. I keep things in and I bottle up my feelings. Here, for the first time in sixty-one years, I let go of all that shit and really cried. It was wonderful."

Barbara and the others had just finished a group-meditation session in which they had tried to enter a trance state and recall their past lives, previous incarnations of their souls.

"You were in a trance and you kept saying, 'Oh, you hurt me, you hurt me so bad,' " another woman, named Lorraine Heier, said to Barbara. "I don't know if you were talking about some man, or about your mother, or what. But you cried and cried and released all that tension. It was good for you."

Lorraine gently rubbed Barbara's back while she spoke and smiled at her. They had come to Sedona together, in search of "a breakthrough experience," according to Lorraine. She worked as a spiritual adviser back home in the little town of Bay St. Louis, on the Gulf Coast.

During their retreat Barbara and Lorraine had studied the healing power of crystals. They had used the sauna and meditated inside a darkened float tank, a coffin-shaped box filled with salt water. They had also received acupressure from John Paul Weber. He had pressed with his hands on various spots on their body, which supposedly corresponded with certain internal organs. The way Barbara understood it, when pressure on a certain place produced pain, it meant that the corresponding organ was somehow not functioning. When these painful spots were found, Weber pressed harder and harder, continuing until the patient reported the pain gone. Sometimes the pain wouldn't go away until the patient confessed a personal failure or recalled some hurtful moment from the past: childhood tragedy, abuse, neglect, defeat. The emotional purging was part of the process; confession preceded the body's forgiveness.

The woman who was sitting with Barbara and Lorraine had just finished an acupressure treatment in which Weber had identified back, liver, and kidney ailments. Clearly exhausted, Vail Kobbe, a gray-haired woman from Los Angeles, sat limply in her chair. Her face was pale and her eyelids were heavy. She said the treatment had lasted two and a quarter hours.

"And I'll tell you, I spent a lot of that time screaming," she said. "It hurt like hell. But old emotional issues came back to me. It's part of the healing process. You store your emotions in your body and the treatment helps you get them out. I've spent the second twenty years of my life healing the damage done by the first twenty years," she said, smiling weakly. "But I feel like I'm almost done."

The women under the dome considered themselves purged, cleansed, healed. It didn't matter if they were physically unchanged. To them, healing did not mean recovery from illness. It meant a psychological and spiritual renewal. It meant getting rid of guilt, self-doubt, depression, and anxiety. It was a way of becoming clean and whole. It was a confession and absolution, a baptism and communion. And if conditions are right, physical healing might take place, too.

Under this definition, the healing center offered its many therapies and rituals, nearly all of which would be considered quackery by mainstream doctors. And, according to this definition, the women under the big dome were confident that they were indeed being healed. As they left for various treatments, I walked downstairs and outside to find John Paul Weber sitting on the front steps of his center. I asked him about the unconventional nature of the care he offered. He admitted that as far as the medical establishment is concerned "these therapies don't work" and then he said he doesn't care.

"I know that what are called 'alternative' therapies do work," he said, smoothing his long, scraggly beard with his hand. "They make people better. They tell me so. But they don't involve the drug companies or hospitals, and the establishment is not about to admit that they work."

Weber's emphatic tone matched Pete Sanders's, and I wondered if the promoter wasn't protesting too much. "I don't need to fight them," he said of regular doctors. "I just want to be a person who helps people heal. I think I can do that better here."

As a nurse, Weber recalled, he had seen few doctors who

demonstrated real compassion and he had seen too many situations where traditional medicine had failed. In the study of acupressure and other unorthodox methods, he found hope.

"We are body, mind, spirit, and emotion. You have to treat the whole person. That just makes sense to me. Of course, it doesn't make sense to the medical establishment, or the insurance companies."

With that Weber announced that he was late for an acupressure therapy appointment. He invited me to return the next day to participate in an Indian sweat lodge ceremony. "We offer any noninvasive treatment that helps people," said Weber. "I just want people to stay well and healthy."

After leaving Weber's domes, I drove up winding Route 89A, through the rocks and tall pines of Oak Creek Canyon, to Flagstaff, where I had coffee and a long talk about vortexes and Sedona's landscape with geology professor Paul Morgan. I was curious about the scientific establishment's view of the Sedona region. I wanted to know more about the rocks, the canyons, and the energy of the place.

A slight, bearded man with a dry, serious manner, Morgan met me at the door of a plain academic office and invited me inside. The room was sparsely decorated, with an old desk and several metal chairs. A large quartz crystal the size of a loaf of bread was on the floor by a window.

Morgan said he could understand the New Agers' fascination with Arizona. With its towering mountains, the Grand Canyon, the red-rock area of Sedona, and the desert, the region is a geologist's beautiful playground. Morgan's particular interest was the Colorado Plateau, a vast, saucer-shaped plain that had once been at sea level but has risen more than a mile. He wanted to understand the forces that had moved the mountains and pushed the huge plateau up and down over billions of years. "Arizona is, I guess, a spiritual environment," he said. "Nature touches something basic in all of us. I have to say that I feel more in touch with my spiritual side when I'm out in the forest or on a mountain."

When I asked him about the energy vortexes, Morgan explained that the Earth has an electromagnetic field, made mainly of energy acquired from the sun and then radiated back into the atmosphere. There are very small but measurable differences in the amount of energy stored and given out by the Earth in different places. Those places with higher energy output could be called vortexes.

Taking me out to the hallway to look at the "Residual Aeromagnetic Map of Arizona," Morgan pointed out the nearest vortex, an abandoned mine in a town called Jerome, about thirty miles west of Sedona. The area was rich in heavy metal, mostly iron stored in basalt, and tended to absorb and then radiate more energy.

"That's where there may be some more electromagnetism, not Sedona," he said, tapping the map with his right index finger.

"But what about the red rocks?" I asked. "Aren't they rich in iron? Wouldn't they hold and then emit higher levels of energy?"

"Did you ever pick up one of those rocks?" asked Morgan.

"Yes. They're pretty light and crumbly."

"Sandstone. The red color is rust. It is iron, but it is in very small amounts that are washed to the surface because the rock is so porous. It oxidizes and makes the red color."

As for the energy that could be derived from rocks, Morgan offered more doubts. "In physics it is true that matter is made up of energy," he said. New Agers use this fact to argue that there is no concrete universe, only the illusion of one. "The problem is, matter isn't both a solid, inanimate object and accessible energy at the same time," said Morgan. "When it's solid, it is there, concretely." Any suggestion that humans can tap solid objects, rocks or crystals, for psychic energy is "pseudoscience," he said.

Then Morgan, the rational scientist, did something surprising. He confessed that he felt a small bond with the New Agers. He had sought spiritual comfort in his struggle with the disease of alcoholism. He had found his peace in a very unscientific set of beliefs, at the core of which is his faith in a Higher Power, a vaguely defined God, that is simply a benign, positive force. For a recovering addict, the Higher Power can be anything, as long as it is more power-ful than man. "A lot of people in the Alcoholics Anonymous program have a problem with the Higher Power. My spon-sor says his is the moon," said Morgan. "Mine is more like a conventional god. I try to meditate every day, and as I drive in to work, I say, 'God, come into my life.' So far, it has really worked."

AA, the Higher Power, and meditation had changed Paul Morgan's life. He said they had moved him from feeling deeply depressed and acting irrationally to getting control of himself and rebuilding his marriage. "If the New Age people are looking for the same kind of answers," he said, "I can't criticize it."

The next morning, in the small town of Cottonwood, which neighbors Sedona, I heard the same kind of ambivalence about the New Agers from another outsider, the historian of the Tonto Apaches, a Native American tribe directly de-scended from the Ancient Ones. A former tribal chairman, Vincent Randall taught Apache history in the Cottonwood schools and had taken on the job of preserving the spiritual traditions handed down by his grandfather and great-grandfather. When I called him to ask about local Indian lore, Randall suggested we meet at a Chinese restaurant—the House of Chin—which he laughingly informed me is known for its hearty Western breakfast, especially the homemade hash.

Although he was rather short, a barrel chest and muscled arms gave Randall an imposing presence as he hopped out of his four-wheel-drive truck at the House of Chin. Inside, he picked his way to a table, nodding hello to the other patrons. He seemed to know everyone. As we sat down, I asked him about the medicine wheels and the Indian lore cited by the vortex tour guides. He paused for a long moment.

"Look, these are some real sincere people and they may really benefit from being exposed to these things," said Randall. "If it creates respect, that's good. But the part I don't like is that so much of what they say just isn't true. There are places where you pay them a lot of money and some guy who says he's a medicine man takes you into a sweat bath. Then there are other people who fool around with the medicine wheel. That's not right. You get the feeling that white people have taken our homes, taken away everything from the Indian, and now they are taking our religion." For Native Americans, medicine wheels are truly sacred places, he said, carefully constructed and then dismantled after each ceremony. "You don't go into the circles and speak out, preach at the people around the circle. That's all wrong," he said. On this point, he agreed with Pete Sanders.

"It's like a bunch of people just one day deciding they are priests and they are going to run Catholic ceremonies. People would say that's disrespectful, but because it's Indian culture we're talking about, no one cares."

Randall had other complaints. None of the places that tour guides described as sacred Indian sites—Castle Rock, Bell Rock, Long Canyon—were in fact important to the Anasazi. "We could teach them the right things, the beliefs and practices that the people here followed, if only they asked us. Here we are a few miles down the road and they don't ever ask us.

"There is one place there, in Boynton Canyon, that is sacred to us. And when they put up a big tennis resort in one end of that canyon, none of those New Age people were there to help us fight the development, and of course we lost."

The way Vincent Randall saw it, the New Agers were just the latest wave of invaders in a land already lost to his people. Like everyone else, he was attracted to Sedona, but he believed he had a stronger claim, a better reason to love the canyons and the buttes.

"I asked my grandfather once, 'Who lived in those canyons?' and he said, 'I did. You did.' You see, the red rock is inside us. It is like we're the Jews, all scattered, and Sedona is our Israel."

I wouldn't tell Vincent Randall that I planned to join a sweat lodge ceremony that afternoon at the healing center. I didn't want him to consider me a New Age invader. And I put his complaints aside as I stood near a huge bonfire, where dozens of lava rocks were being heated until they turned from black to red and finally to white.

Beside the fire, Pat Hendrickson, a medicine man from the Chippewa tribe of the Northern Plains, explained that I was about to undergo a sacred ritual of purification. A large, stout man, Hendrickson had long black hair streaked with gray. He wore shorts and a white T-shirt on which was written, in blue script, NATIF AMERICAINE DU NORD. He said he had picked up the shirt at a conference in Canada.

"We have decided that it's time to open our beliefs up to outsiders, to teach them what we know," he told me. He noted that Earth Day—a national celebration of environmental concern—would arrive the next morning. "We are the original environmentalists," he said. "We have a philosophy that says everything has a spirit: trees, rocks, animals. Our way of life has let us develop along theological lines that give us a responsible role in the world, not ownership." That philosophy would be taught during the sweat lodge ceremony, he said. "You go in, you listen, and we help you participate." He said it would last an hour or two, no more. "When it's over we are spiritually and physically purified. A cleansing takes place, and if it helps people develop a consciousness for the sacred nature of the Earth, that's good, too."

Hendrickson turned away and busied himself with the

eagle feathers, bits of sage and cedar, and the pipe that would be used in the ceremony. I sat on a small wooden bench made out of logs and watched his helpers, nephews named Marvin and Allen, feed the fire and adjust the placement of the lava rock beneath the flames. Ash flew into the air and smoke billowed, drifting up over fifty-foot pine trees.

Behind the bonfire a young woman supervised the construction of the lodge, which would be a low dome, about four feet high and eighteen feet in diameter, built over a round concrete basin where the hot rocks would be placed. The lodge was being built by several of the women I had met the day before at the healing center, including Lorraine and Vail. They started with a frame of crossed branches. On top of the branches they layered strips of carpeting. On top of the carpeting they placed large plastic tarps, the kind used to cover boats in the winter, which were then staked to the ground. More authentic sweat lodges are covered with animal skins or mud or are dug into the earth. But this carpet and plastic dome would serve the purpose and, perhaps, be more airtight, and therefore hotter than anything made of natural materials.

While the women made the dome, Marvin the fire-tender built a small altar of rocks by the flap that served as a door to the lodge. On the rocks he placed an eagle's wing, small packages of cedar and sage, a ceramic pipe that was about two feet long, and a pouch of tobacco. Many tribes used drugs during sacred ceremonies, including parts of the powerfully hallucinogenic mescal cactus, but there would be no drug use during this sweat lodge ritual, only symbolic tobacco smoking.

It was four in the afternoon by the time Hendrickson called us into the lodge. There were eighteen of us, twelve women and six men, including the medicine man and his assistant, Allen. Marvin stayed outside to tend the fire and shovel in the hot stones. After warning us that the heat would be intense, the medicine man invited those who thought they might suffer too much to stay outside. No one moved to leave. Hendrickson then opened the tent flap and, with a wave of his hand, ushered us in.

It was cramped inside the lodge. Our hunched-over backs pressed against the frame of the dome. I was positioned halfway around the circle, directly opposite the door flap, where Hendrickson and Allen sat.

I looked around the circle at the other men and women. The women wore bathing suits and the men had all taken off their shirts. Most of us were holding towels. On my right was a young Indian man who had arrived late and had squeezed into place next to me. To my left was the woman who had supervised the construction of the lodge. Next to her was Vail Kobbe. I wondered how we would all react to the intense heat—sweat lodges can reach about 140 degrees—and the darkness that was to come.

On Hendrickson's command, Marvin shoveled in five rocks. The medicine man placed some sage, and them some bits of cedar, on the hot, loaf-shaped pieces of lava. The offerings literally burst into flame, with a flash of light, and then disintegrated into smoke.

The heat that vibrated up from the rocks drove the smoke into my eyes and my nostrils. Hendrickson offered us a final chance to get out of the lodge and a few of the older women took it. Then Marvin closed the flap and plunged us into smothering darkness. Allen began to sing. The heat quickly rose.

My reaction to the start of the ceremony was probably all wrong, but I couldn't help it. The sweat lodge was, to me, a kind of challenge, a survival test. I planned to remain as still and relaxed as possible, in the hopes that I'd be able to enter the kind of meditative state I had experienced on the vortex tour. I thought of Tibetan monks who can lower their body temperatures and heart rates through meditation. I thought of fire walkers who use meditation to endure the hot coals. I remembered the fire-safety lessons of childhood. The coolest air is closest to the ground.

From the moment the first rock was placed in the lodge, it was obvious that air would be in short supply. A deep breath brought hot, dry smoke deep down into my lungs, where the moisture inside was instantly evaporated. I exhaled, burning the inside of my nose. I stifled a cough, knowing that if I did cough, I would probably gasp in another searing breath and become trapped in a cycle of deep breaths, coughs, and burning. Around me, others were already caught in that cycle. They coughed and gasped, taking in more smoke and heated air and coughing more.

As Allen chanted and sang, I placed a towel over my head, letting it fall down in front of my face. It was quickly drenched in sweat. I sat still, hoping the moisture on the towel would cool the air around my mouth. I closed my eyes, sat motionless, and breathed shallowly, never letting the air down deep into my lungs. This method minimized the effects of the heat, and it protected the lining of my lungs. The shallow breathing didn't provide me with quite enough oxygen, but I decided that light-headedness was better than the burning lungs and suffocating feeling that came with breathing deeply.

When Allen finished, his uncle threw water on the stones, producing a hot vapor that filled the lodge. He then sprinkled the lodge with water. In the blackness, the drops came as a shocking surprise to my body, sending shivers through me, like the chill that accompanies a fever. But the shivers didn't last and I was immediately hot again.

After the water and the song, the people sitting in the circle began, one by one, to pray aloud. Our medicine man started. He prayed to "Grandfather Spirit and Mother Earth" and to the spirits "of all the animals and trees and rocks and all things." He asked Grandfather Spirit to welcome the prayers of the sweat lodge. He thanked the spirits for the gift of the ceremony and then prayed for family members and friends who were sick or in crisis. Finally he prayed for a healing of the planet Earth and for forgiveness of the sins of pollution committed by mankind.

Most of the others followed Hendrickson's lead, opening with the same praise.

"Oh, Grandfather Spirit and Mother Earth."

They prayed for their loved ones and lamented the condition of the environment. One woman literally wept for the Earth, crying about the damage done to "the forests and the rivers and the streams and to all your animal children." Others prayed for relief from illness or addiction. One of the women even recited the Serenity Prayer, the motto of Alcoholics Anonymous:

> *God, grant me the serenity*
> *To accept the things I cannot change*
> *The courage to change the things I can*
> *And the wisdom to know the difference.*

The praying and weeping and praise of the spirits went very slowly. Everyone, it seemed, had much to pray about. After nearly an hour went by and only six people had spoken, Hendrickson announced a break and opened the flap. "The heat builds up too much," he said, "especially for first-timers."

With the light that streamed in through the flap opening, I could see that most of the people in the lodge had laid down, pushing their heads to the outer edges of the structure. The air was probably coolest there. They looked strained, exhausted.

During the short break, Marvin shoveled in seven more rocks from the raging bonfire, bringing the total to twelve. Hendrickson placed more sage and cedar on the rocks. There were more flashes of light and puffs of smoke. The flap was closed, and Hendrickson splashed more water on the rocks. The steam hissed into the air. The temperature rose. I began to wonder how long I could sit still, with a towel on my head, breathing so lightly.

Finally it came time for the young Indian man on my

right to pray. He started with a speech, telling us all that he was often criticized for being too spiritual, for becoming too involved in Native American rites. But he said he was called to the spiritual life and that he was simply following his own nature.

He then launched into a prayer that would, in the intense heat of the lodge, seem endless. It was a long, rhythmic exhortation, begging for the forgiveness and blessing of every spirit imaginable, but especially that of the main deity, Grandfather Spirit. It was also a prayer that revealed a very tortured, troubled life.

I pray for my uncle, Grandfather, that this sweat lodge honor you.

I pray for the animal children, Grandfather.

I pray for my own children, that I may one day see them again, be with them again, Grandfather.

I pray for their mother, Grandfather, that she may see how unnatural it is for us to be apart, Grandfather, that she may see that I should be allowed to see my children.

This went on for at least twenty minutes, as the lodge grew ever hotter. I began to suspect that something more than prayer was going on. How could this man pray so long, in such heat? For that matter, how could everyone else pray so much? It almost seemed as if each of them was determined to be the star of the spiritual show, praying harder and longer while the others murmured assent. Was this a New Age test of endurance, some way to prove who is more spiritual than whom?

Growing exhausted and worried that I was literally being cooked alive, I sank to the dirt floor, putting my head on the ground, my mouth near the dirt, hoping for a breath of cooler air. Beside me, the young Indian man began pounding his legs in rhythm with his prayer.

"I pray for my brothers, grandfather."
Pound, pound.

"I pray for the rivers and the forest, Grandfather."
Pound, pound.

"I pray for the animals, for all your creations."
Pound, pound.

Then suddenly he was quiet. I felt him bend forward, beside me, and place his head on the ground, close to mine.

I felt relieved. At last he had stopped. I also felt sorry for him. I wanted to put an arm around him, to comfort him, but I didn't know if that was appropriate, if I would somehow disturb his spiritual experience. It was also my turn to pray. I had not prayed out loud since I was twelve years old and attending Catechism classes in the Catholic Church. I didn't believe in the Grandfather Spirit or Mother Earth. But I wanted to be a respectful participant. I also wanted to get out of there. Mindful of how hot it was, I summoned up a very brief prayer.

"Grandfather Spirit and Mother Earth. I give thanks to Patrick for inviting me into this sweat lodge and to everyone here for allowing my presence. I pray for all of my family. I pray for the healing of the Earth. I pray for safe passage in my journey through spiritual realms this coming year."

It was all I could muster. I sat back, exhausted, while others in the lodge grunted their approval. Soon there was another brief break. The flap was opened. We gasped for air. More rocks were brought in. The prayers continued.

After more than three hours and twenty-five lava rocks, the last member of our group said her prayer. Hendrickson opened the flap and lit the long peace pipe. It was passed from person to person, along with a plastic butane lighter, which was used to relight the pipe when it went out.

After the first round of smoking, Hendrickson announced there would be more smoking, but that the sweat lodge ceremony was over. He encouraged those of us who wished to leave to do so.

Exhausted, light-headed, and nauseated, I seized his offer. I dashed outside, into warm air that felt frigid against my overheated body.

I looked down at my arm to check my watch and noticed that I was red all over. I had, it seemed, been cooked just a little.

"Good job, man."

It was Marvin, who was still trending the fire outside the lodge.

"I said that was good," he said. "You were in there a long time for your first time."

"Thank you," I answered. I sat on a bench for a moment, too dizzy even to think. I then dried my sweat-drenched body with a towel and pulled on my shirt. As I said goodbye to Marvin, I could hear more chanting emanating from "the sweat."

Inside the lodge, I had focused my emotional energy on the challenge of enduring the heat, the steam, and the smoke. As I drove back to my hotel, I began to realize that the old medicine man had taken risks with my health and the health of all the other neophytes in the lodge, some of whom were middle-aged and not so fit. Although he had told us it would be hot, none of us could have made an informed decision about participating. Three hours is too long for any newcomer to sit in such heat, as my reddened body showed.

Worse was the way he had immersed us all in this test of endurance with little preparation. The whole thing had the quality of a spiritual lark, something unusual to sample from Sedona's New Age cafeteria of experiences. Instead of feeling enlightened and inspired, I felt I had joined in a mockery of a serious ritual. Vincent Randall would have been outraged. I had not entered the sweat yearning to be spiritually cleansed. There were no sins weighing on my conscience, waiting to be purged. And the feeling of relief

I had experienced upon leaving was entirely physical. I was relieved to escape.

Back at my hotel I found myself craving the comforts of the material world. I took a long cool shower and then soaked in the tub. Then I watched television while consuming a dinner of pizza and beer. A tiny, twentieth-century rebellion against ancient spiritual cleansing.

Gradually, my resentments faded and I could entertain a more generous assessment of the sweat. Certainly some of the men and women in the lodge believed they were somehow tainted and needed to be purified, even if I did not. Many religions use punishment, deprivation, and self-mortification in rituals that symbolize spiritual cleansing. Such ceremonies teach lessons in discipline, endurance, and patience. If I wasn't prepared, perhaps that was as much my fault as Hendrickson's.

I did not experience a momentous spiritual renewal in the sweat. But I could understand how that might happen, especially with hallucinogens. And despite the strain of those hours and the fear that I might be made sick by the heat, I was proud of having endured. The ritual had required that I be fully present, fully involved. Few things in life focus the mind so completely.

After the shower, a little pizza rebellion, and many cups of water, I felt calm and relaxed. I could even imagine trying it again.

According to the local paper, Earth Day in Sedona was supposed to begin with a 5 A.M. sunrise service at the town fairgrounds. I rose early and drove over. Only a handful of other people showed up, among them Vail Kobbe, who came because I had told her about it the day before. No one appeared to conduct a service, but those of us who had come stood together and watched the sun rise. One man went to his car and returned with a book of poems about nature. We took turns reading them aloud as we waited for the sun.

It might seem a simple thing, to determine where the sun will rise and then watch it come up, but as we looked out, toward what we thought was a brightening eastern sky, the glow began to subside. Then it seemed to appear again, to the south. The pitiful fact was, none of us was naturalist enough to say where east was. So we watched the birds that soared above us and spied a jack rabbit out for a morning nibble. Once the sun finally did appear, an older man named Tony offered a prayer.

"Let's hope the sun is rising on a new era," he said, "with Earth Day the beginning of us having respect for the environment. Maybe, just maybe, this really is the dawn of a New Age." We then all took to our cars, going our separate ways.

Later in the morning I went back to the fairgrounds to walk around the Earth Day carnival. On this day every city and town of any consequence was celebrating Earth Day with fairs, speeches, parades, and rallies. Hundreds of thousands of people would fill New York's Central Park for a concert. In newspaper pictures of Washington, it seemed as though the entire city had gathered on the Mall for speeches and music. In Sedona, Earth Day was mostly a crafts fair, with a few booths that offered Earth Day T-shirts, crystals, health foods, and other items. Some exhibits displayed energy-saving devices or ecologically safe cleaning products. Students from the university in Flagstaff showed off an electric car they had built. As I wandered around, I bumped into Georgia Gandalf, who was selling her paintings of angels. She gave me another hug and another kiss. I then left for a brunch appointment with Sedona's most prominent psychic, the woman who began the whole vortex craze.

I had called Page Bryant on the telephone the day before and, to my surprise, she had answered. She seemed annoyed by my request for an interview. She had just returned from England, where she led a group on a pilgrimage to Stonehenge. She was tired, tired from all the travel and tired of what was going on in Sedona.

"Everyone has bastardized what I originally said about the vortexes," she had said on the phone. "Frankly, I'm sick of it all. Sedona's being overrun." It took some work, but finally she was persuaded to meet me, if only to set the record straight about the vortexes.

We met for Earth Day brunch at a small restaurant called Irene's. When I arrived, Bryant was waiting there at a table with her husband, Scott. Her hair was black with streaks of gray and it was pulled back into a long ponytail. A large woman, she wore a simple, homey cotton dress, a print of little white flowers on black. She didn't look like a psychic to me. She looked like a small-town librarian.

The daughter of a trucking executive from Conways, South Carolina, Bryant would have likely spent her entire life in small Southern towns if she hadn't encountered her psychic spirit, an inaudible voice she called Albion. She was married to her first husband at the time and raising her two children in Tampa, Florida.

"I was always interested in psychic phenomena, clairvoyance, and things like that," she said as she read the menu. "I read everything I could get my hands on about ESP and the like."

Gradually Bryant became convinced that she was receiving mental messages from an entity called Albion—predictions about the future, insights into the lives of those around her. "The difference between me and the others is I don't say I can explain what it is," Bryant said. "I just call it Albion. It's a presence that speaks through me. It could be my higher mind. It could be anything."

Soon Bryant was acting as a psychic counselor to friends and neighbors in Tampa and building a following by word of mouth. Her big break came when a local radio station gave her a telephone call-in program. She would answer questions from the audience, offering her insights into their problems and predicting their futures. The radio show led to features in supermarket tabloids. She was one of the psychics who every year offer their predictions of world events to the *National Enquirer*. Bryant said she had predicted Nelson Rockefeller's death and the compromising circumstances under which it occurred.

"The tabloids were excellent exposure, even if they didn't print anything about what I actually said," Bryant explained, which is why she quit working for the *National Enquirer*. "I was getting calls from all over the country, day and night." She expanded her business, and eventually the pace of work left her exhausted.

"I got burned out. I didn't want to do that anymore." She moved to Arizona in 1978, where she restricted her work to a radio show in Phoenix. Like everyone else who had ever passed through Oak Creek Canyon on vacation, Bryant had been captivated by Sedona and was determined to live there. Sedona, she decided, would be her retreat from the demands of fame and eager students. She moved there in 1979 and lived quietly for a year. Then Albion told her about the vortexes. He identified seven spots, in canyons and atop red-rock formations, as places where the Earth either emitted special energies or received them from the great beyond. Albion told Bryant to write a book about the environment and psychic phenomena, and she included a reference to the "vortexes" of energy that could be found in Sedona. But the vortexes were not the focus of her book. They were mentioned only in passing.

"Albion said there are places where the Earth emits power, natural power," she said. "Sedona had seven of them, as much as any place in the world. He called them vortexes. I had to look up the word."

(As we talked, it became clear that Bryant was insecure about her lack of formal education. "I could match wits with any of those Ph.D's," she said derisively. "But without the degree, I often don't even get the chance." She spoke proudly of her husband's college degree and referred to him as "the educated one" and herself as "one hundred and fifty percent self-taught.")

At the time of Albion's revelation, Sedona was a quiet,

unincorporated town best known for its scenery and for the apples grown in local orchards. There were no crystal shops or tours of sacred psychic sites, only a few motels and a couple of art galleries.

For the next year or so, things remained quiet. The vortexes received little attention outside of Bryant's small following of clients and students. Then the owner of a local bookstore who had read Bryant's book encouraged her to make an audiotape of her writings on the vortexes. They were offered to visitors, alongside picture postcards and maps of the region. The tape sold briskly, and word of the vortexes spread in the New Age movement.

Soon thousands began making their way to Sedona, mainly from California, seeking psychic experiences in the vortexes. Several enterprising men and women read Bryant's book and established themselves as vortex tour guides. Others wrote their own books, contributing to a sizable body of literature on the vortexes. By 1985, people were trekking to Sedona from around the country and around the world, drawn by the vortexes. New motels and restaurants were built. Real-estate prices soared. By 1990, Sedona was one of the top tourist destinations in the country, with 3 million visitors every year. Travel magazines listed Sedona in their "must see" reviews of hot spots for visitors, and the tourist trade became the dominant industry in town. The vortexes generated tens of millions of dollars a year in tourism revenues. But, ironically, none of this money made its way to Page Bryant. And as this fact emerged in our conversation, she became visibly angry, declaring that money was being made on bastardized versions of her information.

"I kick myself now, when I think about how I should have handled this. If I had handled it right, the information would not have been abused and misused. Now it has all gotten out of hand," she said disgustedly. "We got people here saying, 'Gimme five hundred dollars and we'll go to the top of Bell Rock and go for a ride on the Mother Ship with the aliens.' That's so ridiculous and dishonest."

It wasn't that she didn't believe in life elsewhere in the universe. Bryant said it's silly to suggest that it doesn't exist. Her point was that the vortexes had attracted both real New Age seekers and a lot of hucksters who preyed on the sincerity of pilgrims.

"Let's be realistic about it," she said. "It's a lot of crap what these people are dishing out—dolphin communication and channeling all these famous people. How come no one ever channels someone who was no one? It's always some famous person. Everyone always says, 'I was Cleopatra in a former life.' No one was ever a chambermaid. A lot of it is just crap, I tell you."

Bryant was particularly angry about the tour operators who charged as much as a hundred dollars per person for vortex seminars and made wild claims about what vortexes could do. Only one tour company, operated by one of her former students, credited Albion and Page Bryant for making the vortexes known.

Considering how many psychics, healers, and tour guides were teaching about the vortexes, Bryant concluded that "a whole lot of innocent people, old ladies and such, are being ripped off. It's a matter of respect for the original information. Look what's happened to Sedona. It's out of control. Nobody with an ounce of brains would believe any of it now."

Such a conclusion begged a question. "So why should anyone believe you and Albion?"

"I can't prove that the information is true," she answered. "But you can't prove that it's not. There are just some things, I guess, that are not really open yet to scientific . . . what's the word, honey?"

"Scrutiny," said her husband.

"Yeah, scrutiny," she said.

Then she reached over, patted his hand, and added, "He has the degree."

My pilgrimage to Sedona was almost finished. On my way

out of town, I stopped by the Center for the New Age to say good-bye to Georgia Gandalf. She had struck me as warm and honest and helpful. Unfortunately, Georgia was not at the center when I arrived. The only one in the building was Marlene Myhre, the director. She is a rather dramatic-looking middle-aged woman, tall with bright blue eyes, heavy makeup, and long, ash-blond hair. She had a faraway, even dazed look on her face, and a soft, wispy voice. Myhre is a psychic, a "dreams analyst" who has written some self-published books. (She believes that in dreams the soul ventures through a very real spirit world where conflicts are confronted and resolved.) She had come to Sedona from Wisconsin two years before, to recover from a wrenching divorce that left her penniless. Her story reflects a common theme among Sedona's New Age settlers: tragedy followed by a pioneering journey to a new life in the West. The journey of discovery—the vision quest—is central to the New Age experience, as being "born again" is important to evangelical Christians.

On a much larger scale, the human race has embarked on the same trip, Myhre said. Tragically, millions will perish before the journey's end, because their souls cannot harmonize with the coming spiritual order. "We're on one end of the polarization that's taking place now as we enter the Armageddon period," she said. When the year 2000 comes, she said, those who accept the New Age way of living will happily settle in communities like Sedona. The others "will be so uncomfortable, physically and emotionally, that they will leave their bodies. Individual people might have accidents or have a disease," she explained in her very soft, measured way of talking. "But then there is also famine and AIDS."

I suspected that I was supposed to be shocked by Myhre's vision, but apocalypse is part of so many mystical traditions that I wasn't surprised at all. If fundamentalist preachers and Iranian mullahs can predict the end of the world, why shouldn't some New Agers?

Myhre's beliefs were gleaned from her readings of different New Age books. She had been particularly influenced by art historian and New Age writer José Arguelles, who had organized the international Harmonic Convergence of 1987. Arguelles believed that on August 16 and 17 of that year, certain spiritual forces charted by the Aztec and Mayan calendars converged to mark a turning point in human history. He gathered thousands of like-minded people at spiritual sites worldwide—including Sedona—where they meditated in hopes of welcoming the New Age. Outsiders lampooned the Harmonic Convergence. Cartoonist Gary Trudeau's "Doonesbury" characters called it "the moronic convergence." Yet tens of thousands of Americans had participated and believed, as Myhre did, that it marked the start of a cycle of events that would end in a new kind of world.

The dreadful winnowing implied in all this—agonizing death for the unworthy and utopia for believers—has an obvious appeal for those on the correct side of the dividing line. What better way to establish a sense of security and purpose? If you believe that today's faith will be rewarded by eternal bliss, it doesn't matter if the world considers you strange or eccentric. What matters is who gets the last laugh.

From the days of the early Christians, spiritual minorities have used the same technique, and some have pushed it even harder than the New Agers. In this century many fundamentalist Christians, Jehovah's Witnesses, and other smaller groups have been continually preoccupied with the impending apocalypse followed by the arrival of a millennium of peace. In the nineteenth century, followers of William Miller, a Baptist minister from Vermont, even went so far as to declare a day when the eternal reward would be granted. On October 22, 1844, thousands of "Millerites," many of whom had disposed of their earthly belongings, gathered on hilltops to await the utopia that never came.

Of course, only a minority of nineteenth-century Baptists

shared Miller's millennial dream, and so it is with the New Agers. The typical New Age explorer is concerned, instead, with very personal matters. Indeed, most of those I met in Sedona seemed to be looking for ways to overcome their fears or cope with great losses. Marlene Myhre had lost her marriage and a way of life that had once seemed rock solid. The Finches had lost a daughter and their faith in the traditional American family. Georgia Gandalf had lost her son. The women under John Paul Weber's domes had lost their sense of well-being. Even Pete Sanders had lost his father as a child.

These kinds of losses can strip away the hard coating of denial we all need to keep from being overwhelmed by existential questions. Denial allows us to go about our lives, working, playing, even idling away the hours and years, ignoring our fear of death, the threat of loneliness, the seeming futility of life. Denial is a vital defense mechanism, so important that some psychologists believe it is an organic product of evolution. It is the way in which our brains protect us from our minds. This defense can be destroyed, however, by traumas that seem to threaten us too directly. Serious illness, old age, the death of a loved one, divorce— all these can pierce our denial, deflate our defenses. In rushes spiritual angst. Then begins the quest for relief. Some people turn to the great religions and philosophers. Others turn to the New Age.

Each of the seekers I met in Sedona seemed to be looking for something that would help them deal with change, defeat, mortality, and insecurity. Besides their own personal losses, they were also distressed by a highly urbanized, technological society where the sacred—secure, enduring, transcendent values—had seemingly been eroded. They had all talked about feeling powerless, insecure, and disconnected from others. And they all no longer had ties to many of the old institutions—extended family, church, strong communities—that once might have sustained them.

In Sedona some found hope and a respite from their

pain and alienation. Paranormal power may be one way to begin rebuilding the defenses of the mind. But I suspect that part of Sedona's magic is in its safeness, in its small-town ambience and its welcoming attitude. Life seemed easy here, for the tourists as well as for the spiritual immigrants like Georgia Gandalf, who received instant acceptance and support from the New Age community. It didn't matter that the geologists could find no evidence of the vortexes or that the guides knew little of the spiritual beliefs of local Indians. Here, a New Ager could feel secure, safe, under-stood. In a world of harsh realities, Sedona was a new Lourdes, a place where miracles seemed possible.

# 2 · LOS ANGELES

## Mystics and Healers and AIDS

"WE'VE ALL HAD THOSE LONELY NIGHTS," SAID THE WOMAN on the pink pillows, her soothing voice amplified by a loud-speaker system.

"We all must remember to reach out in love. Love is what we were born with. Love is what we are. And our capacity to love is all we take with us when we leave this planet. None of the rest matters.

"When you wake in the morning, say, 'Today I give love and I receive love because I am love.'

"Tonight, go to bed knowing you gave and received as much as you could.

"And so it is."

From the audience came a reply, in loud unison.

"And so it is!"

The Hayride had begun. At the front of the darkened auditorium of the West Hollywood Public Library was a small table covered with pink fabric and pillows, and upon the pillows sat a blond, middle-aged woman, dressed in pa-jama-like white pants and a long white blouse. Her face was

66

powdery white. Her hair was pulled back. She crossed her legs, Yoga style, and beamed, motherly, upon the crowd arrayed before her.

Beaming back at her, like so many mirrors, were about three hundred people, nearly all of them young homosexual men, the group most affected by AIDS. Some had come in wheelchairs or were connected by plastic tubes to bags of intravenous solutions that hung like giant blisters on metal poles. Many of the men were bony-thin. The vertebrae of their spines were visible through their shirts. Their faces were hollow and wan. Gathered together, they looked like the survivors of some natural disaster finding temporary shelter in a municipal building.

Healing is one of the primary concerns of the New Age. Hundreds of books devoted to spiritual, psychological, and physical healing are published each year, filling whole sections of bookstores. Some, like Bernie Siegel's *Love, Medicine, and Miracles*, offer traditional medical advice and information on the effects of psychological attitude on the body's immune system. But others make outlandish claims about curing everything from cancer to heart disease with "alternative medicine." The New Age has also fostered a proliferation of alternative therapies: herbal medicine, acupressure, Reiki massage, enema therapy, even flower essence treatments. In virtually every case, advocates claim these remedies are based on ancient wisdom and that they bring relief without pain.

The typical New Ager samples these alternatives as he seeks a healthier body and a less troubled mind. But there are believers for whom spiritual healing is a much more urgent matter. In Los Angeles, San Francisco, New York, and other large cities, thousands of people with AIDS turn to New Age healing and alternative therapies as they struggle with a terrifying future. They embrace the New Age because modern medicine offers only the chance to prolong their lives, and because they are, in the eyes of the mainstream American gods, pariahs. In Los Angeles I could not expect to join, directly, in the New Age battle against AIDS. But I could witness the effort first-hand, and try to discover what the movement was offering to people whose every defense against death and despair was under attack.

The Wednesday-night meeting, my first stop in L.A., is called the Hayride, after the woman on the pillow, Louise Hay. Once a little-known author and minister in the New Age church called Science of Mind, Hay formed a support group in 1985 to serve several people she knew who had AIDS. In the beginning about a dozen men met in Hay's living room for mutual support. Given that there was no cure for AIDS, group counsel was the best tool available to those coping with the disease. Word of the "Hayride" spread quickly. Soon more than a hundred men were crowding into Hay's house each Wednesday evening. Eventually the Hayride attracted such a large membership it was moved to the West Hollywood auditorium.

As the Hayride grew, Louise Hay became a New Age star. Her efforts to comfort those with AIDS made an inspiring story, and her best-selling, self-published book, *You Can Heal Your Life*, went through more than a dozen printings, eventually selling more than one million copies. The book spawned a publishing company called Hay House, a nonprofit educational group called the Hay Foundation, and a mail-order catalog business that each year sold millions of dollars' worth of books, audiocassettes, posters, and greeting cards. Hay wrote another book, *Living with AIDS*, and sold audiotapes—recorded meditations called "affirmations"—which many AIDS patients listened to before falling asleep each night. The prayer she was saying as I walked into the meeting—"Today I give love and I receive love because I am love"—was one such affirmation. Through her books and her publishing house, Hay had become not just the main apostle of spiritual healing for people with AIDS, but an angel of self-affirmation for several million others, and the foremost guru of spiritual healing in the New Age.

I quietly took a seat in the back as the opening prayer was being said. I felt uneasy, a bit afraid even, entering a room filled with so many people with AIDS. I wasn't so ignorant that I was seriously concerned about contracting the disease, but I did feel a flicker of worry. What would I say if someone asked what I was doing here? These people didn't want an outsider's pity or concern. Nor was this a freak show, open to any gawker who happens by. I had obtained Hay's permission to attend. I decided that the best I could do would be to express my respect. That would be easy. Looking at these men—all of them roughly my age, all of them struggling with terror—I knew that under the same circumstances, I too just might climb on the Hayride.

After Hay's prayer, the lights were turned on and she asked if anyone in the audience was celebrating a birthday. Hands were raised and runners brought microphones to those in the audience who rose to speak.

"I'm Donald and I'll be thirty-nine this week and I know I'll be around for a while. God bless us, each and every one."

"I'm Lars, I'm forty-five today, and every year is getting better. I think I owe it to the positive affirmations I use. With them the heavens have opened up. I'm grateful to Louise Hay and for these meetings."

"I'm Michael, I'm thirty-four, and I'd like to thank the universe for giving me a year to work on myself. I'm more centered and contented than I have ever been."

"I'm Chuck. I'm thirty-five this week. I've healed my relationship with my parents and my T-cells are up two hundred points."

For a moment, these testimonials made me think that the Hayride was going to be an exercise in happy delusion, a grand denial of the reality of AIDS. They turned out, instead, to be the good news that would precede the real content of the meeting. "Do we have any news of those who have left the planet?" Hay said, signaling a shift in the agenda. No one answered. It seemed that no one from the group had died recently.

"All right then, who wants to share?"

The Hayride quickly took on the tone of a TV talk-and-testimony-show. A thirtyish-looking man with short brown hair raised his hand from the third row. One of Hay's helpers ran over to hand him a microphone.

"I'm Rod. I'm working on forgiving my mother for having had another child when I was young. But I'm having a hard time with it. I still have that resentment."

"That's a wonderful excuse for ruining your life," answered Hay. "You could have a rebirthing session and go back to clear that up." (Rebirthing is an exercise in which a person imagines the experience of being born and, with the help of a teacher, tries to resolve the traumas of early childhood.) "But remember," Hay continued. "You chose to come into a family with this problem to work on. You chose your mother and father and it is part of the stuff you have to work on."

This concept—that each person "chooses" every circumstance of his or her life—is the cornerstone of Hay's philosophy. She teaches that long before birth, the soul chooses to inhabit a specific body, and so follows a certain life course that will resolve the troubles experienced in previous lifetimes. The soul's mission is to achieve a complete balance of good experiences and bad, of vice and virtue. This idea suggests that we are all responsible, at least metaphysically, for everything that happens in our lives.

It was hard to imagine how this seemingly simplistic and deterministic philosophy could ease the spirit of someone who has AIDS. It suggests that one chose to contract the disease, indeed, absolutely had to have it. For a moment I was indignant on behalf of the men in the audience. But surely they all knew Hay's beliefs, and none of them stopped the proceedings to discuss it. Instead the group pressed on. More hands were raised. More problems were aired. Gradually a central theme emerged: This night they would focus on relationships with family members. Many said they had not "come out" as gay to family members.

Others had not revealed their illness. These secrets were a terrible burden.

"I come from a very old-world Italian family," said one man named Tony. "I mean, I think my family knows I'm gay, but I've never actually told them. And they don't know about my illness. Telling them any of this would be horrible."

Many of the men in the audience nodded knowingly.

"My relationship with my parents got so much better after I told them," said the next man. "I told the truth and since then more and more truth is entering my life. I get real support from my family now. Of course, I told them while I was driving the car and my parents were in the backseat. That way, they couldn't attack me because they'd kill us all."

Laughter rippled through the hall.

"You tell them for yourself, not for them," said Rocco, a boyish-looking man with thick curly black hair. Rocco looked about five feet tall and couldn't have weighed more than a hundred pounds. The microphone seemed almost too heavy for him to hold. But he was determined to speak, even if it meant he must pause many times to catch his breath.

"AIDS is enough, man. . . . It's so awful . . . so painful. But for me . . . for me, being honest with people has been beautiful. . . . There are so many people I know who have . . . you know . . . decided to take off. . . . We don't have time to be dishonest. . . . We only have time for the truth."

For a moment the crowd was silenced by Rocco's emotion. No one raised a hand, so Hay took control of the meeting. "We have found that being honest always works best," she said. "Then you can be truly who you are, your family can be who they are, and then you move on."

Obviously, being honest about being gay and having AIDS was not so easy. "I'm an attorney," said the next speaker. "Like a lot of us, my career has been derailed by this. I haven't told my father why. I tell him lots of other reasons. I'm afraid my family will try to take over my life if I tell them. They'll send me to their doctors, try to take control. I had enough of that before."

The issue of control had to be paramount for many with AIDS. They had so little of it. Maybe this is why these men could accept Hay's "soul choice" philosophy. In an indirect way, it restored a sense of order, a sense of control, to their lives. If they couldn't consciously control their immune systems and the progress of the disease, maybe they could feel comforted believing that ultimately their souls were calling the shots.

"Look, I have come to believe that I was born gay for a reason and born into the kind of family I was born into for a reason," said a mustached man named Daniel. "My relationship with them has become so good because I told them about myself and my illness. They needed to learn something. So did I. It has worked."

Daniel was suggesting that AIDS could, at least, break down some of the anti-gay prejudice in families and in the world at large. A dying man evokes the understanding of others, he said. "I have received so much love because I told people the truth."

Love was the message with which Louise Hay opened the meeting and love was the message she wanted to leave behind. With Daniel's testimony hanging in the air, she asked the participants to pick up their folding chairs and stack them against the wall. Then, without being instructed, the men organized themselves to sit in two huge circles, one inside the other. While these rings were being formed, a man dressed in black pushed a bald, withered man in a wheelchair into the center. The man in the wheelchair could have been thirty years old or eighty. It was impossible to tell. His companion, who seemed about thirty years old, stopped when he reached the center of the inner circle and knelt beside the chair. I squeezed into the outer circle and, like everyone, took the hands of the men on either side of me. It felt good to be part of the circle, to not be an interloper, if only for a moment.

Up on her pillows, Hay explained that we had made ourselves into two healing circles and that by meditating together, we could send the energy of our love spinning
around, from one soul to the next. The energy would build
and build, she said, drawing on the spiritual power of the
universe. The circles would send healing love to those who
need it.

The lights were then dimmed, and from the loudspeaker
came more tinkling music, mixed with the sound of wind.
Then came a man's voice, a baritone, singing a one-note
Buddhist chant, "Om."

In the circle we all closed our eyes and joined the chant.
This "om-ing" is a traditional Hindu mantra, or prayer.
The word "om" is a call to the deities. There, in the auditorium of the West Hollywood public library, more than
three-hundred of us automatically "omed," on and on. It
was the kind of display—a bunch of obviously American
adults sitting around chanting like imitation Buddhists—
that outsiders evoke derisively when they criticize New Age
practices. But here, against the reality of so much imminent
death, this chanting was a loving gesture. These men, whose
sexuality was so condemned by mainstream religions, still
needed to reach out to a god of some sort. They needed
the soothing, supportive feeling that comes with communal
prayer. It was as if, for those moments when the "oms"
vibrated in their bodies, fear and despair were drowned
out.

The om-ing produced, in me, a rather pleasant numbness. I thought about the concept of healing love, considered the sincerity of all the people gathered together here,
felt the firm grip of the hands that were in mine, and heard
the power of our voices, joined together and building with
each chant. I understood why the ancients prayed so earnestly for the cooperation of the forces of nature. It didn't
matter that there was no evidence that the prayers worked.

After about five minutes, the music stopped and so did
the "oms" that emanated from the loudspeakers. I opened
my eyes to see that the man in the wheelchair and the one

kneeling beside him were smiling broadly. In the center of the circle, they had been at the focus of the loving intentions of the entire group. In similar circumstances, I might want the very same thing.

As the lights came on, Hay told us to stand. We all did, remaining in our circles. Printed copies of the lyrics of a song were handed out. The men on either side of me put their arms around my shoulders and we all sang, swaying to the music. The song was titled "I Love Myself the Way I Am." Its refrain was:

> *I'm beautiful and capable of being*
> *The best me I can*
> *And I love myself just the way I am.*

With the end of the song came the end of the meeting, practically a frenzy of hugging as the circles broke up and people greeted one another. Several men came to hug me, offering their welcome. None of them asked why I was there. Then Dan Olmos, an aide to Louise Hay who had invited me to the meeting, introduced himself and brought me to meet her. Olmos was quite thin, like nearly all the other men there, and he walked very slowly, as if he were quite fatigued. As we approached Hay, who was surrounded by people, he quietly told me that he had been recently diagnosed with AIDS. "Kind of ironic, isn't it?" he said, smiling.

When we reached Hay, she pulled herself away from the group of admirers to shake my hand and hug me.

"Wasn't that something, those two in the center?" she said, referring to the man and his lover in the wheelchair. She had an excited, breathless tone of voice. "I don't think they have ever been here before, but I think it helped." As several people literally tugged at her sleeves, we made an appointment to meet in two days, at her offices in Santa Monica, for a formal interview. She then turned to tend to those who clamored for her attention. Olmos told me he was surprised that Hay had agreed to the interview. "Not many people do what she does," he said. "There are a lot of demands made on her."

As I left the hall, I passed by a row of tables crowded with men buying New Age remedies—crystals, herbs, flower essences—from vendors. On the sidewalk outside, bunches of men stood talking, the way people do outside of church after a service. I caught snatches of conversation as I passed. The subjects the men discussed were ordinary— where to go for dinner, gossip about friends. What surprised me was how much they laughed. If healing meant deliverance from pain and anguish, some had found it, if only momentarily, at the Hayride.

The next morning I met the Reverend Sandy Scott, another prominent West Coast New Age AIDS healer, at a Hollywood restaurant. Gaudy Hollywood is the hub of New Age activity in the Los Angeles area, and, like Louise Hay, Sandy Scott is fittingly glamorous, in a bright Hollywood sort of way. Blond and tirelessly perky, she wore a bright pink shirt and a skirt. Large ceramic fish dangled from her ears. On her wrist was a Mickey Mouse watch. With her short hair and bubbly demeanor, she looks and sounds so much like the infamous TV evangelist Tammy Faye Bakker that she mentioned it soon after we met.

"I know, I remind you of Tammy," she said. "Everyone says it. I think Tammy is someone like me. Only she got carried away with the money and power. No chance of that happening here. I've gotten rid of the BMW and the big house. That's not what I want anymore."

Scott had been part of the "Prosperity Now" movement that swept the New Age in the early 1980s. Adherents followed various gurus who taught them how to "manifest" wealth through mystical beliefs, spiritual practices, and direct action. The best-known was a former beauty pageant winner named Terry Cole-Whittaker, who developed a huge following and a nationwide TV audience from her Science of Mind church in San Diego. Scott had been one of Cole-Whittaker's assistants.

"It's easy to promote something like that in Southern California," Scott said. "People here are going for success twenty-four hours a day. They get caught up in it, and you know, because deep down they are so needy, there's never enough success to make them happy. It becomes a never-ending cycle."

As Cole-Whittaker's aide, Scott did "financial fluff-ups" for church members, talking with them about why they didn't have the wealth they wanted and helping them plan to get it. It worked for some. For others it meant frustration and even bankruptcy: Following Cole-Whittaker's precepts, some ran up huge debts, assuming "the universe" would take care of the payments. Apparently Cole-Whittaker followed her own advice. She was caught in a financial scandal that ruined her church. As the San Diego ministry collapsed, Sandy moved to L.A. and founded her own church with her husband, Ron, who was also an ordained Science of Mind minister. The specter of what had happened to Cole-Whittaker frightened her. She determined to focus on healing rather than wealth.

Because Los Angeles has been hard hit by AIDS, it was not long before Scott formed a self-help group for people she knew who had the disease. "We call it the Power Group and we don't do death, we do life," she explained as she stirred a bowl of oatmeal. "We try to help people live the best way they can, now. That means we show up at the hospital when they are sick and we go to the City Council meeting for demonstrations." On the day before we met, Scott had joined picketers outside a meeting of the Los Angeles City Council. The protesters demanded increased funding for AIDS programs. Scott noted that Louise Hay never attended protests or marches on behalf of people with AIDS, "and from what I know, she has also stopped going to the hospitals."

It was clear that Scott was competing with Hay. This was

to be expected. After all, supporting those with AIDS is difficult, draining work, and the attention of the press and public is one of its few rewards. Hay had reaped more than her share, perhaps because she stayed out of the gritty politics of the AIDS crisis, a kind of Mother Teresa wafting above policy debates. The problem with this, as Scott pointed out, is that in the battle with AIDS, politics has an enormous effect on the treatment of patients and the search for a cure.

"It's not that I don't appreciate Louise," continued Scott. "She was the first and she has done a tremendous amount of good." Nevertheless, she was angered by Hay's reluctance to go to hospital wards and hospices, where the choices of the soul conclude with death.

"These are young men with good hearts," she said, her eyes welling with tears. "The suffering goes on and on. It's hard to take. When they die, they want you there. But it's very bad sometimes. The smell of rotting flesh is awful. You burn incense and put Vick's in your nostrils and still it's awful. But I've been touched by these men and I can't walk away. Love works. It's about the only thing that relieves the pain. More and more people are finding that out and we are seeing more beautiful deaths."

Behind Sandy's perkiness and phrases like "beautiful death," her work with AIDS patients is a very sad business. Nobody gets cured, at least in this lifetime. Consistent with Science of Mind, Scott teaches that the human soul lives on after death. But beyond that, she can offer no comforting specifics. "Whatever your idea is, as long as you believe it, is as good as mine," she said.

"We don't say you can physically heal every disease any more. We say you can reconcile. I once counseled a woman, a former nun, who I taught, 'You can choose to heal.' Well, that woman had a tumor, and by the time it was finished, it was as big as a cocker spaniel. She said, 'I hate you, I hate you for this.' Eventually we reconciled, before she died. It was then that I realized that death is a healing, too."

As I listened to this last anecdote, I saw that Scott, for

the first time, had stopped smiling. It was also the first time she had relaxed. It wouldn't take a psychiatrist to know there had to be some reason why she had chosen to deal with so much suffering and death. Considering all the drama of her everyday life as an AIDS activist, I had to ask what was behind it all. She responded with the capsule version of her life story. It began with a childhood of sterile California privilege marred by the abuses of an alcoholic mother and a neglectful father. She recounted the rebellion of her early adult life and told how she finally recovered from her own alcohol addiction. It was a sad story, of the kind that is common among ministers, therapists, and other helpers. Like many, she had chosen a career in spiritual healing because she needed so much healing herself.

"Why this kind of ministry at this time?" I asked. "You didn't have to be the one working on AIDS."

"You mean, why the change after San Diego? I guess it's to heal the guilt I felt for being in that other ministry. We knew what was going on there and we didn't stop it. We've got a lot of work to do on that."

Old-fashioned guilt, the staple of traditional religion, had brought Sandy Scott to a life of service. Her AIDS work, and that done by others, was the first example of genuine service I had seen in the New Age movement. And it was guilt, the nemesis attacked by so many "love yourself" workshops, that had brought it about. In the New Age, a movement that can sometimes seem pathologically self-oriented, this was a refreshing change of pace.

Before we parted, I asked Scott if I could meet some of the members of her Power Group. She volunteered two men who, it turned out, had started working that week in the small office her ministry rented just off Hollywood Boulevard. She went to a pay phone in the hotel lobby to call them for me. She came back to say they had agreed to meet. As she turned to leave, I could see that her Tammy Bakker smile had returned.

*　　*　　*

William "Billy" Gonzales and Jeffrey Caine had once been regulars at the Hayride. They both admired Louise Hay and still occasionally went to the Wednesday meetings. But like many with AIDS, they had searched restlessly among many New Age teachers and organizations, taking bits and pieces of spiritual comfort from each one. In the fall of 1989 they both settled in Scott's church and the Power Group. Within a matter of weeks, Billy and Jeffrey, two men living with AIDS, met, dated, and married. At that time they legally changed their names, to William Caine-Gonzales and Jeffrey Caine-Gonzales.

The idea of two homosexual men getting married would shock many Americans. Mainstream churches refuse to conduct such marriages, and they have no legal force anywhere. Before AIDS, such marriages were also an oddity within the gay community. For the last two decades, gay America had fought more for sexual and social freedom than for the institutionalization of its intimacies. But as the AIDS epidemic grew, and the pioneering generation of openly gay men moved into middle age, gay life became less identified with freedom and more synonymous with community. And with community came love, commitment, fidelity—the values of old-fashioned marriage. For Jeffrey and Billy, marriage seemed the reasonable, sustaining, and comforting thing to do. It reminded me of the hurried-up weddings that took place during World War II. Marriage can be a bond that makes the heart grow stronger.

Jeffrey and Billy worked together as volunteers in Sandy Scott's church office, which was in a small plaza of two-story, Tudor-style buildings off Hollywood Boulevard in the touristy heart of the city, near Mann's Chinese Theater and the souvenir shops. When I arrived at the office, I found the door open. Inside, two men were hunched over computer keyboards and staring at the screens while they talked to each other. They had their backs to the door.

"Oh, no! I made all these sentences in capital letters!"

"So what? You can still read them."

"But what if Sandy doesn't want that? Isn't there some way to fix it?"

"I doubt there's an easy way."

The man who had trouble with capital letters was Billy. He was very thin and pale. He had long black hair and he wore a single gold earring, in the shape of a small circle, in his left ear. Jeffrey was even thinner than Billy. On one of his sunken cheeks was a bluish gray smudge of Kaposi's Sarcoma—called KS—a skin cancer common to AIDS patients. They were working on the text of a speech Sandy was to give on the coming weekend. They said they would prefer to be interviewed separately, so the work could continue. Billy and I went out to a sunny courtyard.

Billy pulled a cardigan around himself and buttoned every button. It was seventy-five degrees and sunny, but he was chilled by the gentle breeze that was blowing leaves around the little table where we sat. Billy immediately recited his recent medical history, as if I were a consulting physician. This way of introduction is common among people with AIDS. It breaks the ice and establishes the speaker as an expert. In Billy's case it seemed as though he felt that he didn't have time to be anything but direct.

He first learned he carried the AIDS virus, called HIV, in 1987. He was diagnosed with AIDS a year later by the arrival of spinal meningitis, an "opportunistic infection." His life since then had been filled with so many hospital visits that he couldn't recall them all. He could remember, however, the degrading treatment he received the first time he was hospitalized.

"They were so afraid of AIDS that they wouldn't come in my room," he told me. "They would leave my food on a tray on the floor outside the door. If I could get to it, I could eat. They wouldn't even bring toilet paper to me when I was in the bathroom and didn't have any." After that first experience, Billy made sure to use a different hospital, one that specializes in caring for people with AIDS.

For the first year after his diagnosis, Billy continued to

work, cutting hair at a salon in a department store called the Broadway, but when he suffered a seizure at work, his coworkers began telling his customers that he had AIDS. His clientele dropped 60 percent. Billy left the salon, made up picket signs, and began a one-man protest in front of the store. The *Los Angeles Times* ran a photo of him marching on the sidewalk, and within a few days the store offered him a manager's position in the salon. Billy negotiated with the store's executives until they agreed to give lectures about AIDS to all employees. Then, finding himself too sick to work, he resigned to accept disability payments.

Until then work and the battle with the Broadway had distracted Billy from the reality of AIDS. After he resigned, the drugs he was taking began to work and his seizures ceased. In the calm, he finally had time to become terrified of his prognosis. The hard truth is that the best anyone with AIDS can hope for is to maintain his health and wait for a new treatment that could either cure it or turn it into a chronic illness, like diabetes. This is cold comfort, and it required that Billy reconcile with his fate. That is what "living with AIDS" really means.

In the solitude that came with periods of good health, Billy Gonzales searched for his own way to live with AIDS. Although he had been raised a Catholic, he associated the Church with angry condemnations of homosexuality, so he could not turn to it for support. His family, who had berated him when he told them he was gay, turned their backs on him when he announced he had AIDS.

"This is not just any disease," he said. "If I was dying of cancer, my family would be there for me. They would support me. But they have rejected me because they can't handle the fact that I have AIDS and that I'm gay."

Billy had to wonder why—why this was happening to him. "You want a reason. AIDS can't be just a death sentence. It has to mean something more." He began to search for the "something more" at the Hayride. In those first few Hayride meetings, Louise Hay taught the basics of her philosophy, which Billy then shaped into his own personal outlook on the spiritual meaning of AIDS. He recalled her saying that the soul chooses a family and a life's course. Billy interpreted this to mean that he was living out a divine destiny. Hay also taught that life is affected by a collective spiritual force—"race thoughts"—which are the product of the attitudes of the entire human race. Under this idea AIDS, with its many poignant deaths and enormous social cost, is the result of an evil "race thought": widespread anti-gay bias. AIDS is contributing to the elimination of this bias, said Billy, because it is leading prominent people—politicians, entertainers, artists, and others—to "come out" as concerned gay people. In this way, Billy told me, AIDS forces the world to see homosexual men as fully human beings.

Louise Hay also taught Billy that AIDS carries a spiritual message for the homosexual community. The AIDS crisis has contributed to a reconsideration of the promiscuous life-style many gay men have adopted. Extreme promiscuity is the result of a lack of self-esteem, said Hay. Many gay men, reviled by much of society and even by their families, subconsciously hate themselves, she reasoned. Self-hatred leads to self-destructive behavior and bad "karma" and, eventually, AIDS. It was a neat, circular theory, remarkably similar to age-old American morality. To put it bluntly—we all get what we deserve, even if it is a random disaster.

From a distance, I judged this part of Hay's analysis as simplistic, too condemning. But it struck a chord with Billy, whose life had been filled with self-hatred and tragedy. Raised in a small town north of Los Angeles, he had eighteen brothers and sisters. Several of his brothers had molested him, as did a local priest. He was neglected by his mother and abused by his father. As a teenager he continually thought of suicide and tried to kill himself by running onto busy highways. "I don't know why," he said, smiling, "but the cars always stopped."

Billy had tried desperately to deny his homosexuality. He

even married, at age nineteen, and within a year his wife gave birth to a son, whom they named Lorenzo. Billy said he was devoted to his son and faithful to his wife, but miserably unhappy. After three years, he left them, moving to Los Angeles to live more openly as a homosexual. He had a string of relationships with men in L.A. and pursued his career in salons. Then he discovered he had AIDS.

With no family, Billy found support in the Hayride meetings and the message he received there. He also began going to Hernandez House, the drop-in center for people with AIDS that activist Sally Fisher ran in a residential neighborhood in Hollywood. Finally Billy became a member of Sandy Scott's church, attending her services in a top-floor meeting room at the Hollywood Holiday Inn. He joined her Power Group, about two dozen men with AIDS who meet weekly to study New Age ideas and share friendship. It was there that he met Jeffrey.

From all of his contacts with healing groups and spiritual teachers, Billy had distilled his own blend of New Age beliefs. This was not unusual. The New Age is not like a church with an official set of beliefs and a canon for enforcing them. (It's well known that many churchgoers—Catholics who use birth control, for example—are also selectively loyal to the tenets of their faith. The New Agers are less hypocritical.) The movement presents a long menu of ideas and practices. The believer picks and chooses.

Naturally, Billy seized the beliefs that made him feel good. "AIDS taught me, very quickly, that we are all one human family and I belong," he explained. "I don't think God gave me AIDS to punish me. AIDS is a message, and the message is 'Love one another.' Through our suffering God is teaching the world that gay people are human beings, just like everyone else. We're like the Jews, oppressed and hated. And AIDS is like a plague in the Bible. It's meant as a lesson." This view, of himself as an instrument of God, like the Jews of the Bible, gave Billy the sense that when he died, his life will have had some positive meaning.

He will have been martyred for some purpose. "I also believe that if we come to love each other and believe hard enough, there might be a cure," he said. "You've got to hope for a miracle."

As he thought about belief becoming reality, Billy seemed to reach for a mystical connection that could give him some practical hope. "I think there can be a New Age, a time when people love each other more. After all, reality is consciousness. If we believe in our prayers, we can make them real. Our generation has done enough abusing and killing. Maybe now we can learn to come from the heart. I believe God is a loving God. She's just using a very harsh medicine right now because we've gotten so far away from love that she had to get our attention with something strong."

In the meantime, Billy struggled to live by using both modern medicine and New Age alternatives. He meditated and used visualization to guide the recovery of his immune system. He tried herbal antidotes and he kept crystals on his nightstand. He and Jeffrey also kept a candle burning in their home at all times, "to remind us that there's a light within us, that is everlasting." Billy believed that death is not the end, that the soul and consciousness do live on. "I'm very excited really, about finding out what that's like."

This philosophy didn't always work. When the seizures came and he was hospitalized, or when Jeffrey was afflicted by KS, the terror returned. "Oh, I sometimes wake up and don't really know who I am or where I am," Billy said wanly. "I can't even dress. I say, 'I'm dying and this is all bullshit and nobody is here to care and it's all nothing.' That's how I felt last month when Jeffrey was in the hospital with a fever. He looked like someone who was dying. I went in to see him. The doctor looked at me, and he put me in the hospital, too. I was really low then. But when I come to the Power Group, I feel a trillion times better. It helps you to live life fully, at warp speed, to get it all in. It works."

Just then, Jeffrey wandered out of the office. Billy looked over at him and they both smiled.

"I used to always have this dream about death," Billy continued. "I'd be lying in a coffin and they'd be closing the lid. I'd say, 'I'm not dead! I'm not dead!' Since AIDS, I don't have that dream anymore. I sleep all right. If I wake up, I look at Jeffrey and I'm okay."

Billy went to buy us lunch and Jeffrey sat down, slowly and carefully. He was much weaker than Billy. He had recently been in the hospital for pleurisy and pneumonia. He shuddered in the breeze and put on a heavy coat, covering up a black plastic button that displayed a pink triangle and the message SILENCE = DEATH. During World War II gay prisoners of the Nazi camps were labeled with pink triangles. In recent years the pink triangle has become a symbol of gay pride, promoted by an organization called ACT UP, the AIDS Coalition to Unleash Power. Highly political and confrontational, ACT UP advocates the opposite of Louise Hay's quiet, spiritual approach to AIDS. With his pink triangle defiance and his New Age spirituality, Jeffrey covered all the bases.

Jeffrey had grown up in Los Angeles in a small family. Like Billy, he had tried to be heterosexual, but his relationships with women were always overshadowed by his interest in men. By the time he was twenty, he had abandoned his efforts to live a "straight" life and become part of the gay community of Los Angeles. In 1985 a blood test showed that Jeffrey was infected with the HIV virus. In 1987 he suffered his first AIDS-related infection. After doctors confirmed that he had AIDS, Jeffrey left work and began receiving disability payments. Then he spent much of a year traveling, visiting friends. "You'd be surprised how many people send you airline tickets when they think you are dying," he said, smiling. "I visited a friend in San Francisco. It was a rough trip because a lot of people had died since I had last been there, and that was hard to take. There was a real feeling of death in the gay community there and it depressed me. I told a friend that I wanted to live as long as possible, that I thought I could be one of the long-term survivors you hear about."

Long-term survivors are legendary figures among people with AIDS. Their lives are dissected and analyzed in the hope that some clue, some method for fighting the virus, might be found. Many have come to believe the key to survival is not medicine, not the drug AZT, which suppresses HIV for a while. Drugs are available to all—or at least all who have health insurance or access to government programs—but only a few live with AIDS for eight, nine, or ten years. Many believe it is mental and spiritual attitudes that matter. They think that somewhere in the vaguely substantiated mind-body connection is the key to stimulating the immune system and fighting AIDS.

In San Francisco a friend gave Jeffrey a copy of a magazine published by the Science of Mind Church. He was impressed by the optimism he found in its pages, and by the emphasis on spiritual healing. Something like Christian Science, without the prohibition on medical care, Science of Mind makes selective use of modern medicine while co-opting metaphysical ideas from virtually every religious tradition. Science of Mind began as a book, written by a self-made philosopher named Ernest Holmes. It evolved into a loosely connected kind of denomination—the United Church of Religious Science—with hundreds of churches or smaller "study groups" scattered across the country. One of those churches was Sandy and Ron Scott's Hollywood congregation. When he returned to Los Angeles, Jeffrey and his little dog Gladys went to one of the Scott's Sunday services at the Holiday Inn.

"Sandy was up onstage. I can't remember what she was talking about, but as I walked in I heard her say, 'I'm sick of this fucking shit.' Now I thought, 'If there's a church where people can talk like that, it's for me.' "

Jeffrey and Gladys became regulars at the church and at the Power Group meetings. They were inspired by what the Scotts taught about the power of positive thinking and self-love. "What they said was, 'You can heal your life. Live fully today.' Not that you can heal every disease," recalled Jeffrey. "That sounded reasonable to me. I want to be a long-term survivor and get to the point where they can manage this disease. To do that, I pray at night, most every night. I visualize myself as healthy, happy, whole and complete." When he has trouble sleeping, Jeffrey also listens to tapes of Louise Hay or Sally Fisher, who have recorded soothing messages with "guided visualizations" that instruct a listener to have warm, positive thoughts.

Billy returned with lunch—turkey burgers and fries. Jeffrey seemed relieved to find an excuse to stop talking. He was tired. But he didn't seem dispirited. "I've found a different way to live," he said, "one that's more honest and has a lot more support. The people in the church and at Hernandez House are fabulous." Jeffrey had taken the "AIDS Mastery" course and saw Sally Fisher frequently. "I just wish it hadn't taken this to show me a better way to live."

After lunch, Jeffrey and Billy went back to work and I drove over to Hernandez House. Sally Fisher had invited me to attend a session of her AIDS Mastery course, which would be held the next day, but she wanted me to meet some of the people there first.

Hernandez House is on a residential side street lined with tall palm trees. The house is a large, white, prewar bungalow with a big front porch and a gently sloping roof. Packed in a row of very similar houses, Hernandez House is distinguished only by its front door. It is always opening and closing for a steady stream of people, mostly young men, who come to get information on AIDS care, to attend meetings, or simply to sit around the big living room and talk. The traffic gives the place the feeling of a fraternity house.

Sally Fisher's laugh preceded her as she came downstairs to meet me. A tall woman with dark black hair that softly curled around her pale, angular face, she smiled a lot and laughed loudly. She said she emphasized spiritual freedom over religious dogma and political activism over proselytizing. "We do reality here," she said.

Fisher had gathered half a dozen men, all of whom had

the HIV virus or AIDS. "They're the ones," she said as she directed me to sit with them in the living room. "Talk to them."

Seated on the sofa and in overstuffed chairs were men in various states of health. Some seemed strong and well, others had the gaunt look of AIDS in its more advanced stages. They ranged in age from the bearded young man named Forrest, who was in his early twenties, to Allen, a slightly stooped man of nearly fifty who wore a light brown fedora and looked and sounded like Truman Capote. There was also Jim, a freckly, boyish-looking man with bright red hair, Ron, a man in his forties who had recently come out of the hospital and Tom, a young Southerner who looked and talked like a Marine.

Again I felt nervous approaching a group of men to discuss their battle with a most stigmatizing and deadly disease, but again, my interview subjects put me at ease. They were quite accustomed to talking about AIDS; indeed, they welcomed the opportunity to talk about it some more. After we began, others joined and soon the interview became a free-form discussion of AIDS, homosexuality, and the various stigmas and challenges posed by both.

Like Jeffrey and Billy, these men would invariably revert to asking why: Why was this disease sexually transmitted? Why did it strike the gay community? Why were they the ones who had to confront death in the prime of life? They each answered these questions differently. Some, like Forrest, who had not yet been seriously ill, exuded optimism and strength. They talked about AIDS as a challenge, a call to spiritual growth and change. Others, like Ron, who had been sick for several years, had a more complex, even ambivalent perspective. And Allen, the oldest of the group, waxed fatalistic in the face of so many brave but failed efforts.

"I was spiritually aware when I had those acid trips in the Seventies," he said at one point. "With Louise Hay and that group I learned to love myself. Louise says we're a hundred percent responsible for the disease and it's our choice, our decision. Well then, the decision is made. Now I'm waiting to die."

Sitting back in his chair, looking down his nose as he talked, Allen made the others visibly uncomfortable. Hernandez House existed as a place of hope. Death was not accepted lightly here. Forrest, who worked as a counselor at the house, was angered by Allen's attitude.

"Listen, I can accept that everyone has a different spiritual view," he began. "I can even see what Louise means. But what good does it do to talk about it? If I created it, I did so at such a deep level, a soul level, that it's not worth talking about. Who cares? I believe it's a collective thought that created it, but what does it matter? What matters is living today, completely. Tomorrow could bring a breakthrough, Allen."

Allen presented, in corporeal form, the conundrum of living with AIDS. Healing, in the sense that people at Hernandez House, the Power Group, or the Hayride mean it, requires accepting the fatal reality of AIDS and then living as full a life as possible. But Allen forced the group to see how difficult it can be to live joyfully under a death sentence. Forrest suggested that this challenge could be met through service to others. "I get a lot from being here," he said. "The people here are committed to helping each other and they are courageous. They don't want to die having a lot of regrets. Neither do I. If you get involved in helping other people and helping yourself, you get out from behind your wall of fear."

Allen batted this argument away with a wave of his hand and a single statement: "Wait till you're in my position." Allen needed to be fatalistic. Forrest needed to see a purpose in his suffering. The rest of the group put themselves between the two, turning the conversation to their experiences with mainstream religion (all negative) and concluding that New Age faith helped.

"I think the key is believing in something, strongly,

whether it's a higher power, a Jesus Christ, Buddha, whatever," said Ron, summing up for the group. "It's the act of believing that will save your ass when you are really low. I'm not about to question anyone else's beliefs. And I'm not down on my hands and knees praying about it every night. But I choose to believe there's something more after death."

Dinnertime was near and the group slowly broke up. Allen was the first to go, wrapping a long overcoat around him as he went out. When he left, several of those who remained sighed loudly. It was generally agreed that Allen was more depressed than usual and had needed to express himself. No one condemned his pessimism. They all said that they often had similar feelings.

As others left, I followed Ron and Forrest into the kitchen, where we found fresh peaches in a bowl and a pot of coffee warming on a hot plate. We were joined by another man, named Murray, and soon by Sally Fisher. We stood around the kitchen, eating peaches, drinking coffee, and talking.

"I say, 'Live as if you are going for a miracle, but be prepared to fall short,'" said Fisher as she leaned back against the kitchen counter. "The options range from death to having the virus leave your body, which is in the realm of possibility. But we encourage people to be realistic, to have their eyes open."

Fisher was intrigued by many New Age spiritual ideas. She believed in some channelers—she mentioned the spirit Lazaris, who was channeled by a famous medium from Florida—and she said she had even received some information "on nuclear waste disposal, of all things!" which she was certain came from the spirit realm. "I took it to a physics professor and he said it was interesting, technically, but wouldn't work." She also believed in the Jungian notion of the "collective unconscious," which, through spiritual means, affects both individual development and the course of world events. But she was impatient with spiritual pursuits that might divert attention from concrete action.

"Hey, I took philosophy in college," she said, "and I know that AIDS is a product of our consciousness, just like this table. But it's also real, just like the table, and it's not going to go away. I meditate a lot and work on loving myself, but I still get colds. That's the way it works. We say, 'Pay attention to both, the body and the spirit.' "

Fisher reminded me to return to Hernandez House the next evening to see the opening session of a three-day AIDS Mastery workshop. She then gave me some peaches to take back to my hotel. As I left, Murray followed me to the door.

"So what do you think? What are we, a bunch of deluded mystics?" he asked.

"Mystics, maybe," I answered. "Deluded, no."

"Well, I wouldn't blame you if you thought we were all nuts. But consider the situation we are in."

Murray stood at the door and waved as I walked to my car. He looked like someone standing on the porch of a family home, saying good-bye to a distant relative who had come for a visit. He could go back inside and find someone—maybe a fellow mystic—who could comfort him, perhaps even better than his family could.

The men at Hernandez House were indeed mystically oriented. They sought a utopia of the mind, a place deep within, where fear cannot penetrate. They reminded me of prisoners of war, who use the power of the mind to overcome adversity. Or perhaps they were more like monks gathered together in seclusion, building a life where spiritual concerns are a priority, where they could talk about the collective unconscious, karma, and life after death, in earnest. Mainstream America doesn't have time for these matters. Ours is a nation obsessed with achieving, acquiring, and consuming. It is a youth culture, where the very young and the old, the sick and the dying—those who are often more inclined to spiritual thoughts—are separated from the flow of life. The mystics in our midst remind us of truths so painful that we shut them away. We would rather deny their existence than learn what they might have to teach.

Of course, each of us winds up in this isolation—in the ultimate out-group of the old and the sick—sooner or later.

Louise Hay was sitting at her desk opening mail when I walked into her office the next day. She and a dozen or so aides worked on the sixth floor of a glass and concrete cube in downtown Santa Monica. The view from her corner office included much of the city, to the Pacific Ocean. Behind her, a computer screen glowed with a display of a book in progress. In front of her, a large teddy bear occupied an overstuffed cotton sofa. A quartz crystal the size of a regulation football was resting on top of a large stereo speaker in the far corner of the room.

Hay looked much prettier in the sunlight that streamed in the office than she had in the fluorescent lighting at the Hayride, which had made her look ghostly. Here, her hair looked blond, not white. She wore a long, emerald-green shirt and pants, a heavy silver necklace, large silver earrings, and silver shoes. She glowed.

"Look at this," Hay said, handing me a letter. "This happens all the time." The letter was from a woman in New York. All it said was, "Blessings and great thanks!" In the envelope was a check for a hundred dollars.

"I don't ask for it," she said. "It just comes."

People send Hay money because they have read her books, or seen her on television, and have been moved. *You Can Heal Your Life* had spent many months on the *New York Times* best-seller list. Its main point is that we all are responsible for creating every circumstance of life. Physical or emotional "dis-ease," as she calls it, comes from a lack of self-love and an unwillingness to forgive others. Once a reader understands this concept, he or she can follow Hay's prescriptions—meditations and affirmations—to develop a better self-image and attitude and actually heal the body and spirit. Hay is very specific in her advice. In the back of the book there is a long list of ailments, from acne to warts. Beside each illness is a "probable cause" and a meditation that Hay suggests will cure it. For example, beside cancer, she lists the cause: "Deep hurt. Longstanding resentment. Deep secret grief eating away at the self. Carrying hatreds. What's the use?" Her prescription is the following meditation: "I lovingly forgive and release all of the past. I choose to fill my world with joy. I love and approve of myself."

There is no scientific source for this list of "probable causes" and cures. But those details don't seem to matter to Hay's loyal readers. What matters is the inspiration and the suggestion of control. In this, she is not so different from the healers of the eighteenth and nineteenth centuries who also developed elaborate pseudoscientific systems for diagnosing and treating illness. Phrenologists studied the shape of the skull. Iridologists made diagnoses by examining the eyes. Treatments included herbs, the use of magnets, even hydrotherapy—immersion in water. One of America's most successful nineteenth-century healers was John Kellogg. Long before his cereal company was founded, Kellogg was prescribing vegetarianism and hydrotherapy at his sanitarium in Battle Creek, Michigan. As with most of the other healers, some of Kellogg's patients beat the odds and got better, boosting the popularity of his treatment. But when the cures could not be repeated, Kellogg's therapy fell out of favor. And so it went with all the others.

The difference between Hay and the faith healers of the past is a century of scientific progress. When Kellogg ran his sanitarium, so-called modern medicine had little better to offer many patients. That is not the case today. Today real cures exist for most of the ailments in Hay's charts. This made me think that Hay was simply exploiting the vulnerable, gathering millions of dollars and reaping the benefits of fame, at the expense of those in pain. That would be true if she merely posed as medical expert. But Hay is more than that. She is also a spiritual evangelist and a role model for those who would be healthy, wealthy, and self-assured. She is more beautiful and more successful than most any sixty-two-year-old woman. If she attracts millions of readers, perhaps it is because so many want to be just like her. In the first pages of *You Can Heal Your Life*, Hay offers the best explanation for her huge following. "Everyone," she writes, "suffers from self-hatred and guilt." Louise Hay was there to help everyone overcome these curses.

Hay's life story includes enough hardship to establish a kinship with her most anguished readers. She was born a year before the great stock market crash of 1929 and her childhood was spent amid the poverty of the Great Depression. Her parents, Christian Scientists, were divorced before she was two. She recalls being raped, at age five, by a neighbor who was convicted and sentenced to fifteen years in prison for the crime. Nevertheless, Hay said, she was made to feel at fault for the assault. She ran away from home at fifteen and gave birth to a daughter at sixteen. She endured a series of relationships with violent men as well as a failed marriage. Finally, at about age forty, Hay discovered the Science of Mind and found her calling. She became a minister of the Church in New York and wrote a little book called *You Can Heal Your Body*. Soon after that she was diagnosed with cervical cancer and came to believe that she had cured herself with six months of alternative medicine, self-love, and meditation. Hay then moved to Los Angeles, established a ministry, and grew popular in New Age circles.

The roots of Hay's philosophy are clearly in her mother's Christian Science practice and her own experiences with Science of Mind. But the turning point in her life was the bout with cancer. As the story goes, she was diagnosed by one doctor, but refused treatment. Months later she was reexamined and the cancer had disappeared. A skeptic might wonder if she ever had cancer in the first place. For her, there is no doubt, just as there is no doubt that she was cured, miraculously. It was a miracle that proved her faith. When the New Age movement arose, she was waiting with a spiritual message and personal experience that fit almost too well.

As she told me to take a chair, Hay reached behind her

94

to turn on a stereo. Soothing New Age music—chimes and violins—rose out of the speakers behind me. "I don't know why I'm the one," she said, referring to her status as a superstar healer. "I'm either paying back for a past life, or laying in karmic points for the next one.

"People are interested in the New Age because traditional religion doesn't work," she said of her followers. "Traditional religion is guilt ridden and it was created simply to control people. There may have been a time when humans needed such religion, but we have evolved beyond that now. New religion gives much more power to the individual. It says, 'Here's a new set of laws. If you comply with them, you can take care of life. The universe is here for you.'"

People starve amid the "abundance of the universe" because of low self-esteem, said Hay. A poor self-image is more damaging than one might imagine. The soul projects a person's self-image, said Hay, and attracts the kind of experience that seems appropriate. That's why, she said, women who are raped are responsible for what happens to them. They attract the rapist because they expect and fear an attack. Similarly, she told me, the poor of the world are responsible for their plight, as are those afflicted with AIDS. With the right spiritual approach, she said, any poor person can raise himself up, any sick person can make himself well.

Anyone who has seen real suffering would find this kind of thinking repelling. I did. As Hay spoke I thought of the families who lived atop a garbage dump in Manila, whom I visited while I was a writer on assignment in the Philippines. They were no more responsible for their fate than children of poverty in New York's slums or my wife, who was sexually abused as a child and carried the scars into adulthood. No matter how we wish to control it, life sometimes brings random tragedy. Hay would add insult to injury, blaming the victim. It's the perfect rationale for those who would rather not feel responsible for others.

I thought to challenge her with examples drawn from my

own experiences, but I did not. Instead, I chose something closer to home. I asked her why all the self-esteem generated by the Hayride, the audiotapes, the books, and the affirmations, hadn't defeated the AIDS epidemic. No one had been able to overcome the disease, no matter how much they loved themselves.

Here she fell back on the mysterious matter of "soul choices." It may be, she reasoned, that there are millions of souls that somehow need AIDS. "All the rules don't seem to work with AIDS," she continued. "There has to be an answer. It has to be curable. I know there has to be a good reason, on a cosmic level, to explain AIDS. But even I don't know it yet."

Hay could not accept that something like AIDS might evolve, at random, from natural biological processes. But her search for the spiritual cause had been so frustrating that she had begun to consider any explanation, however bizarre. First she told me that there is evidence that AIDS is man-made, either the product of some diabolical plot or the result of a medical experiment gone wrong. Then she seemed to suggest that AIDS is, in a way, a punishment from God, as many Christian fundamentalists say.

"I was wondering," she said, leaning back in her chair. "What did the people at the Hayride remind you of? What did they look like, to you?"

"Well, some were thin, haggard looking," I answered. "They were skin and bones, wasting away."

"What did that remind you of?"

"The obvious answer is Nazi concentration camp survivors."

"Right."

The inference, given Hay's philosophy, is that people with AIDS may be the reincarnated souls of Nazi tormenters, brought back to endure a fate similar to that of their victims.

"Is that what you think?" I asked, struggling to control my amazement. "You think they might be Nazis reincarnated and this is some kind of karmic justice?"

"I'm not saying that for sure," she answered. "But I look for connections in things, to explain things."

It was an ugly and far-fetched explanation, and it was shocking to hear it offered by this beautiful white-haired evangelist for love. It also betrayed a compulsion to explain things and put them in order, a compulsion that may be the essence of Louise Hay. Her books, with their lists of diseases and recipes for cures, are as much about control as they are about love. In her office, as assistants bustled in and out, seeking decisions and advice, Hay was the picture of control, like the captain on the bridge of a ship in a storm. She presented the same image at the Hayride—calm, steady, in command—while all about her people felt lost and out of control.

"Control, feeling in control, is very important to you, isn't it?" I asked.

"I guess so," she said, chuckling. "You might be on to something there."

Considering the two-year-old Louise who watched her father leave, the five-year-old who was raped, and the fifteen-year-old who became pregnant, it was easy to understand why control was so important to her. She had spent her formative years in chaos, literally out of control. Who wouldn't, under such circumstances, feel a compelling need to explain, order, and control? With AIDS Hay had chosen to struggle with one of the most disorderly, uncontrollable things on earth.

Many of the people Hay attracts have faced similar experiences—unexplainable losses, random tragedies, debilitating defeats—and the idea of gaining control must hold as much power for them. For Louise Hay, the urge for control goes even further, though, to her belief that all of us are capable of becoming superhuman beings. Here her ideas enter the realm of science fiction.

"They say we only use ten percent of our brains. What if we use the other ninety percent? We would all have all kinds of psychic abilities, wouldn't we?" She surmised that one day soon, people would be able to dematerialize, travel telepathically, and reconstruct themselves in some spot halfway around the world. All this is quite wonderful to think about and, she asked, "Why shouldn't we believe it?"

She paused for moment and reached into her desk drawer. She took out a small nail file, leaned back in her chair, and began working on her fingernails. "I'm not saying you have to believe everything I do. I'm just explaining what I've come to believe and it seems true to people. The point is that you have to work out answers that are good for you. Whatever I believe is true for me. Whatever you believe is true for you."

I walked out of Hay's offices and rode the elevator down to the street, where it was a perfect, Southern California afternoon—warm, breezy, cloudless. I walked to the ocean to think about what Hay's work and popularity meant. I was surprised to discover that the park that separates Santa Monica city proper from the beach was inhabited by hundreds of homeless people, men and women in poor excuses for clothes, many of them carrying plastic bags filled with their possessions. They camped in groups, under the trees. They lounged on every available bench or rock.

Discomfited by this park full of pain, I headed back toward Hay's office and my car. On the way I stopped at a McDonald's to use the washroom and had the kind of encounter I had tried to avoid by leaving the park. There, in the washroom, a man called out from a locked stall.

"Excuse me. Is there a man out there? Sir, could you help me? Could you please help me? I won't hurt you."

I asked what he wanted, and he slid a small plastic bottle under the door.

"I can't open this. I need help with it. I'm supposed to wash this every day and I have to use this special water."

The bottle of sterile water bore a label from a Veteran's Administration hospital. As I tried to open it, the man swung the door open. He was a black man who looked about forty years old and was dressed in army fatigues. He was seated on the toilet. His left pant leg was rolled up, exposing a deep wound about eight inches long. The floor was littered with bloody gauze. He explained that he had had a tumor removed from his leg and that he had been discharged to care for the wound himself. He said he was homeless. The McDonald's washroom was his clinic.

I opened the bottle and handed it back to him. He smiled, thanked me, refused my offer of some money, and, wincing, started to work on the wound.

I left, found my car, and began to drive back to Hollywood, contemplating the men with AIDS I had met and the man in McDonald's. All of them were walking symbols of pain, of never-ending struggle. Their problems—AIDS and homelessness—were tragic and frustratingly complex. But they could be understood, in practical, human terms. And I couldn't imagine how "soul choices" had anything to do with them.

That night at the Hernandez House in Hollywood, a group of eighteen people with AIDS or the HIV virus continued their own spiritual struggle with AIDS at Sally Fisher's AIDS Mastery workshop. I attended the opening session of the three-day workshop on the condition that I would not take notes or violate the anonymity of the participants. I can write that among those who attended were three women, several men who were clearly ill, and another who came with an IV setup—a pole, a drip-bag, and an intravenous line—and seemed to be dying. Many said they had attended the Hayride and the Science of Mind Church. They wanted more.

What took place, over the course of many hours, was something like the Hayride, group therapy, a religious service, and an encounter group all rolled together. Before the meeting began, each of the participants received a welcoming gift, an envelope that contained printed instructions and a small crystal. They then sat down in the rows of folding chairs that had been set up in the living room where I had talked with Forrest, Allen, and the others the day before. Sally Fisher opened the meeting with a lengthy speech about the power of honesty and the destructive nature of secrets. It was through honest self-examination, she said, that they would come to "master AIDS," learning to live fully and happily, despite their condition.

The main exercise, which would last well beyond midnight, began with a "guided meditation." Fisher asked the group to breathe deeply, close their eyes, and follow her instructions. She then had them each imagine themselves walking down a long corridor lined with doors. Behind each door was an important memory, a memory that held a key to their current poor self-image. She instructed them to imagine opening the doors, looking at each memory, and then closing them, symbolically freeing themselves of the powerful feelings those memories evoked.

The next step was obviously more painful for the students and more difficult to witness. Each was instructed to stand before the group, offer a brief autobiography, and then reveal something of what was behind their doors. Some spoke of childhood abuse, others mentioned their own drug addiction or the loss of friends and lovers to AIDS. Those who held back, or couldn't seem to recall their childhoods, were questioned by Fisher and her helpers, who shouted their questions from the back of the room.

"What about your father? You didn't mention him."

"Have you told your family you are gay?"

"Have you told them you have AIDS?"

The most uncomfortable exchange of the evening was between Fisher and the youngest participant, a tall, tan twenty-year-old with long blond hair. He stood in the middle of the floor, regaling the group with stories of his oft-drunk parents and his teenage years among the rich children of suburban Orange County. Fisher grew frustrated as she tried to pin him down on the specifics of his condition and his self-image. Then she hit the mark.

"So tell me," she said. "What did you take before you came here?"

"You can tell?"

"What was it?"

"Just a little coke."

"Don't do it tomorrow or you won't be allowed back. You got it?"

"Yeah."

"Sit down," Fisher barked.

From here the members of the group would proceed to examine all the personal qualities they detested and discover that we all share similar faults. I left at about midnight. Fewer than half the people in the group had spoken and it was clear the talking would go on for hours. It was a relief to go and I could sense that the workshop participants were relieved as well when I rose to go. Fisher had invited me, but they had reacted coolly to my presence. During a break, none of them had spoken to me. I understood. They were struggling to reconcile themselves to death and they didn't really need an uninvolved observer.

I reserved the next day, my last among the New Agers with AIDS, for a casual lunch with Billy and Jeffrey Cain-Gonzales and dinner with Dan Olmos, Louise Hay's assistant.

Billy and Jeffrey lived west of the city center, in San Gabriel, an hour's drive from my hotel. As I navigated the freeways, I listened to the news on the radio, which, strangely enough, contained two reports related to the New Age movement. One was about a bomb exploding in the car being used by two members of Earth First!, a radical New Age environmental group that had been battling to save California redwood trees from foresters. Earth First! wasn't above destroying logging equipment, barricading roads, and spiking trees to stop chain saws. The other news report concerned the discovery of a week-old corpse in the apartment of a Los Angeles psychic. The psychic had been trying to raise the man from the dead.

The Caine-Gonzales house was a low ranch on a tiny plot

squeezed between other low ranches on other tiny plots. Billy met me at the door and invited me into the front room, an airy space. Jeffrey was lying on one sofa, his head propped on a pillow. He was wearing a black sweatshirt decorated with the words SILENCE = DEATH and a large pink triangle. I sat on another sofa. Across from me a candle burned on a mantel.

"Excuse me if I don't sit up right away," Jeffrey said. "It was a tough week." It was the first week either of them had worked in more than a year. They were both exhausted. But work was not the only thing that had made Jeffrey and Billy tired. They had stayed out late the night before, attending a play at Billy's son's school. Before the play, Billy drove Jeffrey past his mother's home. They didn't stop. They just looked in the windows. Billy's eyes filled with tears as he told the story.

"I don't know what I expect. Those people there don't want to support me. I guess I want the mother I never had."

Billy and Jeffrey had suffered one rejection after another because of AIDS. Nothing, from family relationships to the mundane chores of everyday life, was the same. To prove this, Billy told me about the time Jeffrey had a seizure in a local supermarket. While Billy was off looking for something, Jeffrey fainted and fell to the floor, cutting his mouth. "I came down the aisle," said Billy, "and he was surrounded by people. They were about to wipe up the blood. I had to yell at them to stop. I said, 'Don't touch that, I'll do it.'" Later, when the paramedics came, Billy had to tell them that Jeffrey had AIDS. They then donned rubber gloves, boots, and aprons before they would touch him. "Ever since that, the people in the supermarket, the neighborhood, everybody it seems, knows we're the guys with AIDS."

As he told the story, Billy sat at the end of the sofa where Jeffrey was lying. He picked up his lover's legs and put them in his lap.

"When you are facing something like this, you go through a lot, maybe ten times as many ups and downs in a week as a regular couple. When you have to go through things like that, life seems pretty challenging."

Billy then got up to call to have a pizza delivered for our lunch. While we waited for it to arrive, he took me on a tour of the house. In their bedroom the double bed was filled with Jeffrey's collection of stuffed pigs. On either side of the bed were little nightstands and on each nightstand was a collection of what Billy called "our God reminders." Crystals, statues of Buddha, ceramic birds and fish, bags of herbs—these were the objects that they looked at to calm themselves in the middle of the long night. On one nightstand there was also a tape player with a headset. Billy and Jeffrey both listened to meditations, spoken by Louise Hay or Sally Fisher, to help them go to sleep.

In the backyard I saw the little patch of grass and the carefully clipped hedges they kept. There was also an empty dog house. Gladys, Billy told me sadly, had recently passed away.

The pizza arrived and we picked at it for more than an hour. Jeffrey never finished his first piece. While we ate, they tried to remember all the alternative therapies they had tried. They recalled herbal remedies, acupuncture, crystals, acupressure, Reiki massage, and special diets prescribed by a psychic. They both said that Louise, Sandy, and Sally had helped them immensely. Jeffrey had participated in the AIDS Mastery course and thought it was wonderful. "When you close the door on those old hurts, during that meditation, it really works."

But while they had consulted with New Age spiritual healers and took alternate therapies, Jeffrey and Billy also sought the most advanced conventional medical care. They both used AZT. Jeffrey had also relied on chemotherapy to treat his KS, with good results. They were covering every base.

"You try what's out there," said Jeffrey. "Take the psychic

diet. I tried it. I couldn't stand it. I love meat. So I eat hamburgers. I couldn't see not eating them. Hey, you're not going to live forever."

A thin smile crossed his face and a laugh bubbled out of Billy. It was the first light moment of the afternoon.

"The most important thing we do is we try things," continued Jeffrey. "We're not passive. You feel a lot better if you try something, anything. And sometimes nothing works. Last week I realized that I could no longer feel God's presence. I was scared. Usually I can just be still, quiet, and I can feel God is there. This time I couldn't feel that. I cried a lot. I prayed a lot."

"When that happens, we'll make a bath for each other," said Billy. "We'll put candles in the bathroom and leave the other one alone in there to feel the hot water and meditate."

To Jeffrey, God's presence was the same thing as sanity. Without it, he would come unglued. He had recovered that feeling, and his equilibrium, during a day of baths, meditation, and listening to tapes. "If it didn't work," he said, "I don't know where I'd be."

Before I left, Jeffrey and Billy asked me to write about them in a way that revealed them as regular people responding to a crisis. Through their New Age studies they had come to believe that every encounter had a spiritual purpose connected with their fate. "If people see that people with AIDS are just human, like them, it will help," said Billy. "It would mean something good came out of this situation."

If Billy and Jeffrey took the "kitchen sink" approach to their illness, Dan Olmos was following the route of the New Age purist. Like Jeffrey, he realized he had AIDS when he discovered a lesion that turned out to be KS. But that evening he said that he hadn't been back to his doctor since his diagnosis. And though he had lost more than twenty pounds, he didn't plan to go back anytime soon. Instead, he was relying on herbal medicine, meditation, and the Louise Hay approach to healing.

(Hay has often insisted that she does not recommend that people with AIDS abandon medical science, but her books are filled with condemning passages about doctors. In *You Can Heal Your Life* she writes, " . . . most doctors do not work with the cause of any illness; they only treat the symptoms, the effects. They do this in one of two ways: they poison or they mutilate." In *The AIDS Book* she writes, "Science is always trying to find a toxin that will kill the disease, not the patient, so look into alternative treatments.")

Olmos encountered Louise Hay and her ideas quite by chance. He had been working as an assistant to a film producer when a friend, who worked at Hay House, called to tell him about a job opening. He declined, but when he lost his film job the next day, he promptly called his friend. The position was still open. He took it, considering it a temporary arrangement. Temporary became permanent as, over the course of three years, he came to follow most of Hay's New Age philosophy of healing.

He met me at a Greek restaurant in Santa Monica. He looked much younger than his thirty years, in part because he was so thin and in part because his face was so pale. Over dolmas and souvlaki he told me he had been raised in a nominally Catholic home, the son of a grocer in the small town of Porterville, California. "My parents were like New Age people. They taught us to be open to everything." At Hay's office Olmos learned about the healing power of crystals and visualizations, but he didn't take it too seriously. That changed when he was diagnosed.

"I suddenly realized, 'I've been at Hay House for a reason.'" That reason, he said, was to find his own way to live with AIDS.

"The doctor wanted to put me on chemotherapy and AZT. But I was feeling fine and I knew those drugs were toxic. I cut off contact with my doctor and I haven't seen him since. I know that sounds amazing. A lot of my friends just don't understand it. But I go my own way in these things, and I feel I know what I'm doing. I feel fine," he said, taking a forkful of food. "And I'm just not going to do anything I don't believe in."

Olmos acknowledged that AZT worked. "My friends who use AZT say it works, but that's because they believe it will. Three years ago, I would have been terrified of AIDS, like them. And I would have immediately gone on AZT. Now I know I have choices, that I don't have to be afraid. That's the difference."

Under Hay's influence, he had chosen to heal himself of AIDS, as best he could, without the standard antiviral drugs. Since leaving his doctor, he had experimented with herbs, vitamins, and diets. He felt healthy and full of energy. And the weight loss, so common to AIDS patients, didn't trouble him. He was certain that it was due to his health regimen, not AIDS. "Taking care of this yourself is all a bit scary, I admit," Olmos said, laughing lightly. "But it bothers my friends more than it bothers me.

"I really believe that when you die, it's not the end. I think reincarnation may be real, or there will be something different than this reality. I'm looking forward to the adventure, actually."

Before we parted, I asked Olmos to tell me his wildest idea about AIDS. He said he sometimes thought it had something to do with creatures from outer space. "I think it's pretty logical to think that they are here—extraterrestrials, I mean. And I wouldn't be surprised if they may have cross-breeded with humans." Olmos said he sometimes wondered if he and the other people with AIDS weren't all really space aliens.

"Wouldn't it be something if AIDS was just the means they used to call us home, back to the mother ship?"

The notion of people with AIDS as aliens was, perhaps, a better metaphor than Olmos had intended. Many gay men must indeed feel alien in a society that so stigmatizes their sexuality. And those with AIDS, who are often isolated as the untouchables of our time, must feel all the more like creatures from another planet. What a relief it would be to escape to a promised land in outer space, another version of New Age heaven.

Of course, fantasy would not help Dan Olmos, and as he left me, I wanted to tell him to reconsider AZT. But I didn't. No doubt he had heard the arguments many times, from those who knew more, and knew him better. He had made his choice. In the end, there is one matter that people with AIDS can still control: their treatment. And, it seemed, each chooses the option that helps them get through each day without going mad. It is a matter of control, or at least the illusion of control. Fantasies aside, many of those who have turned to the New Age obviously have found something of value there. An antidote, not for AIDS, but for despair.

# 3 · PHILADELPHIA

## Lazaris and the Star Seekers

AT EIGHT O'CLOCK ON A WARM SUMMER EVENING IN PHILA-delphia, a chubby, bearded man with blond hair and wire-rim glasses climbed onto a small stage in the downtown Holiday Inn. He sat down in a black lacquer chair sur-rounded by potted plants, took off his glasses, and placed them on a small table. He smiled pleasantly and then closed his eyes, resting his chin on his chest, like an old man sleep-ing on a front-porch rocker.

In the back of the room, where stacks of books, tapes, crystals, and other items were being sold from a makeshift store, the clerks stopped punching the cash registers and the shoppers scurried to their seats. Soon the hundreds of people gathered in the beige and green ballroom were absolutely silent.

Suddenly the man on the stage shivered and stretched, smacked his lips and seemed to peer, through eyes tightly closed, at those before him. He then brought a microphone up to his mouth and, eyes still closed, began to speak in an almost-Scottish accent.

"Weel, weel, awl-rrright now. We ahrrre very pleased to be here for this ti-em togay-ther."

A few in the audience gasped. "Oh!" Some sniffled and wiped tears from their eyes. Nearly everyone smiled broadly, as if a most beautiful being, a delightful child or perhaps royalty, had just entered the room. Still a bit groggy, the man on the stage continued.

"One of the prrroblems that ee-ach of you will confront is anxiety. Anxiety is what we call a wrinkle in the fabric of life. The prrrice you pay for technology. A little rash on the surface." He paused and scratched his hand for emphasis.

"But in fact, it is as dangerous as a melanoma . . . anxiety is increasing in this ti-em in your world, at an exponential rate."

Beside me, a young German named Ernst—we all wore stick-on name tags—placed a small crystal pyramid on the floor under his chair. He then brought out a notebook and began to take notes. All around, in fact, everyone else was scribbling as fast as possible. Most of them had also brought crystals—some even had small collections in leather pouches—and placed them under their chairs. Up on the stage, the monologue continued.

"Let's say your whole Philadelphia harbor is being covered by a seaweed, a slimy moss, and that in a month it would all be covered, exponentially. On the twenty-ninth day it would only be half-covered. With exponential growth, the next day, the whole harbor is choked off. Your anxiety is growing exponentially. Is this your first day or is this your twenty-ninth day? When will you get socked in?"

The question hung over the silent room as hundreds of men and women contemplated it. Some were thinking so hard that their mouths fell open. Not a sound could be heard, except the hum of the hotel air-conditioning system.

The body onstage belonged to Jach Pursel, a former insurance man from Michigan with a friendly, small-town manner. But everyone who had paid fifty dollars to attend a one-night seminar on "The Suffocating Web of Anxiety" knew that the being who spoke through Pursel's mouth was

Lazaris, a formless, timeless, ageless, omniscient spirit-being who inhabits the universe.

Pursel is one of the most successful "channels" of the New Age. And Lazaris (pronounced La-*zair*-us) is a star, the spirit of the moment in Hollywood, and friend of everyone from Sally Fisher to Louise Hay to actress Sharon Gless, who once thanked Lazaris as she accepted an Emmy Award for her work on TV's "Cagney and Lacey." But Lazaris is more than a show-biz spirit. He is also consulted by doctors and lawyers, by AIDS researchers and stock analysts, and even a few bank directors. He is so widely popular that believers from Europe, Africa, South America, and the Pacific fly to the United States to attend his seminars, and his toll-free telephone service is available worldwide. And Lazaris is so productive a spirit that the company formed to promote his insights—Concept:Synergy—needs a thirty-two page sales catalog to list all of his videotapes, audiocassettes, and books.

Pursel and other prominent channels—and their spirit beings—are among the most visible personalities of the New Age movement. They are popular for two reasons. The first is that their strange voices, bold pronouncements, and overpowering personalities make them very entertaining characters. The second reason is that they offer a sure, instant delivery of absolute metaphysical truth. Where vortex energies and herbal cures are hit-or-miss, channeled spirits are nothing if not certain. They always show up when you call them, willing to speak at length on almost any subject, even if you do have to pay a substantial fee.

Of course, the channeling of spirits is hardly a new phenomenon. Everyone recalls, if only from old movies, the "mediums" who once plied their trades in fortune-telling dens and carnival tents. Mediums first appeared in the spiritualist movement of the late nineteenth century. They claimed to transmit messages from the dead through raps on parlor tables and trancelike speeches. Perhaps the most famous of the old mediums was Edgar Cayce, who developed a following of millions who believed in his prophecies and the spiritual cures he prescribed. Casey died in 1945, leaving behind the Edgar Cayce Foundation, which continues to promote his work.

New Age mediums update the jargon of the practice, calling themselves channels—like TV channels—but they work in the same manner as the old mediums. They sit quietly, enter a meditative state, and then seem to be suddenly animated by a new personality. In some cases the visiting spirit identifies itself as a formerly human being now ascended to a higher plane of existence. Others are spirits who have never been flesh. They are pure spiritual energy. All of them are omniscient and unbound by space and time. Considering the nonstop flow of counseling, guidance, and wisdom they supply, they seem one part angel, one part God, and one part psychotherapist.

As the New Age grew in the 1980s, channels arose as the public spokesmen (and women) for the movement. They appeared on TV talk shows and they published books, which sold millions of copies. But their fame was tenuous and mainly dependent on the endorsements of movie and television stars. In the early 1980s the top spirit was Ramtha, an ancient warrior channeled by a former beauty queen and TV executive named J. Z. Knight. Knight and Ramtha were endorsed by actress Linda Evans, who bought a home in rural Washington State in order to be near them. Ramtha grew so popular that Knight built a retreat center, where the interested and the devoted attended days-long seminars. But Ramtha's appeal was tarnished when he reportedly recommended that some believers invest in Knight's pure-bred horses. It was further damaged by reports that Knight had, in an unguarded moment, poked fun at Ramtha, affecting his voice and swagger.

As Ramtha fell from favor, other spirits rode star endorsements to compete for the loyalty of the thousands who would pay as much as two hundred dollars a day to be near them. There was Mafu, the spirit of a leper from Pompeii, who was channeled by former homemaker Penny Torres-Rubin. And there were the various spirits channeled by Kevin Ryerson, who was made famous by one of Shirley MacLaine's books. But none of these entities had the number of endorsements, and the seeming credibility, of Lazaris.

Lazaris has been building his following for more than fifteen years. Concept:Synergy, the company that markets the spirit, employs more than a dozen people and generates millions of dollars annually, through sales of *The Lazaris Materials*: videos (up to $59.95 each), sets of audiocassettes (up to $24.95), and books (as much as $12.95 each). The books and tapes focus mostly on emotional and spiritual concerns, but there are also tapes on such unmystical subjects as making money and dealing with menstruation. More dedicated students pay for telephone consultations with Lazaris ($90 for thirty minutes) or attend one of the ninety or so seminars Lazaris conducts in hotel ballrooms around the country each year. These meetings range from one-night "evenings with Lazaris" to four-day "intensives." Fees range from fifty dollars for an "evening" to six hundred dollars for a four-day "intensive." Transportation, lodging, and food are extra.

Like the old mediums of the past, channels attract a great deal of publicity, much of it negative. J. Z. Knight had been so bruised by critical press reports that her aides refused even to submit my request for an interview. Jach Pursel's assistant, a young man named Andrew William, was not encouraging when I first contacted Concept:Synergy. But after exchanging letters and phone calls, he telephoned to say that Peny North, Jach Pursel's ex-wife and the president of Concept:Synergy, had finally decided to let me come see Lazaris. The only condition was that I participate fully in one of his workshops. The implication was obvious: Lazaris would win me over.

Peny was clearly at the center of the Lazaris phenomenon. In one of his books, Lazaris notes that he came to Earth primarily to be with Peny. Peny was so important, to both Jach and Lazaris, that when she divorced Jach, he happily agreed to live with her and her new husband. For more than ten years Jach, Peny, and psychic Michaell North have lived together and run Concept:Synergy together. Jach goes out on the road with Lazaris, doing ninety seminars a year, while Peny and Michaell stay home in Palm Beach, Florida, running the company. I would meet the Lazaris road show in Philadelphia and attend both a one-night seminar called "Escape the Suffocating Web of Anxiety" and a four-day intensive on "The Sirius Connection."

I went to the "Evening with Lazaris" to prepare myself for the more extensive, four-day seminar. As an outsider who would be part observer and part participant, I was in an ambivalent position. I wanted to make some decisions, in advance of the intensive. Was I going to regard the person onstage as a spirit being named Lazaris? Or would he always be Jach Pursel in my eyes? Would I write "Lazaris said" in my notebook? Could I turn off my critical thinking and simply immerse myself in what the Concept:Synergy brochures called "the Lazaris experience"?

Up on the stage, Jach/Lazaris didn't make my decisions any easier. As he described the problem of anxiety, I noticed that the Scottish-like accent that characterized Lazaris's speech seemed to come and go. The variations made it hard for me to focus on the personality that was Lazaris. Was Lazaris simply a character Jach Pursel invented and struggled to maintain while onstage?

"Anxiety is undefined anger, hurt, fear of pity," he said, the accent fading away. "Women learn not to identify their anger. Men learn not to express hurt."

Then his voice grew softer, more urgent, as if he were speaking more intimately. The accent returned.

"Don't ever admit, not even to yourrrrself, that you ahre hurrt. Don't ever admit, not even to yourself, that you have fears. Too many pe-o-pul, too many pe-o-pul are leaning on you, you can't be frightened."

As I looked around the room, it was clear that few people, if any, shared my ambivalence. The entire audience was sitting silent, focused intently on a being they were sure was a spirit named Lazaris. Many nodded as the person I thought of as Jach "playing" Lazaris continued to describe anxiety. Anxiety was not only repressed emotion. Anxiety also arises, Jach/Lazaris said, "when you brreak, yourrr Dark Law."

Everyone knowingly wrote "Dark Law" in their notebooks. I felt like a stranger in a new church who doesn't know when to sit and when to stand. Fortunately, Jach/Lazaris explained the Dark Law. It is a personal conviction, acquired in childhood, that holds that life will be painful and tragic. A person can break the Dark Law by becoming successful, happy, and content. And yet this transgression against the tragic myth produces an inner anxiety that will force one to sabotage a success, to restore the commitment to the Dark Law.

The final cause of anxiety, he said, "is misplaced trust." At this point Jach/Lazaris introduced some other voices, for comic relief.

"Yeah, I'm gonna trust you," he said in a Southern drawl.

"Yeah, sure, sure I trust you," he added, sounding this time like actor Jimmy Cagney's tough-guy movie character.

"Trust is very fragile. It's a very rare crystal. It breaks every ti-em you drop it, and all the king's horses and all the king's men can't put it together again. Love is the most precious gift. Trust is the most fragile."

Jach/Lazaris could talk country and Cagney. He understood the basic points of popular psychology. He knew the insecurity in all of us. He also knew that deep down, everyone harbors some hurt, some anger, a broken trust or a Dark Law.

But Lazaris brought glad tidings, too. Quickly we learned that the key to overcoming anxiety lay in confronting whatever pain we held within—a childhood trauma, a phobia, a dashed hope, a shattered love—and then, somehow, breaking its hold on our psyches. This is elemental psychology.

But while a therapist would guide a patient through the process over the course of months, or even years, Lazaris would help us reach the goal of resolution in just one evening, through a "guided meditation."

As the lights were dimmed, some of the people in the audience left their chairs to lie on the thick, floral carpet in the back of the room. Others settled themselves down in the aisles, or on several chairs pushed together. People brought out pillows and blankets. One woman took a teddy bear out of a large canvas bag and hugged it tightly under her chin as she lay down on the floor and closed her eyes. Suddenly, the seminar looked like a giant slumber party.

Fortunately, I had watched carefully as the men and women at Hernandez House in Los Angeles had done a guided meditation with Sally Fisher. I decided to try it. So I made myself comfortable, pulling another plastic hotel chair up so I could rest my feet on it. On command, I joined the people who had closed their eyes, and I followed instructions, relaxing all the muscles in my body and entering a still, meditative state.

First, gentle music played through the loudspeakers in the ceiling of the ballroom. In a quiet, mellow voice Jach/ Lazaris then told us a story, a highly visual story in which each of us was the central character. The music played and he spoke in a soft, measured way. The first scene was set on the bank of a fast-flowing river.

"You are standing at river's edge. You take off your clothes and you enter the water, letting yourself float down the river."

We floated down our rivers until we met a giant whirlpool. The background music grew louder and more dramatic as we were sucked in and sank down, down under the water. In the whirlpool, we were to feel the pain of the past, experience all the hurt and anger, falling through it and being engulfed by it. Around me, people began sobbing and crying out.

I fought the urge to stop my own meditation and look around at the crowd. Instead I stayed in my whirlpool, sinking under the water, watching the sunlight above grow dimmer and dimmer. Then I let whatever image my brain produced float above me, blocking the circle of light. I saw an old photograph of myself as a child. I was shaking an angry fist and scowling as my father drove away with a pet dog that had to be put to sleep. I recognized the little shorts and shirt I wore. They were decorated with sailboats. I was four or five years old. I wondered if this was what I was supposed to experience.

"Go dee-a-pah, dee-a-pah," Jach/Lazaris intoned. "In your childhood there is a particular anxiety that is the original debilitator. . . . Go dee-a-pah to the real hurt, the abandonment. Feel it!"

The music grew frenzied, like a whirlpool. There was more crying and moaning around me. I faintly recalled a more painful scene from my past. I was again about four or five years old. I had misbehaved and my mother, momentarily overwhelmed, was pretending to phone an orphanage, to have me taken away. I had obviously been terrified then, and I now felt some of that terror anew. This memory wasn't really new. I had recalled it before. But in the darkness, with the music and Lazaris's urging, I did relive the fear of that time. As an adult and a parent, I had been able to see how desperate a mother with four young children might feel. Here with Lazaris, I recalled how insecure I felt then as a child.

Obviously those around me were having similarly emotional experiences. The crying and sniffling grew louder and louder. We were, three hundred of us, in a trance, reliving childhood traumas. Someone cried, out loud, "Oh no, not that! Oh no!" Then I heard Jach/Lazaris shout, over the crowd.

"Now! Pop! You've fallen through the bottom of the whirlpool. You are safe!"

The rest of the story unfolded on an imaginary riverbank. We stood there, exhausted from the whirlpool, and saw a kind of screen, like a screen door. He instructed us to press our noses against it, to smell the metallic scent, to feel its cool, sharp edges. He told us to press harder, until we actually pushed our entire bodies through the screen, like ghosts passing through a wall. On the screen was left a kind of residue, a "goo" that we were told to scrape off and form into a ball. This ball was our anxiety, our old hurt, our anger. "Hold it over your head until it turns to light and then let it go, release it," said Jach/Lazaris.

A few moments later, we were told to open our eyes. As I did, I felt both relaxed and agitated, a bit dazed and even a little angry. Up onstage, Jach/Lazaris told us that if we had not been instantly cured of our anxieties by this one experience, we could repeat the exercise ourselves.

"Go back, yourself, to the whirlpool and use it over and over again to look for the original anxiety. Play it over and let it bleed." By doing this, someone stuck in the web of anxiety could deflate the powerful events that had caused so much pain and leave them behind. Or so he said. "You might be amazed, absolutely, by what happens."

I had already been amazed, absolutely. I had experienced a potent mix of hypnotic suggestion, psychodrama, and spiritual adventure. I felt emotionally drained, and a bit resentful. A perfect stranger had manipulated me into experiencing something deeply personal and upsetting. Yet there was no one with whom I could discuss what had happened. There was no personal support for any of the three hundred people who had journeyed through their own whirlpool nightmares. All of us were now sitting alone, in the dark. There were only the Lazaris tapes and books for sale on the long tables set up in the rear of the room.

Lazaris announced, "And now we close, weeth love." Jach Pursel was again still for a moment. Then he opened his eyes, to signal that Lazaris was gone. The ballroom crackled with applause. No one else, it seemed, was the least bit resentful. They were ecstatic. They laughed and smiled and cried tears of joy. Beside me, Ernst closed his notebook, picked up his crystal pyramid, pressed it against his forehead, and wept softly. And soon, across the room, sales were brisk at the tables as people filled little purple bags with "Lazaris materials," and a clutch of people pressed against Jach Pursel, who was trying to make his way down the aisle. He hugged those who wished to be hugged and smiled at the others. Then, breaking free from the knot of people, he went straight out the door to an elevator that would take him to his hotel room.

With the star attraction gone, many of the seminar participants remained, talking among themselves. Many greeted one another as old friends. They had met at other Lazaris encounters. Others had come to the meeting together. Perhaps they did offer one another the support they needed in the aftermath of the psychodrama. I sat alone, trying to assess the Lazaris phenomenon and my own experience.

I knew, immediately, that the visit to the whirlpool had not relieved me of all my anxieties. I could understand how the traumas of childhood might contribute to my personal blend of normal neuroses, but when he instructed us to release the little ball of anxiety, I felt nothing. Real psychological change takes much more work.

Who, or what, is Lazaris? There seem to be just three possibilities. One is that he is what he claims to be—a spirit entity from the cosmos. The second is that he is the calculated invention of an entrepreneur who would cynically exploit the earnest seekers of the New Age. The third possibility is that he is a creation of Jach Pursel's mind, but one that Pursel sincerely believes is a spirit being.

No matter what the truth may be—spiritual, psychological, or entrepreneurial—there were obviously two characters here, Jach and Lazaris. So I decided to consider Lazaris an entity separate from Pursel. And, as long as I was going to be spending four ten-hour days sealed inside the Holiday Inn ballroom with hundreds of spiritual pilgrims, I decided to participate as fully as I could.

At the exit, I introduced myself to Mary Beth, the Concept: Synergy staff member who accompanied Pursel on his coast-to-coast tour of hotel ballrooms. She was an imposing woman with a huge head of curly black hair. She wore a sort of caftan and a crystal hung on a chain around her neck. I told her I had many, many questions about what I had seen.

"Don't worry, you'll get your chance," she said. "Jach wants to see you, too. We'll arrange it during the intensive. Until then, just try to enjoy the Lazaris experience."

The intensive, which began the next morning, was called "The Sirius Connection: The Spiritual Vortex, the Ultimate Power Vortex." The brochures I had received from the Concept:Synergy staff said that Lazaris would teach us about the metaphysical power of the star Sirius, the brightest star visible in the night sky. We were going to feel the love of Lazaris and break through our resistance to spiritual growth. "Years of resistance break away. Clarity. Finally, there's clarity. Everyone in the room can feel the light go on. . . . There is a specialness. There is a love. There is a gift." Before the seminar was over we would participate in a "beautiful and magical crystal ceremony" and glimpse "the glimmers of God, Goddess All That Is." Lazaris would show us the face of God.

The crowd at the intensive included some of the people I had seen the night before. Ernst was there. But most of the plainer-looking people were gone. This was a richer, even more motivated crowd that included contingents from Hong Kong, Great Britain, Africa, and Brazil. They came laden with Lazaris books and audiotapes, with pillows and blankets. One woman brought her own special chair, a reclining rounded thing that looked like a giant upholstered cradle. Another woman wore a meditation collar, a kind of padded neck brace that would keep her head from flopping about while she was in a trance.

I took a chair next to Mark, a sandy-haired man, tan and athletic-looking and dressed in designer jeans and a soft silk sport coat. He said he was a screenwriter from the West Coast and that he had been to many intensives, but no, he didn't want to discuss it. He had preparations to make. He turned away to unpack the contents of a leather satchel that was at his feet. He then established a worship area around his chair. First he took out a purple suede pouch that was cinched closed with leather straps. He loosened the straps to make a wide opening that exposed several large quartz crystals. He spread a soft white cloth on the floor under his chair and then put the open pouch on the cloth. Then he took out a second pouch full of crystals—this one was pink suede—opened it the same way, and placed it beside the purple one. Next he pulled out little packages of nuts and granola and set them on the floor in front of him. Then came a green woolen cap, which he turned inside-out to inspect: Small crystals, the size of quarters, were sewn into the hat. Finally he took out a cassette tape player with earphones. He put on the cap, plugged in the earphones, snapped in a Lazaris cassette, switched on the tape player, and closed his eyes.

On my left sat Barbara, a pretty, gray-haired woman, perhaps sixty years old, in a white cotton dress. She said she was from Dallas, that Lazaris had changed her life, and that her family, especially her oil-man husband, didn't understand her New Age interest. "We experience a lot of pain in life, don't we?" she asked. "Lazaris has helped me through mine."

Before I could ask her to tell me more, Jach Pursel came through the door and applause started in the back of the room. It grew louder as he made his way down to the stage and took his place in the big chair. He was wearing blue jeans, sandals, and a green-and-red-striped shirt that he let hang out over his pants, covering his large, round belly. After saying hello to the audience, he removed his glasses, smoothed his long blond hair, sat quietly, and closed his eyes. It was ten o'clock, time to start our four-day adventure.

"Weel, awl-rrright, awl-rrright," he said, signaling Lazaris's arrival. "We li-ek to begin by healing your energy, the energy in the rrroom." He paused for a moment, seeming to reflect. Someone in the audience sighed.

"Now we can say, as we always do, that is a pleasure to be with you. We are joyful to be with you. We welcome you as individuals and e-ach of you in your own uniqueness."

Lazaris began by reassuring us about the value of the four-day meeting. Even though it would be four days spent completely on self-improvement, at a cost of six hundred dollars, this was not a selfish endeavor, he said. "Certainly you are here to work on yourrrself, and some would say that selfish, greedy. We know it is wise. We know that the consensus reality"—meaning society outside the New Age—"that accuses you of personal greed is incorrect." In fact, said Lazaris, the powerful "Sirius connection" would give us the means to help the world. "So what you are doing here is an imperative, a part of your destiny. . . . You are not being selfish or greedy, you are doing your destiny."

Again the notebooks came out, and again everyone was writing everything down, like college freshmen. Lazaris went on to explain that we were going to learn to tap an otherwise unknown spiritual power that flowed from Sirius and contained all the energy of the cosmos. This was not going to be too difficult, because we had all entered this galaxy, as spirits, through Sirius's energy "portal," so we were already connected to the star. "Not everyone is. Fewer are connected than not. But you happen to be, in that sensing, connected. That's what brought you here."

The audience that sat before Lazaris was attentive, even worshipful. Several young women staked out spaces on the floor in front of the stage, where they lay on pillows and just gazed up at Lazaris as he spoke, like children, sprawled on a living-room floor listening to their father tell a story. One woman sitting near me just stared at Lazaris and rocked back and forth, back and forth. Her placid expression never changed. One couple—a middle-aged man and a very young woman—put a blanket on the floor against the back wall and lay down, in an embrace, as they listened. A man in the front row hugged a teddy bear that was more than four feet tall.

As the morning wore on, Lazaris told us about the role Sirius played in ancient religions. Some of what he taught could have come directly from a text on ancient history. The rest was New Age metaphysics. Sirius's movement in the Southern sky, he noted, had helped regulate the ancient Egyptian calendar. The people of Atlantis and Lemuria (mythical places New Agers believe actually existed) tapped the power of Sirius, he said, and so, too, did people in all ancient religions. "Why did they talk of Sirius? Why? We would suggest because there's a power there, a level of truth, in that sensing, that transcends time."

Gradually, I began to note additional peculiarities in Lazaris's speech pattern. First, he always referred to himself, in a royal sense, as "we." In the Lazaris books he explains that all beings have many "selves," including a "higher self," a "future self," a "child self," and others. Lazaris is conscious of all these selves at all times, hence the use of "we." There was also his Scottish brogue, sometimes pronounced and sometimes absent, and the rhythmic interjection of the same odd words or phrases in his sentences. One was the word "sensing." Another was the phrase "We would suggest." Finally, he regularly dropped his direct teaching to play the role of skeptic, or outsider, posing problems and then knocking them down. In this way, he sketched a dividing line between those of us in the Holiday Inn—an elect, elite group—and the outside world.

To warm us up, Lazaris had the lights dimmed and took us through a brief meditation, a "blending" in which his spirit came to be with each of us. "We wait for you on the edge of your reality," he murmured into the microphone while we all sat, eyes closed, then continued:

**We love you.**
**We'll wait for you for forever and a day.**
**We love you.**

As the lights came back up, Lazaris announced a coffee break. Jach Pursel blinked his eyes open and the people in the audience rose to race for the bathrooms, the sales tables, or wherever they would go. On the escalator that led down to the hotel lobby, I followed a pair of fortyish women. One turned to the other and announced, "Well, I've already got my six hundred dollars' worth."

When we returned, Pursel went through the now-familiar transformation. Lazaris appeared to tell us that to prepare for the "Sirius connection" we must liberate ourselves from "negative relativism," achieve true "authenticity," and attain a sense of our own divinity. It took quite some time, more than an hour, for him to explain relativism and its many traps. "Absolute relativism," which says that all truths are equal, all values subjective, "is disabling, limiting, binding," he said. "In that sensing, you say, 'Hey, it's all relative, then I don't have to learn anything I don't want to.' "

In a way, he was right. Relativistic thinking was promoted in the 1960s as a way to protect diversity and individuality, but in some it also produced a sense of moral emptiness because, in a culture where all values are equal, it is difficult to choose. This, Lazaris said, is the negative side of relativity. The positive side of relativity comes from the opportunity to select a set of beliefs and hold them as your own, equal to those held by anyone else.

"All beliefs are true, so pick the ones that work for you," he told his listeners. "If you really believe life is wonderful, that you always win, you will."

Being authentic requires more of a struggle. For that, Lazaris said, we must overcome our fears and heal the wounds of the past that might make us timid and reluctant in our adult lives. To demonstrate how this is done, Lazaris asked to hear the problems of people in the audience, and then he tried to find their sources. The Lazaris regulars seemed to know what to do as they rose, identified themselves, and then submitted their questions.

"Hi, Lazaris, it's Robin."

Squinting in her direction, Lazaris answered, "Yes, yes, awl right."

"Well, see, I've been writing this script with my partner. People read it and they like it, but I can't seem to create the job I want."

"You come close to it, but no gold ring?"

"Yes. The scripts go out, we get all built up, then boom!, it all falls apart."

"You are very talented."

"Well, anyway, we finally got an agent in L.A. He says the problem is timing, that things aren't clicking."

"The conditions aren't right, aren't perfect? Ahhhh. Perfection! You're holding yourself to a high standard, perfection, and in that sensing, you've got to be perfect and only then will you be accepted. Those are the messages you are creating for them to give to you. Who gave you that need to be perfect?"

"I think it was my father. He always said you had to work so hard, pay your dues, be perfect."

"But do you know of a grandmother who stands out in your reality? Maybe a maternal grandmother? How much do you think it came from her?"

"She was a pretty strict Catholic woman, but she was also pretty supportive of me." Robin said her grandmother had died while she was away at college. She had always regretted being unable to be with her at the end.

"Weel, you ahre correct that it comes from your father, but it also comes from your grandmother. There was a bond created between the two of you that was incomplete at her death. Part of you died, too. We would suggest that in meditation you talk to that grandmother and take back what died with her, a certain imaginative, creative spark. She'll gladly give it to you, if you ask."

"Oh, thank you, thank you, Lazaris. I will."

So it went with half a dozen people. A man named Fred, a fifty-year-old, gray-haired accountant in a blue blazer, was typical. He stood, took the microphone, and explained that he had tried to start a new career, as a consultant, but that it wasn't going well.

"You are afraid of being punished if you succeed," came Lazaris's immediate answer. "Who would punish you, your father?"

"He wasn't around."

"What about your relationship with your mother?"

"She neglected me."

"Yes, but how did she do it?"

"Basically, she just turned off."

"How did she do that?"

"Pushed me away." Fred's voice quivered a bit. He started to rock on his heels, nervously. "She made statements like, 'You can't help me support two children and myself. You're no help.'"

"How old were you?"

"Eight."

"Did she lose herself?"

"In her work, yes. I followed suit, constantly focusing on putting bread on the table and not really being alive. I've turned myself off, too."

"You shut down, we would suggest, because of the fear that is so deeply inside you. When the love comes, you are afraid of the pain. With your mother you were clearly being told, 'Your love isn't enough.' We would suggest that you need to go back there and feel the pain. Go back to that eight-year-old. Let him cry. Be there to hold him. Do it several times and then, what do you think you'll feel beneath that pain?"

"Love?"

"What about anger?"

"Oh, yeah. I've got lots of that."

"Do you understand why your mother turned you off?"

"No."

"It could be she was jealous."

"Because I had my whole life ahead of me?"

"Yes, and you didn't have to work your ass off to keep your head above water with no husband. You need to go back to that child and talk to him, explain it to him."

Suddenly a woman in front of Fred leaped to her feet, turned around, and pointed a finger at him. "You need to understand your mother's hurt, too!" she shouted.

"Ah, there's a mother," Lazaris interjected. Laughter rippled through the room. "We understand, but we don't need that kind of comment right now, right?" The woman sat down. "Now then, Fred, does this make sense?"

"Yes it does. I can see."

"Good. Do you hear the difference in your tone? You are more relaxed now, aren't you?"

"Why, yes, I am. Thank you."

Not everyone received such gentle treatment. A gangly young man named Mitch stood up to ask about his troubles with his acting career. Lazaris led Mitch through a discussion of acting as a search for others' approval, the approval he never got from his father. "You are afraid to be real," he told Mitch. "You are afraid that if you stop performing, everybody will find out. But find out what, Mitch?"

"That I'm a phony."

"Isn't that your real fear, that everyone will find out you're a phony?"

"I guess."

"Are you a phony?"

"No, I'm real."

"You are a phony a lot of the time, aren't you?"

"Yes, I'm a phony."

"You're a phony, Mitch. You perform, you play-act!"

Lazaris pressed relentlessly, demanding that Mitch admit his phoniness. Mitch slowly gave way, like a child collapsing before taunting playmates. He eventually began blubbering, "I'm a phony, a phony, a phony." This was difficult to watch, and it made me wonder why Mitch would set himself up for such a public grilling, and why Lazaris was willing to provide it.

It was early evening when we turned our attention to the last item on the day's agenda: discovering our personal divinity. Again the lights were dimmed, the hypnotic music was switched on, and we were told to relax ourselves into a meditative calm. We then traveled in our minds, under Lazaris's direction, to a beautiful tree-shaded pond. At the pond we saw two shimmering triangles floating in the air. One represented our humanity, the other our divinity. The triangles merged, making the shape of the Star of David, which Lazaris said represented a merging of the sacred and the human qualities we all possess.

"Walk through it," he said. "It will change you."

After we walked through the triangles, we flew on winged horses to a beautiful glade where we met a spiritual being called the "higher self." There, we received a precious gift and heard a particular word, a special message. My higher self, or the one I imagined in the exercise, was a faceless kind of man, something like a fencer, in his bodysuit and opaque mask. He gave me a box and inside it was a clock. The word that came into my mind was "patience."

Soon Lazaris ended the meditation. Day one of the intensive was over. We were to go into the night, contemplating the gifts we had received and their meaning. We were to tell no one of our experience. Lazaris didn't say why.

As I ate breakfast the next morning, I decided that the word I had heard—"patience"—was a reminder that I should patiently experience the full four days of the seminar, watching it unfold. I had been restless the day before. Perhaps this was because I didn't believe in Lazaris the way that the others did. I was tempted to leave.

The clock I received in my meditation also seemed to symbolize my feelings about the intensive. There inside the Holiday Inn, surrounded by Lazaris believers, I had lost touch with normal life, and time. It was a very isolating experience, to be shut away in a hotel ballroom, part of a group of three hundred, all intent on an incredibly detailed study of what could be utter nonsense. And certainly no one inside the room talked about anything outside the New Age. On the morning of the second day, I was the only one who walked into the ballroom with the newspaper under his arm. A terrible earthquake had occurred overnight, in Iran, killing tens of thousands of people. The story was the lead item in the *Philadelphia Inquirer*. But no one talked about this, except Lazaris, who asked, as an aside, "Why did the earthquake happen? Perhaps to draw our attention to the Middle East, where there are problems as yet unsolved."

The morning was otherwise consumed by Lazaris's analysis of the symbolism in the gifts and words people had received during the meditation the day before. Each person who sought Lazaris's wisdom seemed to be very moved by what had happened in their meditation. It was as if something very real had happened to them all. One woman had received a key from her higher self. She spoke of this experience with a reverence and excitement that made her voice tremble.

"She said she wanted the lock that was on my heart. It was a very big lock. We called it a deadbolt. I held it in my hands until it turned to light, and then into a white dove, and then it flew away."

Lazaris nodded his approval as she told the story. "How wonderful," he said. "How fantastic."

Others had less light-hearted symbolism hidden in their meditations. One woman said her higher self had given her a bronze statuette of a child, and that she had heard the word "eunuch," but she didn't know what it meant.

"Did you look up the word?" asked Lazaris.

"No. But I asked a friend, but she didn't know what it meant either."

Here Lazaris was momentarily stumped. "A eunuch is . . .

ah ... er ... a person who doesn't have sex. A castrated male is a eunuch," he finally said. "In the Middle Ages, courts kept eunuchs who were thought to be mystical. It was considered mystical to remove that taint and terribleness of sex, particularly in men, and free them to do the work of being a psychic being. Does it mean your sex is gone, or that your power is unable to produce anything? You have tremendous creative energies, but you need to let them rise. You probably have difficulties with premenstrual cycle and so forth. Do you understand?"

"Yes," came the answer.

In many cases Lazaris asked people about troubled relationships or conflicts with parents. And if a problem was not found in this life, Lazaris announced that it resided in a past life. In one instance he asked a woman if she had a son with whom she had a troubled relationship. She had no son, so Lazaris asked about anyone who is "son-like" in her life. Again she could think of no one, so Lazaris launched into a story about a son she had had when she was a peasant woman in the south of France in the year 1035. "There was an attack. Warriors came ... you ran and survived but your son did not. You went back and found his mutilated body. You went off the deep end then, wandering in the woods and calling his name.

"Your problem is in that lifetime, not this one. That woman screwed up and everyone abandoned her then, as a crazy old woman. You can too, now. Does that make sense to you?"

"Yes, it does."

After more analysis of symbols and past lives, Lazaris dismissed us for lunch. Before leaving the hall in search of a sandwich, I wandered by the tables where Concept:Synergy staffers sold the tapes and other items. I overheard one customer explaining that he listened to Lazaris's taped messages every morning when he awoke and in the car driving to and from work. In the evening, he said, he frequently watched Lazaris videotapes. He played tapes in his bedroom, all night long, as he slept. "Thank goodness for auto-reverse," he told one of the cashiers.

Downstairs in the lobby of the hotel, I saw Fred, the accountant who had spoken with Lazaris the day before. I asked him to join me for lunch. As we walked through downtown Philadelphia, on sidewalks jammed with well-dressed businesspeople, we could have been any two office workers on our lunch break. Fred wore his blue blazer and a dress shirt. His gray hair was conservatively short. Only the crystal pendant that dangled from a gold chain around his neck revealed him as a New Age seeker.

As we walked along, Fred told me he had been on a spiritual journey, of sorts, since he was seventeen. That was when he had learned the hidden truth about his long-missing father, whom he hadn't seen for many years. It turned out that his dad wasn't working in some far-off land, as his mother always said. He was in a nearby psychiatric hospital. Fred felt betrayed. He also feared that insanity was hereditary.

At lunch I heard of Fred's lifelong battle with fear. He had tried to cure himself with meditation, yoga, crystals, psychic consultants, and, finally, Lazaris. "Lazaris is the most authoritative one I've encountered yet," he said. "He speaks in a way that is so detailed, so complete. Nothing else has ever sounded so complete to me." He said the intensive was working. He was beginning to feel free of his pain and anxiety, and he even had a sense of his own divinity.

"I feel like I'm ready to make the Sirius connection. I want to know what that's all about."

Before we left the restaurant, Fred asked about my spiritual life. I said that my metaphysical beliefs began and ended with the assumption that there are mysteries none of us can fathom.

"Don't you really want to know what happens when you die, what's out there?" he asked incredulously.

"Like everyone, I wonder," I answered. "But I don't think anyone knows what happens when we die, or whether there is a god or a spirit world. Maybe we find out when we die. Anyway, I have enough questions about what's happening down here, right now, with all us human beings."

"Wow, it's hard to believe you don't really care like I do," said Fred. "I sure want those answers. I've been looking for them all my life."

For the afternoon intensive, I moved to another part of the ballroom and found a chair near two women who were more friendly than Mark, the fellow with the crystals in his cap. Donna and Marie were from Bethlehem, Pennsylvania. Marie was a teacher; Donna worked as a clerk in a hospital. They were best friends who had each saved for a year so they could have their first in-person encounter with Lazaris. They seemed thrilled to be there. I mentioned that there seemed to be more women than men in the room, and I asked if they thought that meant anything.

"Oh, the feminine side of people is more intuitive, more open, more spiritual," Donna said. "You are an unusual man, I guess, which is why you are here. You are probably just more open to your feminine self, which is great."

"I'm not sure how open I am. My feminine self has probably been repressed for some time," I answered.

"Oh, Michelle is in there," she said, smiling and tapping me on the chest. "Let her out."

Up onstage, Lazaris began to speak again in his faux-Scottish tones, explaining that we were all "star children" who had been "seeded" from Sirius. Our destiny was to "manifest success." Then, for the first time, Lazaris turned political. His talk of our status as star children was not idle flattery. We bore the responsibility of using Sirius to lead the world to freedom and self-determination, he said. We were destined to shape history.

"You are working on a destiny to fix, change, and build a world that is self-determined. Like the nations who seek freedom, like Nelson Mandela, who seeks freedom in South Africa." (Mandela was touring the United States like a triumphant war hero at the time, addressing overflow crowds at stadiums and meeting with President Bush.) "Mandela is making a lot of people upset, by seeking self-determination. And the majority in your country is still seeking self-determination. Women, minorities, still do not have it.

"But your planet is on the verge of self-determination. That's what the New Age is. We are now no longer enslaved by the past. It is time for self-determination. You are part of the force that will see it happen. So use this energy. Some would call it selfish. We would call it wise."

Soon, he said, we would open the door of Sirius and the power of the universe would be ours. Unfortunately, though, that would have to wait until tomorrow. Members of the hotel staff, dressed in short jackets and black pants, were standing in the doorway, waiting to transform the room into a reunion hall for the William Penn High School Class of '80. Lazaris was forced to cut the program short.

On the way out of the ballroom I stopped for a moment to make a note. A young man in a dark blue suit came over and introduced himself. His name was Rocky and he was the events manager for the hotel. He had arranged for Concept:Synergy to use the hotel. I told him I was a writer, working on a book about the New Age. Rocky wanted to know just what had been going on in the ballroom. I tried, as best I could, to explain Lazaris and the seminar.

"I've looked in, from time to time," said Rocky. "The guy speaks with so much detail. It makes it sound like it could be true. Then I see the guy walking to his room, joking with people, and he looks like a regular guy. It's weird. How much do people pay to do this?"

"Six hundred," I answered.

"Wow! How many in there?"

"About three hundred people."

"Oh my God," he said. "That's $180,000 and they aren't paying much of anything for overhead."

Rocky led me into an office nearby and pulled out Concept:Synergy's bill. The room cost $540. The total, for four days and one night, would be less than $2,500. "Some deal," he muttered. "Some deal."

The next morning I bumped into Jach Pursel as he was coming off the elevator in the Holiday Inn. He smiled, shook my hand and said he was happy to see me there, and he invited me to meet him in the hotel coffee shop at the end of the day. "I may have only fifteen minutes, but we'll do the best we can," he said, smiling again.

As I went inside the ballroom, I encountered an excited-looking woman, Janet, who asked to see the newspaper that was tucked under my arm.

"Tsk, tsk, tsk. This was bound to happen," she said as she opened to the latest story on the Iranian earthquake. The headline said the death toll had been raised to twenty-five thousand. "There are some real problems that people are denying over there and, spiritually, you know things like this are going to happen until they deal with those problems." There it was again, the New Age connection between spiritual status and disaster. In the same way that many New Age healers believe that emotional distress causes cancer, Janet believed the fortunes of nations rose and fell according to some karmic law.

Janet was a therapist and "ritualist" who worked with private clients throughout eastern Pennsylvania. She performed psychotherapy, helped people with business problems, and conducted ceremonies to spiritually cleanse new homes. "I've been working with the elements of nature—wind, earth, water, fire—for a long time," she said with a smile intended to tell me that "long time" meant many lifetimes.

As Jach took to the stage, I found my place near Marie and Donna. Donna jabbed me in the shoulder.

"How's Michelle?"

It took me a moment to realize she was talking about my "feminine self."

"She's fine, fine," I answered.

Donna smiled warmly. Marie said she had experienced a most moving dream the night before, one related to the gift she had received from her higher self. She positively glowed as she talked about it. "I am so excited about today," she said. "What a wonderful adventure this all is."

The crowd became silent once more as, up on the stage, Jach meditated and became Lazaris.

"Awl rright. Weel, weel, weel. What a night you had. A lot of you went through a lot of changes during the night, even changes you don't remember now. All of you felt that energy, but some of you diminished it, to only that part which you could handle." (I recalled that I had experienced a dream that so amused me that I woke up laughing. Unfortunately, in the light of day I couldn't remember what had been so funny.)

"Others of you may feel guilty because you know too much. You have a Promethean fear because you've found the power of God. Well, the answer to that is that everyone has access to this power if, in that sensing, they step forward to take it."

Others were plagued by what Lazaris called "negative ego," a doubting voice inside. "It's saying to you, 'All right, you've tapped the energy of Sirius, now solve the problems of the world. Set South Africa free, bring peace to the Middle East, solve the deforestation problem . . .' That's your negative ego trying to undermine you."

Instead, Lazaris said, we must have faith. We must believe. "It is part of your destiny to be part of the solutions for the future," he said. "And the time is right." In fact, he said, the democratization of Eastern Europe and the release of Nelson Mandela from a South African prison had taken place because of the spiritual efforts of New Age believers who had "created that reality. It's happening on a physical level because it's happening on a spiritual level and you are part of it all."

Lazaris taught that each individual creates his own reality, the circumstances of his life, through spiritual means. Those who are to receive the power of Sirius are blessed "because they are willing to accept it," he said. Those who will not have the power have chosen that fate. Similarly, those on Earth who are successful, wealthy, beautiful, talented, or influential chose their destinies. So did the hungry, the sick, and the destitute.

"I know what you might think. 'Doesn't everybody deserve a roof over their heads, at least one good meal a day?'" Lazaris asked rhetorically. "Yes. But those people are without those things, not because they don't deserve it, but because they are unwilling to have it."

It was Louise Hay all over again, and once again I found it repelling. If karma is the explanation for everything, then we have no responsibility to actually help anyone else. But the hard truth is that we are all part of the intricate design that produces both gluttonous wealth for the few and suffering for the many. The American who must have bananas for ten cents a pound is partly responsible for the workers in the Third World who receive less than subsistence wages. Closer to home, parents who neglect their children are responsible when they run amok, karma or no karma. In India karma helps maintain the social order. It explains the suffering of the masses and absolves the rich. Perhaps the many New Agers who accept the notion of karma have similar reasons. The suffering among them need an explanation for their grief. The rich need something to soothe their consciences. Of course, what's lost in all this is justice.

For the rest of the morning Lazaris conducted another question-and-answer session. Again, the questions were, for the most part, about problems in careers and personal relationships. Again, some of the answers were soothing while others were quite stern. Lazaris told one woman she was mean and selfish because she rather enjoyed being a bitch. The reason was her unresolved childhood anger at the birth of a brother. Before she could overcome this problem, Lazaris said, "You must own that meanness. You have to say to yourself, 'I am a mean person. I can be destructive. I can shred people's self-esteem.' " Once she acknowledged these qualities, he said, she could forgive herself and begin to improve.

There were also some moments of irony. At one point a man from Brazil, Antonio, presented a rather unusual problem. He said he wanted to become a psychic healer, but he was reluctant to charge money for his services. "In my country," Antonio said, "people believe that you lose your spiritual power if you charge money for your service. They say you are supposed to do spiritual services for free. This has been fed to me since I was a child."

For Lazaris, the universal spirit who set the fees that Concept:Synergy charged for its products and seminars, this was an easy question to resolve.

"A little bit of intellectual work needs to be done," he began. "Everything that exists is really a spiritual vibration, an illusion. To separate money and say it's not spiritual is wrong. You can have all of it you want and still have spirituality. It's like little girls and boys playing tea party. Do they ever run out of tea? No! Money is the same way. You can have all you want."

The look on Antonio's face showed he wasn't convinced.

"Look, work this through," Lazaris said, becoming annoyed. "If money was bad, why should a schoolteacher be paid? Why should a doctor be paid? They are doing very spiritual work. Are you saying the mystical person isn't doing any work? We can't figure out a work that isn't spiritual." The problem, said Lazaris, "is you live in a whole country of martyrs," who denied themselves life's abundance. "That's why you were born there. Martyrdom and guilt are your big problems to tackle in this lifetime," he told the Brazilian healer.

As he answered this and other questions, Lazaris drew on world history, psychology, even popular culture. He seemed to be quite a movie buff. He referred to a number of films, including *Patton* and *Raging Bull*, which he said is "a very spiritual film" because it had been made with such passion and attention to detail.

As this went on, we all knew that one of the big moments of the intensive, our contact with Sirius, was fast approaching. When the Q&A session ended, Lazaris said we would need a brief meditation to ease the building sense of anxiety. He told us to put ourselves in a hypnotic state, to reassure our child-selves.

I had to struggle to stay with the meditation. Sometimes my mind wandered, putting cartoon characters—Gumby, Daffy Duck, and even the old electric-power-industry trademark character Ready Kilowatt—into various scenes. I was also distracted by what was going on in the room around me. People were crying and sniffling. And the music seemed to be botched up. Either the order of the tapes was wrong or they weren't being changed properly, because the louder, dramatic pieces were intruding on the quiet moments of meditation. I opened my eyes and saw Lazaris/ Pursel, leaning on the arm of his chair, talking into the microphone. He was also fumbling with a sophisticated tape player that was on the table beside him. I couldn't be sure, but it seemed that his eyes were open. I was becoming impatient with Lazaris, and much less uncertain about who, or what, he was.

When we returned from lunch, Lazaris announced we would soon embark on the meditative journey to Sirius. We were going to connect with Sirius and put the star's power at our disposal, forevermore. "The channel uses it in this way now," Lazaris told us. "He simply says, 'I ask for this in the name of Sirius.' It works that directly."

This time the lights were turned off completely, except for a few that lighted the stage where Pursel had taken his place. The music started once again. We were told to immerse ourselves in "to-tal re-lax-a-tion."

We started our "seven day" meditative journey at the peaceful place, by the pond. There was the familiar rock, a tree, and a small camp fire. There we searched for our authenticity, our true self, making sure we would approach Sirius with complete earnestness. On the second day we wandered into a nearby wood and found a cave, which was an entrance into the underworld. We entered to discover a beautiful countryside and a long, winding road.

For this day and the next, we would follow the road to a black river where the fifty oarsmen and their barge waited. Along the way to the river we met helpers—an old man or woman, gnomes, elves, a fairy princess—who were there to protect and guide us. The journey was long, through valleys and villages. But eventually we reached the river.

At the river, the long barge appeared, powered by the silent oarsmen. Lazaris described them in great detail, creating a rich picture of a mythical, perhaps medieval land. The oarsmen were black-hooded figures, faceless and silent. They strained against their oars, pulling them up out of the water, plunging them in again, stroking and then pulling them out, creating little whirlpools in the river. As we crossed, through the fog and mist, hounds, hungry hounds that were all skin and bones, howled from the banks.

At daybreak, we found ourselves on the opposite side of the river. Our long walk continued, and it started to rain. This was the longest, most miserable day of our journey, a day that ended with each of us huddled beneath a tree, the wind and rain beating us. We slept, a cold, fitful sleep.

By the time we awoke the next morning, the rain had stopped and our mud-encrusted clothes were drying. We took to the path again and soon stumbled upon our higher self and our future self, sitting by a fire. They welcomed us and we joined them for a meal.

This day was to be dedicated to a kind of purification, in anticipation of connecting with Sirius. We went to a small clearing in a forest. Our higher self was joined by other spiritual beings, our future self, an old man, and many others. These were our "cocreators." They were there to help us tap Sirius and create the reality of our choice. They laid hands on us and gave each of us a crystal cloak, a cloak of strength.

Finally, on that night, we stood in this same clearing and called to the star, Sirius. We stood gazing at it, in the sky, until we saw the triangles appear and merge into a star.

The drama of this moment was heightened by the urgency of the music and Lazaris's voice. When the star appeared, he said, "Look, over there! A star. Look, look!"

The suggestive power of his voice and the highly detailed story he told overwhelmed the people in the room. Many gasped when he cried, "Look!" They really did see the star. I had to force myself to conjure one up, but I succeeded, joining the rest of the meditative travelers, some of whom wept with joy. The music grew louder and louder. Then from the star there came a beam of light, a "cone of power" that fell down on us. Inside this cone, we were to imagine the reality that we wanted to create. Then, at the climax, the cone of power burst into a million spinning, glittery lights that whirled about and filled us with a feeling of strength and grace.

"You know it's yours! Walk into it and become it! You are healed! You get the deal! You have success!"

As the lights disappeared, we returned to our cocreators. They all danced and embraced, celebrating the success. Then it was back to the pond and the tree and the rock and, finally, back to the hotel ballroom.

When it was over, the lights came on and I looked around. Some people held handkerchiefs to their eyes and cried. Others sat perfectly still, their eyes wide open, smiling. Lazaris urged us to "tell no one" what we had experienced. A monument of some sort was being built in that clearing where we had contacted Sirius. We could return there at any time. One woman, said Lazaris, had used the power of Sirius to hold regular psychic meetings with Mandela and President de Klerk of South Africa. He was sure that she was responsible, spiritually, for the progress being made there against apartheid. We were going to go back to Sirius on the last day of the intensive, but until then, we were to keep our experiences secret.

Lazaris left—"weeth love and peace"—and Jach seemed to awaken, rubbing his eyes. Mary Beth handed him a Diet Coke and he sipped it as he was thronged with people, all of them telling him what a wonderful time they had had with Lazaris. Through the loudspeaker came a song, "The Rose," by Bette Midler.

Pursel met me at the hotel coffee shop a few minutes later and we ordered drinks and some spicy buffalo wings. He was a round, almost jovial man who smiled easily and seemed very relaxed. The first thing I asked him was about the spelling of his name. Legally, he said, it was still John Willits Pursel. He had begun using Jach "for numerological reasons." Numerology ascribes psychic meaning, and numbers, to everything—dates, letters, words—and Pursel said he changed his name because the spelling resulted in a better number. Peny, his former wife, had done the same thing (subtracting an *n*) and so had her new husband, Michaell (adding an *l*). Peny and Michaell had also changed their last names, from Prestini to North. With the mystery of the names put to rest, I asked him about his life before Lazaris.

Pursel was born in 1947. He had two sisters and an older brother. His father was a traveling salesman who moved every two years or so, as he was given new territories. His mother taught school in each new community. Jach described himself as "a good boy, so good that I would have been an altar boy if we were Catholics. I never rebelled." In fact, to hear Pursel tell it, his life, up to Lazaris, was remarkably boring.

"I didn't have abusive parents. I loved my childhood. I had an all-American, normal family. I loved it," Jach said, twisting a chicken wing in his mouth and then wiping his hands. "I even enjoyed moving, actually. It was not always so easy the first few weeks of school, but otherwise I liked it." He was a smart boy. "I loved movies, too. Still do. I'd stay up watching them all summer long."

The family eventually settled in Lansing, Michigan, where, at fourteen, Jack met his first and only sweetheart, Penny (with two *n*'s then) Lake. He said that he and Penny were both top students in high school. They went off to the University of Michigan together and Penny became interested in psychic phenomena. She read voraciously, consuming books on Eastern religion, meditative techniques, and psychic practices. In their junior year, Jack and Penny were married.

"For some reason, I think Vietnam had a lot to do with that," he said. "We weren't radical, but we joined the anti-war protests and we were certainly aware of it." College and marriage were both mitigating circumstances that could shield a young man from the draft.

Penny and Jack both planned to be lawyers. A political science major, he dreamed of becoming a powerful politician, or perhaps "a mover and shaker, behind the scenes," he said. "But for some reason, we lost our enthusiasm for it." Jack blamed the war, noting that Vietnam was "like a cloud" that made the future seem, somehow, less important. So instead of going to law school, he took a job with the State Farm Insurance Company, in their local office in Marshall, Michigan. Pursel worked from nine to five while Penny, who had also given up on her dream of becoming a lawyer, stayed home, reading. The two of them never really wanted to have children, he noted. "We thought, with all the problems in the world, we didn't need to do that."

With plenty of time on her hands, Pursel said, his young wife "was engaged in self-education, really. Over time she read more and more philosophy and counterculture stuff."

In 1972, Jach said, "Penny read an article about meditation in *Cosmopolitan* magazine. She told me I should try it, to relax." He attended a class offered by an organization called Silva Mind Control, which teaches meditative techniques. "I was the husband who got dragged along," he said, breaking out in another grin.

Two years later, Jack had become a frequent meditator. One evening in October, Penny suggested that Jack meditate while she asked him questions. It would be fun. He agreed to do it. But as often happened after a long day's work, as soon as he became relaxed, he fell asleep. At least he felt as if he was sleeping. According to the notes Penny made, he had spoken for two hours, in a strange voice, offering all sorts of wondrous insights into their lives.

"Lazaris talked to Penny about her childhood and things going on with her. He said he would be there to talk with her any time. After that, every night for two weeks she would ask me questions. Then, because I was always asleep during this, she played a tape for me. It was hard to believe."

At the time, Pursel said, he had read some of Penny's books, about mediums and psychics. "But I couldn't get into it. Now here it was, happening to me. I was asleep. I knew I was asleep. But there it was."

Lazaris had appeared just as State Farm ordered Jack transferred to an office in Florida. He and Penny left Michigan and settled in Winter Haven, in the central part of the state. They continued to experiment with Lazaris, contacting him and tape-recording what he said. But they were confused and concerned about just what was going on, so they telephoned a friend of Penny's, a psychic she had met just before moving south. It was Michael Prestini. Prestini came to Florida, assessed what was happening to Jack, and declared that he was a true channel, transmitting messages from a genuine spirit being.

"Michael worked in educational films for the state of Michigan, but he also had an extensive background in metaphysics," said Pursel. "He spent four days talking to Lazaris, and after that I stopped fighting it." Lazaris asked Michael to move from Michigan, to work with him. "Michael didn't hesitate," Jach recalled. Prestini moved to Florida and helped found Concept:Synergy as a for-profit company.

They very deliberately chose not to found a nonprofit religious organization, Jach said, "because Penny wanted to avoid all the oversight and rules that come with nonprofit groups. It was to be a profit-making company from the very beginning." Soon they were in business, selling the information that flowed from this being that seemed to inhabit Pursel's body.

As he ordered another Coke, Pursel said he couldn't recall how long it took before Penny and Michael fell in love. "It wasn't long, though. I mean, there was no hanky panky or anything. And I could see that what they had together was beautiful. I could see that she was happy with him."

The way Pursel described it, he and Michael Prestini traded places in a most amicable way. One day Lazaris announced that Jack and Penny should divorce so that Michael and Penny could marry. "It was Penny, Penny and Lazaris, really, who worked it out, and it's been beautiful ever since," said Pursel. "We were best friends, and that didn't stop. I liked Michael, too." He liked them both, so much that even after Penny became Michael's wife, they continued to live together. And eventually they all changed their names, for numerological reasons.

More than a decade later, Jach, Peny, and Michaell continued to live together. They ran Concept:Synergy together, they vacationed together, they even had a joint checking account, with all three names on it.

And for many years, Jach said, he had lived without an intimate romantic love, without a sexual partner. He limited his life to endless weeks on the road dedicated to channeling Lazaris. I gently suggested that he was somewhat like the eunuchs Lazaris had described for the woman who had heard that word in her meditation: a highly spiritual being without the distractions of sexuality. I asked him why he had chosen such a life.

"I dated for a while, but I didn't like it. So I stopped," he said, reaching for another chicken wing. "Other things are more important to me. My life is full. I like my life. That's all there is to it."

"Do you think there's something inside you, something wrong, that keeps you from wanting to be close to someone?"

"If you are asking if it's something deeply psychological, I don't know. I don't understand things to the depth that Lazaris does, but I have never felt the need to see a therapist or anything. I know that Lazaris has a lot of psychoanalysts as clients, though, and I rely on Lazaris." His extra weight, he added, "is probably my padding, my padding between myself and other people."

The "other people" included the millions who followed Lazaris's messages, one way or another. Many of them made him uncomfortable, he said, because they don't understand the difference between Jach and Lazaris. "Hey, I'm just a person, like anyone else," he said, laughing. "It's Lazaris who they should be interested in."

When I asked him why he thought Lazaris was so popular, Jach Pursel, the political science major turned spirit channeler, had explanations from both disciplines to explain the interest. First he offered the standard, New Age response: "People are looking for a spirituality they aren't getting elsewhere, whether it's the churches or whatever." Secondly, he said, "they are looking for a sense of being a success. Our society is based on the idea of upward mobility. Everyone is supposed to be upwardly mobile. That idea of upward mobility puts pressure on people especially now, because things have changed, economically. There's nowhere to move up to now. They can't become more than their fathers were now, because the country has changed." This would explain why, when Lazaris took us to Sirius for that peak experience, he said, "you get the deal! You have success!"

Pursel was right about Americans' obsession with material success. People had good reason to feel obsessed. In real terms, the average American worker's wages had stopped growing in the 1970s. For the first time in modern history there was a generation of young adults who could not be sure that they would stand on their fathers' shoulders—as the expression goes—and move up in social and economic standing. The distress this caused brought people to Lazaris.

These reasons—spiritual hunger and social alienation— explained why both middle-class people and glittery pop stars would be drawn to Lazaris. Pointing to a well-known film director who sat at a nearby table, Pursel said, "Sometimes it seems like everybody has a hole inside that must be filled. Like a lot of people, he's found it with Lazaris. He's very enthusiastic, and very serious about it. I can't explain it any other way."

It was explanation enough and all I was to get from Pursel. Our fifteen minutes had become an hour and he was obviously fatigued. The final day of the intensive was less than twelve hours away.

Before he left, I told Pursel that he seemed to work very hard at his channeling. There were more than ninety dates per year in his schedule, many of those covering three- or four-day "intensives." He stuck to this grueling pace while Peny and Michaell stayed back in Palm Beach, running the business and, in effect, living the good life while running his life.

He admitted it was lonely on the road, but the millions of dollars Lazaris brought in each year made it all okay. "It means I can live in a way I never dreamed I would live," he said. "I like it." Being a good boy who never rebelled had its rewards.

Having touched the power of Sirius, we had just one goal left to reach: seeing God, Goddess, All That Is. Sunday morning would be devoted to this adventure. In the afternoon we would celebrate our spiritual accomplishments with the crystal ceremony.

I took a seat in front of Donna and Marie. Fred the accountant was to my left. On my right was Helen, someone

I hadn't seen before. Helen looked like she was in her mid-sixties. She wore crystal earrings and a crystal pendant. She was a minister's wife from New Jersey, and, she said, she had every Lazaris tape—audio and video—ever made. "I listen to them in the morning, in the kitchen when I get up, and I keep them on in the car," she told me. "I will turn them off when my husband asks me to, though." She didn't have a trace of doubt about Lazaris and his teachings, however. "I know," she said, "because I created a miracle for myself, just as he says you can."

It had been a miracle of healing. Helen had been diagnosed with cancer. But in the weeks before her surgery, she visualized and meditated, determined to "create the reality that I did not have it." She went into the hospital with Lazaris books and tapes under her arms. Further tests revealed that Helen in fact did not have cancer. "That was proof enough for me that what he says, that all of life is an illusion and you can create your own reality, is true," she said, knowingly.

As ten o'clock arrived, Jach took his place in the lacquer chair. He smiled upon the hundreds of faces that were, by now, familiar. But before he removed his glasses and bowed his head, Mary Beth took the stage to remind us that Lazaris was coming to New Jersey in one month, for another seminar. She gave us a sales pitch for an intensive that had a truly intriguing title: Secrets of Longevity, Clues to Immortality, Phase I. The topics Lazaris was to cover included:

Reversing the Aging Process Without Harm
Restructuring DNA: Re-creating the Future
Longevity and Immortality: The Light Side.

On my left, Fred the accountant leaned over to ask if I was planning to attend the New Jersey seminar. He seemed a bit disappointed when I said no. He was already planning to go.

When Mary Beth was finished, she gave Jach the microphone. He immediately fell into his trance. There was no time to waste.

To open the day, Lazaris reassured us that we were all now empowered to call on the energy of Sirius any time we wished. "You have the tools, the techniques, they are yours now," he said. But he warned us against discussing our "Sirius connection" with anyone who might question it. This power was fragile and it could be destroyed by any slip in faith. "Share it with someone you trust," he cautioned. "And when you do share, share the content, not the context or form." Besides, he said, turning playful, "imagine trying to describe this. . . . Well, er, you see there were these triangles and one was humanity and the other was divinity, and they come together and then they are a star and you walk through and then, and then . . ." Feigning breathlessness, Lazaris looked around the room. "Well, it loses somethin' in the translation. I guess you kind of had to be there."

The audience laughed. The point was made. Metaphysical beliefs often wither upon examination. This is one reason the Catholic Church is reluctant to let scientists examine its relics, and the Mormons shroud their institutions in secrecy. Faith is fragile, especially when it's built on a supernatural foundation.

Lazaris then squinted down at the scores of people who jammed the front rows of the room, hoping he would answer their questions.

"Weel, awl right," he said.

The hands went up immediately. The voices were pleading, almost desperate.

"Lazaris, Lazaris, Lazaris! Over here!"

Lazaris was in an expansive mood, willing to talk about issues beyond the narrow concerns of individual lives. At one point he began to ramble about the impact that we could all have on the forces of nature—the environment, earthquakes, volcanic eruptions—through meditation and the power of Sirius. Much of this would depend, however, on the value we placed on our own humanity. If we valued ourselves enough, the very primal forces of nature would be calmed.

"It is true in your world already," he said. "Where the value placed on people is tremendous, not so much damage is done.

"Consider where earthquakes have occurred and caused much damage: Peru, Mexico City, Eastern Europe, Tokyo, Iran, Armenia. Yet in America, in the San Francisco earthquake, the death toll was very low. The damage done is in relationship to the value people hold." The point of this outrageous argument was that in the non-Western world, people suffered more because their cultures held human life in such low regard. It wasn't poverty, or different construction standards, or even geology and climate, he said. It was, in the end, a spiritual matter, and the people in these places were spiritually lacking. The same phenomenon happened, on a less exaggerated scale, even in the United States, he said.

"Hurricanes in your country go ashore in places like Mississippi and New Orleans. There's a lower value on human life there than they hold, for example, in the Northeast."

This was not a new idea. In America, this way of interpreting the vicissitudes of life has been most often identified with Calvinism, a strain of Christian philosophy that grew out of the Reformation. Strict Calvinists believe that one's worldly position is a direct reflection of the soul. Under this definition, then, the poor who died in Mexico City's great earthquake perished because they were sinners. While few modern Christians would call themselves Calvinists, Calvinism remained embedded in American values, so deeply that even in the 1980s, a representative of the Reagan Administration once suggested that the poor and homeless suffered because of their poor spiritual condition.

After his discussion of man and nature, Lazaris returned to the eager questioners before him. A woman took the microphone and posed the most unusual question I had heard during the intensive. She said that she wanted to work as a psychic, but the last time she launched such a career, she behaved so poorly that her clients turned on her. "I hurt people," she said.

"Because, what was your hidden agenda?" asked Lazaris.

"Power."

"You were wanting people to like you. Isn't that where it went askew?"

"Yes," she said, trembling.

"You manipulated them to like you. How did that happen?"

"Getting them to do things, like make registrations, come to my workshops, getting them to depend on me."

It all ended badly for her, she said, with her clients accusing her of fraud and deception. In the end, her business failed. Now she wanted to start again. But before she could, Lazaris said, she needed to understand why she needed love so desperately.

"You did screw people up. We'd not be telling the truth if we didn't say that. But it was not because you were a bad person. It was because you were at cross-agendas. You wanted love. You have to change your motivations, which means find another source of love," said Lazaris. But that didn't necessarily mean romantic love.

Here Lazaris seemed to be speaking also for Jach Pursel, explaining his choice of celibacy, and I wondered if the message wasn't stimulated by my discussion with Jach the night before.

"A lot of you initially think of a love as someone you go to bed with," he said. "But it could be an intimate friend, anyone you can love. That's going to accelerate your growth. . . . You need to create someone to love in your life."

"There are three basic kinds of love relationships," Lazaris continued. The first kind of love he called "one to one" and it is, essentially, like marriage. The second category was "serial relationships" in which a person moves from one lover to the next. "But there is a third group. These people who don't need either of those kinds of sexual relationships. Their intimacy needs are met elsewhere, without sexuality.

"Of course, society says the only decent way to be is one

to one. Those who are not like that are not understood at all. There's something really wrong with you if you aren't like that. Psychologically, you're a mess," he said in an exaggerated, mocking voice. "But the truth is, one-third of the population isn't really interested in sex.

"Most of you have lower sex drives than Madison Avenue says you should," he continued. "You see people on TV drinking Bud Light. You see gorgeous young men and women and you know where they are going after they drink their beers. It's like the Mountain Dew ads. Gorgeous people are at the swimmin' hole behaving like kids, but you know it's not going to be like kids later on."

Lazaris was on a roll. This was obviously a subject he had considered quite thoroughly. And while his monologue was only faintly connected to the questions raised by the would-be psychic, he pressed on.

"Now, the channel was watching a program on CNN recently. There was a woman on who said she was happy living alone. She said, 'I'm not really interested in a man.' Then on came this psychologist who said, 'You've got a real problem, honey. You've numbed out. You need to get to a therapist fast.' Well, the idea that all people need romantic love is just not right," said Lazaris.

The lunch break was coming soon, so it was time for a meditation. Lazaris turned on the tape player and the peaceful music began to flow once more. The lights were dimmed and he soothingly talked us into a hypnotic state of "to-tal-re-lax-a-tion."

We went back to the pond, the tree, and the rock to contact Sirius and "create" our dreams for the world. We could ask that all wars end, that the environment be cleansed, or that hunger cease. "There are those who say the world is coming to an end," Lazaris said, "but they didn't count on you!" Lazaris said that no request would be too big, so I asked for peace in the Middle East. After the wish was decided, the higher self ceremoniously went to the fire and grabbed a small, glowing ember. The ember cooled and became a small crystal in the shape of a tear. It would be our remembrance of what had happened there.

"Now, when I count to five, you will awaken. One . . . two . . . three . . . four . . . five. And as you go to lunch, just feel that energy."

During the lunch break I took a walk in nearby Fairmount Park, where Philadelphia's great museums are located. It was a warm sunny day and the park was filled with people. Children splashed among the copper frogs and fish in the ornate Calder fountain. Vendors sold soft pretzels from pushcarts in front of the museums. For the first time in four days, I was back in what Lazaris would call "the consensus reality," feeling the sunshine on my face and watching children play.

When I returned to the Holiday Inn ballroom, I noticed there was a small, blue-velvet-lined basket on the stage. Lazaris was to conduct a crystal ceremony and, presumably, the crystal gifts he was to give us were in the basket.

"I met the goddess for the first time this weekend, in one of my meditations," Marie told me as I took my seat. She was standing and, as she said this, she began to wobble on her feet. "I've got to sit down," she said shyly. "I have been feeling dizzy like this ever since."

Pursel then entered the room and took the stage for the final time. Before the ceremony, Mary Beth issued some rules. We were to divide ourselves into even groups on either side of the hall and proceed, one by one, to the front. There we would stand before Lazaris for a brief moment. He would adjust our energies—using some motion of his hands—and then give us a crystal. We were not to ask him any questions. We were not to touch him.

Over the next hour and a half, as more soothing music poured forth, three hundred people waited patiently for their moment before Lazaris. As they stood in line, many were shaking, crying, or grinning. When they finally reached the stage and the lacquer chair, many broke down.

Tears streamed down their faces and they simply shook, unable to say anything. I watched several middle-aged men dissolve in tears as they came face to face with Lazaris, whispered their name, and he touched them.

"It's Gene, Lazaris."

"It's Roger, Lazaris."

"It's Peter, Lazaris."

Lazaris would seem to fiddle with the tops of their heads, or he would gently stroke their throats or abdomens, "healing" their energy. Then he would murmur, "Weel yes, yes, awl-right," reach into the basket, and press a crystal into each one's hand. The crystals were supposed to be unique, and Lazaris said he selected each one specifically for the person who was to receive it. Everyone who received a crystal clutched it tightly. Most didn't look at their gift until they were seated again. Then some would hold it and look at it reverently, worshipfully. Others held their crystals up to the light, peering at it for many minutes. Still others placed theirs in their little pouches, with their other crystals. In the back of the room, groups of people were hugging and crying together. Couples embraced and gazed into each other's eyes during long moments of seeming bliss.

Knowing that I lacked the kind of faith that others felt, I thought for a moment that I should leave my place in line. After all, I was not convinced that Lazaris was what he claimed to be. To me, the man in the lacquer chair was the same one who had shared a basket of chicken wings with me the night before. He was Jach Pursel. Then suddenly the line moved, and I was next. I went ahead.

"It's Michael, Lazaris," I said as I reached the little stage. I half-expected Jach to say something about our meeting the night before. But it was Lazaris who spoke, not Pursel.

"Weel, weel, awl-right," he answered.

Then he put one hand on the back of my neck and the other over my head. His hand was hot and sweaty. He waved his arm above my head. Then he put a tiny crystal in my hand, and it was over.

Like the others, I didn't open my hand until I was back at my seat. When I did, I found a small glass bead, tear-shaped. I glanced around and saw that everyone else had beads, too. They were all the same.

For the next hour I continued to study the crystal ceremony. It was very much like Holy Communion in the Catholic Church, where lines of people approach a priest, he utters, "The body of Christ," and they receive the host. But it was also like a much less serious ceremony: a child's visit with a department store Santa Claus. Pursel, with his big tummy and long beard, even looked like Santa.

By now, for me, the evidence that Lazaris and Jach Pursel were one and the same was convincing. First there was the intermittent Scottish accent. Then there was Lazaris's operation of the tape machine. Pursel's eyes were supposedly shut, because he was in a trance. How, then, could he work a tape player? Finally there were all the little things. Lazaris loved movies. Jach loved movies. Jach defended his celibacy. Lazaris defended celibacy.

Not that any of this mattered to anyone else. After all, this was a New Age faith group, and Lazaris's status was not open for discussion. Any suggestion that he might be from the far reaches of Jach Pursel's mind, rather than the outer limits of space, would have caused a riot. It would have been like marching into St. Peter's on Christmas morning and saying that the Virgin Birth never happened. Just as most Christians do not doubt the divinity of Jesus, Lazaris's followers did not doubt his. Besides, Pursel/Lazaris had given them four very long days of spiritual instruction and a certain kind of affection. And as I watched the men and women around me adore the gifts they had received in the crystal ceremony, it was clear that they were satisfied with their end of the bargain.

The intensive was to end with the meditation in which we would glimpse God, Goddess, All That Is. It began immediately after the crystal ceremony.

"And now it's ti-em for the conclu-eding meditation," announced Lazaris as the lights went down and he fumbled again with the tape player. "Let yourself once again enter an altered state. Go de-ah-pah, de-ah-pah. Go to the special place, with the tree and the pond, the rock."

We were going again to the place we had reached on the seven-day journey, where the temple had been built in honor of our connection to Sirius. We went through the door to the underworld and along the path to the barge rowed by fifty oarsmen. But this time we stopped along the river, to pick up our higher self, our future self, and other "cocreators" who waited patiently on the riverbank. We journeyed to the temple and there created a ring of fire by simply pointing our fingers at the ground and tracing a circle. The flames grew high and we summoned the power of Earth, wind, water, and fire. Then the circle of flames receded and we stood, searching for Sirius.

"Let it be done, I am a cocreator," chanted Lazaris as the music accompanying his voice built. He repeated it, over and over. "Let it be done, I am a cocreator. Let it be done, I am a cocreator."

Suddenly a cone of power descended from Sirius. Billions of spinning, flashing lights filled the air.

"The air is filled with frankincense!" Lazaris shouted above the music. "You smell it, even if you don't know what frankincense smells like!"

Then a single, blinding beam of light filled the scene and in the distance, said Lazaris, was "an ancient one" who seemed to float in the clouds. The room was filled with the music and Lazaris's urgent voice.

And in the eyes of the ancient one, for a brief moment, he said, "You glimpse God, Goddess, All That Is!"

I saw an ancient one in my meditation. But when I took the last step, looking for God in his eyes, all I saw was more light, and what seemed to be blue water. I was disappointed. At the very least, I had hoped my mind would create something more original.

Frustrated, I opened my eyes and looked at Lazaris onstage and at the people all around me. They were euphoric. A young man in front of me had his eyes tightly closed, but tears were streaming down his cheeks. He smiled broadly, his head tilted toward the heavens. He brought his hands together prayerfully. He looked as if he was seeing God.

Against the wall, a woman dressed in purple silk robes had her hands in the air and was reaching, reaching with her fingers outstretched. Her eyes were closed, too, and she was swaying gently back and forth. Others in the room rocked back and forth in their chairs. Some lay on the floor, or curled into a fetal position, weeping. Some were laughing out loud, giggling and guffawing. One man, on my left, clenched his fists and pounded his thighs over and over, saying, "Yes, yes, yes," through clenched teeth. He too was crying through eyes that were squeezed closed.

Up onstage, Lazaris was hunched over the microphone, describing what would happen in the afterglow of this ultimate meditative experience.

"You return to be held by your higher self," he said. "Your cocreators come and kiss you on the cheeks and forehead. We appear as a light to be with you and then go up into the heavens and then burst into a billion, billion lights."

And then it was over. Lazaris was saying good-bye. But we could contact him anytime, he reminded us, through meditation. "If it's two in the morning and you can't sleep and you need someone to talk to, we'll be there. Just imagine the light. We're only as far away as your imagination.

"We close. Weeth luf and peace."

In the days that followed the intensive, I was not much concerned with explaining what Lazaris is. Pursel sincerely believes Lazaris is a spirit being. I guess that Lazaris is, instead, the product of Pursel's mind—an alter ego, even a secondary personality. A psychiatrist I know told me Pursel's "Lazaris" is similar to the "characters" that arise in people with "multiple personality disorder." Whatever the explanation, Lazaris was not impressive enough, not smart enough, for me to believe he's an omniscient spirit being.

What interested me more than explaining Lazaris was pondering his followers. The images that remained in my mind were of the pained faces of the people who stood to ask Lazaris for help. For while the Lazaris intensive was billed as a prescription for achieving tremendous power, it was, in fact, a tableau of powerlessness. The people I had seen there were bothered by the same fears and insecurities that have always plagued human beings. Some had been threatened by illness. Many, such as my lunch companion Fred, came from shattered families or had been raised by deranged parents. All seemed to look to Lazaris for a loving parent's acceptance, wisdom, and understanding.

In the end, Jach Pursel's analysis of Lazaris's appeal was probably true. America is a country undergoing enormous economic and social change. Feminism, divorce, global economic competition, even the aftershocks of Watergate and Vietnam, have forced us to reconsider our assumptions about everything from family life to politics. Those larger social forces, and the personal tragedies so common to the human species, combine to create overwhelming insecurity. In Lazaris, some have found reassurances, a balm for insecurity, a friend. In fact, that was how many people—actor Michael York for one—described Lazaris. He was their wonderful friend.

But is Lazaris truly anyone's friend? He disappeared as soon as Jach Pursel awoke from his trance. He was not there to comfort the believers who had to sift through the disturbing memories unlocked during the meditations. Clearly, many people had experienced upsetting, even shocking interior events during their meditations. Their shouts and cries were ample evidence. Who would provide the kind of human relationship one needs for real emotional healing to take place? How did the Lazaris intensive make anyone less isolated, less alienated, less damaged?

Indeed, the philosophy Lazaris preached suggests that there is nothing to consider in life outside the metaphysical. One needn't be involved in anything concrete, especially where the needy or the underprivileged are concerned. Life is a matter of "having fun" and "creating your own reality." Those for whom reality is less than ideal, have only themselves to blame. It is all shallow, and cruel, and ultimately unsatisfying. Lazaris didn't encourage human contact or involvement outside the small group who attended Lazaris events. Even the rituals he performed were isolating. People meditated, with their eyes closed. They stood in line to get their crystals, one by one. Altogether, the Lazaris experience, was like an anesthetic formulated to soothe the loneliness and pain people brought to the ballroom. It was not a cure, but like anything that brings temporary relief, it might keep people coming back for more.

A few weeks after the intensive, Iraq invaded Kuwait and America responded by sending tens of thousands of troops to neighboring Saudi Arabia. All my efforts at using the power of Sirius had not brought peace to the Middle East. Meanwhile, Lazaris was in San Francisco for a lecture on "health, wealth, and success."

# 4 · SIERRA NEVADA

## Earth Tribe Gathering

AYISHA HOMOLKA'S INTENSE ENVIRONMENTALISM IS IN-
flamed by her pagan beliefs, which she explained as we
headed south on Interstate 5, past countless California sub-
divisions and then through the dry grassy hills south of
Oakland called the Diablo Range. Ayisha might be called a
witch, and she once referred to herself that way, but she
had recently begun to consider herself a "free-lance, neo-
pagan ritualist." The title "witch" carried too many negative
connotations, she explained, and she had her seventeen-
year-old daughter, Tamara ("She's a junior police cadet, by
the way") to consider.

"People get the wrong idea. They equate paganism with
evil," she said. On the hilltops above us, hundreds of huge
windmills spun from tall pylons, generating electricity.
They looked like giant lawn ornaments. "Paganism was really the first religion people had. It puts you in touch with
the environment, with the weather, the forces of nature.
It's about being in harmony with the world, respecting it."

As far as Ayisha and other spiritually inspired environmentalists are concerned, humankind is so much out of tune with nature that a state of emergency exists. In response they join others in dramatic protests: blockading logging trucks, occupying timberlands, attacking logging equipment. These ecospiritualists are among the few in the New Age movement for whom belief is more than a private matter. In the tradition of other American reform campaigns, they take to the streets, or the forests, to demand change.

All this demanding is risky business. A few months before Ayisha and I met, two leaders of a radical ecology group called Earth First! were injured when a bomb exploded in their car. Darryl Cherney and Judi Bari had led a series of confrontations with loggers, and it was feared that the loggers had done the bombing. The attack heightened the paranoia that already existed within the environmental movement. It also worried me enough that I decided I needed a guide as I explored New Age environmentalism. Ayisha had agreed to serve and to take me to a forest protest that had been organized by Earth First! but would draw many New Age–style environmentalists.

We met at the Oakland airport. Ayisha arrived in a lurching, dust-covered old Subaru station wagon, California license plate: CRZYLIF. The car sagged under the weight of sleeping bags, tents, boxes of clothes, paper bags full of food (all-natural), books, bottles of water, and various ceremonial items: crystals, an eight-inch-high "goddess" statue with a round belly and large breasts, abalone shells, bits of cedar and sage. A rather large woman with weathered skin and long, shiny black hair, Ayisha wore a black T-shirt and a long blue-plaid skirt. She looked younger than her thirty-nine years.

On the way to the interstate she had explained that this weekend the protesters intended to confront loggers, police, and the National Forest Service in defense of the trees. The event would probably end with mass arrests, but it would also focus the nation's media on the cause. For Ayisha this meant the sacredness of unspoiled nature and the sin of its destruction.

As we descended the Diablo Range and entered the San Joaquin Valley, we passed vast examples of how man has transformed, if not destroyed, nature. Enormous flat groves of almond and fruit trees were irrigated by concrete canals that brought a trough of water from the north. Dozens of trucks sped by, carrying open loads of tomatoes, onions, and potatoes, piled high like gravel. It was hot and the sun shimmered off a road that stretched to the horizon. The long road and the prospect of a five-hour drive seemed to invite storytelling.

"I was raised in a pretty strict family in Milwaukee," began Ayisha. "My father was a Navy man and he treated us like we were recruits. He was an alcoholic, too, and you know what that means. My mom, meanwhile, was always cleaning, or having social gatherings, or volunteering. She was always doing something for somebody. Saint Lucille. I love my mother, though. She's a great person.

"Anyway, in 1970 I went to Stevens Point University in Michigan. I was eighteen years old and I didn't know anything. Pretty soon I discovered philosophy, psychology, drugs, and the counterculture. I loved it because I also discovered myself. I had been proper, subdued, restrained, constrained. You know, crew-neck sweaters with the little white collar sticking out. Suddenly I was able to experiment, be spontaneous. It was exciting."

College life was so exciting and distracting that young Patty (her original name was Patricia Harper) soon lost track of her studies and dropped out of college to marry a man ten years her senior, who had recently finished a term at San Quentin on a drug conviction. "My mother didn't like Fred at all. She kept saying his eyes looked like Charles Manson's," she recalled.

Fred lived up to Lucille's worst expectations. He took Patty on a six-year adventure through remote villages in Europe and North Africa, dealing drugs and dodging the police. As the years passed, Patty took on her Arabic names, Ayisha, a common first name, and Homolka, which means "crazy life." Fred, meanwhile, took bigger and bigger risks, became a drug addict, and he beat her more and more severely. Then, in 1973, their daughter, Tamara, was born in Amsterdam. They were sharing an apartment there with a former military man who dressed in skirts and a woman who preferred to dine nude. With a child to consider, Ayisha finally recognized how bizarre and even dangerous her life was; she began planning her escape. When Tamara was three, she convinced Fred to pay for her to take her daughter to meet her grandparents at Christmastime. They never went back.

The story of Fred and Ayisha abroad sounded like the plot outline for a bad movie about the worst of the 1970s drug culture. It also seemed that Ayisha was telling the truth. She had no reason to fabricate such a story, and she told it only to explain her introduction to paganism. She had also given much thought to her own role in this sordid past. After all, she had chosen to hook up with a violent, drug-dealing criminal. She had placed her child in harm's way and she had stayed in a dangerous, abusive situation for years. "Fred was very charismatic, very controlling," she recalled. "And I'm sure my willingness to get involved with him had a lot to do with my growing up in an alcoholic home. You feel you don't deserve to live any better. You don't develop much self-esteem."

Back in the United States, Ayisha entered psychological counseling, which improved her self-esteem and helped her to resist Fred's desperate and sometimes threatening attempts to win her back. She also returned to college, enrolling at the University of Wisconsin branch in Milwaukee. One evening, as she was telling her life story to a new friend and lamenting the pain she still felt, he said, "I can help you. I'm a witch."

The witch performed a ritual—lighting candles, singing chants—designed to help Ayisha break her emotional ties to Fred. When it was over, Ayisha believed Fred's influence had been diminished. Intrigued by the ceremony, she then undertook an informal study of witchcraft and paganism. She discovered that there are thousands of Americans— witches, goddess worshipers, druids, and others—who adhere to a nature-based spirituality that they trace to preChristian Europe. These "neo-pagans" are not evil devil worshipers, but rather extremely open-minded spiritualists. Most belong to groups founded in the last thirty years. They borrow ideas from Roman and Greek mythology, European paganism, and other ancient faiths. Neo-paganism appealed to Ayisha's feminist impulses because it honors goddesses as well as gods. And its free-lance style of worship touched her creative side. She loved making her own rituals and she was relieved to find the movement had no hierarchy and few rules. She had found a religion, a community of faith, and a way of thinking that gave her a sense of control. Given her childhood and the smothering presence of Fred, it may have been the first time in her life that she felt that way.

"My friend introduced me to the Alexandrian tradition of the craft, which is very ethical," Ayisha told me. (This modern branch of witchcraft was founded in the 1940s by Alexander and Maxine Sanders of England.) "You don't ask for specific things or try to work against someone. You open yourself up to the guidance that is there. The magic we use isn't what people think. It's more like having a ritual to make your intentions clear. It's sort of like visualization. You call on Earth, fire, water, and air, on the goddess and god, call your ancestors, do whatever you need, and use the incense, the candles, movements, words, to put energy into what you want to happen.

"Now I say that I practice an Earth-based spirituality, an old religion that helps me enjoy life here and now. It makes me feel more connected to the Earth, the water, the elements that keep me alive. And I feel like I'm also part of a tribal kind of community with the rituals that make me feel alive."

Ayisha moved to California in 1980. She settled in the
little city of Ukiah, in the northern part of the state. There
she joined a pagan church—The Church of All Worlds—
and became a founding member of an environmental
group called Forever Forest, which was dedicated to saving
the California forests from loggers' chainsaws. It was a short
leap from paganism to environmentalism. After all, pagan
rites revolve around the elements of nature—Earth, fire,
water, air—and they often take place in the wilderness. And
pollution would be the desecration of the temple.

Forever Forest was part of a coalition of groups participating in Redwood Summer, a season-long protest against
logging in California forests. I had called Redwood Summer organizers, looking for New Agers who were part of
their cause. They had recommended Ayisha. A week later
we were driving the three hundred miles from Oakland to
the Sierra National Forest and one of the major events of
Redwood Summer. We were to join several hundred members of Earth First!, which was part of the Redwood Summer coalition. Earth First! planned a four-day wilderness
"rendezvous" that would culminate in the illegal occupation
of an active logging site.

"How are you about nudity?" Ayisha asked. We had just
turned on to state road 198 and were traveling through a
three-foot sea of green tomato plants.

"Is it required?"

"No, but some people like to take their clothes off at
these things, and I hope it doesn't bother you." (Many
pagan groups perform their rituals in the nude.)

"No, I don't think it will."

"Good. These things can get a little weird, especially if
you've never seen one before. There's a lot of howling,
people making their animal calls in the night. And there's
a certain beer-drinking element. I hope none of that bothers you."

As we drove on, Ayisha put a tape in the car's cassette
player and turned it up loud. It was a recording of protest

songs by Darryl Cherney, the Earth First! activist who had
been injured in the recent bombing. The police investigation of the incident had focused at first on the theory that
it was an accident, not an attack. The authorities believed
that Cherney and the car's owner, Judi Bari, had been
transporting the bomb and were to use it somehow to protest destruction of the environment. Earth First!'s violent
rhetoric and aggressiveness invited such a suspicion. The
creation of the organization was inspired by the Edward
Abbey novel *The Monkeywrench Gang*, which is about a group
of environmentalists who blow up bridges, torch billboards,
and plot to destroy dams, all in the name of Mother Earth.
With the monkey wrenchers as role models, the Earth First!
activists had destroyed loggers' equipment by "spiking"
trees and endangered snowmobilers by stretching fishing
line across trails. In 1989 Earth First! founder David Foreman was convicted on federal charges following his arrest
in the midst of a late-night blow-torch attack against a giant
tower carrying electric lines through the Arizona desert.

So the police had reasons to suspect that Bari and Cherney simply mishandled their own bomb. But they had no
material evidence that this was the case. Then an anonymous letter-writer claimed to have done the bombing on
behalf of Christian fundamentalism. Gradually local politicians began complaining that the police were on a political
crusade against the victims of the attack. There were, after
all, plenty of loggers angry enough to bomb the car. In
June the police admitted that their investigation was incon-
clusive and they dropped the charges against Bari and
Cherney. By then the two Earth Firsters were heroes of the
ecology movement.

Cherney's songs were in the tradition of American protest
songs—gospel and folk music rolled together. Ayisha sang
along as we rode past green fields and tractors, past boys
on their bicycles and farmworkers in straw hats.

"You can't clear-cut your way to heaven!" she sang as
we went past the Lily of the Valley Church, where a sign

proclaimed JESUS SAVES. In Poplar we went by a huge Sun-kist fruit-processing factory and another plant that turned turkeys into sausage and salami. "Bullshit! It's all bullshit!" she sang.

Soon we were in Porterville, a hot little town at the foot of the Sierras. I recalled it, too, as the hometown of Dan Olmos, Louise Hay's assistant. We stopped at a supermarket, where Ayisha bought plenty of granola and tofu. I grabbed some canned chicken and beans and eight gallons of bottled water. We then stopped at a little restaurant called The Palms Cafe—orange plastic booths and a soda fountain in the back—for a final hot meal of fish and fries before heading to the forest. While we ate, Ayisha addressed a couple dozen party invitations she wanted to mail before we left town. The invitations, decorated with paper dolls, announced a "Full Moon Tea Party. A playful ceremony to honor the little girls hidden in our hearts. Please wear your favorite dress-up clothes," the invitation read, "and bring something special from your childhood or to the little girl within you now." The tea party would include "hopscotch, jump rope, and running through the sprinkler."

The waitress at The Palms didn't know what to make of Ayisha's paper dolls and tea party invitations. She sarcastically asked, "Can I come to your little party?" Ayisha answered, "Sure, if you're around Ukiah." The tea party genuinely excited Ayisha; it would be yet another ritual, a way to make sacred her childhood memories and those of her friends.

About five miles out of Porterville we started to climb into the mountains. At first the landscape was all dry grass and dirt, but as we went higher, the road became more twisting, and more and more trees appeared until, at last, we were deep inside a forest of towering sugar pine, Douglas fir, and Ponderosa pine.

More than half of California's forests have been felled by logging and development. In the north, around Ukiah, it is easy to make a case against the logging companies, particularly Louisiana Pacific, which has increased its harvest of trees to pay off debts associated with a junk-bond buy-out. It is a perfect parable of the times: Investors bought a lumber company and then accelerated the cutting of the trees in order to pay off the debt. There was little the protesters or even the government could do about it, because it was all taking place on private land. So the Redwood Summer organizers used nonviolent but illegal means—occupying land, sitting on platforms atop trees—to slow the cutting.

The situation in the Sequoia National Forest is more ambiguous. Here the government owns the trees and has control over them. The Forest Service sells logging rights to various tracts, and timber companies come in to cut the trees. Officials insist that they manage the harvest cautiously and that by planting trees and allowing only selective cuts, they ensure the future of the forest. But Redwood Summer protesters believe the Forest Service is allowing too many trees to be cut and causing irreparable damage to the wilderness. An alarming article published in *Audubon* magazine supported the protesters. The article reveals that thousands of acres of forest—including some redwood groves—were being denuded in a practice called "select cutting." The term "select cutting" seems to describe a careful harvest of a limited number of trees. In practice it is much like clearcutting, except a handful of trees are left standing on a tract of many acres.

The largest living things on Earth, the redwoods are a wonderful symbol for ecologists. Naturalist John Muir called them "nature's forest masterpiece, and it is difficult to regard them with anything but awe. They are the longest-living species in the world. Individual trees have stood in California since the dawn of the Roman Empire. They pre-date Columbus, the Dark Ages, the birth of Christ. Though once the redwoods were found in abundance, by 1990 California had fewer than eighty significant groves left. These groves included trees that were more than 30 feet in diameter and more than 275 feet tall. The timber from just one of these trees, noted the *Audubon* article, "could encase the Queen Mary ocean liner in a one-inch-thick box."

Nearly all of these most ancient trees are protected from logging by either state or federal regulations. But smaller redwoods—centuries old, nonetheless—were still subject to logging on private lands and, until a recent law suit halted the practice, in the Sequoia National Forest.

Ayisha loved the redwoods. "They are the Earth's creatures," she said as she drove. "Who are we to decide they should die?"

It was late afternoon by the time we reached the cardboard signs for the turnoff to the Earth First! campsite, which had once been a staging area for wilderness expeditions. A long dirt road led to the grassy clearings where several dozen small tents were already set up. We parked the car under the trees and took a walk around. Drums were pounding in the distance and they were occasionally joined by a howling human. "Owooooo . . . ow, ow, owoooo!" The cries echoed off the mountains.

It was growing dark and Ayisha and I looked around the hilly campground for a level but secluded location for our tent and sleeping bags. We didn't want to be in the middle of the drumming and howling that would, no doubt, go on well into the night. Nor did we want to be so far away that we would miss anything important. We found a spot just a hundred yards down the trail that led to a Sequoia grove. It was a flat area about twenty by twenty square feet, beneath some trees and next to a small grassy meadow—quiet, cool, and just far enough away from the communal kitchen and the main campground.

As she pulled the pieces of the tent out of a nylon bag and I spread a tarp on the ground, Ayisha admitted she was a bit nervous about what would happen in the coming days.

"I'm not sure how many spiritual people are here. The hard-core Earth Firsters call us the 'woo-woos.' Don't ask me where the name came from. I don't know. But anyway, they might not appreciate our approach. It's also a little funny being with someone who's writing down what you say," she added without looking at me.

"I know. It requires a lot of trust," I answered. "I feel like you're giving me a gift. I appreciate it."

"Well, I got a good hit off you when we talked on the phone," she said, shrugging her shoulders. "I'm just going to trust . . . let it happen. Anyway, you must feel strange, too. And what does your wife think of all this?"

"She thinks I have a very strange job," I said, chuckling. My wife had given me a few good-natured warnings about cavorting in the forest with naked women, but her real concern was my safety. "She's worried about what might happen if there's a confrontation with the loggers or the police."

"I think it will be safe and I don't intend to get in any danger," said Ayisha. "There will be a way for us to be part of the action without getting into the middle of it."

With our fears and anxieties out in the open, we silently put up the tent. It was dark by the time we finished. We groped our way back to the car and ate a meal of cheese, bread, tomatoes, and bottled water.

As we ate, a small, wiry man with leathery skin called a greeting from the van parked next to us. He was about forty-five years old. He had golden-blond hair, piercing blue eyes, a long nose, and a quizzical smile on his face. And he wore nothing but tiny, green nylon bikini underpants. Except for the underpants, he looked like Pan, the Greek god of fields, forests, and wild animals.

"My name is Richard," he said. He breathed in deeply and spoke rapidly, exhaling the words. "I'm so happy about being here with these kind of people. I spend most of my time alone. Don't talk much to people. It never works out when I do. I love nature. Don't you? This is where I feel comfortable."

Richard spent much of his time outdoors, living alone in the forests. He also made his own clothes, all out of the same forest-green material. "Ah, I love it here," he said, again inhaling deeply, his chest and stomach bulging and then collapsing like a bellows. He looked up at the canopy of evergreen boughs. Then he wandered away, into the night.

Like Richard, many spiritual environmentalists seem to like nature better than people. As we had driven across California to the Sierra camp, Ayisha had regarded the huge farms and orchards we had passed with disdain: They were a blight and she wished them gone. Her principal concern was the environment, almost to the exclusion of human beings.

Like other New Agers such as Marlene Myhre of Sedona, who believe that much of humanity is unworthy, the spiritual ecologists seem to consider those outside their movement as fatally flawed, sinful, irredeemable. Some even speak of humans as a kind of cancer on the face of the Earth. They view mankind as no more deserving of life than the smallest one-celled organism. Human beings, because of the damage they do, may be even less worthy of life than the amoeba. David Foreman, founder of Earth First!, has even spoken of the need to somehow reduce the human population from 5 billion to about 100 million.

As Richard left I could hear drums and the howling of Earth Firsters imitating wolves and other animals. Ayisha wanted to join the party, so we walked toward the kitchen area, where the sounds originated. There we found a small bonfire and a group of men and women pounding on drums. As we stood and listened for a moment, we were met by two of Ayisha's friends from the pagan community in Ukiah. One was Marylyn, a woman in her mid-fifties who had long brown hair, a lined, weathered face, and a sturdy body. She said she had raised her four children alone— and schooled them at home—on a large piece of land near where Ayisha lived. Next to her stood her nineteen-year-old daughter, Lasara, a redhead who immediately informed me that she was an anarchist.

As we made small talk, another older woman silently

joined our group. (Paganism, like witchcraft, attracts more women than men.) She was a bit of a cavewoman—short and round with long, unkempt, reddish brown hair—and she had a tiny silver monkey wrench attached to her nose like an earring. She wore a woolen cap and a bulky army jacket. During a break in the chatter she introduced herself to me with a "Hiya!" and a firm handshake. Her name was Sequoia and she, too, lived "on the land" up north.

As Sequoia, Marylyn, Lasara, and Ayisha fell into a long conversation about mutual friends, I went back to the tent alone. I figured that I could settle down to sleep while Ayisha stayed behind, chatting with her friends amid the beating drums and the howling. That way we could both have a little privacy.

At our camp I cleared the brush away from a place beside the tent and rolled out a sleeping bag. I took off my shoes and crawled inside. Above me, an awning of evergreen branches swayed in the moonlight. Between them I could see a thousand stars, including Lazaris's bright star, Sirius. In the distance there was more howling. "Ow—ooo, ow, ow, ow-ooo!" The drums beat loud and fast. The Earth tribe was gathering.

With the light of Saturday morning, I could see more clearly the lush green glade where we had camped. As Ayisha slept, I sat up and looked around. Before me stretched a grassy expanse about two hundred yards wide and one hundred yards deep. It was carpeted with Queen Anne's lace, yellow wild flowers, and ferns. A few trees had fallen from the steep hillsides that surrounded the meadow. Birds used them as roosts, resting from their swooping, insect-catching flights above the grass. The only sound that broke the stillness was the cawing of crows until, in the distance, a car horn sounded a five-second blast.

"Breakfast!" a woman bellowed from Kitchen Hill, her announcement echoing off the hillside.

"Ow-oo, ow-oo, ow-ooooo!" came a dozen wolf calls in response.

Ayisha stirred in her sleeping bag. Then she groaned and rolled over. "Ughh. I am not a morning person."

After breakfast we joined a circle of about three hundred in an old cow pasture that was the main camping area, below Kitchen Hill. Most of the yawning protesters were dressed in Earthtones: deep greens, browns, grays. A woman wearing a granny dress and a straw hat played the banjo.

Soon the meeting was opened by one of the organizers, a short, stocky woman in jeans and braids named Kelpie Wilson. Kelpie first reviewed the fire-safety rules (it would not look good if environmentalists set a forest fire) and then went over the method that would be used for making decisions. The weekend would be run by a process called consensus, in which anyone could speak, anyone could propose a course of action, and decisions were made when 80 percent or more agreed. It was to be very democratic, sort of like a New England town meeting.

An older man of about sixty who wore khakis and a cowboy hat spoke up then. "I'd like to remind people that we're in bear country and lion country, so don't bait them in," he said. "Close up your food."

"Yeah, and clean up your trash," added Kelpie. "The press loved pointing out the trash left behind by people at Earth Day."

Half-naked Richard (I again thought of him as Pan) raised his hand and asked people to walk gently around the campgrounds. "Be aware of your movement and the dust under your feet," he implored the group. "Don't cause erosion and rutting. Don't step on the tender young plants. It's all part of your Mother Earth."

"I'm the medic," said the next speaker, a young man with close-cropped hair and glasses. "The first-aid tent is over there, and if you need me, come get me. And oh, if there are any infiltrators here from the FBI, we'll be having a lobotomy clinic after this meeting, so come on over."

The medic was not simply being funny or paranoid. The Earth Firsters who were arrested in the Arizona power-line incident had been undone by an infiltrator, so the group had reason to suspect that there would be informants at every Earth First! gathering. The comment also echoed the confrontational mood of the gathering. The lobotomy joke, the drumming and the whooping—it all reinforced the feeling that these three hundred souls in the forest were righteous warriors standing up against an enormous evil.

Many considered the news media part of the evil opposition, but Sequoia raised her hand to remind us that one of the main goals of the weekend action was to manipulate the press. "First of all, be polite to the media," she said. "Let's work with them. They can help us with our cause and I'm glad they're here. Just be careful of what you say."

"Yeah, be careful," advised a young man in the circle. "At one rendezvous a guy of questionable reputation was talking about political assassinations and that got into the press. We don't want that to happen here."

The day was to be spent organizing "affinity groups" of people who wanted to work together on Monday's protest "action." The meeting ended with no mention of what the action would be.

Afterward I listened to another of the organizers, Mark Huntington, review an agreement that several ecology groups had signed to settle a lawsuit protesting the government's management of the forest. The agreement had created two thousand acres of untouchable wilderness and restricted logging to a quarter of the forest's one million acres. But the Audubon Society had refused to sign the agreement because it barred further suits. "Basically," said Huntington, "we're here to trash the agreement."

Richard/Pan cleared his throat. "We have to have a new system for a New Age," he said. "How do we do that?"

"That's why we're here," answered Mark.

Ayisha posted a sign announcing the forming of a "Spiritual Affinity Group," for those interested in approaching the protest from a religious or metaphysical perspective. We

met in a clearing near the dirt road that led from the highway to the large encampment. At first there were just a
handful, but as Ayisha called out—"Woo-woo, woo-woo"—
more and more people came over to sit in the circle of
people that Ayisha arranged. Eventually there were more
than two dozen, seated in the grass in the shade of a small
stand of trees. In the center of the circle, Ayisha spread a
small cloth and began to build a kind of altar with shells,
flowers, several natural quartz crystals, two small crystal
balls, beads, feathers, and other objects. The people around
the circle placed other talismans on the cloth—crystal earrings, necklaces, little statues, and more crystals—until dozens of offerings were heaped together.

"The presence, the spiritual presence of these trees is
irreplaceable," Ayisha began, referring to the redwoods.
"We call on their spirit to be present to help us." She then
began beating a small drum and chanting.

**We all come from the mother**
**And to her we shall return**
**Like a drop of rain**
**Flowing to the ocean.**

Some of those who had come to join the spiritual affinity
group were old friends of Ayisha. One was a young woman
named Falling Star, who put some sage in an abalone shell,
set it smoldering with a match, and then moved from person to person, ceremonially cleansing each of us with the
smoke. Marylyn was there, and so was Lasara. They knew
the chants and joined in, following Ayisha's lead. Richard/
Pan was also there and he joined the chanting.

The main purpose of this day's meeting was to conduct
a "Council of All Beings." A combination ritual, theater
game, and consciousness-raising exercise, the council was
supposed to heighten our awareness of the natural world.
As Ayisha explained it, we would, over the course of the
afternoon, be inhabited by the consciousness of an animal,

a plant, a rock, or any other element of nature. We would then speak on behalf of these entities, transmitting their concerns and advice to the human race. "Our intention is to heal ourselves and our relationships with the Earth," she said.

Ayisha then invited those in the circle to call on their favorite spirits to join us in the meadow.

"I'd like the call in my guides, and the fairies, the little playful ones," said Marylyn.

"I call in Eros!" said her daughter, Lasara, laughing. "We all know her well."

"I call on the power of Pluto with energies to transform us and power to heal the planet, to empower the people in society who are apathetic and don't feel the pain," said a young woman.

"I call in the mystery of the present moment, of the ordinary and the everyday," cried out Richard.

"I call out the young stag," added Lasara, "the young stag in all of us, so that the King may be challenged."

"And I call the coyote spirit that keeps us on our toes." said Ayisha. "Throw something in our way so that we may be tripped up and out of our numbness. And now we are blessed with their presence. Let's make our intentions known."

One by one, each of the people around the circle stated his or her purpose for the weekend. One, a middle-aged woman with long brown hair, said, "Combining the spiritual with political action gives me a feeling of much more power." Others said they were eager to spend time with others who practiced Earth religion. A young man said the pagan-style rituals he had participated in at other protests "helped me stay sane and confused the hell out of the authorities."

A gray-bearded man with a bandanna around his head introduced himself as "a follower of Jesus who is perfectly comfortable with all kinds of ritual." His name was James Compton-Schmidt, and some in the group called him Reverend Jim. He was a fifty-five-year-old Mennonite minister from Fresno who was determined to put his body on the line for his principles.

"I missed the sixties because I was too busy making money," he said, adjusting the red bandanna. "I vowed that if I got the chance again to get involved, I wouldn't miss it. So I'm here and I'm learning."

Spritely Richard said, "I've always been a loner. The chance to be here with people who feel like I do is healing."

"I'm here to cry for the Earth," announced Morning Star. "But I realize the Earth is not just a victim. She can raise holy hell to fight back, and that's a relief to me."

I told the group that I had come to Redwood Summer as a writer. I was there to both observe and participate, as best I could. There was a brief discussion about my status as a member of the group. Most of the people in the group asked that I not identify them with their last names. Others asked that I not write about them at all. But eventually it was agreed that, as long as I participated in the activities, I was welcome.

After making our statements of intent, we proceeded to mourn the damage done to the environment. "Feel free to cry or moan," Ayisha said as she handed a long, printed list of extinct or endangered animals to those near her. She grabbed her drum and beat out a mournful cadence as they read the list. After each animal was named, one of the men in the circle clanged together Tibetan chimes.

**Thump, thump, thump, went the drum.**
**"Whooping crane."**
**Ting, sounded the chimes.**
**Thump, thump, thump.**
**"Gray wolf."**
**Ting.**

The chimes and drumbeats sounded for dozens of beasts, from the rhinoceros to the jaguar. Around the circle, people began to cry out, moan, and wail. Ayisha closed her eyes, wincing in pain as she kept up the beat. Tears trickled down her cheeks. On and on it went as the Ridley turtle, bald eagle, and others were mourned.

Once the list was read, Ayisha invited us to make our own additions. Lisa, a young woman who, like many others, had taken her shirt off in the hot sun, mourned the loss of the pigeons who had been driven from her neighborhood "by people who said they were a nuisance." Others lamented the destruction of the oceans. And one, a tough-looking, aging biker named Greg, who had long blond hair and a reddish beard, mentioned the loss of "my father and my brothers who died in a meaningless war." Another woman decried "the loss of childhood purity" and "the oppression of the feminist spirit, which has gotten us to the terrible place where we are now."

Loss of innocence, war, misogyny, death, and destruction: The recitation of human-caused ills smothered the circle with guilt. It was now time for us to start the work of redemption. It would begin with what Ayisha called "The Remembering." She asked us to lie back in the grass and try to imagine—"No, remember—when the Earth was created and life began in the primordial seas.

"Can you remember when our life on Earth began? Behold now that lovely liquid jewel spinning in space, Earth."

As we lay back in the grass, eyes closed, she described the evolution of life, from rock and water to tiny animals and plants, all through the chain until the primates appeared. "Open yourself up to a communication from these other life forms. And when you are ready, become one with them. Begin to make the sounds as you believe they would make sounds; begin to move and become that life form."

All around me, people were rising from the grass to imitate animals. Lisa batted the air as if she were a cat or some other creature swatting at an insect. Richard/Pan began to scramble about on all fours, pressing his nose into the dirt, sniffing and scratching. Marylyn began to howl like a mountain lion; her daughter pranced about the meadow.

Lying back in the grass, I became a deer.

I knew something about deer. White-tailed deer lived in the woodlands near my home on Long Island and I had seen them where I had grown up in New Hampshire. (One of the most memorable moments of my childhood had occurred at Animal Forest Park in York, Maine, where I had eaten the "cookies" of feed my parents had purchased for me to give the tamed fawns that scampered about.) I also knew that deer tended toward two kinds of activities: bounding about and standing perfectly still.

I began by standing stock still, with eyes opened wide, inspecting the scene before me. There were people digging in the dirt as if they had paws, and others pretending to wash themselves as cats do. Some were chasing butterflies in the meadow and still others were prowling on all fours, sniffing.

The bounding was a little more difficult. The grass was high, I was not in top physical condition, the mountain air was thin, and I was still human enough to feel a little absurd, in a sixties sort of way. But I did my best, rushing across the meadow in big, leaping strides to take refuge in a stand of trees. I then bounded back. Winded, I curled up behind a tree to catch my breath. I tried to look as deerlike as I could.

The others seemed to become even more like wild animals as Ayisha called for the formal Council of All Beings to begin. We again formed a circle, only this time there was no amiable chatting. Instead I heard growling and whistling, screeching, cooing, and cawing. As we sat down, two of the members of the group each blessed us, with sprinkles of water and the smoke of burning cedar. It reminded me of the use of holy water and incense at a Roman Catholic High Mass.

Ayisha began the council by announcing that she had transformed herself into "dying vegetation," the matter that becomes the nutrients that make the soil fertile. This detritus is the real Earth Mother of us all.

"We are all concerned about the shape our planet is in,"

said Ayisha, speaking for the constituents of primal muck. "The humans are to blame. Maybe there's some way we can communicate to them our feelings and our ideas."

Then, one by one, we spoke as the creatures we had become. The first was a woman who had become a tree. "If they could only feel what it is to be me," she said, "they wouldn't cut us down." Others growled approval. She was followed by a woman who was a frog and then by Richard/ Pan, who was a gray vixen.

"Humans make too much noise," he said. "I can hardly catch a mouse. It's too noisy, too noisy. And you humans foul up the air so badly I can hardly smell a raccoon."

"Excuse me, Mr. Vixen," interrupted Ayisha. "We are not humans in this council. Please remember that."

"Oh, sorry, I was projecting."

Next came a dolphin and a coral reef. They were followed by ex-biker Greg, who was a cougar, and by Marylyn, who was a jaguar. There was an eagle, a pelican, and a man who spoke for all primates.

"The humans don't realize that as they kill us, they are killing themselves," he said. "They torture us for medical science and to test beauty products. They have their genetic engineering and are playing with nature, with genetics. They don't know what they are doing. They are tampering with nature."

At the end, after a turtle, a lion, and a serpent spoke, there was a long pause. It seemed that everyone had said their piece, except me. According to the rules of the council, we were not required to speak. I probably could have remained silent and no one would have noticed, but caught up in what we were doing together, I decided to try.

"I am a deer, the watcher in the forest," I said, rising from the circle and moving to stand behind some trees. "I know the rules of the council say that we can all sit peacefully together, but with my sense of smell, I know there are big cats here and they make me afraid. I am also afraid we are losing our homes in the forest. In the winter we need dense forest to find shelter from the snow and to forage for food. This wilderness is disappearing too fast."

I moved slowly out of the trees and settled back in my place in the circle. "Too many of us get caught in fences or hit by cars as we try to cross the humans' highways," I continued. "I would say to them, give us our homes and let us live."

Ayisha was smiling broadly at me as I spoke. So were some of the others who understood that I was not a fellow traveler in the New Age. They were obviously pleased that I had spoken, and I felt a small bond form between us when I finished.

By letting down my guard and risking embarrassment, I had joined in a process as common as fraternity hazing and the Christian profession of faith. I had signaled my approval for the group, and a desire to be accepted. I had also developed, in an obviously human way, a sense of how wild things might regard the intrusion of man. And I had seen how fully these environmental activists of the New Age were committed to their cause. This was no mere exercise for them. It was spiritual expression.

We closed the council with an oath, the Earth Tribe Oath, taught to us by one of the women in the circle.

With our vision lifted toward the common sun
From the surface of our whirling sanctuary.
In communion with the natives once here abundant
We the Earth Tribe do realize our human duty
To recover all ground with reverence
All water with honor
Under skies unviolated
On behalf of every infant in nature
Now and forever.

Without any concrete information, the spiritual affinity group couldn't plan its participation in the "action" that was less than two days away. So we agreed to get together on Sunday, after the morning's main meeting, at which we hoped to hear some specifics on the protest. After much hugging and kissing we each quietly went our own way.

Although I had felt self-conscious participating in the Council of All Beings, the exercise had made me more a member of the group. I felt a connection with them, the kind of connection that forms whenever people work together on a project. I didn't feel converted to the cause or the beliefs of those in the affinity group, but I did regard them with more respect and some fondness. They were not frightening, violent radicals. They were all-American protesters turning their New Age beliefs into action.

I went back to the car to eat a dinner of canned beans and bread. Ayisha wandered off with some of her friends. I sat on the tailgate of her car and read the bumper stickers that were plastered on a VW bus parked nearby. Among them were:

FEEL IRE
LOVE YOUR MOTHER (*with a picture of Earth*)
VISUALIZE WORLD PEACE
RESCUE THE RAIN FOREST!
EARTH FIRST!
STUMPS SUCK!

After dinner I joined Ayisha and some of the others in the cow pasture to listen to a concert. A half-moon rose over the tall, straight sugar pines as a series of folksingers sang what were actually hymns of ecological spiritualism. Their lyrics were filled with references to God and Goddess, good and evil, sacrifice and martyrdom, a "lost America" and the sacredness of the forest. These were true protest songs, descendants of Woodie Guthrie classics and the songs of the labor movement. They were filled with religious imagery and foreboding.

It was all love and inspiration as the folksingers went through their acts. But when a rock and roll band came onstage, a conflict began to build in the audience. Some of the Earth Firsters were angry about a gasoline-powered generator that would power the electric instruments. It consumed fossil fuel, polluted the air, and made noise. In protest, one of them unplugged the electrical system just as the rock and rollers were beginning to play. The few lights that had illuminated the stage went out and the audience was suddenly in darkness.

As fumbling efforts were made to restore the electricity, a group of drunken Earth Firsters who sat on a small ledge of rock overlooking the crowd, began hurling epithets— "Fuck the generator," "Fuck the band"—and beer bottles at those below.

Very quickly panic and anger surged through the concert crowd. Some people stood and ran. Others began screaming at those on the rock. There were several reasons for the building confrontation. First there was the generator controversy and the alcohol. But more important were the anger and anxiety so many of the protesters brought with them to the wilderness. These people were furious at the logging companies, the government, the consumer society, and all of humanity. No doubt this anger was fueled, in part, by some kind of guilt. They were part of the humanity they detested, part of the fossil-fuel-burning, toxic-waste-producing cancer on the Earth. As they protested the sins of others, they had to sense, on some level, their complicity. This would make some, like the eco-spiritualists, humble. It would make others mean. Finally, there was a certain rabble-rousing, anarchist element in Earth First! Deep in the woods, where there was little organization and no real leader, conditions were perfect for some to lose control and even turn violent.

As another volley of bottles came down from the rocks, a huge inflated ball—it was about fifteen feet in diameter and colored to look like planet Earth—came rolling down

Kitchen Hill, into the crowd. It knocked over a few people. Others began pushing it back up the hill, but they were met by another group determined to roll the ball back into the crowd. The only difference between the two sides of this battle was that one group wanted a rowdy party and the others were frightened. As might be expected, the rowdies prevailed and soon the huge ball was rolling down again, scattering people as it picked up speed.

The Woodstock-style revival took on the mood of a rumble. Earth First! organizers screamed for calm and the people on the ledge—fellow environmentalists—screamed back, "Fuck you!" More beer bottles came flying down from the rock ledge.

In the pitch black, with the screams echoing off the hillside and the ball bouncing out of control, I scrambled away, joining the many others who were fleeing the concert. I felt my way through the trees to where Ayisha's tent was set up. I fumbled for my flashlight, turned it on, and laid out my sleeping bag. Our campsite was safely hidden from the main concentration of tents, screened by trees and invisible in the darkness.

I got into my sleeping bag, glad that we had found a camping spot that was separated from the main camping area by a substantial hill and a quarter-mile hike. I lay back and looked up at the stars. In the distance a chant arose, no doubt sung by the people on the rocks.

**Fuck the human race!**
**Fuck the human race!**
**Fuck the human race!**

On Sunday morning I rose early to join Falling Star, Lisa, and Marylyn in the redwood grove for an impromptu pagan ritual that they would conduct at the base of one of the ancient Sequoias.

As I walked alone in the faint light of dawn, I recalled the old man's warning about the cougars and bears that lived in the forest. For a moment I considered turning back, but then I decided that the Earth First! group had made more than enough noise during the night to frighten any animals away.

Two miles down the narrow, rocky path, I glimpsed the first Sequoia through a screen of other trees. At first I thought I was looking at a wooden wall. But it wasn't a wall, it was the twenty-foot-thick trunk of a single tree that rose more than two hundred feet high. Some of its bark had been charred by fire—redwoods are remarkably fire resistant—and a grove of tiny, geometrically perfect, ten-foot-tall evergreens grew around its base, straight and tall as wooden soldiers. Standing near this immense tree, I felt as small as an elf.

Further down the path I came upon more single Sequoias and then a stand of perhaps a dozen redwoods, scattered over about ten acres amid dozens of smaller trees. Tall, straight, and massive, their trunks and branches formed the pillars and dome of a natural cathedral. Under the branches the air was cool and still. A creek gurgled somewhere in the distance. Such grandeur inspires a feeling of the sacred and stirs the impulse to worship. It instills in the pagan eco-spiritualists a feeling of connection, of being a natural creation, like a tree, a bit of algae, or a deer. This seems to be at the core of their beliefs, and it is a primary motivation for their activism. They want to be in harmony with a natural world that seems pure, unblemished, and sinless in comparison with humanity. Seen in this light, environmentalism is not just a political cause or a point of view. It is a religious calling. And the eco-spiritualists are not just activists, they are prophets, voices that call our attention to a crisis caused, in part, from our dissociation from nature. This is not a new theme in American religion. Indeed, from the Scopes monkey trial to the battle over abortion, conservative Christians have struggled to hold society to their view of what's "natural." Of course, Bible verses about man's "dominion" over the Earth prevents them from embracing environmentalism, but the sense that there is, in nature, something unspoiled is strong in American religious culture. (This idea has been developed by historian Catherine Albanese in a book called *Nature Religion in America*. Albanese shows how the wilderness and America's natural abundance formed the basis for spiritual beliefs that have been part of the country's religious frame of mind since the Pilgrims. She finds nature religion in everything from a 1787 stage play to a nineteenth century singing group called The Hutchinson Tribe to today's New Agers, who continue the tradition of upholding "country virtue." She calls America "nature's nation" in the eyes of those who see God in the natural world.)

Farther along the path I found Marylyn, Lisa, and Falling Star. They were sitting at the base of a tree that was about fifteen feet in diameter and several centuries old. I joined hands with them and picked up their chant:

**Earth my body**
**Water my blood**
**Wind my breath**
**And fire my spirit.**

We sat down in our circle, around a collection of crystals and feathers. Falling Star spread a deck of tarot cards face down on the ground. We each chose cards and Lisa read from a book that interpreted them. Falling Star's card indicated that an operation she would soon undergo would go well. My card indicated that I was being confronted with a serious dilemma. Marylyn related the card to my participation in the spiritual affinity group. "How interesting," she said with a knowing, fortune-teller's smile.

Back at camp, the morning meeting was soon to begin. Kelpie was rereading fire-safety rules. It was less than twenty-four hours before the "action." Many of the people who came to the meeting said they wanted to know what was planned.

"Hey, what about the action? We're all still in the dark," came a voice from the crowd.

"I'm sorry, we're still looking for a site," answered Kelpie." We've got scouting parties out, but we haven't been able to firm things up."

After two days, the members of the Earth Tribe were getting restless. They had their own plans to make, within their affinity groups, and many resented being shut out of planning for the protest. This was not the democratic, "consensus" process Kelpie had promised. But surprisingly, no one complained out loud. They all just listened as various "experts" announced the topics for the day's workshops. The most intriguing suggestion was for a seminar on the problem of elitism in the ecology movement.

It was the first I had heard of the issue, but as I looked at the crowd, I didn't see a single black, Hispanic, or Asian person among the hundreds there. As a matter of fact, in three days I hadn't met anyone who wasn't of white Anglo-Saxon, Protestant descent. The larger New Age movement isn't quite so homogeneous; it includes many secularized Jews and nominal Catholics. But like the environmentalists, the bulk of New Agers tend to be white, upper-middle-class, college-educated liberals. The people at the camp seemed to be an even more exclusive group: the children of the liberal WASP elite.

After the various workshops were announced, several of the more spiritually minded protesters stood to complain about the ruckus of the night before. "Earth First! has a warrior mentality and we should use that energy," said Lasara. "It's good. But we need to respect each other."

The "warrior" is a New Age archetype, an aspect of human character often cited by the champion of the "men's movement," poet Robert Bly. This warrior is not a savage but rather a person who is strong, brave, and a little bit righteous. The nonspiritual Earth Firsters who had come to the rendezvous were no doubt oblivious to the distinction. They were hard-drinking, rowdy environmentalists who favored monkey wrenching over sit-ins and drinking over folk music. Nevertheless, Earth First! was obviously attracting many New Agers and others who were warriors of a different sort. This was a movement in transition and the change was painful.

Of course, none of this came out in the discussion, and soon people started drifting away from the griping. Kelpie declared an end to the meeting, reminding the protesters to join their affinity groups to review plans for the action. Back in the meadow where the "woo-woos" met, many expressed frustration with the organizers' inability to plan a specific action. Ayisha began making a list of activities that could be done almost anywhere. The first item on the "to-do" list was "keening." Keening was Lasara's idea. She thought we should all fall to our knees at some point and wail and moan from the very depths of our beings, to mourn the destruction of the forest. Everyone agreed that keening should be on the list. It would be dramatic, cathartic, and wonderfully attractive to TV camera operators. While the others continued with the list, I excused myself and walked back to the car. Before coming to California I had talked on the phone with officials of the Forest Service. They had explained their side of the debate over the management of the forest, and the man in charge of monitoring the protest, a forester named Lee Belau (pronounced Bay-low), had invited me to lunch at the Ponderosa, a restaurant on the main highway.

I eased the old Subaru out of the rutted dirt lot and followed the winding gravel path to State Road 190. I turned east and drove about five miles to the Ponderosa, a log-cabin-style building that houses a restaurant, a store, a souvenir shop, a coffee shop, a bar, a real-estate office, and a few guest rooms.

Inside, the Ponderosa is a shrine to man's conquest of

the wilderness. The walls are decorated with bear traps and old rifles and there is a small sign that reads WE SUPPORT THE TIMBER INDUSTRY AND THEY SUPPORT US! Almost everything in the Ponderosa—the walls, the ceiling, the floor, the chairs—is made of wood. What isn't made of wood is made out of plastic that looks like wood. There are souvenirs made of pine, like little toilets with the inscriptions BEST SEAT IN THE HOUSE and OLD FAITHFUL.

As I looked around for the forest ranger, I heard a man at the counter bellow to the cook, "I hear they got some naked women over there with them protesters. I might go have a look."

Ranger Belau was waiting at a table in the coffee shop, next to the window that overlooked the dirt parking lot and the gas pumps. He was a gray-haired man of fifty-nine, slim, and about six feet tall. He wore the standard brown military-style uniform of the Forest Service. On the shoulder patch were the letters $U$ and $S$, separated by a pine tree.

"I don't like them much more than they like us," Belau told me as he looked over the menu. "They're always screaming that we're a bunch of incompetents, and you know, I kind of resent it."

Belau and his colleagues were personally offended by the suggestion that they were managing the forest into extinction. Of the one million acres in Sequoia National Forest, he said, only seventy-five thousand were open to logging each year. Actual cutting averaged less than sixty thousand acres per year. By replanting, the Forest Service tried to guarantee "reforestation." This process was not a complete success. Fewer than half the trees planted survived. "But we are seeing adequate growth and the redwoods of any size have not been cut," said Belau. "We are preserving them."

As far as Belau was concerned, the protesters didn't understand forestry or economics. "We could stop cutting trees if people agreed to stop living in houses," he said. "It's a worldwide problem, too. If it isn't cut here, where we can manage how it's done, they'll clear-cut another forest in some other country where they don't manage the forests. Would that be better? I wish it were as easy as these people said, just stop cutting and the problem would be solved. It's not."

If the eco-spiritualists were there, they would have said that Belau didn't understand the ecological crisis affecting his own forest. To them, trees are not just economic entities—so many board-feet of lumber. They are a life-force, part of the sacred system that sustains the planet and everything on it. And their struggle to save the trees amounts to a holy war against infidels such as Belau, who are unable to understand the forest in spiritual terms.

Obviously the battle over the forest is a conflict between two opposing views of nature. One holds that the wilderness is a rich if foreboding place to be used and tamed by man. The other, more romantic view sees nature as kind of a Godhead, a source of all spiritual power and goodness. But Belau did not describe the clash of protesters and foresters in anything but tactical terms. He had enlisted a force of deputies who would respond if the Earth Firsters destroyed property or threatened anyone. Otherwise, Belau said, "We're gonna ignore 'em." The loggers had agreed to take the day off on Monday. The protesters could march onto any logging site they wished. There would be no one there to confront.

"What they want is some kind of confrontation that would get on the news. I'm going to make it so uninteresting that the press won't care. We're not even going to be there. They can go into the woods and do whatever they want. But we're going to frustrate 'em."

It was late afternoon when I got back to the camp. As I drove in, I was met by a small band of drunken environmentalists—the original Earth First! monkey-wrenching variety—who were carrying a keg of beer and drinking tequila straight from a bottle. They invited me to their encampment for a party that would last all night.

In the main camp area, small groups of people gathered in shady spots for the various seminars. Up on Kitchen Hill about a hundred people were learning techniques for nonviolent protest. The elitism seminar was going on near the first-aid tent, but the discussion had turned to the conflict between spiritual ecologists and monkey wrenchers. Ayisha was sitting on the ground there with about two dozen people. She was wiping tears from her eyes as she listened to a man describe the fractures in Earth First!

"I don't know if Earth First! is for me anymore," he said. "I have a lot to give and I care about the issues. But I don't care to be abused and I'm not interested in going off in the woods with a bunch of alcoholics. That's not respectful of people or the environment."

"I got involved from a spiritual point of view," said another man. "I understand that Earth First! was started by a bunch of drunks who were fed up with society. But there are only a few of those guys here now, and they're over in their little camp drinking tequila and beer."

In general, the New Age ecologists look down on excessive drinking and drug use. It's inconsistent with the moderate, save-the-planet life-style they choose. Despite the Saturday-night fiasco, the majority of the protesters seemed to share this view. And even as they lamented the conflict with the rougher activists, the "woo-woos" could see that their ranks were growing larger and more influential within the ecology movement.

The various seminars began to break up around four o'clock. Another general meeting was to begin at six, when we would at last be told the specifics of the next day's protest. I found Ayisha near the cow pasture. She looked angry. She said she was annoyed by the fracas of the evening before, by the lack of organization, and by the conflict between the spiritual ecologists and the original Earth Firsters.

"This whole thing makes me reconsider identifying myself with Earth First!" she said disgustedly. "I care about the forest, but I want to be able to dialogue with people. Earth First! just says to others, 'You're fucked up. We're right. No compromise.' I can see that approach, but that's not the only approach that works."

Ayisha had spent three full days preparing for the action. She had organized the spiritual affinity group, led the Council of All Beings, and planned a complex ritual for the protest. She had also endured the Saturday-night fight and the insult of being kept in the dark about the location and nature of the Monday protest. To top it off, she hadn't even visited the big trees.

It didn't take much to persuade her to use the time before the general meeting to walk two miles down the path to look at the trees. She had seen redwoods before, but they were coastal trees, Sequoia sempervirens. A different type—Sequoia giganteum—grows in the Sierra Nevada. Their trunks are much larger, up to thirty feet in diameter compared to ten feet for coast trees.

We walked quietly. Ayisha stopped from time to time, seeming to breathe the forest into her soul. When we got to the Sequoia grove, she just stood, awestruck. Then her face turned dark and tears came from her eyes.

"Look at these giant beings. They are so magnificent," she said. "Can't you imagine how they feel? What must they think about being cut down, about seeing their family and friends around them all cut down? It must be so distressing. They've stood here two thousand years and now we're going to cut them down?" These were not just trees to Ayisha. They were sentient, feeling creatures for whom she felt great responsibility. They were tall, silent, powerless victims of a cruel human race. She was determined to be their voice, to rescue them.

Gazing at the magnificent trees and understanding that very few remain, I found it easy to share Ayisha's outrage. They must be protected, if only as rare objects of nature's art. But Ayisha's concern was more personal than mine. For me, trees do not feel. They don't have families. Nor do they suffer. Ayisha was certain that they do. Her feelings for them ran so deep that it was as if she was one of the trees herself, a victim of the human world. I couldn't help thinking about the times when Ayisha had needed to be rescued herself. No doubt there were many moments when she would have longed to be rescued from a childhood marred by her father's alcoholism. Then there were those years spent with Fred, years that were desperate, frightened, and confused. No one rescued her. But now, in a recapitulation of her life story, someone would play the rescuer. She would struggle to save these trees.

The visit to the forest had restored Ayisha's spirits. She walked more briskly back to the camp, hurrying along to the general meeting. "These are not just trees," she said to me as she marched. "They are much more than that."

The general meeting—really an Earth Tribe council of war—was already formed by the time we reached camp. Mark Huntington was reviewing the plan.

"The action is going to be at a huge clear-cut, an active logging site," he said. "If there aren't any loggers there, it will still be a great place for an action. If we can get all of these people there and the news media there, it will make all the other Earth First! actions look small. We don't want everyone to be disappointed now if the loggers don't show up."

We were to rise at 4:30 A.M. and form a car caravan that would follow several miles of paved road to a dirt logging trail. We would then hike about five miles to the spot where loggers had been clearing more than a hundred acres of forest. Technically, it wasn't a clear-cut operation. Some trees had been left standing. "But it looks bad, real bad," said Mark. "The media will be impressed. And if the cops are waiting, we'll go in anyway."

For a moment, I considered telling the group what I had learned from Forest Ranger Belau. There weren't going to be any cops. Nor, for that matter, would there be any loggers to confront. In fact, if they really wanted to get arrested, the protesters would be better off massing in Porterville at the Forest Service office.

The problem was that this was really privileged information. Belau had spoken to me as a writer, not a protester. And I was there to record what happened, not alter the course of history. With a touch of regret I realized that even if I had been a deer for an afternoon, I was not really part of this group. I was an outsider, an observer. So I kept my mouth shut and watched the group reach consensus about the morning's action. It immediately became clear that there were many who objected to having a complete plan handed to them at the final hour. The mood of American democracy in action had been broken.

"We're all being told what to do," complained one man. "My affinity group doesn't like this option. We were preparing for a protest at the Forest Service office."

"Well, we wanted to go to the logging site so the media can see a clear-cut," said Kelpie. "We're going to show them the U.S. Forest Service with its pants down."

Ayisha wanted to go into the forest, too. "Our affinity group would like to go to the clear-cut site," she said. "If nothing happens there, then we could go to the Forest Service office. Either way, we're going to create a spiritual happening throughout the day, and anyone who wants to can plug into it."

"If people want to do it, we can go to the Forest Service office, too," Kelpie said.

"Yeah, but I don't like this, the way it was just handed to us," shot back a woman in the crowd.

"You're right," answered Kelpie, wearily. "We're fucked on the process."

"And I don't think we should be calling it a clear-cut if it's not," said Sequoia. "That would look like we're just making things up and it would destroy our credibility."

As night smothered the meeting in darkness, the group raced to a consensus. We would arise at 4:30 A.M. and leave at five o'clock for the logging site. Those who wanted to stage a second protest at the Forest Service office could organize it during the day. The meeting ended with Mark asking for donations. As he passed through the crowd, people stuffed tens and twenties into a hat he held out.

After the meeting, the "woo-woos" whooped it up over in a corner of the cow pasture. Several newcomers joined the affinity group, swelling its number to about thirty. They agreed to meet in the same place at four forty-five, to make sure everyone had a ride in the caravan. They also planned to form a circle at the beginning of the logging road and then march in together, chanting and beating drums. Someone suggested they paint their faces like ancient warriors.

The people in the group were excited about the coming action. Three days together, spent worshipping nature and planning to become defenders of Mother Earth, had bonded them. "When we see the stumps, let's really wail," said Lasara. "Keen like you've never heard it. That'll get on TV." The group parted with a chant.

**Earth my body**
**Water my blood**
**Air my breath**
**And fire my spirit.**

Ayisha, Lisa, and Falling Star invited me to share a bottle of wine with them before sleep. I wanted to join them, but my decision to keep quiet during the meeting stopped me. It had restored, if only in my mind, the professional distance between the writer and his subject. I was not an eco-spiritualist or an Earth Firster. The cause was not mine, and so, I reasoned, the celebration was not mine. "I'm tired, and four-thirty will come fast," I told them. "You go on without me."

As I went alone to the campsite, I met Lasara. She was high with expectation.

"Aren't you so glad you came, Michael?" she asked, slinging an arm around my shoulder. "I'm glad you're here. This is such a trip. I bet you didn't know what you were getting into, with a bunch of pagans in the forest. But it's great, isn't it? I think it is. It's just great."

\*　　\*　　\*

The wolf calls—"Ow-oo, ow, ow, ow-oooo!"—began precisely at four-thirty.

"Let's go to war!" came a scream in the woods.

Off in the distance I could hear the faint "woo-woo" cries of other spiritual ecologists making their way to the gathering area. At the pasture, the members of the spiritual affinity group stood shivering in the dark. They held hands while Marylyn called for the assistance of various spirit beings. Another woman noted the four tall sugar pines that stood nearby. "They represent an unusually strong cone of power," she said. "That's a good sign."

At five o'clock we all went to our cars, ready to join the caravan. Instead, we simply sat in a giant traffic jam beneath the pines. Fifteen minutes passed, then half an hour. No one moved. Finally, at five forty-five, we began to roll. The sun was turning the sky pink and blue.

It took another half-hour for us to drive eight miles to the dirt-road turnoff that led to the logging site. Along the way we passed a banner, strung high in the trees, that read WE'RE ALL IN THIS TOGETHER, WORKING FOR THE ENVIRONMENT. It was decorated with painted paw-prints.

The caravan parked on the edge of the asphalt road. The dirt logging trail was blocked by a locked gate. A sign posted there announced that the area had been officially closed by the Forest Service. Ignoring the sign, hundreds of protesters slipped under, over, and around the gate, and marched on down the dirt road, heading for the cutting zone.

They were like a defiant army, trampling down the road, and on the law, in pursuit of a higher good. Many of these people would be meek and law-abiding if they acted alone, but they had turned fearless and righteous as part of this group. None of them knew what waited at the end of the long dirt road. It could be the police, the National Guard, or nothing. It didn't matter. They were all carried down the trail by their commitment and the power that comes from believing in the rightness of a cause. It was the kind of thing you don't see every day. It was inspiring.

The "woo-woos" stopped at the gate, formed a circle, and chanted. They were a tired and rather dirty bunch, after four days in the forest. Ayisha wore a long, blue peasant-style cotton skirt and a black T-shirt with the words ACTIVE PEACE written on the back. She had taken a felt-tipped marker and drawn three dark stripes, diagonally, across each of her cheeks: war paint.

Ayisha started banging a small drum and led a snake dance that coiled around the intersection. Falling Star lit a big stick of incense and waved it about, filling the air with a sweet smoke. Lisa brandished a crystal-encrusted wand that was about a foot long. Finally, Ayisha stopped the dance and led us around the gate and onto officially closed U.S. Government property. As we marched down the road to our objective, the drumbeat continued and the spiritual affinity group began to chant.

**We are the power—the power!—in everyone**
**We are the vision—the vision!—of what can be done**
**We are the hope—the hope!—in everyone**
**We are the turning of the tide.**

The "woo-woos" were energized and full of camaraderie as they then marched defiantly down the logging trail. I watched them with some envy. Like many writers, I feel more comfortable in the observer's role, watching and recording rather than doing. I had to maintain that pose. I was not one of the "woo-woos." I regretted it, for a moment, because they seemed so filled with purpose and certainty. And they were having so much fun.

The good feelings lasted about fifteen minutes. Then, as the marchers turned a bend in the dirt road, they came upon a large yellow tractor, a grader used to level roads. A massive machine, it had four rubber tires about six feet tall and a twelve-foot-wide flat blade used for pushing dirt. People were scrambling all over the yellow shell of the machine, trying to unplug wires and hydraulic hoses. Sticks had been jammed into the valves of each of the tires and air rushed out with a high-pitched hissing sound. This was monkey wrenching in progress.

When she saw this, Ayisha grew flushed with fury. Although violence against machines was very much a part of the Earth First! tradition, it was not consistent with the absolute nonviolence practiced by the spiritual ecologists.

"What are you doing?" Ayisha asked the men and women who were scrambling around the tractor.

No one answered.

"This is not cool," complained another marcher. "We promised no violence."

"Yeah, we all agreed, no violence," added Ayisha.

"Fuck you, we're just liberating the air," came a reply from atop the big machine. "This isn't violence, it's just slowing 'em down."

It was clear that those intent on vandalizing the grader were not going to stop. Ayisha gave up in frustration. "Yeah, well fuck you, too. You're hurting us as much as you are hurting them," she said, turning to continue down the road.

She walked along in silence for the next mile or so. "I hate it that I did that," she finally said to me. "I was violent back to them and it has broken the feeling I had coming in."

Ayisha was still shaken as we came upon a break in the forest. It was an abandoned logging site, an expanse of dirt and rock—perhaps twenty acres—where hundreds of trees once stood. This was a select cut. About a dozen small trees remained standing, but the rest of the landscape was a giant scar. Foot-high stumps poked out of the dirt like so many tombstones. Tread marks from bulldozers crisscrossed the soil. Near the road, a fifteen-foot-high pile of waste wood was drying in the morning sun.

It was time for keening. Lasara rushed into the field of stumps and grabbed the first stump she came upon. Sinking to her knees and embracing it as if it were a dying child, she began to moan. It was a low, sickly sound that built into a shrill, agonized scream. Then she began to rock back and forth, rhythmically, moaning, "Oh, oh no. Oh, oh no."

Soon a dozen others were wailing in the field of fallen trees. Ayisha ran about a hundred yards until she reached one of the few standing trees, a sugar pine that was about eighty feet tall. The trunk was far too broad for her to get her arms around it completely, but she hugged it nevertheless, spreading her arms across its massive base and pressing her cheek against its bark. She looked like a little child trying to get her arms around her mother.

All around the old logging site, men and women were hugging trees, kneeling in the dirt, and wailing. Marylyn paced in front of the pile of discarded logs, howling like a cat. She was once again the mourning jaguar. She was joined by Richard/Pan, who had stripped off his green pants and shirt and stood atop the woodpile in his bikini, screaming, "Arrrrrrr! Oh, no! Arrrrrr!" On the ground below, Lisa walked around with her crystal wand, waving it at the stumps.

Every person who came upon this stopped and stared. A few TV crews plunged into the field and focused on Lasara and Richard. On the road, those protesters who had brought cameras snapped pictures. A reporter for the Bakersfield newspaper watched and scribbled notes on a pad.

I, too, stood on the road and watched, at first in amazement. The screaming reminded me of TV news footage of mothers mourning their dead children after an earthquake or their soldier sons after a battle. Like those mothers on TV, the keening protesters made a shrill, pained, penetrating sound.

As the various camera crews worked their way around the site, recording the keening, I began to walk to the main site of the protest. I was joined by Reverend Jim, who once again wore his red bandanna, T-shirt, and shorts. He had taken the stick of incense from Falling Star. He waved it about, spreading its smoke in the air before us. Someone beat a drum and someone else began another pagan chant:

Vine and grain, vine and grain
All that falls shall rise again.
Vine and grain, vine and grain
All that falls shall rise again.

Our progress along the dirt road was slow. It was already after 9 A.M. The sun was hot on our heads and our footsteps kicked up clouds of choking dust. I was also slowed by the pack on my back. Ayisha had loaded it with bottles of water and some food and it felt quite heavy. The walk was made even more difficult by the little blockades that the protesters had built every hundred yards or so. Made of logs and rocks, the blockades were intended to stymie loggers on their way to work, but they also slowed the protesters.

It took another hour of walking to bring us to the protesters' objective, the side of a steep hill where an area about one square mile had been stripped of all but a handful of trees. Where the road ended, there stood an iron machine, a metal box the size of a three-story house. Out of the center of this machine rose a steel pillar about thirty feet tall. From this pillar were strung cables that ran down to where the cutting took place. This was a "yarder," a crane that pulls felled trees up the steep incline of the hill, to the road.

The yarder—which was painted beige and orange and had the words LONE PINE LOGGING and THUNDERBIRD printed on it—had already been decorated with branches and banners: STOP WELFARE LOGGING and LOVE YOUR MOTHER and FOREVER FOREST. People clambered all over the machine, jamming sticks into gears and trying to disconnect hoses and wires. One fellow, who called himself "Mud Man" (he was completely covered in black, dried mud), danced around on top of the yarder, screaming, "No more welfare logging!" Sequoia was up there, too, dressed in a homemade spotted-owl costume. She flapped her fabric wings and stomped about on feet covered with claws made from more fabric and cotton stuffing. There wasn't a logger in sight.

Behind the yarder, in the shade created by its bulk, Kelpie Wilson was conducting a news conference. There were a few newspaper reporters there and crews from two local TV stations. Kelpie told them that the site was an example of "a select cut that is really a clear-cut."

"But doesn't the fact that there are no loggers here, no police, and obviously no conflict screw up your plans?" asked a reporter.

"Not at all," answered Kelpie. "I'm thrilled they aren't here. It means we can play here and do what we want."

"But what about the protest, getting arrested? Isn't that all spoiled because no one's here?"

"We shut down all the logging sites for the day. I wouldn't say that our action has been spoiled."

On the other side of the yarder, Sequoia strutted on a little walkway that was part of the machine and railed about the agreement that the Sierra Club and other environmental groups had made with the Forest Service. "I'm just about extinct and they are going to cut the forest down!" she shrieked. "It's all a bunch of owl shit!"

Below Sequoia, Reverend Jim sat on a gravel embankment. A husky man with a bushy beard, Jim had a skull-and-cross-bones tattoo on his forearm from his days in the U.S. Navy. I sat with him and we talked about his commitment to the spiritual ecology movement. He was, after all, the lone Christian among many neo-pagan New Agers, but he said he wasn't at all uncomfortable with the chants or rituals. In fact, he enjoyed them. He liked the impromptu ceremonies that Ayisha organized, the democratic way they were conducted, and the nonsexist, nature-oriented spirituality of the group.

"A lot of what passes itself off as Christianity today is more like American civil religion," he said, wiping his brow with his bandanna. "It's not very passionate, not very connected at all to what Jesus was about. I think that if Jesus were alive, he'd be here. Not doing anything violent, but he'd be here. Environmentalism is right in line with his teachings about freeing the oppressed, only now it's the Earth that's oppressed."

I told Jim that I was surprised by the makeup of the protest groups: white, middle-class, mostly Protestant stock. He said that he too had noticed that there were few Hispanics, blacks, or Asians at the protest. "It makes me uncomfortable," he said. "But there are reasons for it. The mainline Protestant churches are all for environmentalism, at least at the national level. And maybe these people are from families that have been in the United States for more generations. They feel a greater sense of ownership of the country. It's sad that you don't see Latinos here, because so many of them live and work on the land around here," he added.

Just then a TV reporter came over with his cameraman and asked if he could interview Jim. He wanted to speak with a local resident. Jim was from nearby Fresno.

"Jim, as a native Fresnan, this is your backyard. What do you think of what they are doing here?"

"Just look around. There aren't any trees left here. What do you think of it?" Jim responded coolly. This was the important part of the day's work, because, after all, the protest was mainly a media event. If it wasn't reported on the network news, it would be a failure. As I got up to make space for the TV cameraman taping Jim's interview, I heard another reporter call out to Kelpie Wilson, asking for an interview. However, he couldn't recall her name.

"Kibble, Kibble! Over here!" he shouted.

She patiently went to him, politely mentioned that her name was Kelpie, not Kibble, and then, smiling for the camera, submitted to his questions.

While I watched Kelpie and the reporter, Ayisha and the rest of the spiritual affinity group straggled in. They moved a three-foot-high log to a spot in front of the yarder and covered it with a cloth. This would be the altar, and onto it they piled crystals and feathers, fresh oranges, sea shells, bits of cedar, and sage and jewelry. Quickly a huge circle was formed. It wasn't just the thirty or so people who had met in the meadow. More than half the people at the site—more than one hundred in all—joined hands around the makeshift altar.

Ayisha seemed surprised by the response. She shouldn't have been. Without police or loggers to confront, the protesters had nothing to do. The spiritual affinity group was the only one prepared to do anything that would occupy people's minds and hearts and make a symbolic statement to the world.

The ritual began with silence and then calls for the spirits of fire, water, air, and Earth. Lisa called in the power of Earth. She asked each of the worshipers to lick a finger and touch the ground with it, to make a streak of mud to put on their faces. "We call you in, we ask your heavenly presence, Mother Earth," she said. "There is so much healing to be done and we ask you to be a part of it."

Young Lasara again called in the "young stag" to empower our ceremony. "I call in the power of the young stag ... to challenge the establishment, to challenge the king stag, because he has the power and we know what we want. Like the stag, we have the power to save the world! Each of us has the power!"

After Lasara spoke, her mother welcomed the spirit of the "old crone" to help the ritual. Stooped over, a bandanna on her head, she spoke in a croaking voice.

"Crone woman!" she shouted dramatically. "I call you from the shadows to see what your children can create, to see this hillside of pain and sorrow."

And so it went, with the occasional twist. One participant was asked to summon the spirits of the great leaders of the past. She asked the people in the circle to recall their favorite historical figures, and soon names were being shouted into the air: "Buddha! Karl Marx! John Muir! Martin Luther! John Lennon! Gandhi!" Reverend Jim summoned the spirit of Jesus.

Then, as a haggard-looking man with a guitar began to sing an old Irish ballad, the noise of an approaching helicopter intruded. All faces turned upward as the green and white aircraft hovered like a giant dragonfly above the demonstration. Some people started chanting, "Omm-mm-ommm-ommm." Lisa waved her magic wand at the sky. Lasara fell to her knees and began keening. About a dozen women joined her. Others stared up at the noisy chopper or waved their fists at it.

This scene—a hundred or so people gathered around an altar piled with offerings, wailing, om-ing, and moaning beneath the *whirring* helicopter—captured almost every element of the protest and its context. This was the Earth Tribe, gathered in a ritual protest of man's technology and intrusion into the wilderness. None of the protesters on the ground knew who was in the helicopter. It might have been a TV news crew or the Forest Service or the police. But that didn't matter. The helicopter appeared as both a symbol and the material incarnation of man's evil. It provided the proof of the power of Ayisha's ritual.

As the chopper left, the ritual lost its energy. A man who had been watching from outside the circle interrupted.

"We have to have a meeting and decide what to do next," he said officiously.

"Hey, we are in the middle of a ritual," Sequoia snapped.

"Yeah, but we have to decide whether to go to the Forest Service or not."

Someone started a chant, which the others quickly joined, drowning out the worried organizer:

**We are one with the infinite sun**
**For ever and ever and ever.**

This chant continued for five minutes and then again the Earth First! organizers interrupted. This time it was Mark Huntington, who was standing on the gravel embankment, above the ritual gathering.

"Hey, everybody!" he shouted. "People are starting to walk away from the action. We're losing it. We need to have a meeting about what to do next. We have to get back to what we're here to do."

"This is what we're here to do!" shouted someone in the circle. A cheer went up and Mark walked away, disgusted. The eco-spiritualists were taking over the action. Someone in the circle started reading a list of endangered species, the same list that Ayisha had read in the meadow during our Council of All Beings. Then the circle was opened for the prayers of any who wanted to speak.

"I pray for those who are not yet interested," said Sequoia, still in her owl costume.

"I pray for the trees that are not here to shade us," said Reverend Jim.

"I pray for the naïve American dream that has been exploited by corporate greed," said a young man.

With the energy of the ritual fading and an eleven o'clock mountain sun beating down, Ayisha stepped forward to end the ceremony with a blessing drawn from her days as a witch:

**Chant the spell and be it done.**
**Chant the spell and be it done.**
**Chant the spell and be it done.**

In the circle, I heard a man ask the person next to him, "What's the spell?"

She answered, "It's all the things we just did here."

There would be no meeting to plan a further action. Those protesters who had not been part of the ritual had already left, kicking up a cloud of dust that still hung in the air over the road. Slowly the spiritual affinity group and the scores of people who had joined it made their way back to where the cars were parked.

I met Ayisha a mile or two down the logging road. She was smiling, proud of what had happened there and invigorated by the sense of spiritual power she had felt. The stripes on her cheeks were smeared with sweat and her clothes were coated by a thin film of dust. "That closing chant, it was very wiccan," she said. (Wiccan means "witch-like.") "I wasn't sure how people would react," she said, "but I wanted to seal it with that kind of power."

We trudged back in relative silence, past the many barri-ers, past the field of stumps and the vandalized grader. At the gate, Mark Huntington again had his hand out, asking for donations. In his other hand he held a thick roll of bills, which he tried to count as he pleaded for departing protesters to donate more. Just past the gate, a lone sheriff's deputy sat in his patrol car and watched the Earth Firsters straggle out.

The "woo-woos" agreed to come together one last time, in the meadow back at the campsite. They drove back there and formed a circle in the tall grass, beneath the trees. Although no one had been arrested and there had been no confrontation with loggers, they shared a sense of accom-plishment. They had worshiped together, shared a sense of the sacred, and stood to be counted on the side of the trees.

I was invited into the closing circle and joined hands with the "woo-woos" as the final chants were sung. After three days together, I felt comfortable with these people. They had revealed themselves to me and I had done the same. I had chanted the chants and become a deer. With my deci-sion to remain quiet about the forest ranger's plan, I had chosen to remain outside their movement, but I could nev-ertheless admire their commitment, their honesty, and their willingness to turn their spirituality into action. Too much of American political discourse is devoid of passion and a sense of morality. It was refreshing to see passionate believ-ers, who were not right-wing Christians, make an argument based on their view of what's right and what's wrong.

Some of what I had seen over the weekend—the high-handed Earth First! leaders, the Saturday-night ruckus—was disappointing. But those problems arose, in part, because the New Age ecologists were trying to find a role in a cause outside their movement. It is always difficult for those inspired by faith to make alliances with those who are not. But it was clear they were in the battle for the environment to stay, and because their inspiration runs so deep, they may end up being the ecology movement's most-committed troops.

Before we parted, Ayisha asked us to thank the spirits we had invoked and dismiss them. As I watched Lisa, Reverend Jim, Greg, Marylyn, Ayisha, and the others, I was struck by the poetry they spoke. Like plays, rituals are an art form, a means for self-expression. Following Ayisha's example, the woo-woos had each grown more comfortable, and more creative, with their participation. By our last meeting, even those who had fumbled and hesitated before spoke with clarity and grace. They seemed eager to stand in public this way, and speak from the heart.

"Thank-you, south, who gives us the sun," said Lisa. "Thank-you for the fiery passion that burns within us."

"Air, so clear in the mountains, so clear in the valley, thank-you for your energy," said Greg, the rough-edged, aging biker.

When it was over, we all said, "Blessed be" and we embraced. Promises were made. We would all meet again, at some other rendezvous, and the "woo-woos" would create another ritual, celebrate nature, and save the environment through spirituality and protest.

Ayisha and I shared the driving on the long ride back to Oakland. We agreed that the ritual had been a significant part of the protest. Modesty kept Ayisha from acknowledging that her affinity group had, in fact, come to dominate the Earth First! protest. But it had.

She said her group had tapped a deep human need for ritual. "People either have no ritual events at all in their lives, or they belong to churches where the rituals no longer have much meaning for them," she explained. "They are excited when they see that they can plan a ritual themselves, they can decide what is important to say, what kind of spiritual expression they want. It's a wonderful process."

Indeed, in a land where half the citizens are not churchgoers, where faith in institutions has been seriously eroded, the participatory ritual that Ayisha's circle had created had a very strong appeal. It was lively, spontaneous, democratic, and welcoming. And despite all of my wariness, I, too, felt good about having been a part of it.

In Porterville we stopped to buy all the local newspapers, to check their coverage of the protest. The stories were fair and relatively balanced, though one reporter described the protesters as "extremists" and "militants." Then we found a Chinese restaurant for a late lunch. There the conversation turned to the kinds of subjects that occupy good friends— old flames, crazy family members, what makes an ideal marriage.

Back on the road, we raced through Poplar—where a sign read CITY ON THE MOVE, POP. 1,478—and Hanford, where a billboard announced that "Mr. Red Skelton" would appear soon at the civic auditorium. Slowly, we were reentering the world and, slowly, Ayisha and I were preparing to say good-bye. She talked for almost an hour straight.

"I hope you write this in a way that people get the sense of how important the spiritual connection is," she said. "That's where the activism begins, at least for me, it makes it all the more powerful."

New Age spirituality—in her case, drawn from the neo-pagan branch—had given Ayisha much. It had given her a sense of power and control that had long been missing from a life that was shaken by a troubled childhood and a terrifying first marriage. Neo-paganism had provided her rescue. It had also supported her counterculture life-style and her politics. It provided a sense of community and rituals that held meaning for her. The New Age had even given Ayisha a sense that she had a place in the continuum of history, even if only as a descendant of the pagans and druids of yore. She had become part of a tribe.

All of these things—community, history, ritual, faith, political commitment, and a feeling of power and control—are missing from the lives of a great many millions of Americans. And while the eco-spiritual protesters present themselves as opponents of the Forest Service, they are making a much broader statement about the condition of modern American society. Their apocalyptic fears are, in fact, shared by many millions who find life in a technological society to be cold, alienating, and foreboding. Unlike so many others, the eco-spiritualists are trying to do something about it.

Of course, theirs is a humanly flawed movement. They think too little about the welfare of human beings, for example. They are extreme in their criticism of technology and a bit too romantic about the natural world. But every social movement needs a vanguard of people who are willing to be arrested, willing to make a moral issue out of their cause. In the environmental movement, the Earth Tribe is part of this vanguard. They stand on the far edge of the mainstream ecology movement, but by their very presence they move the whole debate about the environment.

As we turned on to Interstate 5, we passed a giant feedlot where thousands of cattle were being fattened prior to slaughter. It was a dusty tract, surrounded by wire fence. It looked like a prison camp for animals. The eye-watering smell of souring dung penetrated the car even though the windows were closed. It was the first time that I had been in Ayisha's car and not smelled the sage and incense and mugwort she carried with her. It was as if God had placed this morbid beef "factory" there to remind us that nothing had changed during our four days in the mountains. People still exploited nature for survival. Despite "right" and "wrong," there were no easy answers. No one spoke for these animals.

Ayisha looked out the window, wrinkled her nose, and sighed. "Welcome back to the world."

# 5 · CAMP OMEGA
## NEW YORK

## Mystic Baseball

*Let someone call you enemy and attack you,
and in that moment, they lost the contest.
It was hard to learn this—perhaps I am only
beginning—but my baseball career was a
long, long initiation into a single secret; that
at the heart of all things, is love.*

Sadaharu Oh

A ZEN WAY OF BASEBALL

IF THERE'S ONE THING I LEARNED PLAYING MYSTIC BASE-ball, it's that sometimes you have to go backward before you move forward. Consider a simple throw from shortstop to first base. First you must focus your attention, shutting out all distractions—the crowd, your teammates, the heat of the day. Grasping the ball, you move your hand down and then backward, toward the outfield. Then you swing it up, in an arc that carries the ball past your ear. At the same time your body rocks forward. If you let go of it at the right moment, the ball flies into the first baseman's outstretched mitt. No sore arm. No wild errors. I mention this, not to teach you how to throw a ball, but to begin to explain baseball played the New Age way at the Omega Institute, a spiritual summer camp for adults in upstate New York.

A kind of spa for the mind, body, and soul, Omega is a resort/retreat that offers serious courses on spirituality, alternative medicine, and psychology. But it is also a place where the New Age could be discovered at play: singing,

dancing, painting, acting, even gardening. Two of the institute's most popular courses are "Beyond Basketball," taught
by Phil Jackson, coach of the Chicago Bulls, and "The Tao
of Boxing," led by Floyd Patterson.

"Baseball: The Spirit and Practice of an American Myth"
intrigued me. First there was the juxtaposition of the game,
an icon of American culture, with the insistently counterculture mentality of the New Age. Second was my own, reflex-
ive response to baseball. My small-town childhood summers
had revolved around baseball, almost to the exclusion of
everything else. I played countless games, and I was a rever-
ent fan of the Boston Red Sox. On many nights I fell asleep
listening to a play-by-play lullaby from the radio hidden
under my pillow. One of the teachers Omega had hired
had been a Red Sox pitching ace. Outspoken and iconoclastic, Bill Lee was nicknamed "Space Man" because of his
eccentric, mystical approach to the game. His teaching partner, Jeffrey McKay, had been a trainer for EST, the controversial and confrontational self-improvement program of
the 1970s, and for Actualizations, an EST spinoff. McKay
had also played minor-league ball and was a college coach.
According to the Omega program, participants in the seminar would "explore baseball as a Way." I signed up.

In the weeks before the course, I hunted up an old mitt
and bought a new Red Sox cap. I also watched the 1989
film *Field of Dreams*, a most romantic baseball fantasy based
on the novel *Shoeless Joe*, by W. P. Kinsella. In the movie,
an Iowa farmer carves a sparkling baseball diamond out
of his fields so that long-dead ball players can come, as
spirit beings, to sprint on the emerald grass and crack the
ball into the cornstalks. *Field of Dreams* turns baseball into
a spiritual practice, a rite of celebration, rebirth and
redemption.

All this might seem ridiculous if you never felt the child-
like bliss of being immersed in the game. In the game, the
body seems full of grace and certainty and the mind is

quiet. Time stands still and there is nothing but the grass, the infield dirt, the sky, and the game itself. This feeling of transcendence has been studied by University of Chicago psychologist Mihaly Csikszentmihaly. He calls it "flow." Athletes feel flow. So do dancers, artists, craftsmen, anyone who is lost in a moment of work, play, or creativity. It's the kind of feeling most of us rarely experience as adults. When we are reminded of it, we long to feel it again.

The baseball cap, the movie, the old mitt—they all filled me with this longing. But as I prepared for what was supposed to be a playful weekend, I also began to worry. Not all my sports memories are happy ones. I had been in too many games where the object was defeating the opponent rather than playing one's best. And I recalled too well the flush of embarrassment when I made errors. Worse were the times when I had humiliated others, especially my younger bother, for poor play. As a child I nicknamed my brother Patrick "Marv" after Marv Throneberry, an error-prone New York Met of the 1960s. I must have spent hours searching in lilac bushes and underbrush, hoping to find baseballs Marv had thrown from right field. As I hunted lost balls, I would pepper him with insults. Sometimes he cried. Baseball can bring out the worst in us.

I had never appreciated the depth of my feelings about the game. But as I considered stepping onto a baseball field for the first time in two decades, I worried about embarrassing myself in front of vastly superior players. What if I threw the ball into the bushes? What if *I* became Marv? Confronted with these fears, I did the only thing I imagined might help. I started practicing with neighborhood kids. In the August sun we played pepper and catch, hit fungoes and shagged flies. I could wear out five ten-year-olds in half an hour.

"Good try, Mr. D'Antonio," they would say as I lunged for ground balls.

"Now you're getting it, Mr. D. Much better than yesterday."

After half a dozen workouts, I could catch the ball consistently and throw with some confidence. At least I wouldn't get hurt. Embarrassed, perhaps, but not hurt.

"You're a writer, not a professional ballplayer," my wife kept saying. "This is supposed to be fun."

But she didn't understand. This was baseball. I had grown up believing that an American male who can't hit or can't field would be ostracized, kicked off the team, denied membership in the fraternity of red-blooded males. I knew this didn't make sense. But the feeling was still there. Modern American boys don't go on vision quests in the wilderness or train to become courageous braves. They prove their masculinity on the playing field. That's why one of the biggest insults in kid sports is to say someone "throws like a girl."

Being an all-American male, I didn't mention any of this to my wife. "Of course, it's all going to be just good fun," I said. But in my mind I saw ground balls skipping past me, pop-ups clunking off my glove.

I wasn't the only one who brought some fear to the cool, leafy Omega camp, a hundred miles north of New York City. Anxiety would be one of the main topics of discussion when our class met for the first time on Saturday morning of Labor Day Weekend. But first we had to endure what every summer camper must endure before the fun starts: orientation.

*Hello Jeffrey*
*Hello Lola*
*Here I am at*
*Camp Granola!*

It was eight-thirty on Saturday morning and a new group of campers was crowded into Main Hall on the eighty-acre campus. Up on stage, a chiseled young man who seemed almost too healthy plunked a guitar and sang a playfully sarcastic song about Omega.

*Just today I*
*Met nine channels.*
*They are on my*
*Teaching panels.*
*While I'm sure they're*
*Very able*
*There's so many*
*That I'm signing up for cable.*

For the next half-hour the Omega counselors reviewed the rules for using the dining hall and other facilities. A conch shell would be blown to signal breakfast, lunch, and dinner. There were 6 A.M. meditation classes open to all, and the holistic health center offered the use of float tanks or the services of a masseuse, for a charge.

From my chair in the second row, I scanned the faces of the crowd. Many had come to study meditation, yoga, alternative medicine, and mythology. But I was looking for the baseball players. I wanted to size them up. What I saw did nothing to settle my nerves. Sprinkled among the more typical New Age seekers were several men who wore complete baseball uniforms—jerseys with numbers, stretchy pants, spiked shoes. These were serious ball players. My heart sank.

After orientation the other campers followed their teachers to various classrooms scattered in the woods while the baseball players remained in Main Hall. Lee and McKay came to the front of the room and told us to arrange ourselves in a circle. We did so and then sat, as attentive as kindergartners on the first day of school.

Tall, muscular, with gray hair and blue eyes, forty-four-year-old William Francis "Space Man" Lee wore striped baseball pants and a T-shirt from one of his several mock Presidential campaigns. (Every four years he "declares" for President as a protest against political windbaggery.) The red-white-and-blue shirt was decorated with a picture of a rhinoceros and the words RHINOCEROS PARTY, BILL "SPACE MAN" LEE FOR PRESIDENT. Lee had pulled a Russian Army cap—drab green decorated with a red star—over his bushy hair. He'd gotten the hat in the Soviet Union, where he and McKay had played several exhibition games the week before.

Jeffrey McKay was smaller than Lee. He had the stocky build of a catcher, which had been his position in the minor leagues. He had blond hair, blue eyes, and a youthful, even boyish face. His face reddened a bit as he cleared his throat to speak.

"There's a poem by Walt Whitman, who must have been a baseball fan," McKay began. "In it, he said, 'I am a teacher of athletes. He most honors my style who learns under it to destroy the teacher.' "

After pausing for us to consider this, he went on. "You know, there is a myth in our society that says an athlete is some special person. He's six-foot-four-inches tall and he's very strong and dominating. But it's just a myth. Everyone is an athlete. All you have to do is balance two things, championship and sportsmanship. Championship is playing hard, with all your skill. Sportsmanship is your regard for yourself and the other players. That balance is what we're seeking."

With a John Wayne cadence, Lee added some of his philosophy to McKay's. "I'm on planet Earth to do one thing," he said, "and that's to play baseball my whole life. I'm in search of the perfect game. Every time you play, it could happen. You walk between those white lines and you have the opportunity to create a game that goes on forever. It never ends." His voice trailed off and he got a faraway look in his eyes. He reminded me of the farmer in *Field of Dreams*. "It's the perfect game. There's no work to go to, nothing to worry about but the game. There's no time limit in baseball. It is the only game unbound by time. It could go on forever.

"Now, my aunt Annabelle Lee is the one who taught me

baseball," he continued. (There was apparently no stopping Lee when he started telling baseball stories.) "She pitched for three ball clubs in a professional league during World War Two. She was the only woman to ever pitch a perfect, no-hit game in hardball. She was interviewed about it and the guy said, 'What was it like?' She said, 'Well, twenty-seven came up and twenty-seven made outs.' She was great. She loved the game."

If spirituality is a belief or discipline that gives meaning and purpose to life, then baseball is Lee's spiritual practice. When he talks about baseball, he speaks with the zeal of a true believer and with the energy of an evangelist. McKay, on the other hand, sees baseball in a broader context. He describes a "community of players," a "safe space for play," and the "power of mutual support." He is interested in baseball as a healing practice, a way to soothe wounds and recover strength. I was drawn to this vision of baseball because it freed the game from the fear and anxiety of too much aggressive competition. It promised to free the player—me—to simply play.

Now of course, these two interests, healing and spiritual development, are at the center of the New Age phenomenon and, true to the movement, the ball players who had come to play at Omega were interested in both. They said as much as they each stood to introduce themselves.

Deb, a thirtyish woman from the small town of Standish, Maine, said she had come with two purposes: to see if she could still hit, and to erase some bitter memories. "I last played ball when I was a little girl," she said. Her voice was masked by a flat, Down East accent, but her story was sharply painful. "My father found out that I was playing Little League and he made me stop. I was one of the best players and I loved the game. But I haven't played it since."

Will, a gray-haired, middle-aged Southerner with a desk-jockey's body, said he had come to exorcise some demons and relive the one high point of his baseball past. "My big moment was a home run I hit in church league when I was maybe twelve years old," he said. "I never expected it. Nobody ever expected something like that from me. But I'll never forget it and I want to recapture that feeling."

Another man, Hank, said that one of the most important moments of his life had occurred at, of all places, the Hall of Fame in Cooperstown. He had arranged to meet an estranged friend there and was able to reconcile with him after twenty years. "We sat in the stands at Doubleday Field and talked and talked. It was one of the best things that ever happened to me."

For Ed, a political consultant from Albany, the baseball seminar would be "part of my effort to recover my soul. I took John Kennedy way too seriously when he said, 'Ask not what your country can do for you, but what you can do for your country.' For the last thirty years or so I've been serving others in one way or another. Now I'm here to reclaim the joy of playing, to find my mystical side. I have a daughter who is nine and a son who is four. They have reminded me what play is and I want to bring back that side of me."

And so it went, with one person after another explaining how baseball had affected his or her emotional or spiritual development. This was mainly a New Age crowd. Several of the women wore crystal earrings. Many of the men had attended other Omega workshops, on shamanism, African drumming, or other topics. And like the other mystically oriented people I had met in my journeys through the New Age, these people were eager for a healing, a transformation. Only this time it wasn't a channel or a psychic that would help them, it was baseball.

"There's a real common thread here," McKay observed before we headed for the practice field. "What I hear is that everybody's ten years old again. People want to heal some of the wounds from back there so they can move on."

"Hey, baseball has its assholes, we all know it," cracked Lee. "I was kicked out of Little League, kicked out of Pony League, kicked off the Red Sox because I stuck up for

Bernie Carbo, and kicked off Toronto because I stood up for Rodney Scott."

The Space Man had been an extremely controversial ball player. In Boston he had annoyed management by standing on his head in center field and speaking his mind to the press about everything from the team's managers to racism in Boston. Lee's book, *The Wrong Stuff*, is the only ball player's autobiography that touches on holistic medicine, the concept of karma, and the teachings of Buckminster Fuller. He writes as much about mystics and psychics and Carlos Casteneda as he does about the mechanics of pitching. On the cover he is pictured winding up to pitch, dressed in an astronaut's suit and a Red Sox cap with a tiny propeller whirling on its peak. My favorite line from the book: "You are the baseball, the baseball is you."

Lee picked up that theme as he continued to expound on his unique approach to the game. "The key is to put everything but the baseball out of your mind when you are on the field. Look at Jody Reed," he continued. Reed, the Red Sox first baseman, is as consistent as the turning of the seasons. "Jody is in a nice Zen trance when he's in the game, at bat or on the field. He's relaxed, centered, his eyes are focused. That's the way you've gotta be."

"There will be a lot of joy here this weekend, but also some tears," added McKay. "Whatever we do, let's support each other. Now, let's play ball."

We split into two groups. One followed McKay to the tennis courts, where they would hit little spongy balls against a fence. The rest of us went into the meadow beside Main Hall to practice throwing and catching. The field was big, about two hundred yards by one hundred yards, and the grass was long, like hay, and so wet with dew that our feet were quickly soaked. It was like the schoolyard where I had played as a boy. In the summer the grass grew so long that a ground ball could disappear in the infield.

Although we were eager to start throwing and catching, first we had to learn to stand. We set our feet shoulder's width apart and put our weight forward, on the balls of our feet. Our knees were to be slightly bent, and our shoulders were to be rounded. "It's called striking the horse," Lee said. "It is the best position to do anything in life." We all "struck the horse," looking like so many bow-legged cowboys with baseball mitts. But standing there, knees bent, my weight slightly forward, I did feel well-balanced and ready to spring into action.

From there Lee showed us the proper way to grip a baseball in order to throw fastballs, sliders, and curves, and he demonstrated the smooth, backward-then-forward method of throwing. Along with the baseball mechanics, there was always philosophy. "The key is to be fluid. I didn't learn to be fluid until I read *Autobiography of a Yogi*. That guy taught me a lot about baseball. You've also got to be willing to fail. Failure is the beginning of success. Besides, if you do it right all the time, you'll be like José Canseco, and then you'll be an asshole."

We paired off to practice throwing. As I threw the ball back and forth with a curly-haired man in blue jeans named Chris, I tried to be willing to fail. I experimented with grips, used the backward-then-forward method, and gave up the stiff-armed, forced way of throwing I had always used. After heaving a few over Chris's head and into the woods, I slowly improved. Soon I was throwing the ball with speed, accuracy, and little effort. My arm was working as a lever, swinging down and back and then forward. And I shut out every distraction. I quieted my doubts and used my mind like a laser targeting device, guiding the ball to Chris's mitt.

Standing there in the field, playing catch with Chris, I felt as competent as I had ever felt with a baseball in my hands. I felt the flow. He seemed to feel it, too.

"Hey, Mike. I'm going to try a curve!" he called.

The ball came in on an arc, curving right into my glove.

"You did it! It really curved!" I shouted.

Then I tried it. It was amazing. For the first time in my life, I could throw a curve ball, or a fastball, or a slider, at will.

After the throwing clinic we went to the tennis courts to

learn hitting. McKay began by having us select bats. Then he told us to throw them on the ground before us. With hollow clunks, eighteen bats hit the dirt.

"Now pick it up, feel it," he said. "Run your hand along its finish. Feel the weight of the bat. Feel how it's balanced. Get to know this bat until it feels like it's an extension of you. It's not just a dumb piece of wood. It's like an extension of your consciousness. It's something that can work with you. Respect it."

All around me, people caressed and shook their bats. Some talked to their bats. Others swung them through the air. I did the same, trying to feel its weight, to feel how it responded as an extension of my arm and my mind.

"The swing involves the power of Earth, fire, wind, and water," McKay continued. It begins with the batter "grounding" himself in the Earth of the batter's box. As batters dig in, they establish a relationship with the Earth. They also begin a ritual that puts them in a state of heightened consciousness, ready to hit the ball. Using a round bat to hit a baseball that's going eighty miles per hour obviously requires extraordinary concentration. The trance heightens concentration in a way that makes hitting possible.

The element of fire is tapped when the hitter "hits from his belly," McKay continued, pointing to a spot below his navel. "You use the fire in your whole body, not just the arms." The element of the air would be expressed in loud exhaling as we hit the ball. Jimmy Connors does this every time he hits the tennis ball. "The Chinese call it *kee-ah*," he said. "And water symbolizes fluidity. It is all one, fluid movement."

For the next hour we practiced the ritual of batting, paying attention to Earth, fire, wind, and water. (One of the pagan chants I had learned from Ayisha—"Earth my body, water my blood, air my breath, and fire my spirit"—invaded my mind from time to time as I did this.) Working in teams of two, we hit little foam baseballs—powder puffs with stitches—against the fences at Omega's tennis courts. With all the grunting and exhaling that went on, we sounded like eighteen Jimmy Connors hitting groundstrokes in a championship match. We also became smoother, more powerful, and more focused hitters.

After these morning drills we answered the call of the conch shell, eating a quick lunch of tofu, sprouts, salad, and broccoli at the Omega cafeteria. I used the time to chat briefly with one of Omega's founders, a woman named Elizabeth Lesser. Lesser began by informing me that she was concerned about my intentions. A *New York Times* reporter had recently visited and wrote an article depicting Omega as a 1960s holdover catering to a rather small segment of the population: self-indulgent liberals with spiritual yearnings. Lesser told me that the *New York Times* reporter "had been a pretty charming guy, too," but that she felt betrayed. "So," she asked bluntly, "where are you coming from on this?"

"I'm not here to trash Omega," I said. "I am here to do something lighthearted. To have fun." But as long as she was speaking bluntly, I added, "The only thing I can see about this place that makes me uncomfortable is it's a pretty elite crowd—all white, all highly educated, all middle or upper class." Indeed, I was starting to think that everyone in the New Age belonged to the same demographic group.

"We do serve a very moneyed group," Lesser allowed. "They are not rich compared with Club Med, but it is a certain upper-middle-class group." Many of them are also professional helpers—social workers, doctors, activists—who are anything but elitists, she added. "They are interested in social change, in making the world a better place. But often those are the same people who need to be healed themselves. They can't be very helpful to others if they are rageful or angry inside. Here they work on it in an environment that is a real community of people who form trusting relationships."

Omega is a place where people explore some of the more painful aspects of life. The institute offers seminars on illness, AIDS, divorce, and the study of death and dying. "These are middle-class people, and you might be cynical about all this, but middle-class pain is real, just as real as any other," said Lesser.

Where did all this pain come from? Lesser believed it came, in part, from the disillusionment that followed the 1950s and '60s. "The baby-boomers were the most well-cared-for generation of children in history. We were so rich. Life was so good. We were supposed to have conquered pain. There was supposed to be no suffering. We didn't see people get born or die. We took the old people out of our communities, and we became very good at emphasizing our individuality. Too good. We destroyed our communities and created very sterile environments."

When the inevitable pain of real life finally visited the baby-boom generation, they became overwhelmed, she suggested. They were not supposed to experience losses or defeats, and when they did, they had no idea how to cope with them. "At the same time, churches and other institutions have declined," said Lesser. "Our lives have contracted into these very limited spheres. Our contacts with each other are very minimal. That's one reason a lot of people come here. They come to find that community that has been lost."

In my case, this would be done through baseball. Mystic baseball promised to be a method—a Zen "Way"—to achieve both inner harmony and outer grace. I imagine this could be done with most any activity—painting, music, writing, work—but baseball had a certain power over me, and many of the others. It stirred both sweet and painful memories that might be used to teach us something about life as play and practice.

I had to hurry from my lunch with Lesser to get a ride in the caravan that would take us all to Rhinebeck High School's playing fields. We were to try the ideas and techniques we had learned that morning in real, nine-inning games.

\*     \*     \*

At the high school we quickly divided ourselves into four teams. It was a sticky, windless, ninety-degree afternoon, and as I waited for the teams to be organized, I felt as though the sun was pushing me down, into the ground. In the harsh glare my confidence began to wane.

Fielding practice only made me feel worse. Taking my position at second base, I promptly called for a pop-up that was coming down about twenty feet behind me. I might as well act like I know what I'm doing, I thought.

I back-pedaled confidently, watching the ball as I moved. Then I made my big mistake. I put my glove up. It blocked the ball from view.

Panic. A hard, heavy object was hurtling toward me like a satellite crashing out of orbit. But all I could see was the sun. I moved my glove down.

There it was, about ten feet above my head. I raised my gloved hand again, to defend myself. I felt the ball slam into the pocket and, for a moment, I hoped that I had caught it.

But there was no reassuring weight in my glove. The ball had disappeared. I whirled to look for it, but I was half-blinded by the sun. By the time my eyes adjusted, the right fielder was picking it up.

I waited for the groans, the complaints, the recriminations. After all, I had called for the ball. It was probably the right fielder's play. Who did I think I was?

"Nice hustle back there, Mike!" shouted McKay, who was over at the bench.

"Hey, good try," said the right fielder. "But I can help you with those. They get lost in the sun."

There would be no criticisms. At first I thought this was a pose, that I was being patronized. But it wasn't so. These New Age ball players reassured every infielder who lost a ground ball and every batter who struck out. They also whooped their approval for the occasional spectacular play. They were sincere.

When the game finally started, I knew that everyone—

both my teammates and our opponents—was hoping I would play well. And I did, sort of. Sure, a few ground balls got by me, and my throws were shaky. But in one inning, three batters hit the ball to second base and I made all three plays. It felt wonderful. I had done something as well as I could do it. It's a feeling we don't often get in real life. I remembered it from my sandlot days. I was ten years old again.

I wasn't the only one. Between innings Will, the gray-haired church leaguer from Memphis, told me he was feeling like a kid again, and it didn't feel good.

"God, I'm in first grade again and everyone knows what they're doing but me," he said. He mopped his face with a towel and swallowed three cups of water. "I've been very interested in the warrior archetype," he said. "It's something we all need, especially men."

(Mythological archetypes—warrior, wise man, crone, maiden, king, and queen—are at the core of widely popular books by Joseph Campbell and the poet Robert Bly. Author of a series of books on myth, Campbell became a household name in the late 1980s via TV interviews with writer/broadcaster Bill Moyers. Building on the theories of psychiatrist C. G. Jung, Campbell argued that mythological archetypes lie within all of us, supplying subconscious inspiration, motivation, and blueprints for behavior. Robert Bly turned Campbell and Jung into poetry and prose about the modern male. He also led so-called "Gatherings of Men," weekend-long meetings at which men explored the archetypes through dance, songs, storytelling, and conversation. These gatherings are part of a growing "men's movement" that is reevaluating the male role in the family and larger society. Bly argues that the Industrial Revolution took men out of the home and destroyed their relationships with daughters and sons. He advocates a stronger male presence in family life and encourages men to be mentors and better friends to one another. Moyers's programs with Campbell and later with Bly kindled such widespread interest in mythology, especially among New Agers, that Will would assume that our conversation about "the warrior within" required no preliminary explanations.)

"What I'm really stuck on," Will continued, "is the fact that the warrior is so skilled. You don't just feel the warrior in you and have it. No, you have to have the warrior's skills, and right now I don't."

In a baseball sense, Will was right. So far, he was no-hit and no-field. But when it came to confronting the pain of his past, he was a very skilled warrior indeed. Middle-aged and out of shape, he nevertheless took to the field doggedly, exposing himself to potential embarrassment, ridicule, and disappointment. Each time that it failed to materialize, the burden of his past grew lighter.

Will seemed like a warrior to me. He was just so mired in self-criticism, he didn't know it yet.

As we chatted, a remarkable display of both talent and errors unfolded on the field. Slow grounders trickled between infielders feet, and outfielders misjudged fluttering pop-ups. But some of the batters hit Lee's pitches solidly, and a center fielder made a series of three running catches. Top-notch players shared the diamond with raw beginners, and no one seemed to care. Somehow, the game proceeded smoothly.

It was not a gentle, passionless game. We played hard. We played to win. In the third inning Chris—my catch-mate from the morning—barreled into me at second to break up a double play. The impact catapulted me into right field.

In between the third and fourth innings, I overcame my pride and asked Jeff for some pointers on throwing the ball. This was more difficult than it might seem. There I was, a thirty-five-year-old man, asking another man to teach me something little boys are supposed to learn by the time they are six years old. But McKay answered me as a teacher, not a competitive male rival. He again reviewed for me the backward-then-forward motion, and he patiently tossed the ball back and forth with me while I worked the kinks out of my motion. When I went back onto the field, I was able to scoop up a grounder and throw the ball to first base with new confidence. But more important, I had asked another man for help and he had responded with kindness and respect. This is the kind of man-to-man exchange Robert Bly and other leaders of the men's movement mean when they talk about new, positive ways for men to relate to one another.

My team lost by one or two runs. I didn't pay close attention to the score. No one else seemed to, either. But I had noticed the "flow." I had narrowed my focus, shutting out all distractions until all I could see was the ball as it left the pitcher's hand, met the bat, and skidded across the grass to my position. Time had seemed to stand still, and my reactions were quicker, surer.

I think others had the same sorts of experiences that day. I know that as a group, we had created an atmosphere that was free of criticism and recrimination. For a few moments, most of us had felt the bliss of being fully immersed in the game, concerned only with what was going on between the foul lines. It was mystic baseball.

Back at Omega that night, I joined some of the players who attended a one-man vaudeville-style show titled "Male Myths and Wise Guys." It was predictable humor about men and their views of women, work, and one another. I left early, deciding my sore body needed some extra sleep. While walking the paths between the cabins, I ran into Chris. When he saw me, he stopped.

"Hey, Mike. I wanted to tell you, I'm sorry about running into you today. I got a little carried away, like I did when I was a kid."

At first I couldn't remember the collision. It was as if the game had been a sunwashed dream. When I did remember, I thought that Chris had done the right thing, knocking me over. It meant he respected my ability. He thought I might actually make the double play.

"Don't worry about it," I told him. "That's how the game is played."

We parted and, I imagine, we both thought more about the difference between playing hard and blind aggression. The aggression that sports could evoke was frightening and destructive. But hard play is part of the contract that binds all players.

I spent much of the evening trying to explain mystic baseball to my brother. Patrick, formerly Marv, rented a summer house less than five miles from Omega. I had told him about the seminar and he volunteered to put me up. After the first day of play, he fed me barbecued steaks (quite a switch from Omega fare) and we reminisced about baseball. I told him I was sorry about the criticism I had heaped upon him when we were boys playing ball.

"Hey, get over it. I have. Anyway, it wasn't that bad," he said.

Before retiring, we watched the Red Sox beat the Yankees on television. I went to sleep, pleasantly exhausted from a day on the diamond, and remembering how I used to feel this way every night as a kid.

The next morning I walked into Main Hall to find Bill Lee and about two dozen disciples contorted into what he called "the Kundalini stretch." The players gathered on the floor were huffing and puffing. The room reeked of clove-scented muscle balm. My own sore spots were confined to my left hand—bruised by catching—and my right shoulder, which was not accustomed to throwing a ball a hundred times a day.

"I rely on a combination of Zen and yoga and I feel pretty good," Lee was saying as I found a place on the carpet and stretched my legs. "Don't compete against yourself. Listen to your body. When you feel your muscles tighten, stop. The burning you feel is good, though. That's the fire building up inside of you. Of course, it's easier for me. I've got four cups of coffee and four Advil in me, and you probably don't.

"Always try to be fluid," he continued. "One day I was carrying two bottles of Blue Nun up the steps in Boston. I slipped and I could tell the cartilage in my knee was getting torn up, but I fell just right and didn't spill a drop. That's what being loose does for you."

Lee was a unique blend of the New Age and jock cultures, Advil and Zen. The most avid fans in our group were especially attentive when he told baseball stories. These poured out of him like corn from a grain elevator. One story described his feud with Craig Nettles: "He wouldn't bat against me in the senior league because he knew I was going to kill him." He told others stories about Billy Martin ("the Rat") and manager Don Zimmer ("the Gerbil").

All this patter was automatic, like a comic's routine, entertaining but at the same time distancing. The rest of us were revealing our physical and emotional shortcomings, but Lee seemed to be hiding behind the banter and his athletic skills. It annoyed me. Lee was a complex and highly educated man. With a superior intellect and an iconoclastic attitude, he had been an outcast among baseball players and a bane to managers. He could quote Shakespeare as well as Casey Stengel. Occasionally, some bitterness and anger would leak out between the anecdotes. But every time the conversation came close to a sore spot, Lee sidestepped it. "I don't dwell on things. The past's the past," he would say.

After morning practice, I cornered Lee and McKay for a lunchtime interview. I wanted to see if Lee would let down the baseball façade and reveal a bit more of the man.

"All right, all right, I would say yes, the whole "Space Man" thing was two-edged," Lee said as he worked his way through a plate of buckwheat biscuits, rice, mixed vegetables, and tofu. "It was funny and I was a little different. But it was also a defense, something to protect myself with. Baseball was a closed fraternity. Closed to me, that is. It hurt me. I had been excommunicated."

As a player, Lee had complained publicly when he thought his teammates were treated unfairly. He poked fun at managers, and he let his feelings about opponents show. He admitted to using drugs and playing under the influence, breaking a code of silence about widespread drug use among athletes. Lee had even spoken in favor of school integration in Boston at a time when the city was the site of pitched battles over a court-ordered busing plan. These were all things that ball players never do.

Lee looked at the game, and the people in it, differently, too. Writing in his book about a teammate who never lived up to his potential, the pitcher becomes a psychoanalyst. "I had the feeling he was carrying around a lot of stuff from his childhood. He spoke with his mother quite often and I got the impression that he never felt he could please her completely," he writes. In another part of his book, Lee even has the audacity to suggest that Americans have gone overboard in their worship of athletes. It "makes me wonder if we're not breeding a society that lacks self-esteem," he writes. "I don't think we pat people on the back enough, letting them know that being able to fix a sink is just as much a skill as being able to get Rod Carew out with the bases loaded. And more worthwhile, if you ask me."

Eventually Lee's attitude—putting personal convictions ahead of baseball—led the Red Sox to trade him to the Montreal Expos. Then the Expos dropped him when he left the ballpark during a game—a serious violation of the rules—to protest the trading of a teammate. After that, "the fix was in," Lee writes. He tried to hook up with several clubs, but none would even give him a tryout.

Years later, Lee was still trying to make a living in the game, but without the status of a baseball insider. No big-league team would give him a job as a coach or a scout, and it was unlikely he would ever want such a job. Still, baseball was the only vocation he knew, and he longed to continue playing. So he played on minor-league teams and in small-town exhibitions throughout the United States and Canada. In 1989 he was player manager for the Winter Haven Super Sox, a team that was part of a new winter league for retired professionals.

Lee's never-ending search for a game to play, a team to

join, had an air of desperation. I asked him if it weren't possible for him, or any other major leaguer, to simply stop being a ball player.

"No. You never stop being the ball player, even if you are an ex–ball player. People never forget. You never forget. Oh, you can go home to some small town in Iowa and sell cars. But you are still the ball player. They always consider you the ball player."

It was true. For better or worse, many baseball players, especially the prominent ones, find it impossible to outlive their pasts. They are always the Babe, the Splendid Splinter, Catfish, Space Man. Lee had seen his fate and, rather than fight it, he had embraced it. "I was put on this Earth to continue the true tradition of baseball," he said. "Real baseball disappeared when TV came into the game. I've been put here to bring it back."

According to Lee's "true tradition of baseball," all playing fields should be made of real grass and the game should be played outdoors. In the true tradition of baseball, players should be athletes, not diversified corporations, and games should be viewed in person, not via television. "They got it right in *Field of Dreams*," said Lee. "That was baseball as it was supposed to be played."

"Television came and the soul flew out of baseball," Jeff McKay interjected. "It's really the factor that changed things. The difference between today and back then is the difference between 'play' and 'display.' Baseball before was play. Now, on TV, it is all a display. It doesn't have the same soul."

I suggested that Lee and McKay were reading too much into the current state of the game. After all, in every arena of life—politics, education, family—there are those who nostalgically pine for the "way it used to be." Lee and McKay sounded like doomsday preachers decrying the evils of modern society. The fact is, the good old days were never as good as we imagine they were, and the problems of the moment are rarely as serious as doomsayers claim.

"No, no, that's not it," Lee protested. "It really has changed. Too much of the life has gone out of baseball, because of the money, because of management, because of a lot of things."

In that moment, between the tofu and the organically grown apples, Lee and McKay seemed like religious fundamentalists determined to restore the purity of a faith that had been sullied by modernity. But, as with every Bible-thumping preacher, there was a personal side to the story. For Lee it was, perhaps, his never-ending battle against his excommunication, his determination to be vindicated. For Jeff McKay it was a matter of reconciling with a profound sense of disillusionment, not just with baseball, but with all of American society.

In a very direct way, McKay was a product of the troubled times in which he had lived. Born and raised in Schenectady, New York, the son of a mid-level manager at the General Electric plant, McKay had a childhood that was consumed with sports and school. He went to Middlebury College, where he starred in football and baseball. "I was a straight, conservative athlete who did everything the coaches told me, even though it was mostly crap," he recalled. A red-blooded, patriotic young man, McKay didn't resist the draft. Instead he served his country in Vietnam and returned to a nation at war with itself.

"Vietnam changed my reality," McKay said. "It changed everything for me. I came back a basket case with a real fuck-you attitude. I decided that everything I had been brought up on, from coaching to school to family, was all bullshit." After Vietnam, McKay immersed himself in the counterculture of the late Sixties and early Seventies. "I was groping, groveling, searching," he said. "Everything I believed in had turned to bullshit and I needed something to replace it."

In the middle of his groping and groveling, McKay made two discoveries. One was the sports center at Esalen, the New Age institute in California. The other was a man named George Davis. Davis is the author of *The Fifth Down: Democracy Through Football*, a radical book that challenges the rigid, authoritarian nature of football. Davis's ideas so moved McKay that he went to California to study with him. It was there that he developed his unusual, open-minded approach to baseball.

"In 1975 I got a job as a coach at the University of Massachusetts," McKay said. "UMass was an amazing place at the time. People were trying all sorts of things. Well, I started gradually, but by the end of the season, the team was voting on who would be captain, even voting on the starting line-up for each day. It was amazing. I had taken the theories and applied them, and they worked."

At the core of McKay's approach is respect for individual athletes. He believes that a player who is conscious of his body, aware of his actions, and open to innovations would one day be able to act as his own coach. "That's the key, to become your own coach, whether it's in baseball or in life," he said.

Another book, by Japanese baseball legend Sadaharu Oh, provided McKay with an Eastern-style philosophy to replace his old war-like approach to baseball. In *A Zen Way of Baseball*, Oh writes of his development as a player and a sports philosopher. Through the study of Aikido, a form of martial arts, Oh learned to regard his opponents as partners in a dance rather than enemies in a battle. He tried to draw on their energies to power his own efforts. Oh also writes about "ki," a Japanese notion about the blending of spiritual and physical energies, and "ma," the interval in space and time between the actions of an opponent and one's own. But perhaps the most important idea Oh describes in his book is the "do," or "the Way" of baseball. Oh used baseball as a spiritual practice to define and guide his entire life. It was, for him, "the Way."

For McKay, who had come back from Vietnam to spend years looking for his own "way," Oh's book was a revelation. He was able to see the "do" of baseball and apply it to his own life. He constantly drew analogies between the lessons of baseball and the lessons of life. He also incorporated many of Oh's spiritual ideas in his coaching. During batting practice, he had urged us to draw on our own "ki" energy, by focusing our bodies and minds fully on the task at hand. When we each swung the bat, we were told to grunt or shout as we exhaled, a martial arts technique.

"The spiritual part is something I have understood only in the last few years," McKay added. "I've studied a lot, even had some out-of-body experiences. I know it's very important and that it translates into performance. I really saw that in the 1984 Olympics. The American baseball team had fourteen guys who are now major leaguers. But the Japanese were so together spiritually that before they even played, I knew they would kick the American team's ass. They did. It was all decided by their spiritual approach."

After lunch, the caravan of vehicles again made its way to the high-school ball fields. On this day, several less-experienced players said they had felt lost the previous afternoon. The games had been played at a high level and they felt inhibited on the field. To solve this problem, we divided ourselves into high- and low-ability groups. I joined the low-ability group, where, even though many players lacked certain skills, enthusiasm and spirit ran high.

Before we played, McKay and Lee tried to help us focus more intently. "It's important to let the natural athlete, who is really the child that's within you, come into play," McKay said. "We all have a number-one self and a number-two self. The number one is that child. The number two is the one with doubts. Number two will run you, and wreck what you're doing, if you let him. Don't let him. That doesn't mean you try to kill that part of you. That's only going to lead to a war inside you. Just take control of what's going on inside your head."

"Look, the Zen of baseball is focus," Lee added. "In the

movie *Bull Durham* they said the secret was breathing through your eyelids. What they meant was that focusing so intently on the ball, nothing else exists. It's Zen. If you are hitting, you see the ball, and boom!"

Walking onto the diamond, Lee lay down in the infield grass near the pitching mound, inviting us to stretch our muscles. As he worked one leg, and then the other, he carried on a monologue.

"Oh! Just feel that grass. It's long and cool and it's giving off oxygen. And those super ball players are all up there in the sky above us. Down here, we're going to get a lot of hits and score a lot of runs."

Feeling more confident, I volunteered to play shortstop for a team that named itself the Tofu Pups. To my right, at third base, was a young man named Noah, who between pitches told me that he had endured endless criticism while playing ball as a boy. But as he had learned the basics of mystic baseball, he had grown more confident. To my left, at second base, was a small, lithe young woman named Ellie, who wore a New York Mets hat, crystal earrings, shorts, and a sleeveless running shirt. At first base was a dark-haired man named Rich who was one of the better players. Our outfield included Bob, a fast and agile player who could cover center and large parts of right and left, and Sharon and Laura, two women who had never before played baseball.

As the game progressed, I watched admiringly as Noah scooped up ground balls and Laura tirelessly chased the pop-ups that went over her head. A near-catch by Laura won her as much praise as one of Noah's smooth put-outs. In fact, the high point of the game came when Laura, determined to overcome her self-consciousness and her fear of getting hurt, stuck her floppy hand up and actually caught a fly ball. She leaped in the air and then danced around as her teammates raced out to embrace her. It was as if she had caught the last fly ball of a World Series.

There were other moments during the game when it was

hard to tell one team from the other. Players in the field cheered the efforts of each batter, and those waiting their turn at the plate applauded the efforts of the players on the field. Deb, the woman from Maine whose father had pulled her out of Little League, was the toughest hitter in the game. She went four for four.

We ended the game with the score tied. The players on both teams seemed perfectly satisfied with that. What mattered was the intensity of the game and each player's small successes—a solid hit, a diving catch. I had scratched out an infield hit, and my fielding had continued to improve. I also had no concern about being criticized or about turning on others as I had once turned on Marv.

Driving back to Omega, Ellie and I relived some of the high points of the day, not the most exciting plays but rather the moments that revealed the changes in the players we were coming to know. There was, of course, Laura's big catch and the celebration that followed. And Will, the gray-haired Southerner, had hit a screaming line drive off of Lee. If that didn't make him feel like a warrior, nothing would. But in Ellie's mind, it was more the tenor of the game that mattered.

"Right now, I'm feeling like I really love the men and the women on our team," she said. "I especially appreciate the men. They aren't behaving like macho guys. They are actually being supportive of each other. I thought only women did that. I think it's great."

Ellie had come to Omega and the practice of mystic baseball as part of her long journey through the New Age. Over the previous few years she had explored crystals and channeling. She had attended other workshops at Omega, practiced yoga, and studied Eastern religion. "I thought baseball would be the least complex and most linear thing I could do at Omega," she said. "I'm finding out that it can be a spiritual practice, just like anything else."

She wasn't the only one who had been moved by a day that was, presumably, all play. The feeling of a mitt in my hand, the dirt of the infield, and the laces of the ball in my fingers had evoked memories that had been long lost. My body seemed to insist that my mind recall the hours my brother and I had spent playing baseball as children. We were so dedicated to baseball that one summer we took shovels and dug the sod out of the infield, hoping to create a smooth dirt surface, like a big-league infield. We also brought a lawn mower to cut the grass and we raked the rocks out of the outfield. That same summer, the summer of '67, I taped a transistor radio to the handlebars of my bicycle and listened to afternoon games while I completed my paper route. The Red Sox won the pennant, and I got Rico Petrocelli and Jim Lonborg's autographs at the grand opening of a gas station in the small city nearest our town.

But there were more distant memories than those. I recalled twilight moments in the backyard with my father pitching underhand as I swung a plastic bat. I was no older than five, and baseball was already such a part of the mythology of my childhood that in my eyes, my father was a big leaguer. The fantasy grew so strong that for a time I was convinced that he indeed had been a larger-than-life figure, a professional ball player.

That night at Omega, our group met for a review of what we had learned, and I discovered that others were sensing flashes of childhood, feeling a connection to the game that had been laid down in those early years, when experience makes deep, lasting imprints on the brain.

"I had a very strong feeling of connection to my father out there," said Nate, a man of about forty. "He died recently, at the age of ninety. We used to sit and watch the Dodgers games on TV. It was wonderful just to be with him. Now I do the same thing with my kids. I know when there's a game on, they're with me for hours. And you know, we're not too old to go out and play ourselves. Sometimes we forget that."

Jeff McKay said that one of his most important memories

was of a Little League tryout. "I was in third grade and I was very nervous," he said. "But I remember my father taking me there, to tryouts. In one hand I had my catcher's mitt. In the other was my father's hand. I felt great."

For Ed, the political consultant, the game had brought back some unpleasant memories. "I went back into the time when I had a bad attitude about sports. Today I was batting against Alan, who is a very good pitcher. I didn't appreciate him and his skill and then do my best, too. Instead I did what I did when I was a kid. I hated him. I hated everyone who was better than me. But it's good for me to realize that, because I know it doesn't have to be that way."

Chris, the runner who had crashed into me on the first day of play, had a similarly negative experience at first. "Yesterday I felt like I had a real sixth-grade mentality. I have to apologize for taking Mike out at second base. I had been ignoring the context of what we are doing here. Today was much better. It was amazing how good it felt to see that I was competent playing, and watching someone else do well was a real thrill. It felt great."

"This is an exploration we're doing here, an exploration of baseball and of ourselves," added Jeff McKay. "This spring, in short order, I visited the Vietnam Memorial, went to my twenty-fifth college reunion, and re-met my ex-wife after twenty-two years. I felt a lot of pain. But when you get a chance to experience pain, as some of you have this weekend, it's a chance to deal with it. Experience it. Don't try to avoid it. The avoidance of pain will only lead to more pain."

This idea is a primary tenet of the New Age. New Agers, who readily blend psychology, mysticism, religion, and philosophy, firmly believe in analyzing and confronting the painful past in order to promote spiritual growth. Jach Pursel and his channeled spirit Lazaris seek to accomplish this with guided meditations. Sally Fisher and the other AIDS workers do it with visualization. Space Man Lee and Bill McKay use baseball. In each case, progress is a matter of going backward, to examine one's beginnings, before moving forward.

After the meeting I sat with some of the players to ask them more about baseball as a spiritual practice. Nate, who had spoken earlier about his father, said the weekend on the diamond was just the latest step in a long process of seeking. "My spiritual awakening happened several years ago, when I was about twenty-seven years old," he said. "I was brought up Jewish. My father went to an Orthodox temple and we observed the holidays. But I was also a product of the Sixties and I was interested in discovering more."

He discovered "more" on a trip to India, where he studied philosophy and religion with a number of gurus. "I found out that the spiritual is something beyond body and beyond mind," he said. "Believe it or not, I think you can get that feeling playing baseball. Yesterday it was hot and I was wearing a sweatshirt. But I didn't realize I was so hot and sweaty until I stopped playing. I had been so completely in the game, I didn't feel other things. I liked that."

The ritual of the game and its tradition gave Nate the sense that the world had some order, that some values were timeless. These were rare commodities in an era marked by so much technological and social change. "Baseball is a ball and a bat and it's played the way it has always been played," he said. "I like the continuity, the idea that I'm part of something that has gone on for a long time."

Others agreed that at Omega, baseball had taken on a spiritual quality. Louis, who had played in the outfield against the Tofu Pups, said he had been deeply moved by his teammates. "There's been a collapse of community support in the country—at least that's the way I experience it," said Louis, who lived in a sprawling Connecticut suburb. "But there's still a wonderful energy you feel when you do something spiritual in a group." Louis said he got that feeling of community, at other times, by participating in Sufi dancing, a spiritual celebration performed by believers of the Sufi sect of Islam. At Omega he had found the same sense of community celebration while playing baseball.

Laura, a novice outfielder, said she had discovered she didn't have to mask her inadequacies with a show of defensive bravado. "I came here thinking I'd have to be tough— one of the guys—and I knew I could fake that and get through. But I didn't have to do that. No one was doing that macho sports thing, so I allowed myself to be supported and lifted up by the team. I never felt that way before. It was great."

The games had dredged up different emotions for some of the men. Several mentioned that they had felt like outcasts as boys, because they were not star athletes. "When you choose up teams, some guys get left out, and that feels like shit," said a man named Steve. Another man said he had spent much of the past weekend reflecting on his relationship with his father. "My father was just not there, and he never showed me things like how to throw a ball," he said. "But if you're an all-American boy, you're supposed to know how to do these things automatically. I felt like being here, under these conditions, was pretty healing."

It was hard to believe that baseball could have such a profound effect on its players. But then again, this was not ordinary baseball. It was mystic baseball and it was having an effect on me, too, despite my writer's defenses. The infield dirt beneath my feet, the smell of the grass, the sound of the ball popping into a glove—all of it had returned me to the simplicity of childhood. With the techniques Lee and McKay taught, I had acquired new skills and come to understand that I hadn't been a baseball failure. Rather, I had been a small boy caught up in a winning-is-everything mentality. In revisiting those experiences, I had gone backward in order to reconcile with my past and move forward. Mystic baseball did not make me a New Age convert. But it did teach me that even grown-ups need to play, and that there is, indeed, much more to a sport than winning and losing.

Of course, like a stage play or a religious rite, the game was just a representation of life. It wasn't quite real. In real life, we rarely experience something as satisfying and decisive as a base hit. In real life, no one applauds you when you do your job well, and it's often difficult to tell who is on your team and who is not. Nevertheless, for a brief time I had been free of the pressures and distractions of modern adult life. Like a fallen-away Catholic who once again smells the incense and hears the Latin Mass, I had been transported back in time, to a moment when I believed.

"What did the slave say to Julius Caesar just before stabbing him? He said, 'All glories flee.' Remember that today."

Space Man got his Shakespeare wrong. Caesar was first stabbed by Casca, who cried, "Speak hands for me." But still, the sentiment was appropriate. As we met in Main Hall on the morning of our last day, many of us were flushed with the excitement of our accomplishments and filled with a sense of camaraderie. But our weekend of mystic baseball had been a carefully constructed experiment, calculated to bring out our best. We were supposed to support one another, and we had. We were supposed to focus on the practice of baseball, not the goal of winning. We had done that, too. In fact, through mystic baseball, we had escaped entirely from the Darwinian world of work, from family responsibilities, and from everyday worries. Soon, however, the experiment would end and our glory days would fade.

It was Labor Day, the last real day of summer, and a cold front had moved in from Canada during the night. The haze and heat of Sunday were replaced with the melancholy cool of autumn. The hollow morning light filled me with a sense of things—time, the season, the spell of mystic baseball—all running out.

On the baseball field the grass was wet with dew and the wind blew strong, carrying whirlpools of dust from home plate out to left field. It was a good morning for right-handed pull hitters.

The Tofu Pups all smeared sun-reflecting grease under their eyes and took to the field looking like so many raccoons. Both teams played tentatively. Of course, some of the hesitancy was due to sore muscles. But it was clear that many of the batters were just a little distracted as they faced the Space Man on the mound, and the fielders sometimes seemed to have their minds on something other than the game. They were, no doubt, thinking about their weekend of play coming to an end.

Between innings I chatted with McKay, who sat on some metal bleachers behind the backstop. He said he wanted to make sure I understood his approach to sports. "There was a small movement to revolutionize sports in the 1960s," he told me. "It was part of the whole Sixties thing. They wanted to attack the megalith of sports, the Dallas Cowboy mentality, the corporate dominance. But it was all based on pissing and moaning and saying 'Fuck you' to the establishment. It didn't go anywhere."

With the advent of the New Age movement, he said, came a different kind of reaction to sports: the philosophy of noncompetitive games. "I tried all that stuff, too," he said. "I played the role of New Age male, but that was just as much a pain in the ass as the old redneck way. It was as limp as the other was rigid."

Finally, McKay settled on a blend of intense American competitiveness and Eastern-style respect, balance, and harmony. "The point is, winning matters. It matters very much. But it's not the only thing." In mystic baseball, the idea is to play hard, play to win, but regard one's opponent as gifted, human, and worthy. That way, a player can complete the game feeling the same way about himself.

On the field, we practiced what McKay had preached and achieved remarkable results. Will used the strong wind to lift a ball into the outfield for an extra-base hit. It wasn't a home run, but Will had produced that clear, crisp sound of a bat hitting the ball fully. Later, Noah turned in a sparkling play in the field. Reacting with pure instinct to a hard-hit line drive, he snared it in his glove and then threw it quickly from third base to first to catch a runner in a double play.

As I watched the others overcome the limitations they had brought with them on Saturday, I reviewed my own progress. I had improved my fielding by adopting the Zen trance approach, focusing only on the little white sphere of the baseball and shutting out everything else. My throwing had also improved, because I had been willing to admit that I was having difficulty and I had practiced the "backward-then-forward" method. But I had not gotten a solid hit all weekend. I had not mastered the mystic baseball approach to batting. In the last inning of play, I got one final chance.

As I came up to bat with the Pups one run behind in the bottom of the ninth inning, I realized that I had been distracted at the plate by all the things that a well-prepared batter can ignore. I was distracted by the sun, by my cheering teammates, by my own inner doubts, and by the friendly, taunting monologue Lee conducted on the mound:

"Oh, the bases are loaded! Can he do it, folks?"

"Here it comes, watch him hit the ball on the ground."

"All right. Pop up. Get ready. I'll make him pop it up."

Suddenly I realized that Lee wasn't speaking to the fielders. He was speaking to me. He was trying to help me. I had fallen into the habit of swinging at the first pitch every time I came up to bat. And Lee had always started me off with an inside pitch that was almost impossible to hit. I decided, this time, to wait for a good pitch. But Lee wasn't throwing. He just stood there, smiled, and put his gloved hand on his hip.

"So, are you going to swing at the first pitch?"

"Not this time," I answered, with mock seriousness. I laughed for a moment, then struggled to focus again on the game, letting everything else fade away in a fuzzy blur.

"It's going to be a good one," came the taunt from the mound. "You're gonna like it. Here it comes."

Lee had proven that he could put the ball where he wanted, when he wanted. During warm-ups he had shown off by hitting the center post of the backstop from near second base. This time he threw it across the center of the plate, waist high. A perfect strike.

I didn't swing. I didn't say anything. I scraped a line in the dirt and nestled my right foot solidly in the Earth, grounding myself. After two more pitches, I saw a curve ball looping toward me. I swayed backward for a moment, then started moving toward the ball. McKay had taught us to "hit the ball where it's pitched" rather than try to redirect it. So I swung the bat out a bit, to catch the ball as it crossed the outside of the plate. I exhaled loudly and I twisted my body from my midsection, using the fire within. I tried to move as smoothly, as fluidly as water.

The ball jumped off my bat and flew over the head of the second baseman, into right field. A clean, well-placed single.

When I reached first base, the Tofu Pups were cheering wildly. So was someone else, out in the outfield. I looked into right field to see three people cheering from a small set of bleachers. It was my brother and a couple of friends. They had come to watch me play. When they got my attention, they gave me a "wave," rising one by one and throwing their hands in the air. I doffed my cap, like Ted Williams.

The game ended with me stranded on first base. The Tofu Pups couldn't bring me home, but on the last out, I raced around the bases and slid into home, just for fun.

# 6 · FAIRFIELD
## IOWA

---

# Maharishi's Heaven on Earth

---

*At whose behest does the mind think? Who bids the body live? Who makes the tongue speak?*

THE UPANISHADS

SOON AFTER I LEFT OMEGA, THE FIRST OF THE ARTICLES appeared in the *Los Angeles Times* and the *Wall Street Journal*. They were followed by stories in newspapers in Miami, Chicago, and other cities. Peace was coming. World harmony was at hand. It would begin in Fairfield, Iowa.

Fairfield is the home of Maharishi International University, a college founded by Maharishi (great sage) Mahesh Yogi. If anyone can claim to be the original New Age leader, it is Maharishi, the Indian guru made internationally famous by some of his early students—John, Paul, George, and Ringo. It would be more that a decade before the term "New Age" would be fashionable, but in the 1960s the Beatles and others eagerly consumed Maharishi's predictions of the dawning "Age of Enlightenment." Amidst the counterculture revolution, the Maharishi toured the world like the flower children's Billy Graham, promising permanent, all-knowing bliss through natural, "transcendental meditation."

Hundreds of thousands of Americans believed, enrolling in TM courses and becoming devout meditators. Meditation did calm the mind and soothe the body, but it did not produce "the one sure cure to eradicate all sufferings" that Maharishi had promised. Gradually most of the celebrities lost interest. The crowds thinned, and with his finances under government investigation, the Maharishi retreated to an Italian resort, declaring an end to his personal crusades.

Though he faded from public view, Maharishi did not cease working. He expanded his philosophy, developing elaborate theories about TM's boundless benefits. He also used millions of dollars donated by his disciples to build schools, medical clinics, housing developments, and businesses. In 1974 he purchased the entire campus of the bankrupt Parsons College in Fairfield for about two million dollars. MIU became a mecca for serious meditators who flocked to Fairfield to work at the university or attend retreats, courses, and conferences.

It was at one of these conferences—the Heaven-on-Earth Assembly—that peace was supposed to break out. Three thousand meditators would use TM to end a military crisis that began when Iraq invaded Kuwait and America responded by sending more than two hundred thousand troops to defend Saudi Arabia. Maharishi and his aides proclaimed that the Heaven-on-Earth Assembly would stop the impending war. And that would be only the beginning. They planned to establish a world peace center in Fairfield where seven thousand meditators would guarantee continuing peace through constant meditation. This would cost just $1 billion, which they hoped would be paid by the U.S. Government.

To promote the peace initiative and his return to public life, Maharishi held a telephone press conference from his home in Holland. He also gave an interview to *Life* magazine, which published an article announcing "The Return of Mr. Bliss." Finally, leaving nothing to chance, he bought space in newspapers around the world. The ads declared, "Maharishi Offers SOLUTION TO THE GULF CRISIS and a Practical Formula to Create PERMANENT WORLD PEACE."

\*     \*     \*

Despite the publicity, I was the only out-of-town writer to join the TM pilgrims who trekked to Heaven-on-Earth in Iowa. Bordered on the north by endless cornfields and on the south by the town of Fairfield, MIU is a typical-looking college—except for the domes. In the middle of all the brick and ivy sit two enormous golden domes, perfect twin circles two hundred feet across and six stories high, squatting like giant mushrooms in a field of green grass.

At Henn Mansion, the administration building, I opened the door on a frenzy of activity. Women in conservative dresses and men in dark business suits were rushing to send fax messages to local media, announcing a press conference that would be held the next day. Assistant publicity director Anne Melfi was much too busy to talk. Besides, she said, any discussion would be pointless, since I had not been "oriented" via videotape. She gave me a campus map and pointed me in the direction of the library, where I could view several programs about the college.

"Watch the tapes," she insisted. "Before you ask any questions, watch the tapes. There's a lot to learn and it's much too complicated to get into now."

How complicated could it be? From what I knew, TM is a meditative discipline that has a calming effect on the mind and body. It eases complaints related to stress, such as high blood pressure, and it helps focus the intellect. I assumed that the thousands who were part of the assembly were using their meditation to, in effect, pray for peace. This didn't seem so difficult to understand. But in the spirit of being a gracious guest, I dutifully went to the library, which was in a small wing of the science building, found the video room, donned earphones, and turned on the tapes.

From the first moments of the first tape I realized Anne Melfi was right. There was much more to TM, the university, and the Maharishi than I realized. Maharishi is serious about creating world peace, all-knowing bliss, a real Heaven-on-Earth. And he insists that he has a tool, a "scientific technology," for doing it in short order. Not only that, this technology could make people fly.

All of this is explained by the students and professors who appear on the tapes. Between the footage of idyllic campus scenes, they describe how Maharishi has combined the practice of meditation and an advanced concept of atomic physics called the "Unified Field Theory." The theory suggests that all matter and energy flow from a single, unified source. The source has yet to be identified and the theory remains just a theory, but mainstream physicists believe it is a stepping stone to the eventual discovery of new laws that will connect several separate views of physics.

As the tapes reveal, Maharishi envisions the Unified Field as a kind of place that one can visit through deep meditation. Once it is blended with the Unified Field, a person's mind can have access to the wisdom of the universe, and it can influence the course of events. This is a mystical notion grafted on to science. But the students and professors on the tape don't see it that way. They accept the Maharishi's suggestion that there is a place called the Unified Field, and that meditation is the means, the technology, by which they can go there. "With the Unified Field, you know that everything comes from your consciousness," explains one of the well-scrubbed students on the video. "If you don't like something, you can change it because you can influence everything in the world."

Unified Field Technology is at the heart of everything taught at MIU. English professors at MIU teach it; so do history professors. MIU is the only school in America where one can earn a masters degree in study of the Unified Field. Indeed, at MIU it is meditation and contact with the Unified Field that make an educated person. That's why everyone is required to visit the domes twice a day, seven days a week, for three hours of group meditation, to support individual private meditation. Meditation takes so much time away from course work that catch-up classes are held on Saturdays, to please accrediting authorities.

In the Unified Field meditators could also learn to fly. The tapes show dozens of men sitting cross-legged on the floor of a gymnasium. After a few moments of stillness they begin to rock. Then they use muscles in their upper legs and torsos to roll up onto their knees and hop into the air. The effusive narrator on the tape says that this hopping is the first stage of "yogic flying," another proof of the power of the Unified Field.

I left the library in a state of shock. The way the Maharishi looked at it, the Unified Field is a magical place one can reach through a journey in the mind, something like the planet B612 in the children's book *The Little Prince*. How could a fully accredited university function with a curriculum based entirely on this mysticism dressed up as science? Didn't anyone question the Unified Field Technology or the claim that meditators could fly?

These questions forced me to reconsider my exploration of this corner of the New Age movement. The curiosity I had felt upon arriving on campus had been replaced by the dread sense that I was witnessing a gigantic delusion. But I fought the impulse to leap to that conclusion. After all, TM is not a new spiritual fad. It has been around since 1955. And the Maharishi is no Jim Jones in the jungles of Guyana. Over the years millions of people have used TM, and I had never read of any complaints. As I walked through the yellow autumn leaves on the path from the library to Henn Mansion, I thought that perhaps I had misunderstood the videotapes. Surely people here would allow that much of the Maharishi's message was simply a way of speaking, a metaphor.

At the administration building, Anne Melfi led me to an office she shared with a tall, middle-aged man named Pat Hardigree. With her hair mussed and her dress slightly askew, Melfi seemed distracted and anxious as she sat down on a small sofa. Casting for an easy question that might help her feel at ease with me, I asked her about "flying" meditators. "Flying is really just a figure of speech, isn't it?"

"Oh, no," she said. "Maharishi teaches that flying is possible through meditation. What you saw was the first stage of flying. Many people don't consider flying normal, but we know that we use only five percent of our real potential. Why shouldn't the use of the other ninety-five percent allow us to fly?"

Melfi made the same argument when it came to TM's benefits. Through meditation, she said, one could reverse the aging process, unleash dormant genius, and find a life of total bliss. "You get fulfillment and self-actualization, which mean different things to different people. But no matter what your definition is, you get it."

Each point Melfi raised prompted a question. But after a while, she didn't seem to hear any of them. It was as if a thick wall of glass separated us. While I spoke, she gazed out the window. Her answers had nothing to do with my questions. She could see me, but she didn't hear me.

"Do you think everyone has the potential to be a genius?" I asked.

"Maharishi has said there has been something missing in the Western approach to life. There is knowledge and then there is the knower. It's the knower, in the process of knowing, that we have been ignoring."

"But can everyone become a creative genius?"

"From Vedic teachings, we know that life should be bliss, that harmony is natural. That is what we are talking about."

Sometimes Pat Hardigree would add something to Melfi's remarks, amplifying a point with an example or a reference to some study. But neither of them answered questions directly.

"We focus on the benefits of TM," continued Melfi. "It makes you more creative, it helps you develop every part of you. You don't have to be overly stressed to benefit from it. Even if you are in perfect health, the aging process reverses. We have three hundred different studies to prove this. You can be twenty years younger than your biological age. Studies prove it."

As they talked, Melfi and Hardigree opened file drawers and pulled out pamphlets and booklets and mimeographed papers, which soon grew into a foot-high stack on the table in front of me. These were some of the studies that proved the wonders of TM. One was titled "Growth of Higher Stages of Consciousness: Maharishi's Vedic Psychology of Human Development." Another was called "International Peace Project in the Middle East: The Effects of the Maharishi Technology of the Unified Field." (This paper claimed that through TM, which was called "the Maharishi Technology," meditators had reduced violence in Israel and Lebanon.)

The papers, like the videotapes, seemed intended to preempt discussion, to indoctrinate rather than illuminate. Realizing I had reached a dead end, I asked about sitting in on the Heaven-on-Earth Assembly and interviewing MIU students. Here I met another wall. It was unlikely I would be allowed to see any of the assembly meetings. The same was true for the group meditations in the domes. And if I wanted to do interviews, they would be arranged for me. Visitors were not allowed to walk the campus and strike up conversations.

After Melfi turned down all my requests, I made one last effort to get beyond her pat testimony about TM. "How did you get involved with TM, Anne?" I asked her.

"I first saw him on the 'Merv Griffin Show,'" she explained, her face softening into a smile. "It was 1977. I was living in New York City and getting totally bowled over by the stress there. I was unemployed and very down. I saw Maharishi and I thought, 'I need that kind of dynamism to keep up with the pace of New York.' I went to a free introductory lecture and then did the training." She went on to study an advance version of meditation called the "TM Sidhi" course. She had come to MIU to study more. She took a job in the MIU publicity office in exchange for free housing, tuition, and a stipend of about fifty dollars per week.

"The entire staff here is volunteer," she added. The professors, administrators—everyone but the service workers drafted from the local community worked for room, board, and a small stipend. "That's why we think the government should give us a grant, for salaries," added Melfi, "so we can have a full-time community of creators of coherence." These people would make meditation their occupation and, in exchange for government support, would literally create world peace via the Unified Field. "They couldn't do other work because they need to preserve their nervous systems in a rested state," said Melfi. "But we are quite sure the investment would be more than worthwhile. Think of all we could save in defense spending!"

Melfi had trouble understanding why no one had seized Maharishi's offer of a global utopia. "Maharishi has said that all political attempts at peace have failed and all military attempts have failed. Why wouldn't the world try something that is proven to work and costs so little? It would make every nation invincible."

At the morning press conference the president of MIU and some of the school's leading academic lights would once again plead for some nation—or some billionaire—to volunteer to finance the peace plan. But now, said Melfi, the hour of meditation was nigh. It was time for everyone to go to the domes. Pat Hardigree promised to meet me for dinner. In the meantime, I was on my own.

In minutes I was on the sidewalk in front of the mansion. Looking across the campus from the hilltop, I could see thousands of people walking to the golden domes. They poured out of the dormitories and classrooms, from the student union building and the library. As an early-autumn dusk smothered the campus, a parade of cars, their headlights blazing, worked its way from downtown Fairfield up Route 1 to the campus and the parking lots. These were the meditators who had come to Fairfield to live and work near the domes. They were part of the MIU community, even if they worked off campus, and they attended the mass meditation twice daily, like everyone else.

I was forbidden to enter the domes, so I just stood there, watching the campus shut down. Lights went off in buildings. The last administrator came out of darkened Henn Mansion, locking the door behind him. A few stragglers rushed along the sidewalk. Soon all was quiet. No cars passed on the roadway. No students walked the paths from building to building. In the stillness, I went to my car.

Just a few blocks from MIU, Fairfield bustled in utter small-town normalcy. People hurried in and out of the post office and shoppers visited the stores that lined the town square. I went to a motel, checked in, and sat for a moment on the bed in my room, trying to sort out my reactions to what I had seen and heard. Of course, world peace is a wonderful ambition and I admired the meditators' idealism. But I worried that for the first time in my journey through the New Age, I had encountered, if not deception, delusion on a grand scale. MIU was called a university, but it was not concerned with the academic endeavors that mark real colleges. There was no room for questions, or doubt. And despite all the meditation, there was little bliss evident in my first visit on campus. In four hours I hadn't heard anyone laugh.

I returned to MIU that evening to meet Pat Hardigree in an old gymnasium that housed a fair put on for the Heaven-on-Earth Assembly. The floor of the gym was partitioned like a flea market, with wooden barriers marking off stalls for hawkers. In their various booths vendors offered everything from crystals and gems to special foods marketed under the Maharishi brand name. Other merchants sold cotton clothing (Maharishi recommends all-natural fibers), incense, and books. A meditators' real-estate company offered tours of homes for sale, and Sidha Travel Agency was available to book return visits to Fairfield. The smell of curry wafting from a makeshift kitchen in the rear of the gym added to the bazaar-like atmosphere.

It turned out that Pat Hardigree was required to man the display of books, brochures, and videotapes run by the MIU admissions office. He arranged for me to meet an old friend of his, Michael Howell, a businessman from Florida. Afte we were introduced we bought some Indian food—curry rice and vegetables for him, a sweet yogurt drink called lassi for me—and found a place on the floor to sit and talk.

A tall man with pale skin and reddish hair, Howell wore a suit and tie like every other man in the hall. The women all worse dresses. Everyone at MIU seemed outfitted in a kind of studied normalcy, as if someone had examined what Middle America might look like and then tried to create it. The students and staff I had seen earlier in the day had the same look—uniformly neat, clean, indistinguishable.

"It's not a rule or anything, but Maharishi expects us to dress our best, to represent TM well," Howell said as we settled in. "That's why there are no beards, no long hair. It's a little funny when you think about where we all came from, back in the Sixties."

He was right. Here was a crowd of about four hundred former flower children, men and women who had originally flocked to Maharishi in part because they were rejecting all that conventional society—their parents' society—stood for: the old religion, the old values, the old fashions. But twenty-five years later, they looked just like their parents, right down to their adherence to a suit-and-tie dress code.

As he ate rice and vegetables, Howell tried to explain what he was doing at the conference. "We're here to create coherence. By meditating as a large group, we can impose an order on the Unified Field." That orderliness, he explained, would then dominate world events. Through meditation, and union with the Unified Field, the participants would bring mankind into alignment with natural law, he added. "And the laws of nature are very orderly."

Howell was able to participate in this group meditation because he was a "Sidha," a meditator who had learned the group of practices called "the Sidhis" (pronounced Sid-ees), which make up the advanced TM program. These techniques, which include yoga exercises and meditations, are supposed to lead to yogic flying. They take an hour and a half to complete, and were done, en masse, twice daily during the assembly.

The training to become a Sidha can take months and cost thousands of dollars, compared with four hundred dollars for basic TM training, which is accomplished in a few evening classes. But Howell said TM is such an important part of his life that he never hesitates to sign up for more training. In fact, it had taken him less than two years to become a fully qualified TM trainer.

Howell had been introduced to TM in 1971. He had been discharged from the navy, had grown his hair long, and was touring the country with a friend. They both played guitar and they hoped to become rock-and-roll stars. "I had spent my time going after one thing or another, and then never feeling satisfied when I got it. I didn't want to deal with my family, my friends. But I wasn't sure what I wanted either. But I never felt relaxed, fulfilled.

"Anyway, in Colorado I met someone who was into TM. I went to a free lecture and it made sense." After the lecture came the course in TM. TM is a relaxation technique. A person sits quietly and recites a single word or phrase—called a mantra—over and over, clearing his mind of thought. It takes about twenty minutes and produces a profound sense of relaxation. The mantra is supposed to be kept secret and is given to each student by his teacher. For years TM teachers insisted the mantras were meaningless words, important only for their sounds. In the 1970s the movement's leaders admitted that many mantras were the names of Hindu gods. According to Hindu practice, the chanting of a god's name brings its power to the meditator.

"I liked TM from the beginning and I did it every day," continued Howell. "Pretty soon, I began to feel good inside. I no longer felt that uneasiness. I had found a way to create an evenness in my life. My mind had always been so busy, easily distracted. But after a few days there weren't the ups and downs I had experienced before. I was able to focus much better."

While his friend continued to play music and eventually became a guitarist for several successful bands, Howell gave up the quest for stardom. "I decided I could go back to Florida, back to everything I left behind, like my family. I got home and I actually felt good, even working construction. It all seemed to be the TM, so I said to myself, 'If it's this good, I want more.' That's when I decided to become a teacher."

About twenty years later, Howell is an established member of the American TM community. He had attended countless training sessions and seminars. He even spent five months at a center the Maharishi operated in Spain, during the 1970s. At all these meetings he listened to live and videotaped lectures delivered by the Maharishi, performed countless hours of meditation, and made lasting friendships with other meditators.

"His holiness, he's considered a saint. To be with him is the only way to understand. He speaks in simple terms and yet communicates so profoundly. The pictures you see of him around here are there because he deserves the credit for bringing this knowledge to the world. For thirty-five years he has given his every waking moment to teaching it."

"Would you say TM has given you the sense of peace you were seeking?" I asked.

"Not a sense of peace. Real peace," he said, correcting me. "There's a big difference."

A "real peace" would be also created for the world during the Heaven-on-Earth Assembly, he added. "Efforts at achieving peace through politics have failed. They haven't been able to use military means to create peace either. That's because as long as people aren't peaceful within, as long as they aren't in harmony with nature, someone will rise up and cause problems. But there is a collective consciousness in the Unified Field, and everyone, including Saddam Hussein, is part of it. The TM Sidhi process creates coherence, orderliness, in that field, and it will affect Hussein whether he's aware of it or not.

"We have to try it. Based on the efforts of the past two thousand years, nothing else has worked. We have to do something. We have much better means for destroying the world now than we ever had, with nuclear weapons. In fact, did you read in *Newsweek* recently that in 1983, the Russians really thought Reagan was going to make a nuclear attack? They were considering a preemptive strike. We were on the edge of destruction and nobody knew. By creating coherence, we're going to make conditions where that won't be possible."

In TM, Howell believed he had found a channel for his idealism, something he could do to make the world better, safer. "I'm open to the possibility that it would work, in part, because I've always been open to new ideas," he explained. "Someone might say 'UFOs are baloney.' I say, 'Why not UFOs?'" In TM Howell had also found community of belief, a shelter from a world that seemed dangerously chaotic. "Here the people are very friendly. You feel more blissful," he said, looking around the hall at fellow Sidhas, who were all eating or shopping. "They act like they know you, even if they don't. It feels good."

It was eight o'clock and Howell told me the Heaven-on-Earth Assembly would convene again in fifteen minutes. He was determined to attend every lecture and participate in every meditation during the week-long session. Evening meetings often included entertainment, he said. The night before meditator/actor Eddie Albert, most famous for his role in the TV comedy "Green Acres," had read poetry. "It would be great if you could come with me, but Security would never let you in."

When we walked over to the Grand Assembly Hall, we were met at the door by two linebacker-sized men. They wore business suits and carried walkie-talkies and they checked every person who entered to make sure they had proper, MIU-issued identification cards. When I asked about taking a peek inside the hall, they answered with a firm "No." Over their shoulders I could see people passing through metal detectors, the kind used at airports. Howell said good-bye, then strolled through the metal detectors and disappeared.

The next morning's press conference was held in Carnegie Hall, a brick building with a white-columned entrance that once housed the first Carnegie Library established west of the Mississippi. MIU had converted it into classrooms. The conference room on the first floor was furnished with several dozen wing-backed chairs, all covered in a golden-colored fabric. To the left of the lectern, another golden chair held a three-foot-high framed photo of a tired-looking Maharishi, his drooping eyes circled by dark shadows. He was shown smiling blissfully and holding a red flower. To the right was a small sofa, also golden.

At 11 A.M. Dr. Bevan Morris, MIU's president, stood at the lectern to make an announcement. He was joined by Professors David Orme-Johnson and R. Keith Wallace, who sat on the golden-colored sofa. Before them were thirty empty chairs and four journalists—one from the local paper, the *Fairfield Ledger*, two from local TV stations, and me.

"Today we are here to discuss the offer which his Holiness Maharishi Mahesh Yogi has made to solve the crisis in the Persian Gulf," Morris began. He was a gray-suited walrus of a man, tall and rotund with jowly cheeks and huge dark circles under his eyes, just like the circles under the Maharishi's eyes. His voice, liltingly British, was high, soft, and breathy. He pronounced the word "Maharishi" the way a Hindi-speaker would. He said, "Ma-har-shee," not, "Ma-ha-ree-shee," as most Americans say it.

"We are having for this weekend assembly thirty-seven hundred experts in the advanced program to TM Sidhi and thirty-three hundred other meditators, for a total of seven thousand. We are doing this to create a very big wave of coherence, to create irreversible peace on Earth."

Morris went on to explain that by meditating, the Sidhas and the others would enter the Unified Field and establish a "wave of peace" that would literally becalm the opposing factions in the Middle East. This was not a fantasy, he insisted, but a "technology" proven effective over the preceding decade. In fact, the world was already seeing the results of other mass-meditation projects, said Morris. "The end of the rivalry between the superpowers and the recent great happenings in Eastern Europe are two results of the Maharishi effect," he said. "I was in Berlin when the reunification of Germany took place. It happened after an assembly like this one. In the preceding year [East German leader] Erich Honecker was overthrown on the second day of an assembly." Closer to home, Morris pointed to lowered crime rates in Iowa and even in Fairfield, all caused, he said, by the meditators.

"But clearly the effect is not large enough yet to produce total world peace," he continued. Total world peace would require 7,000 meditators working every day, 365 days a year. The number 7,000 represented the square root of one percent of the world population. It was Maharishi Mahesh Yogi's guess that this number of meditators would be adequate to produce the proper effect. "Maharishi doesn't want to create a passing effect," said Morris. "He wants to create a permanent solution." A permanent solution would be possible, if only someone offered up the $1 billion needed for facilities and salaries for the peacemakers. The Maharishi did not approve of sending a few hundred meditators to areas of conflict—such as the Middle East or Northern Ireland—because the entire world deserved everlasting peace. "We don't want to be like a fire brigade, rushing here and there. But there is no doubt that this is the way to solve the problem of war which, so far, no one in history has been able to resolve either through political or military means."

Morris stopped talking, stepped back from the lectern, and smiled broadly. Seeing no raised hands, he made way for his two star professors, who briefly outlined the "scientific proof" supporting the Maharishi technology. Keith Wallace, a physiologist, reviewed studies confirming the health effects of TM. Wallace is slightly built, with short, receding dark hair, glasses, and a very youthful face. He looked bright, alert, and excited as he discussed changes in metabolism, blood pressure, etc., caused by meditation. Tall, with sandy hair and a mild manner, David Orme-Johnson, a psychologist, reviewed the social science research that he said supported the effectiveness of the Maharishi technology. Again there were references to the scientific studies of TM, but this time the claim was that there were not just three hundred or four hundred but five hundred studies supporting the Maharishi.

While I didn't feel qualified to assess reports on physiology, I felt on firmer ground when considering Orme-Johnson's social science. In brief, he was claiming that half a dozen indicators of social conditions—traffic accidents, the tenor of newspaper headlines, crime reports, etc.—improved when meditators gathered to influence the Unified Field. This had taken place, he said, in Israel and Lebanon during a group meditation intended to employ the Maharishi effect to quiet the armed conflict there.

Taken at face value, the report might seem convincing. If you add statistics indicating reduced fighting in Lebanon as Sidhas practiced in Jerusalem, the notion of a "Maharishi effect" becomes even more compelling. But even if the facts were reported accurately, Orme-Johnson could not claim cause and effect. This is because he could never control, or account for, all the other factors that affect events like traffic accidents and the Lebanon war. Society is not a laboratory where academics can carry out clean experiments. This is why those in the hard sciences—physics, chemistry, biology, etc.—derisively describe their colleagues in the humanities as "so-called scientists." The fact is, no matter how one tries, cause and effect is all but impossible to prove when it comes to human behavior.

Orme-Johnson's claims were preposterous. But when Bevan Morris asked the reporters if they had any questions, no one moved. Finally, after a long silence, a young man from a TV station asked, "Is there anything more you'd like to tell us?"

"Yes," answered Morris. "We hope that you will take this notice and take it especially to the people of the world. Their leaders have not yet responded, but we feel the people would."

That was it.

No further questions came from the local reporters. As I sat, watching, I realized I might not get another opportunity to talk with these men. Working with the campus press office had been a laborious affair. It could take them days to arrange an interview. With this in mind, I raised my hand.

"If you want your offer to be taken seriously, you need to make a credible argument," I began. "But you are making the kinds of claims—claiming to affect the flow of history—that no other academics or scientists would make. How are people supposed to believe this?"

"I'd like to address the concept of collective consciousness and try to make you believe it's possible," volunteered Orme-Johnson. "Think about the atmosphere within a happy family compared with that in a business where there's conflict. You go into the home of a happy family, and you feel it. In a business where there's conflict, you feel that, too. Now, physics says that if there are coherent elements present, they are more powerful than those that are chaotic. They impose orderliness. Similarly, you need relatively few coherent people to create coherence in a society."

Orme-Johnson was suggesting that human beings will behave like atomic particles, falling into line with those who are peaceful and calm. I could see how the presence of peaceful people would influence a society, but that's not what he was claiming. He was saying the effect took place through meditation in the Unified Field. But before I could ask about this, President Morris jumped into the discussion.

"Listen, what we are saying is that here's a situation, once again, where old ideas don't work. There has never been a successful military or political peace. We're saying, 'Try this.' "

This was the fifth or sixth time I had heard the apocalyptic-sounding argument that mankind had never achieved a workable peace. I couldn't resist pointing out the various instances where peace has been achieved, without the help of the Maharishi effect.

Morris grew visibly angry. He came out from behind the lectern and walked among the golden armchairs. He bent over me and jabbed a finger at my face, like a lecturing traffic cop.

"If you have a better idea, a better system for creating world peace, then let's hear it," he said, his voice rising to a shout. "We aren't here to be criticized by those who don't have open minds. Can you offer some proof of any other peace plan that works? Nothing has solved the cause of war! Nothing has eased the suffering! We're offering a solution!"

In the silence that followed, Morris looked around the room like a man who was suddenly discovered to be somewhere he was not supposed to be. I was embarrassed for him, and as he went back to the lectern, I explained why I had questioned his claim.

"I'm not trying to attack you," I said. "But you are making some pretty extreme claims here, and you have to admit that the world isn't responding the way you would hope. No one has come to you with the one billion dollars. Don't you worry that you have a credibility problem?"

Keith Wallace, the calm bespectacled scientist, intervened.

"The credibility problem itself is based on the collective unconscious. There aren't enough open-minded people yet to tip the balance. And besides, whenever there's a really good idea that is unusual, you have a very difficult time convincing people. That's why it's good we live in a world of science, where we can prove ourselves."

"Okay," I replied. By this point I was aware that the local journalists in the room were staring at us. I had turned the press conference into a personal interview. But since I had already crossed the line, I decided to press on.

"MIU goes to great lengths to note it is an accredited university, like every other. But you are the only ones who teach what you teach. Take Dr. Orme-Johnson. He's a psychologist. But doesn't his argument about the Unified Field contradict the foundations of psychology? Even George Bush has said that Saddam Hussein is crazy. But what you are saying is that the fact that a leader is psychotic is irrelevant. Everything is a matter of the Unified Field."

"Well, yes, Maharishi says that underneath the apparent cause of a problem—say, psychosis—there is the deeper cause that's related to the Unified Field," answered Orme-Johnson. "A government leader is the innocent mirror of the collective consciousness of a society. If, through the Unified Field, you change the society, you change the leader."

"So you would say you are rejecting the accumulated wisdom of your profession?"

"I guess I would have to say yes. But they have no proof that anything they say, any of their theories or therapies, really work either."

"Come now. You ought not debate this here," Bevan Morris interrupted. Calm once more, he was again striking the pose of mature university president. "You should sit with these scientists and hear them out. At the very least, any intelligent person such as you would study it fully. That's why we like to have people like yourself here to explore."

Spotting another opportunity to exploit the forum, I then asked Morris to help me with my exploration.

"It would help if I could see something of the Heaven-on-Earth Assembly," I told him.

"Of course. That can be worked out. Contact my office."

With the press conference concluded, the TV reporters packed up their cameras and microphones. The reporter from the *Fairfield Ledger* closed her notebook and hurried away. I lingered to thank the president and the professors for their time. Morris and Orme-Johnson left promptly, but Professor Wallace hesitated a moment. "We should talk more about this," he said. "I don't want you to leave with the wrong impression. I'll get in touch with you through the press office."

The press office had arranged for me to tour the elementary and high schools—Maharishi Schools of the Age of Enlightenment—which MIU operated for the benefit of meditators' children. The university catalog said that these schools "create ideal citizens, individuals who fulfill their own interests and the interests of society simultaneously." Because they learn to access the Unified Field, the catalog explained, these children discover "that all the subjects they study are different expressions of their own intelligence." This struck me as a rather unique approach to education, so, though I was late, I rushed over to the school complex hoping someone would show me around.

The two schools occupied a single L-shaped, three-story brick building in the southwest corner of the campus. The larger wing was new, having opened only a month before I visited. It housed all the younger children, five hundred or so, from kindergartners to eighth-graders. The sixty high schoolers attended class in the older, smaller section of the building. The school was funded by tuition, which ranged from $2,000 per year for a first-grader to $3,350 for a high-school senior.

It turned out that I was too late for the tour arranged by the press office, and the school did not allow visitors to walk around the building unescorted. But elementary-school principal Roxanne Teague was showing a couple of people from the assembly around and I tagged along.

Even at first glance, this was obviously a different kind of school. Posters and charts illustrating the Unified Field Theory had been hung throughout the building, and the Maharishi smiled down from photographs that seemed to be everywhere. This immensely pleased one of the others on the tour, a gray-haired man named Phil. A Californian, Phil was attending the Heaven-on-Earth Assembly and contemplating relocating to Fairfield. He had two young children who would attend the Maharishi school, and he seemed determined, even desperate, to see the school in the best light. In the library, where most of the shelves were empty, he found a few nature books and declared them "a wonderful example of concern for our environment." Upstairs he kept repeating that everything in the school was "so sweet!" The drawings in the art room—"So sweet!" The poster declaring THE WORLD IS MY FAMILY—"So Sweet!" And when Phil saw some letters from Russian students, he pronounced them "so sweet!" as well.

Phil also approved of the uniforms the children wore— blue jumpers for girls, shirts and ties for boys—and he appreciated the strict separation of boys and girls, who occupied separate classrooms. He was also pleased to discover that many of the subjects taught were based on ideas drawn from ancient Hindu scriptures call The Vedas, or "The Truths." Some devout Hindus regard The Vedas as the bedrock of civilization, the source of all knowledge. The Maharishi school combined the interpreted wisdom of The Vedas with more modern concepts in the same way that the Maharishi combined mysticism and physics. The result included courses in Vedic history, Vedic science, even Vedic math.

In one classroom a teacher demonstrated Vedic math with a multiplication problem involving two two-digit numbers. By adding one combination of the numbers and multiplying another, she produced the answer on a single line. Although she insisted that her method was much simpler than standard math, none of us could follow what she had done to arrive at the answer. To help us, she drew four points on the board and a web of lines, which indicated which numbers were to be added and which should be multiplied. I don't think any of us, even Phil, understood.

In other classrooms we saw teachers conducting lectures before quietly attentive children. Our guide wouldn't allow us to speak with any of the students or teachers, but she assured us that the children here were superior students, even though the educational establishment had yet to recognize the value of Vedic education. "Once we show them the research based on what we're doing here," she said, "then they won't be able to pooh-pooh it."

This emphasis on creating a research report that would prove to the world the superiority of the Maharishi school surprised me, but it shouldn't have. After just two days at the school, I had heard countless references to the studies that proved the effectiveness of TM and the "Maharishi Technology of the Unified Field." Seemingly scientific studies were more valuable than anything to the people at MIU. Clearly many in the TM movement were obsessed by this effort to connect science and belief. Why should those who ran the elementary school be any different?

After the tour, Phil asked me about my reaction to MIU. It was the first time anyone there had asked for my opinion about anything, even the weather.

"I feel like I've seen a lot," I told him, "but not what I came here to see, the Heaven-on-Earth Assembly."

"I don't know about that. But if you'd like to see the Grand Hall, I'll show it to you right now."

A white metal shed about as long as two football fields and perhaps one hundred twenty feet wide, the Grand Hall was nestled in a ravine, behind the student union building. There were no security guards at the door when we arrived. The assembly had been interrupted for a lunch break and the meditators were not expected back for two hours. Phil led me inside to a maze of steel shelves flanked by the walk-through metal detectors. Following his lead, I took off my shoes and put them on one of the shelves and followed him through the metal detectors.

On the other side was an enormous white expanse. The windowless shed was illuminated by fluorescent bulbs, and the floor was almost entirely covered by foam mattresses with white sheets. It looked like one enormous, glowing white bed. Each mattress was obviously space enough for a single meditator. On most were little, legless folding chairs, backrests for participants who would spend long hours on their mattresses. All of the chairs faced the long east wall of the building, where a massive altar-like stage had been built.

Seventy feet across and thirty feet deep, the stage was a plushly carpeted, dazzling display of flowers, fountains, bunting, and twinkling Christmas-tree lights. The steps leading up to it were covered with hundreds of potted plants, flowers, shrubs, even little trees. Huge TV sets on both sides of the stage were arranged so people on the floor could see them. Next to them gurgled small fountains, four-foot-wide ponds with jets of water rising about a foot high in a circle. On these jets of water were balanced hollow plastic balls, each painted to look like the planet Earth. Behind the TVs, the potted plants, and the floating globes were rows of golden armchairs, arranged as if for dignitaries. In the center of all this, raised a few feet higher, was a white silk sofa, on which rested a five-foot-high framed picture of the Maharishi. Near the sofa was a large American flag on a staff and a large brass bell inscribed with the words "Bell of Invincibility."

The stage was made to look even more dramatic by the special lighting and decoration that framed it. On the wall behind the stage arched a rainbow fifty feet high, flecked with golden glitter and strung with blinking white Christmas-tree lights. The lights extended out to a ten-foot-wide golden globe that was suspended from the ceiling. They created the illusion of a twinkling awning, suspended over the flower-strewn platform.

As Phil and I sat together on the huge bed that was the floor, it was easy to imagine the Maharishi reclining on the sofa like an Indian prince surrounded by twinkling lights and bright flowers and speaking softly to those gathered around him. This was how the Maharishi was often pictured in the media. It was all very regal, exotic, and luxurious. Phil said that meetings of the Heaven-on-Earth Assembly were about half meditation and half lectures. Some of the lectures were given by the Maharishi, on videotape. Others were given by Bevan Morris and visiting experts. He said the lectures were mostly on the need for meditation and its effect on the Unified Field.

"I sit here now and I can't help think, 'My, how people need this,'" Phil said with a sigh.

Just then a security guard appeared and asked us to leave. Phil and I bounced our way across the foam-covered floor to the metal detectors. As we put on our shoes, he pointed to a very serious-looking man who was speaking into a walkie-talkie.

"Whew, good thing he wasn't here when we came in," Phil said, sounding like an errant schoolboy referring to a grim assistant principal. "He never would have let you in."

Back at Henn Mansion, I quickly discovered that my press conference performance had had the effect of a sharp stick jabbed into a wasp nest. Anne Melfi coolly told me that I was "obviously not getting all the information" I needed to understand the Unified Field. So she had enlisted one of her superiors to help me. His name was Mario Orsatti and he would meet me in the reception room across the hall from her office.

Melfi led me to the reception room, which was decorated like a formal dining room with a large mahogany table and chairs. After showing me a chair, she turned and left, closing the door behind her. For a moment I felt a bit like a child awaiting punishment for some misdeed, but as I waited and waited, I became more angry than anxious. So much about MIU seemed calculated to manipulate. Though he was thousands of miles away, the Maharishi controlled the life-style, finances, and thinking of the staff at MIU. Most sent their children to the Maharishi's school, and they submitted themselves to his rules for eating and dressing. Other New Age leaders wielded tremendous influence, but none that I had seen had such a complete hold on their followers. The MIU people seemed unnatural in conversation and robotic in their carefully contrived ordinariness.

And every encounter devolved into a discussion of Maharishi and his theories.

After a long wait, in came a slightly built young man with dark hair, glasses, and an angular face. He wore a tailored blue suit and a red tie. He had a perfect white smile.

"So, I heard we had a smart Italian guy from the East Coast in here. I'm Mario Orsatti and I'm a pretty skeptical Italian guy from the East Coast myself," he said, flashing a smile and shaking my hand firmly. He told me his family owned a famous restaurant in Atlantic City and that he was a commonsense kind of man. "So, let's you and me talk." He sat down and proceeded to give me an hour-long lecture on the Maharishi, science, and the Unified Field.

"Look, you turn on the light and electricity makes the light come on. It's there for everybody. You don't need a degree in physics to understand it. It just works. The Maharishi technology is the same. It's there for everybody. That's what makes the Maharishi unique. He's saying it's there for everyone, this knowledge. He's a radical. He's saying that this meditation is here for everyone, it works, and it's down-to-earth practical."

Through meditation, Orsatti continued, a person can turn off the intellect and become one with the very basic elements of nature—in essence, blend with its atomic structure.

"Now, imagine you are Alice in Wonderland. Would you do that for me for a minute? You are descending into smaller and smaller levels of existence, down into the atomic and subatomic level. As you fall down, down, deeper and deeper, you see there is nothing but forces, force fields really. When you are there, you can see that this table is an illusion. It's just particles of energy, and the space between the particles is much greater than the particles themselves. At an even smaller level, you encounter the Unified Field. So you can see, the table is an illusion, all of reality is an illusion. The only thing that's real is intelligence. Existence is a field of energy that is intelligence. That's what the Unified Field is."

This was almost more than I could bear. The staff and students at MIU might be accustomed to a social order in which they could be kept waiting in a sitting room for half an hour and then be subjected to an hour-long monologue on an absurd view of physics. It is absurd because Orsatti and the others make the same basic mistake that many philosophy students make when they consider the physics of the atom. They confuse energy with light and thereby conclude that there is no such thing as concrete matter, that the table is not really there. In fact, energy exists as either stored energy—hard stuff such as the wooden table—or as energy in use, such as light or heat. In fact, the table really does exist, whether my mind "makes it real" or not. And it would continue to exist as long as I didn't convert it into energy in use by, for example, burning it to produce heat and light.

But Orsatti didn't give me a chance to discuss the nature of matter and energy with him. He talked too fast for me to interrupt him.

"If you go beyond the subatomic level to the Unified Field," he said, "you discover something amazing. You discover that you are part of the Unified Field."

Here he held up his hands, on either side of his face, cupping his fingers to make them look like puppets.

"When you reach this level," he said, looking first at one hand and then the other, "the observer and the observed become one." He tilted each of his hands, moving them as if they had eyes and were inspecting each other. "The knowledge and knower and the process of knowing are all one."

There was more, but none of it any more convincing. When he finished, Mario asked if I had any questions. I said "No," because I did understand and I didn't want to fall into another difficult dialogue about the basic assumptions of the Maharishi's science. But I did use the opening to push for a look at the Heaven-on-Earth Assembly.

"I still would like to go to one of the assembly meetings. How about tomorrow night? It's the last session."

"Hey, *paisan*," Orsatti answered with a smile. "I'm going

to be singing with a group that night, so I'm going in early. Meet me at the door at eight o'clock. I'll get you in."

As I left Mario Orsatti and Henn Mansion, the sky was turning purple and once again the buildings on campus were emptying and the domes were filling up. Driving back through Fairfield, I stopped at the police station. I wanted to investigate the claim that meditators had created a "wave of coherence" that lowered the crime rate. If that was going to happen anywhere, I figured, it would happen in Fairfield, a city with a larger percentage of meditators than any in the world.

Police Chief Randy Cooksie, an informal young man who wore a bulky sweater and blue jeans, invited me into his tiny back office. There he pulled some records out of a metal filing cabinet. They were annual "call reports," which indicated how many times people asked for police assistance with a crime, accident, or incident. There had been a steady increase through the 1980s, and there was no sign of any slackening in 1990.

"In fact," said Cooksie, "I would say most of our traffic problems have to do with MIU people themselves. They all come from the East Coast and the West Coast, and I swear, they must not enforce the traffic codes there because these people just ignore all the rules. It's not that they aren't intelligent people. But we wind up giving half the tickets we write to MIU people. Maybe they're just caught up in worshiping the Maharishi or something. They sure aren't paying attention to their driving." He said the campus had its share of crimes, mostly theft, and that the three rapes he had investigated in the past year involved either victims, or suspects, from MIU.

Cooksie said he had no serious complaints about the MIU faculty and students in general, but as he considered the meditator's claim that they had lowered the crime rate in Fairfield, he became annoyed.

"If you want to get the whole story," he finally said, "you should talk to some people on the other side." He then gave me the names of several people who had been publicly critical of the university. One was a fallen angel of sorts, a former Sidha named Larry Rails who had formed an organization to support those leaving the TM fold. "Now, he might be really interesting."

The next morning I telephoned Larry Rails to arrange an interview.

"Are you the one in today's newspaper?" he asked.

"I don't know what you mean."

"Well, check the paper and then come over. If you're the one, I'd be happy to see you."

On the front page of the *Fairfield Ledger* was an article about the MIU press conference. Much of it was concerned with the exchange between the university officials and "a New York writer on campus for a week of observation . . . who told the speakers point-blank that he didn't believe their theory."

The article went on to describe my challenges to Morris and company and their reactions to me. The *Ledger* noted that MIU officials are accustomed to skeptics but were taken aback by my questions. Generally "they look upon disbelievers with amused tolerance and write off critics for not being 'enlightened,'" the piece said. "Their response seemed a little more testy Friday."

Larry Rails was holding a thick manila folder under his arm when he met me at the front door of his home. A tall, thin man, with gray hair, a scraggly gray beard, and weathered face, he wore baggy denim overalls and a white T-shirt. The folder contained copies of a newsletter published for what he called "ex-TMers" and copies of various documents that he said revealed "the many deceptions" perpetrated by MIU and the Maharishi.

"It was October 8, 1967, when I went to my first meeting," Rails said as we sat together at his dining-room table. "I know that because they keep a file on everyone who becomes a meditator, and right before I got out, I went and looked at mine.

"Anyway, I was living in California and I had seen a flyer

that said, 'Increase Your Happiness, Expand Your Potential.' Hey, it was Berkeley in the Sixties. Everybody was into that. And this is where Maharishi is so psychologically keen." Rails held up two fingers, making the V-shaped sign for peace. "Remember this? Everybody wanted peace but didn't know how to get it. Then this guy comes along and says, 'I have a way.' If that's what you want out of life anyway, it seems logical to go along.

"Anyway, I got into it, and after five years I realized that I no longer needed marijuana and drugs. I think it's because meditation is a kind of high and you find you don't need the drugs. There's a euphoria you get after real intense meditation that's a lot like drugs. Anyway, it worked for me, like it did for a lot of people. It made it easier to get clean." It worked so well that Rails became a teacher and then a Sidha, practicing the most advanced TM techniques on his own, every day.

Rails, his wife, Barbara, and their daughter, Shanti (Sanskrit for "peace"), moved to Fairfield in response to an appeal by the Maharishi and Bevan Morris. "They sent out several letters appealing to everyone to move to Fairfield or there would be a nuclear disaster. Maharishi used to say, 'The signs are not clear,' and unless we came together to meditate, there would be a big disaster."

The Railses came to Fairfield, enrolled Shanti in the Maharishi school, and supported themselves with a variety of odd jobs. They fell into the pattern of life typical for meditators in town. Parents rise early, drop children at day care at 6:30 A.M., meditate at the domes until 8:30, and then rush to get the children to school by 9 A.M. Evenings are similarly rushed as parents try to finish dinner by 6:30, arrange for a baby-sitter, and then meditate in the domes from 7 to 8:30 at night. On weekends, parents must still find someone to care for their children during morning and evening meditations. And often there are study groups, lectures, and social affairs at MIU after the evening meditation. Attendance is not required, "but they make it pretty clear you should go," said Rails.

In the kitchen Barbara Rails, who had been listening, called out. "It's murder on the kids and it causes a real breakdown of the family." She came to join us in the dining room.

"TM makes you feel like you are someone you are not, that you have limitless capabilities, so you must be too good for any job you get," she said. Her husband nodded as she gave him a sideways glance. "If you structure your own reality, you are like a god. There's no limit to your creativity, your abilities. Why should you listen to your boss?"

Over time both of the Railses noticed that the promises of the movement were rarely achieved. Life was hard for them in Fairfield. The influx of meditators made work scarce and Larry kept losing jobs because of his attitude. Then Barbara developed a serious back problem, which never improved, even though MIU experts insist all meditators can enjoy perfect health. Finally, Larry began to see "that the ideal society they say they are building is far from ideal. I just noticed in the obituaries that TMers die. On campus I could see that they lie and are manipulative." He got nowhere when he tried to discuss his discoveries with others. "I realized that the idea of TM is to make you passive. They have this kind of self-induced hypnosis that's addictive, like a drug."

The drug analogy was apropos. Prolonged, intense meditation can alter the chemistry of the brain. It can produce pleasurable sensations as well as a kind of numbing. "It puts you in a state of euphoria that is like a morphine feeling," Rails recalled. "You get so you want to do it a lot, and you aren't operating on a normal basis. Several people at MIU have had to be involuntarily committed to mental hospitals because they snapped."

(Weeks later I would confirm this claim with court officers in Iowa. And I would read an account of a young woman's nervous breakdown in a first-person book on TM training written by playwright William Gibson. Gibson attended several weeks of training with his son at the same center in Spain where Mike Howell had studied. Gibson writes that even those running the program were worried about the negative psychological effects of an intense form of meditation they called "rounding." TM officials were so concerned about rounding that they carefully limited its practice and kept a psychiatrist on staff to help with those who were damaged by it.)

"If you look at the people in TM, they are mostly people in their thirties and forties who were part of the whole Sixties thing of drugs and dropping out," continued Rails. "I think we needed some kind of escape, maybe because we were the first generation to deal with nuclear weapons, the terror of it. Hell, people take drugs for all sorts of reasons, but mostly to escape reality. It's the same with TM. I think the Maharishi started out with something very good, very innocent. But it's like anything. It gets big, a lot of money comes in, and it gets corrupted. Like this whole thing of saying it's a science. It's not science, it's religion. But they became willing to deceive like that to continue getting the money and power over people."

The papers Rails gave me seemed to illustrate that deception. One relatively minor example was a copy of an MIU advertisement, which claimed that *U.S. News and World Report* had named it one of America's best colleges. Attached was a letter from one of the magazine's editors noting that MIU's claim is "at odds with reality."

More serious was the letter written by the former head of MIU's physics department, Dennis Roark. Roark writes that MIU's entire academic program is based on "crackpot science. There is no evidence or argument that could connect some sort of universal consciousness to be subjectively experienced with a Unified Field of all physics. In fact, the existing scientific work suggests just the opposite." Roark also describes the manufacture of bogus scientific reports by MIU researchers and the suppression of research findings that contradicted the Maharishi's teachings on the power of meditation.

Other damning documents in Rails's file included a report from a former TM movement official to the North-

Central Association of Schools and Colleges, the agency responsible for accrediting MIU. Albert Miller writes of misused funds, doctored studies, and library censorship. Finally, there was a nine-page affidavit from MIU's former legal counsel and director of grants, Anthony Denaro. Denaro charges that the school engaged in "a systematic, willful pattern of fraud, including tax fraud, lobbying problems, and other deceptions." He suggests that MIU's original accreditation as a bona fide university was tainted by the subsequent appointment of the accreditation team's chairman to the school's board of trustees. During the accreditation team's visits, he writes, "the course content, syllabi, course descriptions were so seriously tampered with and camouflaged to make them appear bona fide and academically sound that a willful, systematic fraud was present."

Despite the lawyerese, it was plain that Denaro, formerly a very committed member of the TM community, had been thoroughly disillusioned by his work inside MIU's administration. His affidavit suggests that the deceptions were perpetrated in order to "sell or market TM," and he warned of the risk of "serious psychological and physical trauma" faced by MIU students.

All of these documents, and more, had been compiled by a network of former meditators who were contemplating a lawsuit against MIU and the TM organization. The ex-TMers, many of them former MIU students, believed they had been defrauded by a religious cult disguised as an academic discipline. Perhaps the most prominent member of the group was Albert Miller. Miller lived in Iowa City and, using Rails's phone, I called him and arranged to interview him before leaving Iowa the next day.

"Please push through the deception," Larry Rails said as he stood in the doorway of his home to say good-bye. "It is like Alice in Wonderland. Nothing is what they say it is."

When I arrived back on campus that afternoon, Professor Keith Wallace asked for one more shot at convincing me.

We met at Henn Mansion, in the same formal room where Mario Orsatti had taken me to Wonderland. Although it was Saturday afternoon and classes were over for the week, Wallace met me dressed in a suit and tie, the uniform of extreme normalcy prescribed by Maharishi. Wallace began referring to me as "a very intelligent man." Hearing this again, and remembering that both Bevan Morris and Mario Orsatti had told me how smart I was, I feared another hour-long, hectoring speech. But Wallace was not going to lecture. He said he wanted to tell me that he had been hurt by my questions at the news conference.

"You seemed receptive at first," he said, "but you didn't take us too seriously. I thought that was fine. But then you acted like so many intellectuals who prefer to laugh at us rather than understand. I felt it especially when you asked if we feel isolated here. That left me feeling bad."

I told him I had asked about the professional isolation of scientists at MIU because I wanted to understand the people behind the institution. The MIU faculty routinely challenged the collected wisdom of every academic discipline. I wondered why so many would be willing to take such a risk and endure the professional ostracism that would follow.

Wallace allowed that he had always faced an uphill struggle within the scientific community. Indeed, before 1970, most medical experts denied that there was a connection between the mind and the body. As a student Wallace had published one of the first studies confirming TM's beneficial effects on health. Today it is widely accepted. "But in the beginning, we were going out on a limb. Nobody believed it until they saw the research and it was replicated."

Now, Wallace said, the TM community faced a more serious challenge with regard to the Unified Field Technology. "We know that people laugh at it. But there are people who have an open mind. They support us privately, but not publicly. They won't risk losing their jobs. I used to go to conferences and feel like I didn't know why I was there. Lately there have been more people willing to talk with me, especially in private."

"But how can you be sure they aren't just patronizing you?"

"I can tell. That used to happen, but it's different now." After this brief interlude of humane conversation, Wallace quickly turned to a recitation of the proofs that the Unified Field Technology works, citing all the same flawed studies everyone else at MIU cited. I couldn't help thinking about how much his loyalty to TM had cost him. Bright, articulate, well-educated, Wallace had scored a remarkable success when his first paper was published by a prestigious journal just months after he received his doctorate. But the research for that paper was the last work he would do under the aegis of a major mainstream university. Since then his coauthor, Harvard's Herbert Benson, had published further reports showing that the benefits ascribed to TM could also be achieved through other meditation techniques. Benson had even published a book, *The Relaxation Response*, which teaches readers to chant the word "one" in order to get the same result a TM practitioner gets with a mantra. Benson had gone on to professional prominence. Wallace became the Maharishi's scientist. Inside the movement, he was a shining star, but outside the TM community, Wallace had wondered why he went to professional conferences.

Wallace's choices only make sense when they are viewed as an expression of faith. His sacrifices are insignificant if what Maharishi teaches is true. Faith also explains Bevan Morris's response to my challenges and the dogmatic explanations everyone at MIU offered when discussing the Unified Field. MIU is more like an ancient seminary than a modern college. It exists to foster belief. Much like the scholars at church-sponsored universities of the Middle Ages, MIU's professors blend religion and science quite freely. And when the two conflict, there is no doubt about which will prevail.

This view of MIU and the TM movement as religious institutions was reinforced by what I saw that night at the Heaven-on-Earth Assembly. As he promised, Mario Orsatti met me at the door and escorted me into the Grand Assembly Hall. "I don't want to tell you what will happen," he said, "but you're going to love it."

I sat in a folding chair in a special area near the altar reserved for MIU faculty and guests. The fountains sprayed their streams of water, balancing the plastic globes. The Christmas-tree lights twinkled. Quickly the hall filled with thousands of people, all of them dressed quite formally. The women wore long dresses and the men wore suits. Some even had on tuxedos.

As the well-dressed crowd settled in on the bed/floor, various dignitaries assembled onstage. Bevan Morris, attired in a stunning all-white suit, opened the meeting by introducing the trustees of the university, major benefactors, and longtime meditators who had become respected elders of the movement. Morris also introduced two Indian musicians who would provide the entertainment for an evening that would celebrate the close of the assembly. One played a sitar and the other the tabler—a sort of high-pitched drum. Their music was called Maharishi Gandharva-veda music. Morris explained that the sounds of Maharishi Gandharva-veda music were the same sounds that created the reality of the universe. Listening to Gandharva-veda music was not mere entertainment, he added, it was a way of entering the Unified Field.

Standing up on the altar-like stage, dressed in his white suit, Morris had an air of gentle, prosperous authority. His voice was measured and mellow, but also earnest. He seemed especially earnest when he reported on a telephone call he had received from Maharishi himself, to discuss the Heaven-on-Earth Assembly.

"Maharishi said, 'I want you all to remember that by enlivening the field of consciousness, you are playing a parental role. People may not recognize what we're doing, but it's not their fault. Just go ahead as a parent would, instructing a child who does not seem to listen."

In the audience, hundreds of heads nodded. The meditators appreciated the reassurance. If they thought of themselves as parents to a world full of ungrateful children, perhaps they could continue with their work, even though no one had come forward to fund the seven thousand permanent meditators and no one outside their movement took the technology of the Unified Field seriously. As wise parents, superior to a world full of ungrateful children, they could wait out a long period of childish rebellion. Of course, the meditators I had met seemed too much like children themselves—the Maharishi's children—to be parents to anyone. But if he told them they were parents to the world, then that would be how they would think of themselves.

"And Maharishi said the main effect of this assembly was that you all came back to the self," continued Morris. "You all enlivened the self."

As for the goal of the conference—peace in the Persian Gulf—it seemed Maharishi was experiencing a change of heart. "He said our present mood is that we will cease to be a football of situations or circumstances created by others," Morris told us. "The field of politics is not worth our while to spend half a minute in it. So what we will do is stabilize world peace on a permanent basis, not run after Kuwait. But we won't worry about these things. We have a process for living in a state of enlightenment."

If the Maharishi's message was not enough of a payoff for those who had come thousands of miles and given many days to the assembly, they could take some satisfaction from the report then given by Michael Thompkins, Minister of Information and Inspiration of the Maharishi Government of the Age of Enlightenment. Thompkins recited a long list of world events, news items really, which he said proved the effectiveness of the Heaven-on-Earth Assembly.

"The world is moving very quickly to become a world-unified family," he said. As evidence he cited the reunification of Germany and Albania's opening to international exchanges. "For fifty-one years you couldn't visit Albania. It was stamped right there on your passport. But now you can." (Actually there's no notice about Albania on U.S. passports, but everyone in the audience understood Thompkins's point.)

Turning to Iraq, Thompkins noted a "definite improvement" since the assembly began meditating. "In the Iraq crisis, world unity is strengthening. For the first time, Sweden and Finland joined the economic embargo. The headline in the *New York Times* yesterday was 'Iraqis Hint at Compromise.' " Thompkins went on with more good news from South America, Africa, Central America, and Europe. All of it was due to the Heaven-on-Earth Assembly, he said.

But as Thompkins spoke, a United States ship was chasing an Iraqi merchant vessel, enforcing the embargo of Iraq. Later in the night it would fire across the ship's bow, an act of aggression that would heighten tensions in the standoff over Kuwait. In the weeks to come, President Bush would send one hundred thousand more troops to the region, swelling the American forces there to more than three hundred thousand. The war clouds were, in fact, darkening over the Persian Gulf, but everyone at MIU believed the region was bathed in the light of peace.

Of course, none of this really mattered. This was a gathering of people who required good news, even miracles, to reinforce belief. Thompkins's chief responsibility was inspiration, not information. He gave it to them. Looking out over the thousands of happy-looking faces, I was reminded of a packed church and a congregation listening to comforting Bible stories. The difference here was that the stories were not from Scripture. They were twisted accounts of current events. And the presentation was not a moral lesson or the application of a timeless truth to modern problems. It was, instead, a propaganda effort, an exercise in information control worthy of the old Pravda.

The highlight of the night was to be the Gandharva-veda concert, but before the solemn music began, Bevan Morris made a brief appeal for wealthy meditators to move to Fairfield and become part of a permanent group of seven thousand. "If you can't stay, when you go home, send someone else back here," he pleaded. Then Morris announced a performance by the group he called "the Lifeguards."

The Lifeguards were Mario Orsatti's singing group. He bounded onto the altar carrying a surfboard and accompanied by three other men. They quickly began singing parodies of Beach Boys hits. The first was a takeoff on "In My Room."

> *There's a place where we all go*
> *To maintain world peace*
> *In our domes*
> *In our domes.*

Another was based on the song "I Get Around" and included the following lyrics:

> *None of us guys miss program*
> *'Cause it wouldn't be right*
> *To leave the world in chaos*
> *Every day and night.*

The people in the audience came to life for the Lifeguards. They clapped in time with the beat and some even sang along. And they roared with approval when the group was joined by none other than Mike Love, a member of the Beach Boys, and meditator. Love was dressed in an expensive suit (the TM uniform) that made him look more like a banker than an aging rock-and-roller. But with the parody lyrics in hand, he added authenticity to the group's sound. He also boosted the star-quality of the Heaven-on-Earth Assembly. So what if peace was late in arriving, they had a real-life Beach Boy.

After a half-dozen songs, the Lifeguards ran out of material. Though many in the audience called out for an encore, Bevan Morris firmly ushered the singers off the stage to make way for "the bliss of Gandharva-veda." I slipped behind a curtain and found Mario Orsatti backstage. He was flushed with excitement, out of breath and sweating.

"I loved it," he said. "I could do this all the time. It's so much fun." He told me he had been a theater major in college and had been thrilled by his work on the stage. He seemed wistful as he thought about what he gave up to become a volunteer administrator of a small college in the middle of the cornfields. I asked him why he did it.

"My father, who has killed himself in the restaurant business, asks me the same thing sometimes," he said, laughing. "He doesn't understand. He says, 'Why don't you get a real job?' " Although his father had doubts about his son's career, he supported him enough to send him money to help meet his expenses. And, Mario recalled, when a local priest told his father that his son was involved with a cult, "My father told him, 'What do you know about religion, anyway?'

"He supports what I do, but he can be funny about it, too," Mario continued. "I'll give you an example. I really like cars and he knows it. One day we passed a nice blue Fiat Spyder. It was beautiful.

"He said, 'You like that car?'

"I said, 'Yeah.'

"He said, 'You really like it?'

"Now I start thinking that he's going to buy me one. This was very exciting. So I said, 'Sure, I really do.'

"So he tells me, 'Get a job and buy yourself one.' "

As Mario finished telling me this story, the Gandharva-veda musicians began to play. We stood together and watched their performance for a while. It was pleasant enough. Perhaps with enough experience I could have enjoyed it enough to stay for an entire concert. But after half an hour I arranged to meet Mario for breakfast and then said good night. As I made my way across the giant bed and to the door, I noticed that most of the people in the audience were quietly talking to one another or reading.

Bevan Morris was right. Gandharva-veda music is not entertainment.

My final encounter with the TM movement—or rather, with its effects—took place the next day at a subsidized housing project for the elderly in Iowa City where Albert Miller lived. Miller had been manager of operations for the Capital of the Age of Enlightenment in Fairfield. Several such "capitals" are located around the world. They operate as field offices and training centers for the TM movement. The one at MIU is one of the largest.

A small, white-haired man with blue eyes and a stubble of white whiskers, Miller met me at his door dressed in shirt, shorts, and high white athletic socks. His home was cluttered with books, magazines, and filing cabinets filled with documents relating to MIU, TM, and Maharishi. By the window was a small desk with a typewriter. He made some tea and, as it steeped, went to his filing cabinets and began pulling out documents. The first was the long letter he had written to the Midwest accrediting agency, charging fraud at MIU and urging an investigation. There were other affidavits, newspaper clippings, articles from Indian magazines, even scientific critiques of the Maharishi's theories of consciousness and physics. While all of these papers made up an impressive indictment of the TM movement, Miller's tales of personal experiences were more illuminating.

"I started in 1971, in Laguna Beach, California," he said as he moved about the cluttered apartment gathering papers. "I had gone through a divorce. I was lonely. And I found the TM movement to be wonderful therapy. It settled my mind. I became more focused and for the first time in my life felt a calmness. I had been through a lot, including childhood traumas, and nothing worked like TM. It was instantaneous relief and I said, 'Wow, this really works.' "

Figuring that if a little meditation did wonders, a great deal would work miracles, Miller studied advanced meditation techniques and went on several TM retreats. "I noticed that some people had strange reactions to the intense meditations—roundings, we called them. They would go off someplace and not know how they got there. They would sometimes talk incessantly. I didn't think much of this until it happened to me.

"I was working in an engineering office at the time. I had been to a three-day weekend retreat where we did six hours of meditation a day. I went home when it was over and went to bed. The next morning I got up and drove to work. In all that time I didn't talk to anyone. Then, when I saw my secretary, I said 'Good morning' and just kept on talking. I couldn't stop. The more I tried to stop, the more I talked.

"It was nonsense, what came out, but it made me feel very strange, paranoid even. The more I talked, the more intense my feelings became. I was aware of myself being different, not normal, but I couldn't change it. I just made myself leave the office and go home."

At home, Miller recalled, "I spent two days trying to get a hold of reality." He had recurring hallucinations of being lost at sea, swimming against a strong current and being drowned. Gradually the hallucinations went away and he returned to work.

"I told my TM teacher about it and he said it was all a good thing. 'You got rid of some stress,' he said." The experience had chastened him, but Miller decided that he had probably just done too much rounding. After a break of a few weeks, he resumed his daily meditation and he continued to be a TM enthusiast.

In 1983, when he retired, Miller moved to Fairfield to spend a few months in residence as a nonregistered student. At any one time, as many as a thousand such part-time students are at MIU attending the "Creating Coherence Program." They pay two hundred dollars per month and perform a few hours of work each week in exchange for room, board, and classes. The students are like monks,

spending hours in the domes and otherwise living very as-
cetically. Some eventually join the Parusha, Maharishi's
corps of celibate monks, or Mother Divine, a similar group
for women.

Though he didn't feel called to be a Parusha, Miller nevertheless found a niche that would allow him to live in the
safe haven that was the MIU community. Starting as a four-
hour-per-week laborer, he worked his way up to director of
operations for the capital. His ascent was easy, he recalled.

"They didn't know the first thing about business, and the
physical plant was falling apart because everyone was too
spaced out from meditating to do the work. Nothing was
getting done." Contrary to what I had been told by Mario
Orsatti, Miller said, "everything there was always screwed
up. If they had a banquet, the food arrived three hours
late. They couldn't get the laundry to run right or the cafe-
terias. And from what I heard, putting up those domes was
a disaster."

Miller blamed the incompetence he witnessed at MIU on
the long-term effects of intense involvement in the TM
movement. Everyday meditators can use the twenty-minute
TM routine to focus their lives. Those who commit much
more time and effort to TM "start seeing their options narrow," he said. "Those who are heavily into it for years and
years stop questioning, stop thinking. They don't seem very
capable of working outside TM. And they seem to believe
everything the Maharishi says. I was getting like that. I had
my doubts, but I didn't question any of the teachings, because they came from Maharishi."

It was an odd series of events that broke Miller's compla-
cency. On a visit to the MIU library, he checked out several
books by Indian sages whose interpretations of ancient
Hindu scriptures were different from Maharishi's. He returned the books and then, weeks later, noticed they were
missing from the shelves. When he asked about the books,
he was told they had been removed from the collection. He
protested, but the librarian was steadfast. Those books had

been banned. This censorship made Miller question MIU's status as a university, and it quickly led him to give thought to long-buried doubts about the whole TM movement. When officials on campus refused to answer his questions, Miller embarked on an investigation that led him to develop a new view of the Maharishi and his work.

"The original work Maharishi did, in India in the 1950s, described TM as a religious movement," he said, handing me a copy of "Beacon Light of the Himalayas," a 1955 booklet published by Maharishi. (A close reading does show that "Beacon Light" promotes TM as a strictly religious and spiritual practice.) "The Maharishi came to the U.S. and promised everybody the moon, everything short of physical immortality. But when TM started to slump, he saw it had to be repackaged. That's where the science part came in. Keith Wallace got his paper published and the Maharishi had an opening. Wallace didn't falsify his data, but he didn't use rigid controls. Since then the same results have been achieved by people doing different kinds of meditation."

Having discovered the books, articles, and studies that conflicted with MIU's claims, Miller felt the anger of a betrayed believer. "I wouldn't care if they were honest and said it's a form of meditation that works and that the philosophy is based on Hinduism," he said. "It's the deceptive packaging that bothered me. MIU is no more a college than Clown College."

In this new light, Miller understood the dazed attitudes and bizarre behavior he had often witnessed at MIU. "There were a lot of people there suffering from too much meditation, or rounding. They would babble incoherently, on and on. Some even made sexual advances in the wrong setting. But everyone just ignored the way they acted. No one helped them. They just denied it was going on."

Following his disillusionment, Miller left MIU but for a while continued to live in Fairfield. He wrote many letters to the editor of the local paper, criticizing MIU's claims and critiquing the paper's coverage of the school. He became well-known among former meditators, and MIU students who were experiencing crises of faith contacted him frequently. But he felt alone and isolated in Fairfield. Former friends treated him coolly and the prospects for establishing new friends seemed dim. He moved to Iowa City, where the University of Iowa is located, hoping the college town would be a good place to start life over. "But I'm not a very outgoing person, so I can't say I have many friends here," he told me. "The TM movement gives you instant friends, instant connections. I've lost all that now."

Albert Miller had paid a price for his intellectual integrity. At age sixty-six, far from his home in California and low on money, he again faced the loneliness that had first compelled him to join the movement in 1971. "No one is lonely and isolated at MIU. People act very supportive, except if you have doubts. Then you have to leave."

My odyssey in Iowa ended in Albert Miller's subsidized apartment. He gave me a long list of other dissenters, but I didn't need any more evidence to prove that MIU, TM, and the Heaven-on-Earth Assembly were not what they seemed. What I needed was to make sense of what I had discovered. The Maharishi had been one of the first to suggest that the Sixties generation could forge an age of enlightenment. His ideas about meditation and personal growth had led directly to the broad social and spiritual development called the New Age. He had helped many Westerners recover their sense of spirituality and sacredness, and he had awakened us to the connection between mind and body. At the Heaven-on-Earth Assembly, I had hoped to see his philosophy turned outward, to accomplish some idealistic purpose. Instead I had found a place of illusion and delusion, where individuality and creativity were blunted and human insecurities were exploited.

Of course, power and money do corrupt, and what happened with the Maharishi might be expected. According to a *Times of India* article that Albert Miller gave me, the

Maharishi's holdings are worth about three billion dollars, more than enough money to lead a man astray.

But the deception I uncovered at MIU was more disturbing, on a personal level, because the people I met there were somewhat like me. They were educated, seemingly open-minded, and idealistic adults. They were well aware of the challenges that science and reason posed for religion, but they still ached for spiritual comfort. So they had sought a middle ground, a spiritual practice supported by empirical fact. Such a middle ground would appeal to me. I, too, have been disillusioned by the conflict of reason and religion, and I also feel the hunger for spiritual comfort and community. I would have welcomed the discovery of a middle way, a path to spirituality that was consistent with reason.

But TM, as it is practiced at MIU, isn't a middle ground. It is like the worst of religion: unreasonable, repressive, authoritarian. And knowing this, I had to acknowledge that these people, my peers, were vulnerable and fragile human beings. They were as vulnerable as any of the born-again Christians who were duped by TV evangelists in the 1980s. They were just as fragile as the frightened, impoverished believers who sent millions of dollars to the Depression-era radio priest Father Coughlin, who preyed on the fear and disillusionment of his time.

For the first time in my travels through New Age America, I worried that I was observing a cult rather than a culture. None of the followers of Lazaris or Louise Hay had given over so much to a leader or a group. MIU and the Maharishi would take control of everything—right down to matters of food, shelter, and child-rearing—for the most devout.

What would lead a person to the Heaven-on-Earth Assembly and MIU's vain attempt to control the universe with the Unified Field Technology? The true believers obviously fear that humankind is incapable of solving its problems. They are so certain of this depressing view that they can take no comfort in such hopeful events as the reunification of Germany unless they credit the Maharishi. And they are so disillusioned that they believe that only something as fanciful as a Heaven-on-Earth Assembly can forestall nuclear annihilation.

The meditators' responses to these insecurities have followed a predictable path. They have accepted rigid, authoritarian control in exchange for security. Far from being a place where individuals grow and innovate, the Fairfield TM community is regimented and constricted. Everyone treks to the vast, whitewashed domes morning and night, seven days a week. The Maharishi's teachings, right down to the Sunday-best dress code, are accepted by all. All conflict, doubt, perhaps even all genuine emotion, is stifled and covered over with a pleasant veneer. As Mike Howell said, "They act like they know you, even if they don't."

The regimentation extends to include the meditators' children, who are consigned to schools where boys and girls are separated, children wear uniforms, and the visage of the bearded guru smiles down from the classroom walls. One might argue that these children are no more affected by their isolation than students in any other private school, but it is more reasonable to expect that their adjustment to the outside world will be long and painful. Regular college will be difficult for anyone indoctrinated in the Unified Field Theory as interpreted by the Maharishi. Relationships with nonmeditators, and life in communities other than Fairfield, will pose real challenges. No doubt some of these children will feel compelled to rebel in ways that are so extreme that even parents who were young rebels themselves in the Sixties will be shocked.

All of it—the hunger for orderliness, the strict control of debate, the massive denial of doubts, the blind fealty to TM's hierarchy—is a complete repudiation of the values of the 1960s. Gone are the notions of self-expression and creativity. Gone is the mistrust of power and control. They are replaced by conformity and a kind of comfort.

The most troubling part of all of this is the squandering of so many lives. The people who are drawn to the Maharishi and his message of hope include some of the best and the brightest. Beneath the buttoned-up suit and behind the fixed smile, Mario Orsatti is a lively young man with no small amount of show-biz talent. He is intelligent enough to recognize the futility of materialism and he is sensitive enough to search for meaning in an age of unbelief. Perhaps it was the fear of following his father to an overworked old age. Maybe it was his reluctance to face the long years of failure and uncertainty that await every would-be actor. Whatever the reason, like the others, Orsatti has followed his leader into a retreat from reality. With the Maharishi, they have turned Transcendental Meditation, the tap root of the New Age, into a grandiose, narcissistic dream, a form of intellectual bondage, which they call enlightenment.

# 7 · NEW YORK CITY

## Cruising the Expo

FOR THE MOST PART, THE NEW AGE IS CONCERNED WITH making life lighter, with healing, even playful pursuits. Even the most devout can laugh about the sillier aspects of "past life" theories or channeling. In contrast, the relentless, blue-steel certainty of the Maharishi's followers was humorless and cold. And as I left Fairfield, I longed for the earthy, flawed, thoroughly human kind of adventures I had had in other quarters of the movement.

Fortunately, I returned to New York in time for the opening of the largest New Age fair in the country, the Whole Life Expo. A sixteen-page program announced a schedule of more than a hundred speakers, everyone from Timothy Leary, the counterculture cheerleader of the Sixties, to Bernie Siegel, surgeon and evangelist for love and miracles. Besides the lectures, there would be literally hundreds of sales booths offering all-natural food, crystals, "brain spa" machines, even something called "Angelic Technologies." The Expo promised the variety, magic, and hope that were more characteristic of the New Age than the severe atmosphere of MIU. On a cold and wet Saturday morning, the Expo had transformed the New York Penta Hotel into a glittery, swirling, spiritual carnival.

Most glittery of all were the star children. In a large banquet room that was jammed with displays and browsing people, the star children shone as if spotlights followed their every movement. They wore bright white robes and halos made of thin wire and hundreds of little silver and gold stars, the paper kind that elementary-school teachers paste on the best of my daughters' homework.

I followed a haloed man to a small booth, made of folding tables, where dozens of people were buying the paper-star headgear—five dollars per halo—and picking up literature published by an organization called Star-born Unlimited. A tape player on the table broadcast a kind of theme song for the group:

*We are all angels*
*Bringing love to everyone.*

A white-robed young man named Steve told me that Star-born Unlimited is an organization of people "who know they originated somewhere else in the universe." The Star-born are preparing for an evolutionary leap forward, which would take place before the millennium. Soon, he said, Earth would be transformed by a number of planetary events, similar to the 1987 Harmonic Convergence. The Star-born were looking forward to "the 11:11," he said. "It's a door, an entrance into a new dimension, a new energy where we'll have a thousand years of peace." The 11:11 would open, making this ascendance possible, on January 1, 1992. It would close on December 31, 2011.

It was difficult to talk among the crush of people seeking to buy halos, and Steve had to return to twisting wire and pasting stars. The demand was far exceeding the supply. I grabbed a pamphlet which explained the Star-born in more detail. It says the Star-born are led by a prophetess named Solara, who has written a series of books about the Star-born. Solara has called for a gathering of 144,000 Star-born souls at the Great Pyramids of Egypt in January 1992. By gathering together, these people from the stars would open "The Doorway of the 11:11," allowing for "our mass ascension into new realms of consciousness." Until then, the pamphlet says, we could prepare by forming groups, reading Solara's books, listening to her audiotapes, attending semi-annual "Angelic reunions," and donating our time and money to Star-born Unlimited.

The idea of star people was not new to Solara. The New Age idea that many humans have descended from space creatures goes back to 1976 and a book, *Gods of Aquarius*, by author Brad Steiger. Steiger, a former English teacher, first began writing short stories for fantasy magazines in the 1960s. Since then he has published more than a hundred books on UFOs and psychic phenomena. In *Gods of Aquarius,* Steiger concludes that beings from other galaxies have interacted with humankind since prehistory. "Star People," Steiger writes, are the product of human matings with these visitors. Their purpose is to help the world through a coming "Great Purification," which would be something like the battle of Armageddon expected by some Christian fundamentalists. While the fundamentalists believe Armageddon will be followed by the Second Coming of Christ and one thousand years of peace, Steiger writes that after the Great Purification, humans would enter a New Age of enlightenment. In subsequent books Steiger published predictions of worldwide famine (1982), a pole shift (1982–84), World War III (1982–85), and Armageddon (1989).

The 11:11 theory of the Star-born builds on Steiger's conclusions and establishes a practical framework for action. And while there is a decidedly commercial bent to the Star-born organization, it also offers some soothing New Age benefits. As the pamphlet says, believers become part of a "Starry family," a select group with a grand purpose in life.

"Knowing that you are an Angel consciously serving on Earth definitely lightens your burdens and clears your path." Of course, few of the people who bought the halos (Angelic Technologies) seemed much interested in the 11:11 or the work of being an angel. Most just liked the shiny, star-covered hats.

From the Star-born halo table I wandered through a warren of displays for spiritual wonders and miracle cures. I listened for a few minutes as a crystal salesman from Sedona answered questions from a female customer. He turned rough-cut crystals into amulets tuned to the "vibrations" of each buyer. The amulets ensured good health and good fortune. Of course, it wasn't necessary to custom-order. If one of the ones on display appealed to her, he said, it was probably a perfect vibrational match. The amulets cost between twelve hundred and two thousand dollars.

At another booth, a young woman named Kathy grabbed my arm and thrust a little plastic cup into my hand.

"Drink it, go ahead, drink it. You'll feel better."

The substance in the cup looked like molasses and smelled like compost.

"But I don't feel bad."

"Drink it anyway. It makes everyone feel good. You'll feel more energetic and sleep better at night. Haven't you read about the cancer rate? Aren't you concerned?"

I took a swallow. It tasted like it smelled.

"What does it taste like to you?" asked Kathy.

"Decaying plants."

"Right! That's because it's made from plants."

Kathy was selling a drink called Km, which is a combination of potassium and fourteen different plants (K is the atomic table's symbol for potassium). According to Kathy, Km is like rocket fuel for the body. "And even if you don't need it, you need it." At Kathy's insistence, and in order to get away from her sales pitch, I entered my name in a raffle for a free bottle of Km, worth thirty-two dollars.

After buying an all-natural strawberry soda to wash the

taste of Km out of my mouth, I quickly looked at a few more exhibits. Several booths were selling "brain machines"—heavy goggles that create a miniature light show and headphones that play special meditation music. Other vendors offered vibrating water beds, or photographed and interpreted your "aura." A Polaroid picture of my aura—it was a yellowish light around my head—showed I was "intuitive, healthy, and spiritually grounded," said the man who stood me in front of a lighted curtain and snapped the picture. I took his interpretation as a compliment.

With all the hawkers and gawkers turning the convention floor into a frenzy of trade, I headed for one of the hotel conference rooms and the first of three lectures I planned to attend. At twenty-seven dollars per ticket, I had chosen my seminars carefully. The first would be Timothy Leary's free-form talk, which had the rather grandiose title of "American Culture, 1950 to 1990." After a brief break I would then explore the burgeoning men's movement with John Lee, a psychotherapist and author of books on men. Last I would try to get in to see Dr. Bernie Siegel, who, according to the woman who sold me the ticket, was the hottest draw on the program.

Timothy Leary was not a big attraction. Only about fifty of the three hundred seats set up in the meeting room were occupied when I arrived. A few more listeners straggled in before the start of the lecture, but even with them, Leary came into a room where the empty chairs far outnumbered the people.

He looked surprisingly old. Of course, everyone has aged since the Sixties, but Leary, the counterculture rebel and champion of psychedelics, looked, well, frail. He was extremely thin, and the skin of his face was stretched taut over a beak of a nose and a jutting chin. His cloudy blue eyes were shaded by deep sockets.

"I became seventy years old Monday," Leary began. He hunched over the lectern in a way that made his brown wool sweater bag at the shoulders. "Perhaps you will indulge me in expressing a feeling welling up in my mind and my heart this week. In three score and ten years on this planet I have never seen a situation where everything seems so fucked up."

The audience howled approvingly at Leary's profanity.

"I read the *New York Times* and think it would be a Monty Python comedy if it weren't so real.

"I debate Gordon Liddy a lot these days, and if there's one thing we agree on, it's that the system isn't working. At the same time, I have to say I've never seen so many good things happen, like in Eastern Europe. There are real revolutions taking place, and they are led not by generals with airplanes but by kids in running shoes.

"Now, I read in the paper that several hundred Russian born-again Christians are coming to the U.S. to convert us. Doesn't that boggle the mind? Doesn't it all boggle the mind? I am becoming convinced that in the countdown to the year 2000 everything will just get crazier and crazier."

Millennial fear, social confusion, portents of gloom. So far, Leary wasn't saying anything different from other New Age prophets. The world is in crisis—threatened by pollution, nuclear weapons, AIDS, famine, take your pick—and only the dawning of a New Age would save it. But then he offered his solution, and it was, in terms of the New Age movement, unique.

"It's technology," said Leary, sounding like the businessman in the film *The Graduate* who declares that "plastics" are the key to the future. "Within four or five years, certainly within ten years, an avalanche, a wave of new technologies, is going to wash over the world. The Japanese electronics industry is out of control. Soon we're all going to have home film-editing/idea-processing equipment that is all hand-held. Information will be pouring out of fiber-optic cables and into our homes cheaper than water. A new language will appear, a multimedia symbolic language that will use letters as icons. And a poor kid in Harlem who wants to talk to someone in China will be able to do it in an instant, for pennies. That's power!"

In a disjointed and halting way, Leary went on to describe the development of a new approach to computers called virtual reality. Virtual reality is what the phrase suggests, a nearly real world created by powerful computers to be manipulated by human beings. Some virtual-reality computers have already been developed. In these systems, earphones and huge goggles with 180-degree computer screens inside are connected directly to powerful computers. You put on the earphones, the goggles, and a special glove, which is lined with sensors that are also connected to the computer. When the machine is switched on, you get the sensation of entering a make-believe world, which you can manipulate with a wiggle of the head or the flick of a finger.

With these machines, students reading Twain would be able to crack open the text like an egg and see images of Tom Sawyer or Huck Finn. They could talk to the characters, make a film of the book, or change the plot to see what would happen. All of this would be done in virtual reality. These kinds of machines will bring about the global village envisioned in the 1950s and '60s by Marshall McLuhan, said Leary. McLuhan argued that every epoch of social development was marked by changes in communication technology. Movable type created the era of print, which lasted until the advent of radio and TV. In the coming century, McLuhan said, electronic media—TV, radio, computers—would bind together people who are scattered around the globe. He predicted the rise of an international "information society" less constrained by political boundaries, language barriers, and cultural differences.

This is the New Age of Timothy Leary. And it flows directly from his acid-dropping days in the Sixties. "Virtual reality is like LSD, but better. All this technology is going to encourage and empower the diversity of people." It will also bring them together. People will meet and share adventures in Virtual reality. "My brain wants to get in touch with other brains," said Leary, "and most of all, it wants to do it through the eyes."

From this more or less coherent monologue, Leary proceeded to take questions from the audience. Suddenly we were back in the Sixties, a place most of his questioners apparently never left.

"What new, better drugs are being developed for mind expansion?"

"Oh, there is wonderful research going on, into all sorts of designer drugs. Of course, if one-half of one percent of the money being used for the drug war were spent on research, these better drugs would be here already."

"How about dedicating your lecture to John Lennon?"

"Do you know that when Yoko was in Moscow, Gorby told her, 'Isn't it a shame we don't have John here to sing "Give Peace a Chance?" ' My wife, John, Yoko, Tommy Smothers, and I sang the first version of 'Give Peace a Chance.' And he called me to sing it with them at the 'bed-in' for peace."

Leary talked about his drug arrests and prison terms served in California. "I felt honored. The Sixties was a great time to be in prison." There were also meanderings about immortality and the nature of the soul. "The soul is in the brain," Leary pronounced. "But it's not physical. It's energy, like electrons. Sticks and stones may break your bones, but electrons will really fuck up your brain."

Eventually someone announced that Leary's time was up. He departed with the kind of parting shot that seemed designed to mollify hostile conservative audiences at the Gordon Liddy debates. It was corny and sentimental and surprising.

"You know, I consider it my duty to lug my brain around and experience life. Like Lou Gehrig, I feel like I'm the luckiest guy who ever lived. America's still a heavenly place to live and we're lucky to be here."

I had just a few minutes to grab a vegetarian egg roll at one of the vendors' stalls and get back to the meeting room for my second twenty-seven-dollar lecture. But as I followed a shortcut across the convention hall, I couldn't help but notice large crowds gathered around televisions at two of the Expo booths. A close look revealed that one TV was showing a videotape of literally hundreds of naked people romping around at a nudist camp. The booth was for the Metro Naturist Society. Across the aisle a larger crowd was gathering around a TV set displaying a graphic tape of an extremely athletic man and a remarkably flexible woman having sex. A sign at this booth announced THE TANTRA SOCIETY and its *Jewel in the Lotus* video.

I didn't have time for a close study of the *Jewel in the Lotus*. It would have taken too long to work through the crowd. But the signs at the display table said that for a fee, the society would teach anyone exotic Hindu sexual techniques that would lead to spiritual and sexual ecstasy.

I had my sights set somewhat lower. As I walked into the Georgian Ballroom, John Lee was already explaining "what's going on with men today." Actually, he was talking about some men, those involved in the "men's movement" fostered by Robert Bly. Bly rejects both the macho-man image and the overly sensitive feminist man, raising up, instead, the ideal of a strong but gentle, assertive yet intelligent, self-assured male. This ideal is the goal of the New Agers, the intellectuals and the psychologically oriented, who make up the bulk of the men's movement.

Just as feminism begins with scathing critiques of society's mistreatment of women, the men's movement starts with an analysis of the constrictions the culture places on men. Bly observes that boys raised in the typical American family are denied meaningful contact with fathers, who spend nearly all their waking hours out of the home. They are left to define manhood for themselves, and usually rely on media images and fleeting glimpses of the men in their lives in order to accomplish this task. As adults, these self-made men are insecure, anxious, unable to trust other men. They inhabit a lonely world of incessant competition where they survive by muting their emotions, becoming half-alive, machine-like beings. And then they wonder why their friendships, marriages, even their relationships with their children, seem hollow.

The men's movement got a big boost in the summer of 1990 when the *New York Times Magazine* published a long feature article on a weekend-long gathering of men in Texas. Many men wrote letters to the magazine to comment on the article. Some described the members of the movement as "life's losers" or men unable to take individual responsibility for their lives. Others greeted the arrival of the movement as a sign that some men were looking for fuller, more satisfying lives outside stereotypical roles.

The latter assessments, and much of what Robert Bly has written, ring true with me. As a child of the Fifties and Sixties, I grew up in a world largely abandoned by adult men. Weekends and two-week vacations were not enough for me to learn from my father all I needed to know about being a man. Instead, I guessed my way along, watching him, reading, studying television. This was not something I understood until I read Bly's work. But I felt, as I read, that I could have made each of his points. And several of my friends who are in their thirties and forties also believe Bly's writings illuminated their lives.

A gregarious Texan with salt-and-pepper hair and a full beard, John Lee is a disciple of Robert Bly. Although he is director of the Austin Men's Center, he is best known for his book *The Flying Boy*. An account of his own failing efforts at love, *The Flying Boy* follows Lee's discovery that many of his emotional problems could be traced to his ideas about the nature of men. The son of a rageful alcoholic, Lee had grown up believing that real men don't show love, never make commitments, compete with every man in sight, and accept a lifetime of stoic isolation.

"What's the number-one game we little boys—four or five years old—played more than any other?" Lee asked the audience of about two hundred people.

No one raised a hand.

"Oh, come on. We played this game night and day, every day."

A few of the women in the audience suggested baseball and football. Lee shook his head and then walked over to one of the men in the front row.

"Any man can tell you. Watch."

The man stood up and said one word: "war."

"That's it," said Lee. "We might have called it army, or cops and robbers, or cowboys and Indians. Whatever we called it, we pretended to kill our friends or got killed ourselves every day. We were little boys—four, five, six years old. Those are the years when you learn everything, and we were killing or getting killed, every day."

By pretending to kill, over and over, boys prepare their psyches for all the competitions of adult male life, up to and including actual combat. War-play is the best way to learn how to numb your feelings, said Lee. Society demands this of boys because, as men, they may have to carry out some awful duties.

"The play helps make it possible to do the real thing one day, say in the Persian Gulf of the desert of Saudi Arabia. That's why the leading toys for boys are still military related: guns, knives, plastic machine guns. The little boys are preparing to fight, kill, and die, if necessary. If you don't believe it, watch them. You know, way down inside, I still have these ideas about how, if I'm ever captured, I'll be able to escape from the prison camp."

The steady numbing or desensitizing of male children is also accomplished through shame, ridicule, beatings, and rejection. The process is not selective. Eventually it anesthetizes men to every emotion. "The result of this is most men cannot feel their feelings most of the time. They think instead," added Lee. "Men think a lot. They even think when they're having sex. They say to themselves, 'I know how to do this. I know the techniques. Hey! Wait a minute. I'm about to have an orgasm. Maybe I'll do some multiplication.' "

When the audience stopped laughing, Lee described his own life as a shut-down, emotionally paralyzed man who had been unable to sustain relationships despite a deep yearning for love. He quoted Austrian psychoanalyst Alice Miller, whose many books were eagerly consumed by many in the New Age. Miller argues that most adults replicate the abuse of their own childhood when they raise their offspring, practicing a "poisonous pedagogy." Lee said that his mother "looked into my eyes to see a savior, a husband, a genius, anything but the little child that I was."

The journey to emotional awakening begins with a confrontation with the painful past, Lee continued. "Here is where I depart from a lot of New Agers. They always want to go up, ascend. They don't want to go down. They don't want to feel the fact that they were 'incested' at age five. They don't want to feel the abuse of the alcoholic father.

"When I started to do this, it was powerful. I took a plastic bat and a pillow and I just started to beat it, like it was my dad. I said, 'I hate you, you son of a bitch,' over and over. Tears were streaming down my face and then I said, 'I hate you, because I loved you so much and you weren't there.'"

All this was fairly basic modern psychology, but it was presented in a way that seemed to touch the men in the audience deeply. They sat in rapt attention. It is practically a cliché to say so, but American men remain, for the most part, a constrained, silent species. And Lee was probably correct in his assessment of their silent suffering: the price they pay for the loss of their emotions. In this crowd, Lee's story moved some to tears. It prompted others to speak of how they were abused, abandoned, or neglected. One man mentioned that he had been just three years old when his father left his family. Another spoke of being berated and humiliated. Several mentioned their inability to succeed in love and marriage.

"Is there any wonder?" asked Lee. "How many of us had good models for relationships? How many were told how to tenderly love a woman? This is what my father said on sex: 'Get as much as you can, as often as you can, but don't get 'em pregnant.' Thanks a lot."

The personal anecdotes gave Lee's "workshop" the quality of a twelve-step meeting. Twelve-step groups—fashioned after Alcoholics Anonymous and its "twelve steps for recovery"—are becoming increasingly popular. Loosely connected to holistic health and the New Age movement, these groups rely on highly emotional storytelling, in which participants reveal their history of struggling with one tormenting addiction or another. The programs are vaguely spiritual—one of the steps calls for reliance on "God or a Higher Power"—and they make use of prayer and meditation. They can be effective, mostly because they provide a community of support for difficult personal change.

The twelfth step of AA encourages members to bring others into the group, and Lee concluded his presentation with a similar pitch for the men's movement. "A woman can't model healthy male behavior for me. Only other men can do it," he explained. Then he said, "Thank you. If anyone wants to give me a hug, that's great for me."

I glanced back as I left for the next seminar. More than a dozen men were lined up to embrace John Lee. They would get and give only the most fleeting kind of support, but the contact would be a signal of approval and encouragement for their reassessment of maleness. What more could you expect from an hour-long introduction to a process that could take a lifetime?

Upstairs, Bernie Siegel was about to begin a discussion of "Peace, Love, and Healing." Siegel is the biggest star in the field of New Age healing. Like many, he might be a bit uncomfortable with the New Age label. He tends to emphasize his credentials as a surgeon formerly affiliated with Yale University. But Siegel's message of spiritual healing resonates with New Age concepts. The doctor is a staple for New Age magazines, gatherings, and institutes. He is a regular at Omega and a headliner at every Whole Life Expo. He is quoted by Louise Hay and courted by every New Age author eager for a book-jacket endorsement.

But Siegel is also an important "crossover" figure. He has brought New Age, holistic thinking to millions of mainstream Americans who would never associate themselves with the movement. They buy his audiotaped messages, attend his seminars, and keep his books on the best-seller lists for months and months.

It is hard to overstate the impact Siegel and other New Age writers on the mind-body connection have had on both public attitudes about health and the medical profession. Building on ideas first suggested by TM researchers Wallace and Benson, these writers have popularized research that draws connections between certain mental or emotional states and health. There is credible evidence suggesting that the immune system works more effectively when we live balanced, fulfilling lives. It also appears that a diet more like the vegetarian style favored by New Agers helps you live longer and healthier.

These holistic ideas have gained such wide public acceptance that modified diets, meditation, group therapy, and the use of guided imagery are commonplace among cancer patients, even those who know nothing about the New Age. Even characters with cancer on mainstream television dramas have used these techniques.

Siegel's books, largely accounts of apparently miraculous recoveries from life-threatening illness, are an appealing mixture of anecdote and argument, science and spirituality. The first, *Love, Medicine, and Miracles*, is based on his work with a group of cancer patients he calls "exceptional." These patients defy their illnesses and the toxic nature of cancer treatment and live. Siegel argues that they use their minds and their hearts to help heal their bodies.

The scientific evidence on the connections between mind and body is still hotly debated. In the end, the link may not be as certain as Siegel and others suggest. Nonetheless, Siegel's argument appeals to a New Age sensibility about the way things ought to be. If we create our own reality, as

Maharishi, Lazaris, Louise Hay, and all the others suggest, then that certainly includes matters of sickness and health. It also suggests that we should be able to cure ourselves, and that this ability is not just physical, but spiritual.

This spiritual dimension is why Bernie Siegel is something more than a doctor. In the five years since the publication of his first book, Siegel has become a spiritual leader, a preacher, a New Age evangelist who talks about miracles as much as about medicine. He is also a hero to those who want to connect New Age spirituality with reason. Like Professor Keith Wallace at MIU, he has the proof, the scientific proof, to support hope.

Siegel and his message of hope are so popular that when I arrived at the meeting room where he was to speak, every seat was occupied and the line to get into the room was about fifty feet long and five people across. Those waiting in line included people in wheelchairs and several who had the gaunt look of cancer or AIDS patients.

"We paid thirty dollars, weeks in advance, to get a seat. We sure as hell better get in!" one man shouted at a woman who guarded the glass door to the hall. Behind her, hotel workers hurriedly set up more chairs. As each new row was completed, the guard at the door let in the same number of people. Each time the door opened, the sound of music, something like gospel music, flooded the anteroom. The whole crowd inside was singing.

> *Love, radiant love*
> *Replaces our fears*
> *Makes everything clear.*

Eventually the angry man and I were let inside. He sat on my right, folded his arms on his chest, and stared straight ahead. To my left were a woman of about fifty in a wheelchair and a man who was, no doubt, her adult son. I looked across more than eighty rows of chairs, and past perhaps a thousand heads, to see a man on a small stage, strumming a guitar and leading the song. He wore one of the Star-born halos. Next to him was Siegel. I knew it was he because of his shaved head, the crisp white dress shirt, and his broad smile. I had seen many photos of him, I had watched him on TV talk shows, and he always looked this way: warm, brainy, self-assured.

As Siegel made some preliminary remarks, the young man on my left leaned over to ask his mother if she needed her medication. "I don't take it until six," she said. She reached into a plastic bag that was on her lap and gave him several brown plastic pill bottles. "Okay," he answered. "I'll have them ready."

The two then turned again to Siegel, giving him their full attention. By then the doctor was explaining how, many years ago, a patient he was treating for cancer had told him that her main problem was coping with the intervals between visits to her doctors. She needed to know how to "live" with her illness.

Siegel had never considered this issue, and it prompted a reconsideration of some of his assumptions about medical practice. Many doctors approach patients as the victims of an illness that must be defeated. The emphasis is on staving off death. Siegel wondered if this paradigm couldn't be changed, so that both doctor and patient emphasized the quality of the patient's life, while also fighting the disease. He had seen his exceptional patients do this. Many had prevailed over tumors that should have killed them. He began to look for their secrets to success. He discovered that these patients were vibrant, lively people who had so much to live for that they refused to die. Such people do live longer, added Siegel, and even the *Journal of the American Medical Association* says so.

"There was an article in *JAMA* called 'Postponement of Death Until the Symbolically Meaningful Occasion,'" he explained. "This is like the woman who says, 'I want to wait until my son's wedding before I die.' Time and time again, this is what happens. The will to live keeps them going."

It happens because feelings, all feelings, "are chemical." They create physical manifestations in the body, some of which are beneficial, some of which are deleterious. "There were forty-five thousand patients in one study of mental-health care. Those who received mental-health care along with medical care had one-third less money spent on them for physical illnesses. If you are happy in your marriage and happy in your work, you don't show up at the doctor's office. If both are screwed up, you get a serious illness.

"Or how about when you laugh? We know that there's an increased level of neuropeptides in the body when you laugh. You feel good and your whole body knows it, even the lining of your blood vessels."

So, Siegel argued, the open expression of emotion is intimately connected to health. This is why the lady who must live to see her son married often does. It is also why, said Siegel, "women with the same cancers as men live longer." Women are better at expressing emotion. On the negative side, he said, a trauma, a bad marriage, a childhood of misery, take their toll on the body as well as on the heart. If these problems are not resolved, either through psychotherapy or other means, they result in illness, even death. Here Siegel, like John Lee, referred to Alice Miller.

"In the last paragraph of one of Alice Miller's books, she says, 'The truth of our childhood is stored up in our bodies.' I think this is true. A lot of us have been used and abused. Now I'm going to call out a dozen problems, and as I call them out, when you hear yours, stand up."

Even from a great distance I could see an amused look on Siegel's face. He was stifling a laugh. The hall, which was already very quiet, became absolutely silent. After a long pause, he said, "Of course I'm not going to be doing that. But that silence means we all belong in group therapy. If you were born and grew up with guilt, fault, blame, and shame, you need to understand that you were born lovable, and you still are."

Beside me, the woman in the wheelchair nodded and her

son put his head in his hands for a moment. Siegel went on to recite a spiritual/medical parable.

"God gave me these three-by-five cards. They were purple and gold. They said, 'The bearer of this card is entitled to live to be one hundred years old.' The only thing is, you are going to live through a lot of pain. It is painful to live. But if you consider your disease a wake-up call, a blessing that calls you to live fully, it helps people to live their lives, get on the path."

Remarkable patients are the ones who, upon receiving a diagnosis, begin living as if each day is precious. If they always wanted to live in the country, they move to Colorado. They take the violin lessons they never had, quit their nine-to-five jobs to be artists, or begin, for the first time, to take their relationships seriously. "This is the group that survives," said Siegel. "They don't give up one of their days and then they keep getting more and more and more."

Remarkable patients also take charge of their treatment, said Siegel. "Make sure they identify you as a person, not a patient," Siegel told the audience. "Keep your clothes on. Ask questions. Become assertive with physicians. Maintain your power. Patient means submissive suffer. If you are a good patient, you are in trouble."

To support his many points, Siegel reached for anecdotes about people with cancer. One was about an indomitable woman who had thirteen operations and is still working as a special-education teacher. She had survived, even thrived, because she "became real, like the Velveteen rabbit." Then there was the woman who each week arrived at her doctor's office wearing a different joke-shop rubber nose. "The third time, her doctor smiled."

The stories of miracles and of saintly patients, the singing and occasional references to God, made Siegel's talk seem like a revival meeting. He was there to exhort the people to hope, and he used all of the preacher's tools—humor, storytelling, rhetoric, and God—to do it. He was also there to accept the adulation of people who saw him as a prophet of miracles. There is something of a huckster in the doctor, what with his many books, audiotapes, weekend retreats, and standing-room-only speaking engagements. He is charismatic, a compelling speaker, and, by all accounts, demanding and temperamental. And he has become wealthy on the sale of his ideas.

Not all of Siegel's ideas are kind or reassuring. He says that cancer doesn't just happen to you. It is brought on, in part, by the process of denying one's true feelings. Every sick person is guilty: guilty of not "processing" his feelings, guilty of harboring resentment, guilty of not following her "bliss." It is cruel to blame cancer's victims for the disease. Surely there are well-adjusted, loving, happy adults who get cancer. Perhaps the woman in my row was one such person. And what of the person who doesn't have it in him to respond to cancer by entering psychotherapy, or quitting a job, or moving to Colorado? Are they to be labeled "unexceptional cancer patients" or, worse, failures?

Of course, the opposite side of this problem is the hope that we might all be "exceptional." Siegel describes illness as a call to a better way of life. Those who respond by seizing life's opportunities for love and expression might prevail. And even if they don't, the robust pursuit of life has to be more rewarding than the meek acceptance of inexorable death. Almost anyone would choose Siegel's path of hope.

This hope is the reason why hundreds of people jammed the hotel ballroom and dozens more still pressed against the glass door. It is why Siegel is not just a doctor but a spiritual healer and a leader of the New Age. It is the reason why, in 1987, I gave a copy of Siegel's first book to a friend whose mother was dying of cancer.

By calling people to live fully and responsibly, especially when ill, Siegel also tries to protect them from the ravages of an often inhuman medical system that can reduce life-and-death issues to matters of technology and calculation. "My grandmother is the ideal example of a patient," he said, grinning. "After she's been in the hospital for a week, the nurses look terrible."

Life is a terminal condition, and Siegel's advice applies to all. Like John Lee, he would argue against the numbed, emotional sleepwalk that many of us make out of our days. This advice is difficult to follow. It's much easier to buy a halo, join the Star-born, drink Km. But given the size of the crowd in the ballroom, and the hundreds pressing at the door, there are many who would choose Siegel's more difficult path. Unlike other New Age evangelists and sales-men, Siegel isn't offering either a magic potion or magical thinking. He insists that we fight the hard fight.

Two weeks after the Expo, an envelope arrived with the return address of a small town in New Jersey. It was from Kathy. I had won the Km raffle. All I had to do was fill out a form and send it back. My twenty-nine-dollar bottle of Km would arrive in a matter of weeks.

Along with her note was a little pamphlet published by the manufacturer of Km. It said that I could become a Km salesperson. One couple had made $350,000 in one year selling Km. Another had earned $500,000. "The time has arrived," it said. "The opportunity is at hand. It's your move."

# 8 · NEWPORT
## VERMONT

---

# Ice Cream Capitalists

IT WOULD HAVE BEEN A RISKY PUBLIC-RELATIONS MOVE FOR any nationally known corporation with Wall Street investors and Main Street customers. But there it was, on Christmas Eve, a full-page advertisement in the *New York Times* challenging President Bush's Persian Gulf policy and pleading for peace. War was unnecessary and avoidable, the ad read. "Take the more difficult and more courageous path to victory through patient, diplomatic effort." At the bottom were the names of more than a dozen sponsoring companies. The only one that most people outside the New Age movement would recognize was Ben and Jerry's Ice Cream.

In early 1991, Ben and Jerry's was a $90-million-a-year company famous for its Cherry Garcia and New York Super Fudge Chunk flavors. *Time* magazine called it the best ice cream in the world. Less well-known, but more remarkable, is the company's standing as a leader in New Age capitalism. Of course, New Age notions have seeped into millions of individual businesspeople's lives. The media has documented the widespread use of crystals and psychics by stockbrokers and investment bankers. Half a dozen prominent business consultants promote courses in "empowered management" or "healing the workplace." And as the Whole Earth Expo demonstrated, there are thousands of entrepreneurs serving the New Age market. But Ben and Jerry's is different. It is an entire company organized around New Age values, not offbeat spiritual ideas, but ideals that include ethical business practice, humane personnel policies, and the goal of being a positive force in the community. The company's mission statement includes three distinct purposes. The first is to "improve the quality of life in a broad community, local, national, and international." The second is to run a profitable company. The third is to make the best ice cream.

Ben and Jerry's sells an all-American product to the American masses and makes lots of money. But even so, much of what Ben and Jerry's does runs against the capitalist grain. Purchase contracts are made not with the lowest bidder, but with struggling concerns that aid social causes: nut-pickers in the Amazon, Indian farmers in Maine, a bakery that employs the homeless. Executive salaries are limited to five times the lowest-paid worker's wage. Seven percent of pretax profits are given to community organizations. Another one percent goes to peace groups. When the company went public, it restricted stock sales to those living in the firm's home state of Vermont. The typical investor antes up just a hundred and fifty dollars.

In line with this record was the *Times* antiwar advertisement. The country was careening toward war with Iraq. The sale of American flags was running high. By standing against the patriots who pounded the drums of war, Ben and Jerry's took a substantial risk. It took some time to reach company spokesman Rob Michalak, to ask him about this. I kept getting a cheery answering machine message: "Hi, this is Rob Michalak, Ben and Jerry's P.R. czar. I'm either at a meeting, or doing TM, so leave a message and I'll call back." When we eventually did speak, Michalak said the decision to place the ad had been automatic.

"One of our goals is to be holistically involved in the community, whether that's locally, nationally, or globally," he said. "Ben says that business is the most powerful tool there is for social change. With the war, we're just trying to express our concerns. A lot of us are worried about what that means—first, to human resources, and second, to economic resources. We feel we have a responsibility to speak up, before it's too late."

The bombing of Iraq and its occupying forces in Kuwait began at 6:30 P.M. Eastern time on January 16, 1991. At nine o'clock President Bush went on TV to announce "the liberation of Kuwait." Thousands of combat missions were flown in the first few hours of the war in what was the most intense air attack in history. Like millions, I watched television late into the night, transfixed by the reports on the massive offensive.

The next morning, as I drove from New York to Ben and Jerry's factory in Waterbury, Vermont, the radio brought a steady stream of war news. No allied planes had been lost and the reports suggested stunning successes for Western fighters and their high-tech weapons. Missiles had been fired on Baghdad. Bombs were killing thousands of soldiers and civilians. But none of the newscasts provided details of bloodshed and death. This would be a high-tech war and the view was from afar, from thousands of feet in the air. The running commentary of the announcers sounded like the play-by-play for a football game, enthusiastic reports of "hits" on "targets" and "missions accomplished."

The news of war made almost everything else—a visit to a New Age business, for example—seem frivolous. Many of the people at the plant had the same reaction. Red-eyed from a sleepless night before the TV, a receptionist was on the telephone talking about the war with a friend. In a conference room a television blared with more reports from Cable News Network. Dozens of workers were crowded into the room and those who passed by asked about the latest developments. Like me, they were horrified by the tragedy

of the war and fascinated by the combat technology on display: smart bombs, map-reading missiles, laser-guided war-
heads. It was a strange juxtaposition—war and an ice cream
factory—made even more graphic by the kitschy design of
the Ben and Jerry's plant. Outside, the modern metal building was painted in bright pastels with big patches of black
and white, like the pattern of a Holstein's hide. Inside,
workers somberly spoke of war while the production line
clattered away, spitting out quart containers of Chocolate
Fudge Brownie ice cream.

"This morning is hard for everybody," Rob Michalak said
as he led me through the plant on a private tour. "People
are in a state of shock." Michalak is a tall thirty-five-year-
old man with long brown hair and wire-rim glasses; he wore
a sweater, corduroy pants, and no tie. Through glass windows we could see the white-coated workers manning the
production line. Michalak showed me the cozy company
cafeteria. Local ladies came in each day to make home-
cooked meals. In a hallway I noticed a four-page memo
pinned to the bulletin board, in between a notice for a winter solstice party and an advertisement for massage therapy.
It was written by the company president.

"To: Everybody. Re: War in the Gulf. While watching
events last night on TV, it became clear that as events unfold, the need for a support network will probably grow."
The memo went on to announce meetings for support
groups. It also offered free, company-paid counseling, paid
time-off for those doing community service work, and tips
for helping children cope with the war news. "Even if you
don't have an emotional reaction to what's happening, it's
probable that someone near you is troubled," the memo
concluded. "This is the time to check in with people. I hope
you will take some time today to touch base with your coworkers and let people know that you'll be there for each
other."

"We make ice cream, but the company is made up of
people," Michalak explained.

Our tour ended in a small trailer in the back of the plant,

by the loading docks, where Michalak left me with Randy Yantz, the thirty-three-year-old plant maintenance supervisor. Yantz is a small, wiry man with a mustache and a wary attitude. He takes his job seriously, and he was not entirely pleased by my interruption.

"I know where every piece of pipe and tubing in that plant goes, and what it's for," he told me. "I've put a lot into my job here, and they've put a lot into me. It's a good deal and I wouldn't say anything to jeopardize it."

Yantz had come to Ben and Jerry's after two years in the army and half a dozen years in dead-end jobs. He had worked as a mechanic and then as a maintenance man in a cheese factory. "The cheese plant was so bad," he said. "They didn't care about the people and they didn't care about the product. I wouldn't eat their cheese. I know how they make it."

A help-wanted ad brought Yantz to Waterbury, where he met both Ben Cohen and Jerry Greenfield, the founders of the company. He was struck by two things. "The first was, they were very serious about making the best ice cream possible. The second was, they were so supportive of people. You were supposed to call them Ben and Jerry, not Mister.

"When I came to work here, they were just building the plant. I spent a lot of time with Ben. He wanted me to learn every pipe in the place, and he gave me the time. Now I do. He also supported me learning new things. They care about you developing here, moving up. It wasn't like that anywhere else I ever worked."

On the desk behind Yantz was a small Apple computer. He pointed to it and told me that he was teaching some of his workers how to use it, so they might also be promoted. "Management had asked me what I wanted to move up to. I wanted to run maintenance, so they helped me learn the computer and other things I needed to do it. Now I'm doing the same for everyone in maintenance. It makes you feel good, to help someone learn new skills, move up."

Suddenly Yantz was interrupted by a loud message that

crackled over the intercom that was part of the telephone. Someone sang "Happy Birthday" to a worker named Claudine.

"See what I mean? That's the 'Joy Gang.' They're always doing stuff like that." The Joy Gang plans and carries out activities to lighten the workday. They had been responsible for a Dress Like Elvis Presley Day, a winter solstice party, Valentine's Day flowers, and the company picnic. The Joy Gang also gives prizes to various departments. One marketing group had been given a gas grill for lunchtime cookouts.

"The pay here is a little bit higher than at other places, but not that much. It's the other benefits that are unusual," added Yantz. They include free health-club memberships for everyone, not just executives, free health and dental coverage, profit sharing, wellness programs, free psychological counseling, tuition aid for college classes, even three pints of free ice cream each day. "They also have all these things, like one percent for peace, and the Ben and Jerry's Foundation that gives away seven percent of the profits. I like that. It makes me feel good about the company I work for, because they are really trying to make a difference."

Though Yantz was not a New Ager, he knew about the movement and observed that "we've got a lot of them here. I don't know what Ben and Jerry's beliefs are. I do know they want to create a better world, and that you don't run into that with too many bosses. They know we have to make profits, but they don't take that much money out. That's not the number-one thing. The number-one thing is people."

Rob Michalak knocked before opening the door to the trailer-office and taking me off to lunch. As I went out the door, Yantz told me, "I can't imagine working anywhere else."

On the way to lunch, more war news poured from the radio in Michalak's car. He switched the station to find classical music. As he drove, he told me the short version of the story of his coming to work at Ben and Jerry's.

"I was news director at the NBC affiliate in Burlington, but I was getting burned out," he said. "The news thing isn't complete. You aren't really able to give the whole story and you often don't feel like you're helping anything." In the summer of 1989 he read an advertisement for the job of public-relations coordinator at Ben and Jerry's. He knew the company, so he applied.

"They put you though *some* interview process," he added. "I was interviewed first by mid-level managers, then by upper-level. Then I met with all the people I would work with directly. Then I met with the people I would work with indirectly. With each step it was like they were trying to see if you are the kind of person who could work here." A Ben and Jerry's kind of person accepts the salary limits imposed by the five-to-one ratio, said Michalak. A Ben and Jerry's person believes in the company's mission, "which is to define what a socially responsible, caring company can be," he said.

"Anyway, after all these meetings I finally get a call from Ben. It was a Saturday and he was getting ready to leave for the Amazon rain forest on that day. He said he wanted me to meet him at a doughnut shop in Essex. We talked about media, world issues, the distribution of wealth, everything except ice cream. The interview was about who I was and how I thought. When it was done, he hired me."

The way Ben Cohen hired his new public-relations director reflected his entire approach to business. He focused on Michalak's attitude, trying to discover if he was both caring and competent. "I told him I wanted to work at a place that had a conscience," Michalak said, continuing the story over lunch. "You spend a lot of your life at work. It should be something you can feel good about at the end of the day."

This very altruistic attitude was a product, in part, of Michalak's vaguely defined spiritual view, a grab bag of New Age and alternative thinking that included a belief in the Hindu concept of karma and fealty to the Golden Rule. "Our soul is part of the larger, universal soul," he explained. "And this life is a chance for us to reach our fullest expression. For me, that means living by the highest sense of ethics in every part of my life. I need to be gentle with people, gentle on the environment. Unfortunately, most businesses don't operate that way."

This philosophy had come to Michalak very gradually. Raised in the Polish Catholic community of Buffalo, Michalak said he had to develop his own, free-lance religion because the church's message didn't touch him. "Jesus' message was good, but he was talking to a certain demographic through parables," he said, lapsing into public-relations–speak. "If you translate it into today's language, it comes out sort of Eastern, sort of New Age.

"The people in production may not talk much about this stuff, but some of us in marketing do," he explained. He was one of several people in the company who shared books and videotapes by different spiritual teachers. Michalak had just finished a book on Native American religion, and he was interested in seeing a tape by a local guru, which was making the rounds. He said he had also enjoyed reading *Emmanuel's Book*, a comforting presentation on everything from relationships to reincarnation, "channeled" by a psychic named Pat Rodegast. "I'm not willing to say what channeling is," he said. "But there is some very interesting material in that book."

Suddenly Michalak stiffened, as if he had caught himself in a professional lapse. He said he wanted me to understand that Ben and Jerry's is a serious business, where the focus is on humane management and a social, rather than spiritual, agenda. "I'm skeptical about a lot of the spiritual stuff. But the heart of the New Age, when it talks about living and working responsibly, is very good."

It's also very good public relations. That afternoon I spent some time with Lee Holden, perhaps the only ice cream company employee in the world with the title of "company filmmaker." Holden makes training films and documentaries on company projects, such as the student tour the company sponsored in the Soviet Union. He also makes arrangements for the many TV crews that troop to Vermont to do pieces on the company for various news shows. In the past few months, he said, all three major networks, plus documentary producer Bill Moyers, had sent cameras to Ben and Jerry's. The founders had also appeared recently on NBC's "Today Show" and "CBS This Morning." Holden helped generate this publicity, which also happened to be priceless free advertising. The process was simple. First the company tried something innovative, its all-natural waste-water treatment system, for example. Then a press release describing the project's success went out. Newspeople, eager for upbeat business stories, responded. The publicity stimulated ice cream sales, which brought in more money to experiment with something else.

Besides being a public-relations whiz, Holden is a serious meditator and a follower of a guru named Maharaj Ji, whom he discovered when he was in college in the early 1970s. (Maharaj Ji began teaching at age eight and built a following of hundreds of thousands before he was twelve.) "Maharaj Ji teaches a way of going inside and tapping the energy that keeps you alive," said Holden. "Energy is some kind of unidentified power that is in every atom in the universe. It is inside of me. Is that God? I don't know. But when I picture this idea, it gives me a spiritual clarity I never experienced before." Holden had been a student of his guru for more than fifteen years. He corresponded regularly with him and attended annual meetings of disciples from around the world. At Ben and Jerry's he tried to show, by example, the benefits of his meditation.

"I'm trying to find the balance necessary to be a spiritual being in a material world. That's hard to do when you have to work for a living. When I worked in the film industry, the end product was often something very negative or exploitive, and the focus was money, money, money. There was nothing I felt proud of. Here I see my work as service, to other people in the company and to the community.

That gives you a sense of purpose you don't get at most companies."

Holden, Michalak, and Yantz were pleasant, likable men, but the repetitive happy-talk began to grate. Ben and Jerry's is an ice cream company, not a scout camp. Certainly there had to be some problems in Camelot. Even scout camps have problems. After nearly a full day with people who had nothing but praise for their employer, I was beginning to feel as if I had stumbled upon the business version of a cult, like Mary Kaye Cosmetics or Amway. Everyone seemed so incredibly happy to be working at Ben and Jerry's. They loved Ben and admired Jerry. They didn't mind working for less money than they might earn at a place without a five-to-one salary cap. There were no management problems and none of the petty jealousies that dominate most companies. This was a New Age workplace, where higher values prevailed and, to use the old leftist saw, people came before profits. The company even placed a "social responsibility statement" in its annual report. In 1989 the report included an almost-confessional section analyzing the company's relationship with suppliers, employees, and franchisees. It addressed the firm's "obligation" to assure suppliers and franchise operators a fair profit and reasonable business relationships. "We believe that we are doing a good job of developing the social conscience of this company," this section concludes. "We commit to celebrating our successes without self-righteousness, and facing our deficiencies without fear."

The report, the posters, the enthusiastic employees—it all added up to an unremitting message of goodness and light, until I met Pam Root, from the sales department. Root was able to criticize the company, if only a little.

"Oh, come on," she said. "It's not like that. There have been times when I've thought, 'Everybody is really screwed up here. Everybody.' "

Pam Root was leaving a conference room where a group of people had been watching a news program that included a clip of President Bush's speech. "Can you believe that man?" she said as we walked to a nearby office. In the hallway I saw a poster of Martin Luther King, Jr., and the quote: "We must pursue peaceful ends through peaceful means." Root was furious about Bush. "He was actually smiling. Smirking. It's absurd. How are we supposed to feel? We've got a lot of people here who are really committed to peace. No one believes we were wrong to take out the ad. But we are pretty stressed out today." When we settled in to talk, I told Root that I was a bit skeptical about all the glowing reports of harmony and bliss at Ben and Jerry's. "Oh, people are screwed up here, too," she said.

"Three years ago I experienced a rude awakening. "I was working for a new marketing director, a guy who had come from a very big food company." At the time, Ben and Jerry's was expanding rapidly. It had gone from a single store in a renovated gas station in Burlington to a major regional ice cream maker in eight years. "This guy didn't operate in the spirit of this place," said Root. "He did that male thing of never admitting a mistake, never asking for help. He also pushed people to meet unrealistic goals. I began thinking, 'This is just like any other company. They just have a different image.' "

The high-pressure techniques bothered Root even more because the company had promoted an image that was the opposite. Ben and Jerry said they were more concerned with people than quotas. And until the arrival of the new marketing director, the firm had practiced a kind of anti-selling. In fact, they had just finished displaying this counterculture business strategy in a battle with the giant Pillsbury Company, which makes Häagen-Dazs ice cream. It seems Pillsbury had been pressuring ice cream middlemen—warehousers and distributors—to get them to stop handling Ben and Jerry's products. Pillsbury had a lot of leverage, because it could pull an entire line of frozen foods from a distributor's shelves. Making a choice between Ben and Jerry's small-scale ice cream business and the huge Pillsbury lineup was easy for anyone who worried about staying in business.

Such predatory business practice—some might call it extortion—is also almost impossible to stop, because proof is elusive and witnesses are reluctant to testify. An aggressive court challenge to Pillsbury would have cost Ben and Jerry more than their company was worth, so they tried something more creative. First they put a cryptic message— "What's the Doughboy Afraid Of?"—on the lids of their ice cream cartons. Then they went to Pillsbury's corporate headquarters for a two-man protest march. Soon their complaint was getting national media attention, the cute little Doughboy's image was being sullied, and Ben and Jerry got their distributors.

This approach to business—open, honest, funny—impressed Root. But when the new, hotshot marketing director began pushing for ever-higher earnings, she worried that the company was losing its soul. "We were becoming really successful, but everybody, including Ben and Jerry, struggled with the success. Coming out of the Sixties, they wanted to run the kind of business they liked. But here it was, getting big. Suddenly we had three hundred people working here and national distribution. I was afraid it was getting too big."

The tension between growth and the original values of the company lasted until the summer of 1990, when the marketing director was asked to leave. Soon another key manager, the one who had trouble resolving the problem in the first place, announced he would retire, too.

"I think it was a case of everybody being too nice, in a way," said Root. "Nobody wanted conflict, but there was a problem here we had to fix. I'm glad it's over, because things are getting better."

Pam Root had a long-term view of the company. She had starting working with Ben and Jerry when they were still scooping cones at the gas station in Burlington. "I thought, 'Hey, these guys are really fun,' and working there was fun." In those days, they used to show free movies on the wall of the shop on Saturday nights. They gave all mothers free ice cream on Mother's Day. Everyone got a free cone on the company's anniversary. Root was there to watch Ben and Jerry develop their recipes. (The ice cream is heavily flavored because Ben's sense of taste was damaged by his constant use of nasal sprays to fight allergies as a child. He kept insisting on more flavoring, because he couldn't taste what Jerry mixed.) She also witnessed the design of the distinctive, hand-lettered pint packages that feature pictures of Ben and Jerry and the motto "Two Real Guys." While Pillsbury and Kraft were selling premium ice cream with made-up, Nordic names—Häagen-Dazs and Frusen Gladje—Ben and Jerry sold sincerity and knock-you-down flavors. Ben and Jerry thrived.     .

"The outside world could look at it and say, 'Well, Ben Cohen was a marketing genius. He saw that sincerity would sell, and he did it,' " said Root. "I don't think that's what happened. They weren't trying to use a gimmick. They were just being who they were. Sometimes I think that if they could, they would go back to those days, before it got so big. Some days I feel like I would, too."

The company's stress counselors had helped write the Gulf war memo I saw posted in the hallway. The next morning they led a 7:30 A.M. support group meeting for first-shift workers at the plant. The production crew, about a dozen men and women in white coats, hair nets, and white hard hats, crowded into a conference room on the second floor of the ice cream factory. Most squeezed into the chairs that surrounded a twenty-foot-long table. A few paper clips flew across the table, fired by rubber-band-wielding snipers. I could hear some nervous talk about the war.

"Hey, it's your birthday today. How old are you?"

"Too old to be drafted, thank God."

Dennis Leisenring, the company psychologist, began the meeting and, as it turned out, did almost all the talking. A tall man in his late forties, he wore a bulky wool sweater and khaki pants, and he leaned against the conference table as he spoke. He is a veteran of the Vietnam War.

"As you all know, the nation is in a crisis of unprecedented proportions. For the first time, we're seeing a minute-by-minute account of one of the ugliest things in civilization: war. I was in the previous one and, regardless of your political orientation, it is not a lot of fun. We wanted to let you know that we are prepared to help people cope. We're going to start support groups, for people who are veterans, for people with children, for people with someone over there, for everyone."

When Leisenring asked for comments, the men and women around the table were suddenly shy. Eyes were averted. Throats were cleared. One woman quietly described her husband's struggle with nightmare memories of Vietnam, which were suddenly fresh in his mind.

"That's true what he said," the woman told the group. "My husband was in Vietnam for two years, but he never said much about it. Now he's talking about it all the time."

From across the table, another woman said that she was worried about her children. "They go to watch cartoons and instead it's the war. What do you say to them? How do you make 'em feel safe?"

"We all need to talk about our feelings, especially when it seems to be on the TV every time we turn it on," said Leisenring. He advised parents to reassure children about their personal safety, to tell them that the war was halfway around the world and that they would continue to get their parents' care. "We are plugging into a statewide network about this, getting information about meetings, places where you can volunteer to help. There are things we can do to help each other, too. I don't want people to be alone, especially watching the TV news. We need to support each other here. Talk. Spend time with each other. This is a hard time."

When Leisenring asked if those in the room were interested in forming a group that would meet regularly to discuss the war, about half the people raised their hand. He promised to put a group together and then reminded them that the company counseling service was available to anyone who was especially distressed. "Don't think this doesn't affect you. It affects all of us," he said. "We need to take care of ourselves."

As Leisenring finished, the crew chief for the morning shift pulled out a clipboard and opened the weekly work-review meeting usually held at that hour. I left the room with Leisenring and we stood in the hallway for a moment, discussing his work at Ben and Jerry's. He said his main focus, in recent months, had been on getting people to work less.

"People overwork here, then the quality of what they do suffers," he explained. "It's especially true of the marketing and management people, who aren't on shifts. A lot of them come in early and stay late. We have to chase them out, force them to rest." Well-rested workers are more efficient, creative, and healthy. They use fewer sick days, need less medical care, and make fewer mistakes. These facts are well known in American business, but few companies actually try to get their workaholic employees to slow down. "Instead, they just use them, letting them burn out," added Leisenring. "That's not good for people and it's not good for the company." For the same reason—long-term employee well-being—Ben and Jerry's give every worker a free health-club membership. It is intended to counteract the effects of all the free ice cream.

The group in the conference room finished its business and began to leave. One of them, a diminutive man who wore a quilted snowmobile suit, interrupted my conversation with Leisenring.

"Are you Mike, the fellow doing the book?"

"Yes."

"I'm Mike Pastina. I'd like to talk with you. I'm busy, so can we do it now?"

In the conference room, with the door closed, Mike Pastina presented the most unique view I would hear in my brief visit to Vermont. He said that Ben and Jerry's is a wonderful place to be employed. Working conditions are ideal. The ice cream is wonderful. The good works done by the company are all real. But Ben and Jerry's is also a den of New Agers who are ultimately destined for hell. "That is, unless they are saved. And I'm hoping to help some of them because I'm sort of a double agent for Jesus here."

Pastina, who worked in the subzero cold of the storage and shipping area, is a devout born-again Christian who has worked at the ice cream factory for four years. At about five foot two, with red hair, a full beard, and a cherubic face, he looks positively elfin. "I'm a very upbeat person," he said, grinning. "I like to show, by example, the power of the Lord. I don't push it on people. But if they see how happy I am and want to know why, I tell them it's because I let Jesus into my heart.

"Now, when I got here I thought this place was a little weird. They have a different spirit in this place. A lot of the people have asked Ben and Jerry's to come into their heart. You see it in them. It's very spiritual, in a leftist sort of way. They love this company and they'll do whatever is asked of them. They believe in Ben and Jerry and believe in what they are doing, with this social responsibility idea."

Social responsibility—safeguarding the environment, giving money to charities, treating workers fairly—was a good thing, he allowed. But it wasn't enough. Because Pastina interpreted the world in an old-fashioned, Biblical way, he considered the New Age approach to business to be evil. "Oh, there are tons of evil spirits floating around this place," he said. "That's what the New Age is, the effect of evil spirits. You see it in the advertisements for meditation that these people put on the bulletin boards. Some of 'em wear crystals, too. The only way for God to get in here and work against it is through his people, like me. When I came here there were only two born-again Christians in the whole place. Now there are six. That's progress."

Pastina continued this running spiritual assessment as he led me to the warehouse area, to show me where he worked. He found a down parka and some gloves for me. Then we went to inspect the freezer rooms, which, at forty below zero, put frost on my beard and took my breath away. All the time, he talked about the difference between the "worldly" good done by Ben and Jerry's and the spiritual evil of the place.

"On a worldly level, I love working here," he said. "I've got a Ben and Jerry's T-shirt and a Ben and Jerry's hat. You can go as far as your abilities take you here. It's a very encouraging environment. Ben and Jerry's never left the Sixties. They believe in human life, in making love, not war. It's very attractive."

So attractive, that Pastina had to struggle to remind himself that the company was based on values he believed were un-Christian. "All the good stuff is a problem," he shouted over the noise made by a refrigeration machine. "It makes the New Age way of thinking too attractive. The New Age says you can be whatever you want, do whatever you want. It's like you are God. But I have to remind myself that it's very selfish. It's not something of God's."

Mike Pastina's obsession with the battle of good and evil, with notions of God and the spirit world, are not so unique. Millions of Pentecostal Christians and, for that matter, millions of devout New Agers live with a similar attunement to the metaphysical. These two groups are remarkably similar. Both are preoccupied with the idea of a magnificent transforming moment: for the individual, through spiritual awakening, and for the world, through the Second Coming or the dawn of the New Age. Both groups believe that God may continue to reveal spiritual truths in our time. Both emphasize personal choice in spiritual matters, personal interpretations of scripture teachings, and personal expressions of the sacred. And both groups are inheritors of an

American philosophical tradition that runs from Emerson's call for "a religion by revelation to us" to Oral Roberts's regular visits with a living, talking Jesus.

But as far as Pastina was concerned, only one group was on the side of true good: the Christians. This view extended even to his assessment of the Gulf war.

"I'm probably the only person here who is not upset by it," he told me. "For me, it's just God's plan unfolding. It's all in the Scripture and now the prophecy is coming true." The prophecy he was referring to is known as "end-times," or Armageddon prophecy, and it involves the apocalyptic writings of the Old Testament. Millions of born-again Americans believe that the Gulf war is a precursor to the Earth-destroying battle of Armageddon. They are not troubled at all by this because, according to the popular Scripture interpretations by leading evangelists, Christians would be supernaturally protected from the destruction, surviving to live in a utopia reigned by the returning Christ.

"The war doesn't bother me at all," Pastina continued. "I know what's happening and I know I'm saved. I also know that support groups and meetings like they had this morning aren't going to really help people. Frankly, I think a Bible study would be more effective."

I spent most of the morning with Mike Pastina. He introduced me to his boss, a twenty-nine-year-old woman named Wendy Yoder. She had come to Ben and Jerry's in 1983, after earning a degree in "resource management" and working for the U.S. Forest Service. She had stayed because "the ideals of the company and the teamwork made me feel as excited as I did in college." She described the Ben and Jerry spirit as "caring humanism." She added, "When people ask you how you are doing, they really want to know." Yoder's spiritual life was focused around the Alcoholics Anonymous twelve-step program, which was loosely connected, by many people, to the New Age.

"I consider myself spiritual, but it's not an organized thing. For me, spiritual people are those who have been to

Hell in their lives and don't want to go back." Her superiors didn't object if Yoder left work during the day to attend an AA meeting. Many of her coworkers encouraged her to stay with the program. "I haven't experienced anything here but encouragement," added Yoder. "They support you a lot, with things like those war discussion groups. I really supported the peace advertisement and I became very depressed when the war started. It's harder to work because I'm distracted. The support groups help with that and I think that must be good for productivity. It's good for people, and it's good for business." All of this—the support groups, the easy acceptance of her AA program—distinguished the company. But while she recognized that this kind of support was unusual, she stopped short of "asking Ben and Jerry's into her heart," as Mike Pastina put it.

"Look, a lot of people say this is a family or something like it. It's not. It's a company," she said as I was about to leave her. "The reason it's so successful, I think, is they have a really good product and they've exploited the press with some of their ideas. The image of the company is almost bigger than the company itself. Only three people in this whole company have any experience making ice cream. The real genius has been in the promotion."

As I left the warehouse and shipping departments, I passed through the manufacturing area, where two lines of machines, operated by half a dozen people each, continually spit out cartons of ice cream. The people who worked on the lines managed their own shifts. They each chose their tasks for the day, to limit the boredom and repetition. And each one had the authority to stop production if a problem arose. One of the workers told me that these policies made her feel more as though it was her ice cream coming off the line. She also offered me a taste, which I refused. It was a curious thing. Amidst all this ice cream, my usual craving for the stuff disappeared. In two days there, I would sample just a few spoonfuls.

The afternoon was to be spent with one of the artists who

designed the distinctive, hand-lettered packages and posters the company used. And finally, at the end of the day, I would meet Ben Cohen. Jerry, it turned out, was out of town. Before these final encounters, I had lunch with Lee Holden and Rob Michalak. We spent the hour talking, not about Ben and Jerry, but about the war.

The second day of Desert Storm had brought reports of the overwhelming success of American military technology. The videotapes showed pilots directing bombs literally through the doors of buildings and down air shafts. The aircraft worked flawlessly. The ordnance was incredibly accurate. The pilots were fearless. Their commanders took great delight in reporting the many successful bombing runs. I had seen all of this on the TV in my hotel room before I left for the ice cream plant. Holden and Michalak had seen it, too. And they had been disturbed by one thing: the excitement they felt.

"We really stand for peace here, and the thought of thousands of pounds of explosives dropping on human beings is very upsetting," said Holden. "But it is impressive, and you find yourself admiring the power, the skill." Michalak agreed. He had felt a twinge of patriotic pride as he watched American successes, and he had begun to think in terms of the Gulf conflict being a just war. "Saddam Hussein is a bad guy and he couldn't be allowed to just take over another country," he said. While Michalak still believed that President Bush had acted too soon, that he should have waited for economic sanctions to work, his pacifism was withering.

Much of our lunchtime discussion was taken up with this conflict between peace politics and the seductive grandeur of war. Neither man seemed close to resolving the spiritual crisis this created. But it was clear that Lee Holden, at least, was working his way toward a reconciliation that allowed for the use of force against an evil enemy. "The Bhagavad Gita takes place on a battlefield," remarked Holden. "Krishna told his disciple to fight, that it was all right to fight, but that he must be conscious of the creator as well."

Michalak, who wasn't nearly as serious about his spiritual pursuits as Holden, was left to sort things out without the Bhagavad Gita or a guru. "I don't think we're out of line pushing for peace," he said. "But I also think you have to be realistic and recognize there are bad situations in the world that have to be confronted. I'm not really sure, though. This is a very hard thing to decide."

The conflict that Michalak and Holden felt might surprise critics of the New Age, especially those who harshly condemn it as irrational and impractical. Like anyone else with strong, religious convictions, these New Agers struggled to apply them to a very practical, concrete problem. They did not express a knee-jerk rejection of the war. Their beliefs allowed for good and evil, even for a just war. But they were also so self-aware that they were distressed by the excitement they felt while viewing war images. This excitement revealed an inner quality which neither man liked. Their struggle was not just with the rightness of the war, but with the content of their own character.

Back at the Ben and Jerry's art department, where half a dozen people labored over tilted drafting tables, Sarah Forbes wasn't feeling at all ambiguous. She considered the war a tragedy, a huge example of the male ego run amok. This was the kind of analysis one might expect, however, because Forbes was among the few women at Ben and Jerry's who followed the highly feminist spiritual path of wicca, or witchcraft.

"It probably started when I was given a set of glass balls, witches balls, that you hang in your windows to ward off the evil eye," Forbes told me. "I was curious about them and I looked into it. Being interested in feminism, I was obviously drawn to the wiccan tradition. It reinforced my feminist values. Of course I don't accept all of it. A lot of it is bullshit. But a lot of it isn't."

Like the women I met at the Earth First! protest in California, Forbes didn't call herself a witch. She didn't look like one, either. Tall, with razor-cut blond hair and dressed in a businesslike green blazer, thirty-year-old Forbes looked more like a young Republican. "I was a Yuppie for a while," she confessed. "I had the car and the clothes. I ran around doing free-lance artwork around Philadelphia. But none of the people I knew could talk about anything serious, anything spiritual. I really want to know how people manage to get over the really rough spots in life. How do people handle death and loneliness? No one out there talks about these things."

Forbes had moved from Pennsylvania to Vermont in order to be with a boyfriend. The relationship ended, but she wanted to stay in the rural Northeast. There were few jobs for graphic artists in the state. Ben and Jerry's was one place to try. After doing some free-lance work, she came to believe that it was one of the few places where she would ever feel comfortable working full-time. When the job offer came, she seized it immediately.

"This place attracts misfits. It's a very odd crew," she said. "People here will talk about anything. If you're having a bad day and you need to cry, it's okay. If there's a crisis in your life, people will take you into an office, close the door, and talk about it. How many places are like that? Can other people cry in the office and know that it's all right, that nobody will judge you? I think this is the way a lot of people would prefer to work, in a company that's more like a community. Everybody knows that the meaning of life is not money. We're the ones who have decided to live that way. This is a New Age company, and it works."

On another day, Forbes might have talked more about the virtues of New Age business practice, but right now she was too preoccupied by the war. No matter what I asked her, our conversation always returned to her belief that the bombings ordered by Bush were premature and probably unnecessary. Even though the whole country seemed to be rallying 'round the troops, she remained convinced that Ben and Jerry's antiwar policy was the right one. "We are not completely isolated in our opinions. A lot of people feel the way we do. They just didn't have the money, or the courage, to say where they stood. We weren't afraid. I'm proud of that."

It seemed rather arrogant to suggest that an ice cream company in Vermont should be a source of wisdom for a country on the brink of war. The business of business is business, not social policy. This argument might be a fair criticism of Ben and Jerry's, if there wasn't ample evidence that American business is a major player in every national policy debate. Business has a stake in war and in peace. Business, especially big business, exerts extraordinary influence on politicians through campaign donations, lobbyists, and personal contacts. Executives help shape tax laws, health-care programs, economic policies, and trade programs. This process is so pervasive that it's almost invisible, like the atmosphere. The difference between Ben and Jerry's lobbying and the ongoing efforts by the rest of corporate America was that Ben and Jerry's was very public in its attempt to influence the process. It was not much different from their approach to the Doughboy battle. Rather than operate quietly, in courtrooms, they tried to seize the moral high ground and take their case to the public. There was nothing idle or accidental in this strategy. It was inherent to Ben Cohen's outlook on business. He said as much during the hour we spent together in his office at the end of the day.

Cohen's office was in a low ranch house, shrouded by tall pine trees, that was part of the property the company had purchased for the ice cream plant. From the front porch, one could look back at the plant, with its pastel metal walls and cowhide-design paint job, rising high on the snow-covered hillside. Inside the house, Cohen shared the space with a few assistants, his partner Jerry, and some other executives.

Cohen looked like anything but an executive as he emerged, ice cream bar in hand, to lead me back to his office. His receding, scraggly blond hair loops into curls in the back, before falling down over his collar. He has a full, bushy, nest of a beard that looks as though it has never been trimmed. His wire-rim glasses were slightly askew. His baggy, khaki pants were slung under a rather large belly, which was covered with a bright blue T-shirt. From his appearance, one would conclude that he was a shift-worker or maintenance man, not the chair*person* of the board.

The office was even less businesslike than the man. Papers and cardboard boxes littered the floor. On his desk were a plastic banana, empty ice cream cartons, and a knapsack full of compact discs. On the opposite wall was a bookcase with dusty books and ice cream cartons that looked as though they hadn't been moved in years.

"Excuse me while I taste this," Cohen said, holding up one hand to stop our conversation and using the other to nibble on the ice cream bar. On a notepad he wrote, "Not enough STBs." STBs were "special tidbits," the chunks of chocolate, cookies, or other ingredients mixed into the ice cream. Cohen, who approved or rejected every new product, was about to send the "Rainforest Crunch Bar" back to the development lab for more work.

Product development is just one of Cohen's interests. While his partner Jerry Greenfield has withdrawn from active management, focusing solely on matters of company morale, Cohen remains at the center of the firm. He monitors everything—the quality of the ice cream, contracts with suppliers, employee enthusiasm—making sure everything is working according to the three-part mission statement and the general philosophy of the founders.

"All of this is the product of conscious decisions we made back when we began in the gas station," Cohen said when I asked about the counterculture business strategy. He and Greenfield had both embraced anticapitalist thinking long before, so when they decided to run a business, there was no question about challenging all of the norms. They wanted to use their business to support themselves, create something enjoyable, and redistribute wealth. That last item—redistributing wealth—is anathema to American business, which tends to oppose even progressive income taxes, but Cohen and Greenfield both found morally repugnant the lavish advantages and million-dollar salaries enjoyed by executives who employ thousands at subsistence wages. They wanted to make a company that would reward all of its workers, and its community, with its wealth.

This approach was not based on any one book or teacher, said Cohen. "It was more from the miasma of the counterculture. We were coming out of the Sixties generation. I was very aware of civil rights issues and sensitized to the way society treats people. We were very aware that most businesses are run solely for profits, to make income for the owner. If that happened to be at the expense of the employees or the community, that didn't matter. The one thing we did know when we started was that we weren't going to do that."

Indeed, the team of Cohen and Greenfield knew how they wanted to do business before they knew just what their business would sell. Childhood friends from Long Island, they were both nearing thirty when they began seriously planning to open a business. Having failed to complete a college degree, Ben had supported himself as a potter, a cab driver, a cashier, and at many other odd jobs before becoming a crafts teacher at a school for disturbed boys in upstate New York. Jerry had graduated from Oberlin College and worked as a lab technician. He had wanted to be a doctor but couldn't get into medical school. Unhappy with their work, they decided to move together to Burlington and open something that would be as rare there as a palm tree: a bagel shop. The bagel shop would provide pleasant work and a good income for the two friends. But the bagel-making equipment cost too much, so they switched to ice cream, learning the basics from a five-dollar correspondence course sold by Pennsylvania State University.

Ben and Jerry had planned to run a neighborhood business, keeping prices low, employing local people, and giving as much back to the community as they could, in the form of free ice cream and charitable donations. Sheer luck would have it that they happened to make terrific ice cream—rich flavors with huge chunks of chocolate, cookies, candy, and nuts—at a time when a national ice cream craze was starting. In a matter of months, restaurants and local grocery stores were asking them for supplies. In 1981 their ice cream was called the best in the world by *Time* magazine. A few months later they opened a second shop, in Shelbourne, Vermont. From there the company expanded like a child's balloon. In twelve years it grew from a two-man business making ice cream with an old-fashioned rock-salt mixer to a $75-million-a-year firm with national distributors, three hundred employees, stock offerings, and foreign franchises.

As he described the growth, even Ben Cohen seemed amazed. "We kept asking ourselves what was happening, how it was happening," he said, his voice rising as if he was asking a question. "It was hard to figure out. We didn't know anything about how to run a business and yet we were successful." It may have been difficult for two young, antiestablishment radicals from the Sixties counterculture to see why they had succeeded so dramatically, but the fact was they were bright, capable men whose fathers had both been part of the business world. Cohen's father was an accountant, Greenfield's a stockbroker. And though they had trouble keeping up with the accounting and banking, they were smart enough to hire a general manager to get control of their financial operations. When they needed capital, they were savvy enough to pull off a do-it-yourself stock offering for Vermont residents only. This sort of thing was evidence that Cohen and Greenfield had picked up some business sense somewhere along the way. But when I suggested as much, Cohen brushed the idea aside.

"We really didn't understand business. That's the thing. The biggest shock came when we realized we were no longer ice cream men, but businessmen. There was a lot of money flowing through this place. I was on the phone hammering guys down to get the lowest price on supplies. We looked at ourselves and our first reaction was, 'We've got to sell everything and get out.'"

At the time, Cohen was scouting territory for a second manufacturing plant. He was contacted by an eccentric old businessman who had some land for sale in Brattleboro. The old man operated by instinct, succeeding when logic said he should fail. When Cohen met him, he was in the process of turning an abandoned diner into a successful gourmet restaurant. "Maurice was a great guy. I told him I didn't like the way the company was going. I thought it was getting so big that it was losing its soul, that it would inevitably exploit people. People were already working too many hours and in conditions that weren't what they should be. I felt guilty about it. You know what he said? He said, 'Why don't you do it differently?'"

That simple question led Cohen and Greenfield to redouble their efforts at spreading the wealth generated by the company. "If it was going to make a lot of money, that meant we could do a lot more with it," said Cohen. "In order to improve conditions for the employees and the community, we needed to grow. So we went ahead."

From a simple policy of charity, Cohen and Greenfield moved toward aggressive giving. They founded the Ben and Jerry's Foundation, using thousands of shares of their own stock and donations from company profits. "The difference was we would be actively helping, rather than just 'not screwing' people," he said. The Ben and Jerry's Foundation gave money to housing programs for the poor, to peace groups, to veterans' organizations and environmentalists. Ben and Jerry also institutionalized the policy of

using the company's normal business activities for some social good. By purchasing milk from small cooperatives, they
supported family farms. By purchasing blueberries from
Maine Indians, they supported struggling tribal businesses.
They also began thinking in bigger terms, using the money
and the cachet of the company to pursue such things as
"ice cream diplomacy" with the Soviet Union. In 1991 Ben
and Jerry's would open its joint-venture factory and scoop
shop in the Soviet Union. Profits from the operation would
pay for more student exchanges.

The antiwar advertisement and the "Peace Pops" that carried peace slogans on their wrappers, were part of this
business-as-social-activism approach. Cohen didn't separate
his life as an ice cream maker from his other concerns. He
lived holistically. "I'm a businessman, but I'm a man first.
That means I put what I think is important first. And we
thought it was important to tell people that the solution to
conflict is not war. I am aware of the fact that the polls said
that half the people didn't want war, but now that it's
started, eighty or ninety percent are for it. That doesn't
matter. We stand for peace and if we didn't say something,
it would have been hypocritical."

The most jarring bit of recent war news concerned Iraqi
missiles, which had been fired into Israel in an effort to
broaden the war. Iraqi officials had long sought to link the
problem of Israel's annexed Palestinian territory to any resolution of the Kuwait problem. Knowing that Cohen and
Greenfield were Jewish, I asked him if attacks on Israel,
which might eventually include deadly chemical bombs,
might change his mind about the war. He stood his ground.

"Israel annexes Arab lands. That's cool. We invade Pan-
ama. That's cool. Now that dude annexes Kuwait, and it's
not cool. Where's the justice in this?"

These assessments, which were not much different from
some of the statements made by Iraq's leaders, would have
placed Cohen in a very small minority among Americans.
But he was not afraid to express them, nor was he concerned about the effect on business. The way he saw it, all

businesses were involved in the political process. The problem was, all the others were pushing policies that were bad for people.

"There is no doubt in my mind that business is the most powerful force in society. Our society is the way it is, the military industrial complex is the way it is, because that's the way business wants things. If business didn't make tons of money based on war, it would never happen." This attitude prevailed in business because those who opposed it— liberal thinkers, radicals, the religiously inspired—stayed out of the business world, said Cohen. "Traditionally, people like me have stayed in social services, the arts, or small companies. They saw business as uncaring, unhumanistic. I agree with that. But here we're saying, 'You can have a business that is caring and humanistic and works.' I think a lot of people are going to be attracted to this. People want to work in this kind of environment, even if they make a little less. Working in traditional business is just too stressful and dehumanizing."

Just then the phone rang. Cohen picked it up. "Yo!" he shouted.

He paused for a moment, listening.

"Yo!"

Another pause.

"Yo. Yo. Yo."

He "yo-ed" for several minutes, never uttering another syllable and never cracking a smile. When he hung up, the train of our conversation was broken. He said he had to leave, but invited me to ask one more question. I asked if he had been influenced by any counterculture books, leaders, or movements.

"Right now I'm reading *The Lazy Man's Guide to Enlightenment*, but that's just for fun. As I said, it all came to me more by osmosis. I was influenced by lyrics from the Grateful Dead and Paul Simon. But it was not very specific. I just knew I didn't want to live and work the way everyone else seemed to. That didn't seem like much fun to me."

\*     \*     \*

Cohen and Greenfield had created a holistic, New Age business, one that considered the mental, physical, and emotional health of its employees, its suppliers, its customers, even its competitors. All of this had been described in spiritual terms by Greenfield in an interview with *New Age Journal*. "We're all brothers and sisters, and what's in you is in me and we're all part of everything, of the Great One," he said. Because all of humanity is spiritually connected, he said, he had to avoid unethical business practices.

Less philosophical and perhaps more practical, Ben Cohen seemed to see his company in political terms. He was determined to prove that business could be part of improving communities, part of the "healing" process that so many New Agers talk about. He wanted to show that the world of work didn't have to be "business as usual."

So far, Ben and Jerry are succeeding. Their 1991 sales were projected at more than $90 million. Consumers are obviously happy with the ice cream. The beneficiaries of Ben and Jerry's donations had to be pleased with the cash.

But what stands out most is the attitude of the employees at Ben and Jerry's. They seem happier than any workers I have ever met. In every company I have ever worked for, rank-and-file workers existed in a state of resigned unhappiness. They checked their hearts and minds at the door, put in their hours, and accepted their paychecks. Most felt ignored as individuals. They knew they labored primarily for the benefit of high-paid executives and anonymous investors. This is clearly not the case at Ben and Jerry's. Indeed, the company is so equitably run that the only real problem for workers might be that they could become too happy. A worker who signs on at age twenty might be so satisfied that he doesn't reassess his career for decades. Meanwhile, opportunities might be lost and adventures passed by.

Of course, this is a nit-picking criticism, one that loyalists would say ignores the primary difference between New Age capitalists and traditional entrepreneurs. People who come to Ben and Jerry's and stay, seek a way of life, not a way to make money. Sarah Forbes had it right, and her words bear repeating:

"This is the way a lot of people would prefer to work, in a company that's more like a community. Everybody knows that the meaning of life is not money. We're the ones who have decided to live that way. This is a New Age company, and it works."

# 9 · DETROIT

## Stopping Briefly on a Road
## Well-Traveled

IMAGINE FREUD AND JESUS CHRIST IN THE SAME ROOM. Better yet, imagine them in the same person. This is M. Scott Peck. Or rather, this is the philosophy that Peck, psychiatrist and best-selling author, has tried to create. It's psycho-spirituality—not quite religion, not quite therapy, but definitely an idea with enormous appeal for New Agers and many others.

Peck's first book, *The Road Less Traveled*, has been a best-seller for most of a decade. Subtitled "A New Psychology of Love, Traditional Values and Spiritual Growth," it includes advice about spiritual and emotional development, love, marriage, and responsibility. Another of Peck's books, *People of the Lie*, argues the existence of true evil in the hearts of men and women. These books are so widely popular that I have encountered people reading them on airplanes and in restaurants, in college classrooms, and Sunday schools. I even know a police sergeant who assigns them to his rookie cops. He thinks they move recruits to be more noble and humane—genuine peace officers.

Of course, Scott Peck is not the only one working to fuse psychology and spirituality. The two have been slowly coming together since the turn of the century. At first, it was religion that began to accept psychology. For decades priests, rabbis, even evangelical ministers have taken seminary courses in psychology and have made liberal use of therapeutic techniques in their counseling. More recently psychotherapists began to notice the limitations of psychology and the value of a spiritual life. As they reconsidered the religious nature of humankind, they turned to the New Age because it seemed different from hierarchical, dogmatic religion. Irene Siegel, the psychotherapist/shaman of Smithtown, Long Island, is an example of this trend. So is Los Angeles psychiatrist Stanislav Grof, the author of many books on the subject, who redefines some psychiatric disorders as "spiritual emergencies." Such emergencies, which can include hallucinations and out-of-body experiences, are true mystical events, not evidence of psychosis, he writes.

Like the clergy who have learned that therapy works, the thousands of spiritually attuned New Age counselors I met in Sedona, Los Angeles, and elsewhere believe that spiritual practices work. There is some evidence to support this belief. The extremists at MIU notwithstanding, many solid studies have found that meditation does have benefits for the body and the mind. It can lower anxiety, as well as blood pressure, and it can both focus the mind and free it from obsessions. Eastern-style meditation is also becoming one the remedies most often prescribed by psychotherapists.

Scott Peck goes further. While others would struggle to be "value neutral" and avoid anything reminiscent of traditional religion, Peck borrows heavily from mainstream Christianity. He even extracts old-fashioned moral lessons from the Bible and other religious texts and applies them to modern life. He tells people there are such things as good and evil, right and wrong. Indeed, sometimes he sounds like a born-again evangelist. What makes Peck essentially New Age is that he seems to value all religious traditions equally. He's as comfortable with pagan myths as he is with Scripture. And he goes beyond spirituality, to prescribe psychotherapy as a cure for the psychoses and neuroses that dwell beside the evil in men's lives.

All of this is in Peck's books. But there is more to the Scott Peck phenomenon than million-seller self-help books. Each year Peck takes his message on the road, becoming the Billy Graham of the New Age. He conducts seminars for huge audiences in cities across the country. People came to his day-long seminars, which cost eighty-five dollars per person, to be educated, analyzed, inspired, and uplifted. Peck almost never gives interviews or appears on TV programs, and his speaking engagements are not advertised to the general public. Nevertheless, they always sell out.

As I expected, the mauve and green ballroom at the Detroit Radisson Hotel was packed to overflowing when I arrived for M. Scott Peck's one-day seminar there. I had contacted his staff months in advance in order to get a ticket. Speaking with the doctor would be impossible. "He just doesn't do that, ever," his executive assistant had told me. But I was welcomed to attend, listen, and speak with any of the seven hundred or so people in the audience.

After looking over the sales tables full of Scott Peck books and audiotapes in the back of the room, I found a seat up front, in the middle of what I soon realized was a group of about two dozen autoworkers from General Motors. Some wore navy blue jackets with the UAW Local 22 logo. Others had on blue UAW sweaters. All of them had yellow notepads and clipboards.

Soon Dr. Peck, cane in hand, hobbled into the room. Applause began to build as he struggled lamely onto a small stage. By the time he reached a high-backed swivel chair where he would preside over the day's events, many in the audience were standing. Peck stood for a moment, seeming bemused and moved. He is a pale, frail-looking man with

ash-blond hair, and he was dressed like a middle-aged executive—gray suit, a pink shirt, a pinkish tie, clunky black
shoes. He looked completely at ease, like a confident college
professor presiding over the last session of the most popular course on campus.

After an effusive introduction, Peck finally sat down, clip-
ping a small microphone to his lapel as he settled in. "I
apologize for the fact that I'm sitting down," he began. "I
have a disease of the spine, which like most diseases is partly
psychosomatic. I am a nervous psychiatrist."

After an eruption of giggles, Peck proceeded to lay down
the rules for the day. Most of them had to do with his
relationship with the audience, and they suggested that the
doctor had suffered in some of his contacts with awestruck
fans. "Please don't grab ahold of me during break time. I
need that time to get my head together. After all, I'm a
genius," he said with mock seriousness. "And I'd be happy
to sign copies of my books, but I won't have time to write
inscriptions like 'To Beth and Harry, keep on truckin'.' I've
clocked it and it takes six times longer. We would never get
out of here."

Peck's rules led me to worry that I was surrounded by
dependent groupies, self-help junkies who were there as
much to worship as learn. I was reassured when I introduced myself to the UAW man sitting on my left, Joseph
Granberry. Granberry, thirty-one, told me he was a former
assemblyline worker at a General Motors truck and bus factory in Pontiac. He had recently became part of a union
team that counseled workers who were having problems,
both on the job and off. All of the UAW people at the
meeting were part of the same counseling service. They had
come to learn more about helping others, not to bask in
the glow of Peck's fame.

"That's the best part of what I do, helping people get
their stuff together," he said. "There comes a point in everybody's life when you got to realize what's important. I
like being there when that happens for somebody." An alco-

holic, Granberry had stopped drinking with the help of Alcoholics Anonymous. Since becoming sober, he had worked hard to help others recognize their drinking problems and use AA to recover.

"I've been around enough alcoholics to know that without some kind of spiritual belief, they don't get better," Granberry said. "But it's not just the individual who has a problem. It's the whole society. It's sick. Everybody wants more of everything—more, more, more. That drives people crazy and never makes 'em happy. I've read his books and this guy here knows a lot about that," he continued. "Maybe I can pick up something today that would help me in my work."

It turned out that aside from a handful of Scott Peck groupies, the audience was almost entirely made up of people like Joseph Granberry. They worked in counseling, psychology, or the ministry. They tried to be healers and, like Granberry, they were eager to find something more for their clients. Addiction and depression seem epidemic in America today, and curing them is almost always a long, difficult process. Peck suggested that there is another tool they could use to help.

Up onstage, Peck began the day-long lecture by admitting he was uncomfortable with his evangelist role. "I recently realized, to my absolute horror, that I have become an evangelist. It's the last thing I ever expected to become. And an evangelist is probably the last person you'd expect to pay eighty-five dollars a day to listen to. But it is not my intent to convert anybody. I bring good news about all religions."

From this point Peck went on to a familiar New Age theme: the importance of myth. From Carl Jung to Joseph Campbell, many modern experts in myth and the mind have argued that certain stories and archetypes exist in every culture and religion. Jung believed they reside in a "collective unconscious," ready to be used by anyone and everyone. Myths are one way people have tried to understand themselves and fashion some ideas about gods, the origins of the Earth, and the destination of the soul. Some experts even argue that myths are an evolutionary necessity, a mechanism for keeping the individual sane and society well-organized. New Agers are intrigued by these theories on myth, in part because they provide an intellectual justification for spiritual interest.

"People know that myths are stories that aren't true. They are fairy tales that are found in culture after culture, age after age," said Peck. "But all myths embody some kind of truth. Take the use of dragons in mythology. They are found in the myths of every culture and they are a symbol of one aspect of human nature. They stand for the darker side. So are worms and snakes with wings. We have to accept that we are seven hundred or so dragons gathered here this morning."

Peck paused for a moment to let this inside joke sink in. Any New Ager worth the label knows enough about myth—either by studying Carl Jung or Joseph Campbell—to recall that the image of human dragons is familiar, and pleasantly wise. We are all part dragon. A wise man understands this. When the giggles subsided, Peck continued.

"One of the biggest myths is in the Bible. It's Genesis. Are there any closet creationists here? If there are, I apologize, but God—he, she, they—didn't have anything to do with evolution. Genesis is a myth. It teaches us that we cannot go back to Eden. We can only go forward, through the desert. Psychological pathology, drinking, drug abuse: They are all attempts to avoid the pain of the desert, of life, and go back to Eden. It's a seeking form of what Dietrich Bonhoeffer called 'Cheap Grace.' It's an attempt to regain that warm, fuzzy sense of oneness that we experience as infants. We can try that, or we can go forward into the desert, to deeper and deeper forms of consciousness and our own salvation."

Peck's choice of Bonhoeffer was illuminating. A German theologian who ceaselessly opposed Hitler, Bonhoeffer was eventually hanged by the Nazis, who accused him of plotting to kill the Führer. Before his death, Bonhoeffer concluded that traditional notions of God and religion are meaningless. He advocated the creation of a "religion-less" church that would retain Christian values but lose much of traditional dogma and doctrine. It would be a religion for the modern age, a religion, perhaps, for the New Age.

From Bonhoeffer, Peck proceeded to spend the morning on the subject of pain and psycho-spiritual development. "Pain is essential," he said. "Most people run away from it and hide. They say, 'I don't want to grow, I've stopped learning.' These are the people you see who look like adults but who are emotional children in adult clothes. They think they have found a safe place to hide, but their pain comes with them. You have to go through the desert first, before you feel the bliss."

Joseph Campbell speaks of bliss often. So do many in the New Age, who use the word to describe not euphoria, but a state of relaxed attentiveness. Bliss was the goal of the mystic baseball players and the MIU meditators.

Peck's "desert" of modern life is mostly a realm of bliss-preventing distractions and anxieties. He was rather orthodox in his approach to the origins on these troubles: They typically begin with childhood abuse or neglect, he explained, and they worsen if they are denied or ignored. The process of discovering, discussing, and healing these wounds takes place in psychotherapy, which Peck held up as an almost sacramental act. "I am not a pain freak, but this process involves constructive suffering, a willingness to go through it," Peck added. "And this path is really quite selfish. Instead of avoiding pain, which is stupid selfishness, you experience constructive pain in order to have the bliss that's on the other side."

This is the core of Peck's message. Through therapy you discover the truth—about yourself, your parents, the darker side of human nature—and the truth sets you free. The acceptance that follows these discoveries eases anxiety and fear, even the existential fear that haunts us all. And God is not lost in all this. Once freed by the truth, life becomes more sacred, more serene, and one finds it easier to follow a moral, Godly path.

Unfortunately, Peck said, modern society, with its many legal and illegal painkillers, seems obsessed with avoiding even constructive pain. In our high-tech, well-fed existence we have "lost the sense that existential pain enhances our existence. As a result, some parents try to raise children without having them experience guilt. What a terrible thing to do. We need a certain amount of guilt—not neurotic guilt but healthy guilt—in order to exist well in society. The jail in my community is full of people who are there precisely because they don't experience guilt. We need a certain level of anxiety to exist well, too."

Through psychotherapy and spiritual practice—prayer, meditation, study—we can reach a "higher state of consciousness" that allows us to live life more fully, he said. "If you stay with it and go farther into the desert, paradoxically, the more joy you will have. We can only go forward into the desert, to deeper and deeper forms of consciousness, for our own salvation. We cannot lose, once we realize that everything that happens to us has been designed to teach us holiness. What better news can there be?"

With this talk of "deserts" and "states of consciousness," Peck was trying to connect with ancient mystics. All the great religions feature some form of meditative practice. Through their meditations, mystics seem to find an energizing serenity that is both a spiritual and a psychological state. Though he is a psychiatrist, Peck was not afraid to speak in language that described this process in religious terms. Where other therapists might talk about "personal growth" and "self-worth," Peck spoke of "holiness" and "higher consciousness." Higher consciousness, it seemed, is an awareness of self-worth, and it comes to those who persevere, who take the "road less-traveled" by being honest, loving, and disciplined. This is the essential message in Peck's book, which opens with a line from the Four Noble Truths of Buddhism: "Life is difficult." The book goes on to argue passionately for responsible, self-disciplined living. Peck taps every major world religion to make the case for metaphysics, and he predicts the eventual union of science and religion, which many New Agers await as eagerly as born-again Christians await the Second Coming. In a chapter titled "Scientific Tunnel Vision," Peck challenges psychology's rejection of religion and even suggests that the psychic phenomenon, so readily rejected by science, deserves more serious study.

Like his book, Peck's lecture was a gracefully presented mixture of psychological and religious ideas. He continually referred to the Christian metaphor of the desert as place of challenge, purification, and renewal. But always he described spiritual growth as a psychological test. "Salvation is the ongoing process of becoming increasingly conscious," he said. "It is an ongoing process, not a one-time thing. Purgatory," he said, stopping to call attention to his punch line, "is a very well-appointed psychiatric hospital."

The audience of earnest professional helpers eagerly consumed Peck's message. He took their language, the language of therapy, and infused it with a religious spirit. He elevated mental health to an eternal process, gave it a deeper purpose and meaning. He praised the work they all did, describing their efforts to help those society often rejects as "controlled folly," a risk that must be taken. All of this seemed to excite the people in the crowd, who sat so quietly that the occasional cough or sneeze seemed amplified many times. But while they were attentive, they did not seem as frightened as those who flocked to see Louise Hay or as vulnerable as the people at the Lazaris intensive. Hay, Lazaris, and, for that matter, the Maharishi were much more charismatic figures, who used the power of their personalities to attract followers. Peck didn't have followers, per se. He had students. His appeal was in his ideas, not his bland, wheat-stalk personality. And he never took refuge in the metaphysical. He never left planet Earth.

Still, as with Lazaris and Hay, Peck used psychological exercises that seemed as much about emotional manipulation as instruction. During one, he asked us to close our eyes, listen to a treacly Cat Stevens love song, and imagine that God was singing it to us. The music was intended to create a mood of warmth and trust. No one resisted the exercise. As I looked around, I saw people smile. Some had tears of joy rolling down their cheeks.

At another moment in the seminar he asked for questions from the audience. One woman who responded seemed awed by Peck's call for them to endure life's difficulties like mystics wandering in a literal desert. He seemed eager to assure her that this was not the case. "As one of the great Muslim Sufis said, 'When I say weep, I do not mean weep for days.'" Another questioner asked for a more specific formula for right-living, which Peck refused to give. This refusal put further distance between Peck and the Maharishi, Lazaris, and Louise Hay. A third person had a fan-club kind of question: "What does the 'M' in M. Scott Peck stand for?" The answer: Morgan.

The program was a combination of a mental-health lecture and a revival meeting. Peck's choice of music, which he played before and after breaks, ran toward popular tunes with universal messages of love. He played them at well-timed intervals, to energize the audience the way gospel music revitalizes a church congregation. They were also familiar to his listeners and served as unifying inspirational reference points. Before lunch he asked us to close our eyes and sing along with Bette Midler's "The Rose," the same song used by Lazaris. But unlike Lazaris, Peck invited his audience to sing along, and the room was filled with the lyric.

During the break I bought a sandwich and a soda from a buffet table the hotel had set up in its lobby. I sat with several people from the lecture audience, including a psychologist, a minister, and a woman who said she was a "wonder consultant." She said she helped people develop a sense of wonder that makes their lives happier. Her main resource was *A Course in Miracles*, the twelve-hundred-page book that was supposedly dictated to a now-deceased author by a spirit entity that appears to be Jesus Christ. The course is promoted by a nonprofit foundation and used by hundreds of New Age study groups. The wonder consultant was devoted to the *Course* and used its teachings in her work. But she hoped that Scott Peck would teach her new ways to instill a sense of wonder in her clients.

The psychologist said he had come because Peck was one of his heroes. "When we psychologists threw out spirituality, we created a big void," he said. "This fills it."

The minister, who wore a clerical collar and a silver pin carved to look like a dove, said he found Peck's work to be very consistent with Christianity. "If I didn't see the Christian message in this, I wouldn't be here," he added.

The afternoon lecture brought more of Peck's simple but sensible psychology and theology: Life is hard. Neurosis is normal. God loves us. True evil, he said, lies "in militant ignorance, militant unconsciousness. Paradoxically, the further you go into the desert, the more it hurts. But the best measure of a person's greatness is his or her capacity to suffer. Pain is a quintessential part of life and we ignore it at our own peril."

Throughout his talk, Peck moved easily from religion to psychology, using one to define the other. When someone in the audience asked if he believed in the concept of karma, he said that he did, but then he explained it in psychological terms. "I'll give you an example. It involves a boy who killed his brother with a twenty-two that his parents gave him for Christmas. His karma was set when they did that." The child had been born into a family where "his soul was spiritually diminished." The gift of a gun, and the killing, were just the final, inevitable acts of a cycle set in motion by the family's values and the relationships between the parents and the children.

From karma Peck went on to breathe psychological life

into a dying religious concept: the notion of sin. "If we can acknowledge our sins with contrition, they are forgiven. The slate is wiped clean. It can be a new day, every day. Sin is a matter of missing the mark, falling short of our ideal, and by that definition we are all sinners. The key is to do what Saint Therese said, to bear serenely the trial of being displeasing to yourself."

Almost all of what Peck dealt with was focused on the personal. He spoke of the importance of "soul development" and "self-worth," the feeling of being worthy of self-respect. Occasionally, though, his message went beyond the self, to stress commitment to the community. "I emphasize personal, spiritual growth because that's where the market is," he confessed. By "market" Peck didn't mean an economic market, although it is true that there are billions of dollars to be made in self-help. He meant, instead, an intellectual market. By appealing to self-interest, he hoped to find an opening to present a larger concern. "There is a greater need," he said. "Our country needs different solutions for its problems. And we are going to have to provide the solutions because our government is spiritually and morally bankrupt."

This description of a world deep in sin could have been uttered by Rev. Jerry Falwell or Oral Roberts, and it marked Peck as an evangelist willing to use some very traditional rhetoric. It also served to identify those who took "the road less-traveled" as brave and virtuous, if not exactly better than others. He urged the audience to realize that they were good people, able to overcome the social pressure to become mired in materialism and addiction. "Nothing holds us back more from mental health, from spiritual health, from God, than the feeling that we are not worthy. Let me end by telling each of you how beautiful you are, how important you are, and that you are desired in ways you cannot imagine. You are beautiful."

There would be one more brief exercise, a trust-building experiment, for those who wanted to stay. Peck encouraged those who were on a schedule to depart. With this, the autoworkers rose en masse and made for the door. I wouldn't get a chance to ask Joseph Granberry what he thought of the program.

I spent the last half-hour of the seminar with a woman named Sue Kachorek, an executive from a local hospital who said her family didn't understand why she had taken a day off from work and spent eighty-five dollars to sit on a hard chair in a hotel ballroom to listen to a psychiatrist talk about God. "My family doesn't understand, but I have friends who do and a lot of us have come here today," she said quietly during a pause in Peck's presentation. "We are all reflective people. We think about what's important, and I've realized it's definitely not having the house, the car, the job, and all that. There has to be something more than selfishness."

After about half the crowd departed, Peck told us we should turn his lessons into action to help others. He asked each of us to exchange phone numbers with another seminar participant. I exchanged numbers with Kachorek. He then directed us to telephone each other in three weeks, to report what we had done to become more responsible, more contributing members of society.

That was it. He said good-bye. "The Rose" came pouring out of the ballroom's loudspeakers and dozens of people rushed forward to have Peck sign copies of his book.

Watching the eager crowd of people around Peck, I could see that he is a hero to a segment of America that struggles to find something to replace or augment traditional faith. He tapped the right sources—psychology, mysticism, Eastern religion, and mythology—to make his approach consistent with the New Age. But his use of traditional Christian ideas, especially as they related to suffering and sin, were comfortable and familiar. Similarly, Peck was the first major New Age leader I had heard who valued old-fashioned sacrifice—for the sake of our children, others, the future. And where other New Agers looked to energy vortexes or some other magical power, Peck asked that we look within and develop realistic expectations.

This rigorous approach to mental and spiritual health explained why Peck appealed to such a well-educated audience. With all the therapists and ministers in the room, there were more advanced degrees present than people. These more sophisticated seekers—the intellectuals of the New Age—choose Peck because he is intelligent and demanding. He doesn't offer psychic solutions. Instead he suggests a philosophical acceptance of life's pain and a commitment to honesty, self-discipline, and, ultimately, love. According to his books, this will lead to a psychological and spiritual awakening, and the happiness all people desire. But there is nothing easy in this, a fact that confounds the critics who consider the New Age nothing but a carnival of spiritual magicians and psychic sideshows.

By combining the serious business of therapy and the rigors of spiritual honesty, Peck has constructed a therapeutic form of religion. While orthodox believers from both realms might object to this fusion, it is not as revolutionary as it might seem. In the traditional church, rites such as confession or Communion have a powerful, psychologically transforming effect, especially on the devout believer. This was perhaps even more true in past centuries, when everyday people were less affected by rational science and more open to superstition and magic. These ceremonies simply wouldn't work on the psyches of those who considered them primitive or irrelevant. For a modern audience, Peck has discovered a new kind of ritual—psychotherapy—and he has enriched it with a sense of the sacred. In the process, he has given intellectuals license to explore a spirituality which they have rejected in mainstream religion but still feel within themselves.

This approach to spirituality made more sense to me than any I had seen in my long exploration of the New Age. Scott Peck didn't need to go into a trance or invoke the spirits. For him, spiritual expression could be realized in

meditation and an honest, moral way of living. The rest—
the nature of God, the soul, life after death—was in the
realm of mystery to be divined by the individual. I was also
impressed by Peck's effort to avoid a cult of personality.
The rules he announced at the beginning of the meeting
put distance between him and the audience, a distance that
was probably good for all concerned. And while he focused
intently on the individual, he did not advocate selfishness.
Indeed, he seemed to be saying that a rewarding life lies in
transcending self-interest. This is one of the primary truths
of all great religions and Peck had presented it without
obscuring dogma and superstition.

Three weeks after the seminar, I realized that I hadn't
heard from Sue Kachorek. She hadn't heard from me, either. And for a moment, I felt some of the "good guilt"
Peck had discussed. It was "guilt" because I knew I had
failed to keep a commitment that had meant something
when it was made. And it was "good" pain because it reminded me that there is still, inside of me, something good
that demands I live up to a certain moral code.

# 10 · ANANDA VILLAGE

## The Risk of Utopia

IT DOESN'T QUITE LOOK LIKE UTOPIA. ON A COLD, WET winter day the unpaved streets at Ananda World Brotherhood Village become rust-red bogs. Paint peels on the wooden siding of the older houses. Roofs sag and porches droop. The sun-bleached frames of unfinished structures loom like dinosaur skeletons in the misty rain.

If the New Age movement leads to one, ultimate destination—in physical, spiritual, and social terms—it may be this tiny mountain village eighty miles north of Sacramento, California, on the Yuba River. Ananda is supposed to be a model community for the New Age, an example of what life could be for us all in some future, enlightened era.

Of course, the rutted dirt roads and half-built homes suggest that the New Age has yet to dawn. Still, Ananda has grown steadily in recent years, and newcomers are building more permanent houses. The few tepees still standing amid the trees are romantic reminders of Ananda's beginnings. The village was founded in 1967 by yoga master J. Donald Walters, a student of Parmahansa Yogananda, one of the

first Indian gurus to settle in America. Yogananda lived in
the United States from 1920 until his death, in 1952, at
age fifty-nine. He attracted thousands to his Self-Realization
Fellowship, which operated more than forty yoga centers
nationwide. More important, he wrote *Autobiography of a
Yogi*, the mystical book that has captured "Spaceman" Lee
and millions of other readers.

The book traces the spiritual journey of a young Indian
boy named Mukunda Lal Ghosh who enters a guru's hermitage, becomes a Hindu monk, and takes the name Yogananda (bliss–ananda–through divine union–yoga). It
recounts his lifelong effort to bring Kriya Yoga to the West,
and reveals a darkly apocalyptic view of world affairs. Yogananda believed that before the year 2000, a cataclysm would
strike the Earth. He hoped that a combination of Indian
spiritual practice and American know-how would save
mankind. That salvation would take place in little utopian
communes. The yogi died before founding such a village,
but Walters—whose Hindu name is Swami Kryananda—
gave life to the dream. He founded Ananda and remains
its ultimate leader, guiding both the spiritual development of its citizens and the physical development of the
community.

To outside observers, the most remarkable thing about
Ananda is that it still exists, years after nearly all the other
counterculture communities of the Sixties have disappeared. Literally hundreds of communes and experimental
settlements have failed, often because of infighting, lack of
leadership, or impractical ideals.

Ananda lives on, in part because it operates several successful businesses. The center of life in the village, and a
key source of cash, is a kind of spiritual resort called Ananda's Expanding Light. Each year thousands come to the
Expanding Light to attend programs and workshops, to vacation or to enjoy days of uninterrupted meditation. The
center offers everything from daily personal retreats to
four-week programs for "Ananda Meditation Training."

Visitors can take courses in yoga, nutrition, nature, even the "Secrets of Success." They might also receive massage therapy, marriage counseling, chiropractic care, or spiritual counseling. Fees range from $34 for one day to $1,634 for a month. Like other resorts, it has a toll-free number for reservations.

THE GUEST IS GOD, says a small sign by the front door of the Expanding Light. (Anandans believe everyone is part of God.) I entered and was met by William LoCicero, one of the center's managers. He had invited me to visit for the January celebration of Yogananda's birthday. A thin, almost frail-looking man in his thirties, LoCicero walked noiselessly and spoke in a half-whisper. "We are more like a monastery than anything else," he said as he led me back to his office.

When I asked why Ananda survived, LoCicero first mentioned the many businesses—the retreat center, a publishing house, several stores, a builder's guild, a medical clinic, even an auto repair shop—that made the commune self-supporting. It was as if by reciting these worldly successes, he would demonstrate that Anandans are self-sufficient, sensible, normal.

"But what really makes Ananda work is that we practice nonattachment to the material world," he added. "Instead, we look for a more God-filled life. When everyone is living that way, you don't have the same conflicts. Everyone here was, at one time, searching, searching for something. Here, we are people who have found it and have decided to live together."

"It" means direct contact with God—the same thing promised by Lazaris at the Sirius weekend. The difference is that Lazaris brings people to God via group meditations and seminars while Walters claims that you can have blissful encounters with God through hours of daily meditation and a monastic way of living (since Anandans also believe that God exists within, this is also called "self-realization"). The commune facilitated this process. By sharing work and wealth, the villagers were able to spend less time making money and more time meditating.

LoCicero's face darkened when I asked him about his own path to self-realization. He looked down at the floor.

"I don't see why that's important. You are here to write about Ananda, not about me. Let's keep it like that."

"But Ananda is its people, including you."

"Yes, but it's more a way of living. That's what you should be explaining."

"How about if you just tell me some of the basics? For example, how old are you and where do you come from?"

"I don't see why that's important. Yogananda never told people how old he was. He said that people just use it to judge you, to put you in a category. Besides, I'm not what's important here. Individual personalities aren't as important as God."

LoCicero's reticence wasn't a matter of suspicion. He was trying to be humble. What is important to him is the faith, not the faithful; the teacher, not the student; the community, not the individual.

We tussled a bit more. I explained that to understand Ananda, I needed to know where the villagers came from, in every sense.

With halting responses, LoCicero sketched the thinnest outline of his life. He was born and raised in Youngstown, Ohio, in a family of first-generation Italian Americans. His father worked in a steel mill and his mother raised her three children—two boys and a girl—"to do good and be good." He recalled that she read him the Bible at night. He had been a very religious little boy.

"Then, all hell broke loose with me when I was a teenager." LoCicero rebelled against his parents, the church, his teachers, the middle-class values of financial security, career, and prosperity. "I wasn't attracted to money or to a big job. I didn't know what I wanted, but it wasn't the life I saw around me." He attended college in the early 1970s, but he was unable to settle on a major and he failed to graduate. He drifted.

"Then one Christmas, I took some books on yoga out of the Youngstown library," he said. As a teenager, LoCicero had been fascinated by India. He had also had a vision, a dream perhaps, of an Indian man in meditation. He devoured those first few books on yoga and went back for more, on Hinduism, Indian culture, anything related to yoga.

At the time, Youngstown's steel mills were closing. Thousands of workers were being laid off. Entire neighborhoods began to crumble. LoCicero moved to Houston with some friends, hoping to find work. In contrast to Ohio, Houston was awash in money. The first Arab oil embargo was in force and the subsequent run-up in prices had made for a Texas oil boom. LoCicero quickly found a job that paid much more than he could have made in Youngstown. Secure in his new life, he spent much of his free time at the Yoga Institute of Houston. It was there that he first met Kryananda and heard him speak.

"He had long hair and he was wearing these robes and he had a group of singers with him," LoCicero recalled. "My intellectual mind said, 'This is really weird.' But I closed my eyes and listened and my heart said, 'Yes, this is it!'" LoCicero closed his eyes again as he told me this. "I was inspired, uplifted. I had never felt that way before."

LoCicero stayed at the center to meet Kryananda and sign up for a weekend-long course. At the end of the course he had dinner with Walters and some of his longtime students. By late Sunday night, he was helping plan the establishment of an ashram in Houston. The ashram didn't work out, but LoCicero had found his spiritual path. He soon attended a two-week retreat at the Expanding Light. A few months later, he moved to Ananda.

"I had been living with what Yogananda calls 'An anguishing sense of monotony,'" he added, glancing at a picture on the wall. It showed him standing with Walters, who had his arm around LoCicero's shoulder. "Here we have a harmonious family, where we try to bring out everyone's potential."

Which doesn't mean there aren't moments of crisis and conflict. In 1978, the year LoCicero arrived, a forest fire destroyed most of the small houses the original settlers had occupied. Many who lost their homes left. Those who chose to rebuild soon faced another crisis when more than nine hundred cult followers of Rev. Jim Jones committed mass suicide in the utopian village they had built in the jungles of Guyana. The Jonestown disaster cast a shadow over all religious communities. The families and friends of the Ananda villagers warned them that it could happen again.

"Some of us said, 'Hey, we should keep a lower profile, hide out.' But Kryananda said we were nothing like Jonestown and we had nothing to hide, so there was no reason to fear."

While LoCicero talked, a young woman brought in pizza—whole-wheat crust with tofu instead of cheese—which he invited me to share. "Every Friday night is pizza night here," he explained. "We like to have fun, too."

The all-natural, meatless, and tasteless pizza met Yogananda's vegetarian diet standards. It also symbolized the almost relentless pursuit of wholesomeness at Ananda. Anandans do not watch television, nor do they smoke or drink. They view only "uplifting" films, and their musical tastes run toward American folk songs and Hindu-style chants. "We try to live in the world, but not be of it."

All this implies, of course, that there is something terribly wrong with the world, and it establishes the Anandans as a people apart. There is nothing unique in this. Christians have struggled with this problem—of being "in" the world but not "of" it—for centuries. So did the followers of Jim Jones. The difference between Jim Jones's followers and everyday Christians, between a cult and a religion, is a matter of degree and personal control. As a group falls further into social isolation, and authority becomes more concentrated in a single person or clique, it becomes more cultlike. Under this definition the Jim Jones group was the ultimate cult. The Maharishi's followers in Iowa may be a cult, and the Anandans run the risk of becoming one.

After we finished our meal, LoCicero asked a woman who was at the front desk to show me my room at Serenity House, one of the guest cottages. Susan Dermond and I walked under a star-speckled sky to a low, wood-shingled building that was about one hundred yards downhill from the Expanding Light. The night was clear, still, cold.

My tiny room was more like a cell than a hotel room. It was furnished with a single bed and a nightstand. Light came from two wall-mounted fixtures. The only bit of decoration was a four-square-inch framed portrait of Yogananda, which stood on the nightstand. It was a room designed for a cloistered nun.

In contrast to LoCicero, Dermond was warm and friendly. From South Carolina, she had once been a librarian at Furman University. She had first learned about Kriya Yoga when she read Yogananda's autobiography. Her efforts to learn more led her to a Kriya Yoga study group and Kryananda's many books. After visiting Ananda a few times, she sold an elegant old family home, quit her job, said goodbye to her friends, and moved to the New Age community. She built a small house and taught in the village elementary school, which had just sixty-five students. She was so open, exuberant, and direct that I imagined she was a good teacher. I also got the feeling that she was delighted to meet someone from outside the community. I asked her about what LoCicero had said, about the underlying harmony at Ananda.

"Oh, don't get the wrong idea," she said, laughing and running her hand through her hair. "We have problems. People get divorced here. They get sick, too. But day to day, we cooperate to reach certain goals, while in the world people compete with each other to see who has the nicest job, the best house. I know. I was part of that. And my family still thinks I was crazy to move here. But I tell my father that this is like the small town where he grew up, where you don't lock your doors and the kids walk to school through apple orchards."

Though safe and serene, Ananda was also very isolated. The nearest department store was an hour's drive away. The only real source of news was the radio. "For the first couple of years I'd have to go to town every week just to look at stores," Dermond confessed. "Now I don't do that. I find this setting idyllic, really." Single and childless, Dermond believed she had found a safe, nurturing place to live out her life. "It's not lonely. And living among people who sense God, well, I guess it's like being part of a Catholic order. It feels very good."

Life in a religious order can be safe, nurturing, orderly. It can also be stultifying and oppressive. Many an old-fashioned nun lives in the convent because she is afraid of the world, and vicious battles can rage behind monastery walls. For these reasons and more, Catholic monastic orders have seen their ranks dwindle to the point where many may soon die.

But there will always be those who yearn for a contemplative life. America has always had such groups: The Shakers, the Amana colonies, even the Amish are examples. They all recognized the price of life in a complex, materialistic society and chose, instead, the plain and the simple. Alone in a room that reflected perfectly the asceticism of Ananda, I thought of the village as a modern version of a Shaker community. And the villagers seemed like monks of the New Age, seeking the plain and the simple as antidotes to modern worries. But I was not convinced, as Bill LoCicero is, that Ananda is immune to the problems that isolation and the abuse of authority brought to both the monasteries of yore and to Jonestown.

"Gong. Gong. Gong." Saturday-morning meditation was announced by the sound of someone beating on an empty acetylene tank, which had been hung from a tree near the Expanding Light. Almost everyone at Ananda meditated for an hour or more each morning. The gong called visiting devotees to the center at 7 A.M., where they would silently meditate together until nine o'clock.

Morning meditation was intended for the devout, not for me, so after the gong jarred me awake, I had some time before the dining room would open for breakfast. I dressed and drove over to the nearby town of North San Juan, where the only restaurant in town was open for breakfast. My trip to North San Juan was motivated mainly by my desire for caffeine, which was not available at the retreat house. It is worth mentioning only because of John, the middle-aged logger who talked to me almost nonstop as I sipped coffee and scanned the front page of the local paper, which was filled with news of the war in the Persian Gulf. Without any more than a "Good morning" from me, John volunteered that the Persian Gulf war was evidence that a larger, more traumatic shift in the world order—an apocalypse perhaps—would soon take place.

"Something big is going to happen, a Depression, a nuclear world war," he said as a waitress refilled a mug inscribed with his name. Dozens of "name mugs" hung on a special rack for regular customers.

"The way people live must change," he continued. "There are too many people out of work, too many people who do work but don't really make anything. Everything's all out of whack. Nobody makes anything anymore. It's all computers and mass production, and that's not natural. We've gotten too focused on money and things. We have to live more simply, like we used to."

Though he was not from Ananda and had never studied the Yogi's works, this proto–Paul Bunyan sounded surprisingly like Yogananda discussing the impending apocalypse. His words also recalled the "Armageddon theology" of fundamentalist Christians, who believe that an earth-destroying war and the return of Christ are imminent. When I asked John if he had any religious or spiritual beliefs to support his thinking, he said that he didn't belong to a church or follow any religious teacher. He said he found God in nature.

"I go out and sit in the woods. Sometimes I see deer or fox. Once I even saw a mountain lion. I feel better out there, closer to God, I guess."

These beliefs, that the world is hurtling toward disaster and that God could be found in unspoiled nature, were based on "gut feelings," John said. They also resonate with the fears and beliefs that abide in the American character. From the Millerites and Mormons of the nineteenth century to Elizabeth Clare Prophet's followers in Montana, a certain segment of religious America has always lived in expectation of The End. Likewise, from the Deists of the Revolution to the New Age neo-pagans, Americans have found God in nature. Indeed, if TV commercials are any measure of American values, we all find nirvana (along with a new car, beer, or soft drink) on a mountaintop or beside a sylvan lake. Whatever the sources, these notions about ultimate doom and the Godhead of nature are common enough to drift into casual conversation at the North San Juan café.

Back at the Expanding Light, a breakfast of fruit, cereal, yogurt, and bran muffins was served monastery-style; in silence. The dining room had been decorated for the "Master's Birthday Banquet" that would be held the next day. Framed pictures of the long-haired guru had been placed on every table. On one wall there were another two dozen photos and paintings of him in various poses and settings. Altogether, there were more than fifty photographs of Yogananda in the room. Purple and pink fabric had been draped over the windows and life-size plywood cutouts, painted to look like elegantly bejeweled Indian women, had been placed near the door. From the kitchen came the muffled sound of Indian chanting, played on a tape player. The old photos, music, and decorations made the dining room into a gaudy shrine to the departed guru. It all made me a bit uncomfortable, in the way that the mouldering bones of saints on display in St. Peter's in Rome make me uncomfortable. There was too much worship implied in the decorations, too much adoration.

At about ten o'clock a tall, thin man with curly brown hair came into the room, clapped his hands, and announced the start of a lecture on "Yogananda's Path for This Age" in the adjoining temple. We rose and followed him into a small anteroom, where we all took off our shoes, and then into another domed, hexagonal room that was the sanctuary.

The bright, white-walled chapel had thick, dark blue carpet, which softly padded the steps of our bare feet. The windows were edged with squares of blue and red stained glass. The space was almost empty, except for a small altar on the wall opposite the doorway. The altar was really a series of steps, which were decorated with candles, flowers, and dozens and dozens of pictures of Yogananda. He was shown sitting, standing, reclining, speaking, embracing followers, flanked by dignitaries, alone in meditation. On a shelf behind the altar, high enough to be seen even from the back of the room, were several framed pictures. In the center was a picture of the bearded face most Christians recognize as Christ. This picture was flanked by pictures of the four yogi masters who were respected by Yogananda. On the far right was Yogananda himself.

Rather unsubtly, the decorations illustrated a core principal of the master's teaching, that over the centuries God has reached out to humankind through such teachers, who speak for him. Yogananda was the latest in this line. This explained the shrine in the banquet room, the atmosphere of unrestrained adoration. As far as the villagers were concerned, Yogananda had been much more than a teacher. He had been a living Christ, perhaps a god. No wonder they were so unnervingly devout.

Our lecturer, an Ananda minister named Rich McCord, arranged some chairs in a circle and invited us to sit down. He fetched a small organ from a corner of the room and played a few chords. Soon he began to sing, in a flat, sing-song voice:

*Joy, joy, joy, joy
Ever-new joy, joy.*

The song went on for several minutes. We in the semicircle closed our eyes and joined him. McCord never seemed to breathe as he sang, he just went on and on, first fast, then slow, first loud, then soft. I tried to keep up. The vibration and the slight oxygen deficiency that resulted had a pleasant, mesmerizing effect. When he stopped playing and we all fell silent, I was light-headed, slightly warm, relaxed.

"Very few teachers ever bring anything totally new," McCord said when he stopped singing. "Instead, they bring something appropriate for the people and the time in which they are teaching. The age we are in now is best reflected in science." Science has shattered many old religious assumptions, he said. "So people are reaching out for deeper levels of understanding. On the surface, it may look like we're in chaos, but really, what started in the 1960s and Seventies is a sincere search for understanding, and it continues today."

McCord described Yogananda as the prophet of a new approach to religion, one that would supplant a dying Christianity. "Entrants into the Catholic priesthood have declined by eighty percent since 1960. It's because people are no longer satisfied with dogma or rules. They want experience with God. The purpose of yoga is to get away from dogma, away from belief. The bottom line is personal experience of God. How will you know when you've touched God-consciousness? As Master said, you will know."

Reaching the ultimate meditative state of "samadhi," or "God-union," requires years, even decades, of meditation and pure living. But when it happens, "the energy that is you is joined with the energy that is the God-consciousness," said McCord. "People in the New Age movement understand this. They understand that all of creation is flowing energy and that we are part of the flow. Wrong-living can obstruct the flow. A deep practice of Kriya Yoga, with its energization exercises, improves the flow."

He said that it is the combination—right-living and deep meditation—that one sees at work in the village of Ananda. "Yogananda tried to start a community, but unfortunately the people weren't ready for it. Still, he said it was the way of the future, and that with the coming cataclysm, the destruction of the modern way of life, we would be forced to again live in small communities. Our cities would become nightmares to live in and the viable alternative will be communities like this."

McCord then switched on a television set as big as one of the stained-glass windows and played a tape of a lecture given by Swami Kryananda. Normally Kryananda would appear in person at a celebration of Yogananda's birthday, but he was recovering from an illness, kidney stones, and would not be seen in public for some months. On the tape, the American swami had the bearing and the appearance of an Episcopal bishop. His face was pale, soft, kindly. He wore a white robe and he smiled reassuringly as he spoke.

Apparently addressing a community gathering, Kryananda suggested that Ananda is at the center of a historic turning point for civilization. The energy of spiritual renewal is filling the universe, he explained. We merely had to tune into the "collective unconscious" and make the New Age ours. Yogananda had started the process. Those who were receptive to his "energy" were continuing it. "If you feel the attunement, go with it. It's a rare blessing." Kryananda repeated that his master is nonsectarian. His path is open to all. But he also hinted that the villagers of Ananda are, nevertheless, special. The Anandans are "warriors of light," representing God in a world of darkness. "There's so much darkness in the world, so much real evil. People laugh at higher values. They sneer at you." Though millions don't know that "something tremendous is happening," said Kryananda, "the ages to come will see and they will bless you."

When the video stopped, all the others clapped their hands. I sat still, stunned by the grandiosity in what both McCord and the videotaped swami had said. They are the warriors of light, the ones who know God.

McCord clasped his hands at his chest, bowed, and smiled. As the others left, I lingered to ask him about the cataclysm, which apparently didn't interest anyone else. With television news programs displaying the Persian Gulf war in terrible detail, I wondered if he believed that what the guru had predicted was coming to pass.

"I can't really say if it's now, or even if it is going to happen with this war. Yogananda wasn't that specific," McCord said as he led me into the dining room, where we sat down at a table. "But he did say that before the end of the century there would be another world war, a U.S.-involved war. He also said that Boston would wind up having a tropical climate, and that the people in the world would wind up having half the wealth they have now. He also said that because of good karma, the United States and India would come out on top." Some combination of American technology and Indian spirituality would be man's salvation and ensure centuries of undisturbed peace.

Yogananda's predictions made sense to McCord, but he didn't dwell on them. He was, instead, consumed by the pursuit of God. "I'm an all-or-nothing kind of person," he explained. "I had these questions: What is God? Is he knowable?" In 1982 he read *Autobiography of a Yogi* and he found reason to believe that God can be experienced. "I had gotten out of graduate school and I had a very good job as a management consultant in Palo Alto. I had everything, but it wasn't making me happy. I remember when I was about six years old and I went with my parents to one of their friends' houses. We lived in a small town in Minnesota and people lived the same. But when I looked at them, they didn't seem happy. I knew then that a regular, middle-class life wasn't for me. When I grew up and began living it myself, I had that same feeling again."

In another time, McCord might have become a Roman Catholic monk. But the twentieth-century Christianity he knew in the Presbyterian church of his childhood never captured him. He was an all-or-nothing person and the church seemed to offer only halfway answers. "I didn't want a part-time spiritual life," he said.

Kriya Yoga, with its intense meditation techniques, exercises, and "postures," appealed to McCord. He studied for two years and then visited Ananda. In 1984, he came to live in the village, occupying a one-room cell and adopting a spare, renunciate life-style. He became a missionary of sorts, accompanying Kryananda on some of his speaking tours, and made a pilgrimage to India.

"All the dirt, all the noise, the overcrowding—I could see why Yogananda loved it so much. I felt it was home to me." The night before, Susan Dermond had mentioned that she had made a recent pilgrimage to India. She too had felt "at home." McCord explained that everyone at Ananda believed they had lived in India "during a previous incarnation." This, in part, explained their attraction to Yogananda. They had been the guru's disciples before, in another life.

"But don't think we do this big Indian thing all the time," he said, waving his hand at the decorations in the big hall. "This is the one time of the year when we do all this Indian-style stuff. Usually there's none of this."

As McCord talked, another Ananda minister came to sit at the table. Bent Hansen was a young Canadian with short blond hair, a thick mustache, and pale blue eyes. In contrast with the other, sunken-eyed, anorexic-looking people I had seen at Ananda, Hansen was a robust, even muscular man. And he seem fascinated by a question I asked about Kryananda's videotaped lecture. I wanted to know about the dark forces, the evil he had mentioned. A former meditator had once told me he encountered evil spirits while practicing yoga and had subsequently given up the practice. I wanted to know if such encounters were common.

"There are dark forces, lower astral entities," Hansen volunteered. "Catholic saints dealt with demons all the time. Some people call them tramp souls. They are real." The tramps can enter a meditator's consciousness. "That's why it's important to meditate with a purpose of seeking God, rather than simply going blank and letting anything happen."

As we talked, the kitchen staff chanted along with an Indian tape that blared out of a small tape player. The large dining room was empty, except for us three and the chants reverberating off of the rafters. The combination of the chanting, the big empty space, and the ghost talk gave our little meeting a spooky aura of mystery.

"This is why it's important to have a master and be in a community that is seeking God," continued Hansen. "I have never heard of this kind of thing happening with any of our people." The teachers, the Ananda ministers, the entire structure of the community—all are designed to direct the spiritual life of its members. Drifters, the unstable, and the disturbed "are weeded out," he said. The weeding takes place during the interviews, courses, and long periods of training that precede a new member's acceptance into the community. Newcomers must spend a year in intensive study and meditation as postulants. They live at an old retreat center, which is several miles from the main village, and they are closely supervised. For the next four years they are novices, conditional members of the community. Only after five years are they invited to take formal vows to become a lifetime member of Ananda. These requirements, which were established when the community was first founded as a Hindu monastery for single men and women, now extend to the married couples and families who come to settle there.

With the kitchen crew laying out lunch, Rich McCord left

and Hansen volunteered to show me around Ananda. He drove my rental car and talked nonstop as we wended our way along the paved main road and the many rutted, gravel paths that serve as side streets.

The center of the community and the heart of its everyday commercial life is the handful of wooden buildings that borders a wide, open pasture where several boys were tossing a football as we approached. On one side of the street a small house serves as the village administrative office, and beside it is the tiny Ananda post office. Near the post office is an old barn that is used as an auto-repair shop, and next to that is a small house that has been converted to a school for seventh- and eighth-graders. The elementary school occupies two new buildings on a hilltop overlooking the village center. Ananda's children go to public high school after eighth grade.

The most important commercial building in the village is Master's Store, a refurbished farmhouse that is a general store, café, delicatessen, and laundromat. As we walked through, two women were folding laundry and stacking it on top of the washing machines and dryers. A couple drank herbal tea in the sunny greenhouse where little white tables and chairs were arranged to look like a sidewalk café. Sales of organically grown vegetables and tofu were brisk.

In the old days, said Hansen, all the vegetables and fruit eaten at Ananda would have been grown in the huge garden that once covered the hillside behind the store, just beyond the old men and women's shower houses. But as Ananda and its residents grew older, amenities such as indoor plumbing became quite popular and the shower houses fell into disuse. Something similar happened to the garden. It took an extraordinary amount of time to cultivate and manage acres of gardens and one of the nation's largest compost heaps. Eventually the gardeners realized it was cheaper to buy vegetables from local growers who pledged them to be chemical free, and by abandoning the garden, the Anandans freed themselves for other work—in the publishing company, the builders' guild, or even in the Ananda gift shops in nearby towns—that made them money.

The decision to let the garden become a fertile nest of weeds was symbolic of an overall change that had taken place at Ananda. In the 1980s the village had been transformed from a hippie-style commune into a middle-class town. As Hansen explained the change, and how Ananda now functioned, he sounded like a town father, perhaps the head selectman of a New England village, discussing taxes and public-works projects. He was proud, chauvinistic.

"The people who settle here permanently pay a single, lifetime fee," he said. "It's based in part on the ability to pay, but usually it's between two thousand and three thousand dollars. After that, there is a monthly service charge of two hundred or three hundred dollars on all the residences. Businesses pay similar fees, usually ten percent of their earnings. The money is used to build roads and community buildings like the schools." The fees also paid for electricity and other services. "And it pays for things like that," Hansen said as he pointed to a basketball court where several children rolled around on skateboards.

Clearly, Ananda was organizing itself into a sort of municipality. There was a village board, elected by residents, and frequent community meetings to settle major issues. "Kryananda is the president for life of the village council, but he has never voted. He really prefers that we lead ourselves," he added, in a tone that made him sound like an obedient son.

As he talked, Hansen drove us down winding roads to the Crystal Hermitage, Kryananda's home. A long, low building that clung to a steep embankment, it is the finest house in the village and it seemed that Hansen took me there for that reason. He was showing off.

With a swimming pool, a sprawling layout, and a spectacular view of the Yuba River Valley, Kryananda's house was quite impressive, especially when compared with the tepees,

small cottages, and clustered apartments that other Anandans occupied. The view was breathtaking and the land-
scaping gave the grounds the atmosphere of a quiet
monastery or seminary. It recalled Assisi, where Ananda
has an ashram and where Kryananda had spent much time.

When I noted the contrast between this "hermitage" and
the rest of the housing at Ananda, Hansen quickly reassured me that no community money had been spent on the
place. It had been built with money Kryananda had inherited upon the deaths of his parents. Many other Ananda
residents had also built homes with money sent from parents or received as inheritances. This was due, in part, to
the fact that the community's members were growing older.
The average age of an adult in the community was forty,
said Hansen.

"A lot of people have the assets you have going into middle age. You know, they may have inherited a house or
some money. But we also face some of the problems of
middle age."

The main problem is health care. As the Ananda community ages, the need for doctors increases, and so does the
possibility of serious illness. In an age when one long-term
illness can run up hundreds of thousands of dollars in hospital bills, the prospect of one or more residents developing
cancer or being injured in an auto accident was frightening
to those who managed the community's finances. Most of
the residents are uninsured. They receive low-cost medical
care at a village clinic and hospitalizations are paid for by
the community. "But we have been lucky," said Hansen.
"We haven't had to pay for anything really big yet."

Plain luck has spared the community's three hundred residents serious health problems, but luck will have no effect
on the aging of the community. With many citizens already
in their fifties and the majority about to enter middle age,
Ananda faces the challenge of caring for hundreds of people of retirement age. Surely many will continue to work,
but a large number will not. And the number of young

people joining the community is small, so they can't be counted on to help support their elders.

Ironically, Ananda faces the main problems that are slowly destroying Catholic orders: an aging membership and too few newcomers. Ananda is a sort of refuge of spiritually minded veterans of the 1960s. And Yogananda's message resonates best with those who have seen him in person. Succeeding generations might not be so moved by the yogi's ideas, and young people born long after the end of the counterculture revolution might not feel the same need for a radical life-style.

Bent Hansen didn't recognize that there might be something lacking in Yogananda's message or in the Ananda way of life. He saw the looming demographic crisis as a transient inconvenience. "It's a problem, but we're having trouble focusing on it," added Hansen. "It's not something that is right here and now, so it doesn't feel immediate and it's hard to say what should be done."

That night, at a "flower ceremony" held to mark the eve of Yogananda's birthday, it was easy to see why the villagers had trouble attending to the retirement issue. The sanctuary at the Expanding Light was filled with hundreds of people in their early forties, in the prime of life. There were many families with young children, and dozens of young couples.

The ceremony was conducted by four ministers, two married couples actually. Ministers Vidura and Durga Smallen were in charge of the day-to-day affairs of the village. The others were Devi and Jyotish Novak, who were, next to Kryananda, the spiritual leaders of Ananda. (Their first names are Hindu, given by Kryananda.) Like many of the couples at Ananda, Jyotish had been a monk and Devi had been an Ananda nun before their marriage. And like many couples, they shared a single job, so that they could manage both work and family life easier.

"Saints of all religions, we offer the flowers of our devotion, gently at thy feet," Durga said in the opening prayer of the ceremony. "Help us to remember that you are always with us, that you are our dearest friend, that in our pain and joy, we are yours and you are ours."

There followed a long, urgent chant of "Om master, om master, om master." Then Jyotish, who looked and sounded very much like the Kryananda I had seen on the videotape, instructed us to meditate silently, together. He closed his eyes and an expression of bliss came over his face.

"Focus on that spot between your eyes and call to Master," he said. "When your mind is calm, feel the love. Feel that peace, that deep friendship, that unconditional love."

The feeling of unconditional love, like the perfect love a mother offers her infant, is often mentioned by New Agers as the ultimate evidence of God's presence. Looking around the crowded sanctuary, I saw hundreds of people with their eyes closed, trying to feel that love. Some smiled broadly, as if to signal that yes, they had made contact with God. Tears trickled from the closed eyes of a woman next to me. In the back of the room a baby cried and her mother quickly carried her to the vestibule. No one else moved.

Jyotish signaled the end of the meditation by noisily breathing in and exhaling. As eyes were opened and people reached for hankies to dry their tears, someone turned on a tape player. Through the loudspeakers that hung from the rafters came the crackling voice of Yogananda, recorded more than thirty years before. The yogi sounded as if he were speaking from the bottom of a well. It was impossible to make out precisely what he said, but I could hear enough to tell that he was relating a story about the sufferings of St. Anthony, the Catholic mystic.

St. Anthony continually sought God "even when he was overwhelmed by grief," said the guru. In the end, he reached "God-consciousness" because "he had followed his activity with a pious life, and he went after God." We too should pursue God with boundless vigor, said Yogananda. The tape ended as Yogananda recommended that all people end their days with "the deepest gratitude" for their spiritual guides. "God,

Christ, gurus," he said, chanting the order in which they should be honored. "God, Christ, gurus."

With the chant still hanging in the air, the tape was switched off and Jyotish Novak increased the level of adoration. Yogananda's birthday should be like Christmas and New Year's rolled into one, he said, "because Master is an incarnation of great love and great will."

But what could be done to honor him? he asked. "What do you get for the man who *is* everything? He is more ourselves than we are ourselves." Yogananda's soul was so highly evolved, so pure and good, that he had no need to return to Earth for another life, he added. He was residing in bliss. "What he really wants us to give him is that which keeps him from realizing him . . . in self-offering, we close the cycle." Self-offering meant making a solemn vow, a commitment to the Ananda Church of God-Realization. The hundreds in the room stood and, reading from a paper they had been given at the door, recited in unison:

*I offer myself in service and devotion to your cause*
*and to the ray of divine light*
*as it is represented by Your channels,*
*Jesus Christ, Babaji-Krishna, Lahiri Mahasaya, Swami*
*Sri Yuketswar, and Parmahansa Yogananda.*

*Accept me into this family of Self-realization*
*and make me also, through them,*
*an instrument of Thy blessings.*
*Thus, as I receive,*
*may others be blessed, also to receive.*

*I will join my energies to those of my gurubhais*
*my spiritual family on Earth.*
*I will cooperate with them, and especially*
*with the living representatives and guides*
*of my divine line of gurus.*

*Discipline me, guide me, purify me.*
*Teach me to attune myself to Thy ray, until at last,*
*through daily meditation, service, and devotion,*
*I unite my soul with Thy Infinite Spirit.*

When the vow was finished, the villagers went to the altar, where scores of small candles had been lit to illuminate the pictures of Yogananda. One by one, the villagers each laid a single flower next to a photograph of the great guru. The flowers, Jyotish explained, symbolized the flaws and failings that each member relinquished to Yogananda. (Christians similarly "give" their sins to Christ, who absolves them through his death.) As the flower procession slowly continued, the devotees sang a simple chant, over and over:

*Om Master, may Thy joy fill our days.*
*Om Master, may Thy wisdom guide our ways.*

When it was over, Devi announced that the kitchen staff would be offering pieces of birthday cake to anyone who wished to take them home. "Take some birthday cake in silence, and go home in meditation."

Not a word was spoken in the little foyer outside the temple, even as hundreds of people struggled to find their shoes in the mountain of leather and canvas outside the door. The cake-givers stood holding huge trays of sheet cake covered with white icing. Almost everyone took a piece before they slipped into the cold night.

I walked silently to my little cell, not meditating but contemplating what I had seen. The ceremony had been a remarkable fusion of East and West, just as Yogananda's teachings are a fusion of both Hindu and Christian symbolism. The chanting, the pictures of the guru, the bare feet, all recalled Hinduism. But the references to God and Jesus Christ, the use of old English words such as "Thee" and "Thy," evoked austere, old-fashioned Protestantism. The oath, or vow, seemed decidedly Christian, something like the Apostles Creed. But the adoration of a "master" is a decidedly Eastern phenomenon.

The constant references to a "master" chafed against my American, intellectual sensibilities. I am the product of a culture that reveres individualism, self-reliance, equality. It is also a culture in which, in the main, religion or spiritual practices are private matters often restricted to one morning on the weekend or, perhaps, a meeting or two each week. In general, Americans are not very open about their faith and they tend to curb any expression of it in their everyday life. We are even more reluctant to call any leader "master" and dedicate our lives to him. The exception to this rule is Jesus Christ, who many born-again Christians believe has a spiritual reign over their lives. But this belief does not involve a man of the twentieth century whose words are tape-recorded and whose chief disciples, and inheritors of his authority, walk the earth. The way in which so many willingly accepted Yogananda as "master" was unnerving. And I wondered if there weren't many villagers who had, without exactly meaning to, ceded control of their lives to Kryananda and his closest students, Jyotish and Devi Novak. I wondered if a photo of J. Donald Walters might one day be added to the pictures of Christ and the gurus which decorate the Ananda temple.

At dawn I could hear the rhythmic scratch of someone sweeping the wide porch and steps in front of the temple. Whoever it was swept so hard it sounded as if he might scrape the paint off the wood. I looked out the window to see an older man wielding a broom and a young woman tacking yards of bright yellow ribbon to the porch railings. The sound of rattling dishes broke the still air. Somewhere dogs were barking.

Master's birthday was one of the more important holidays of the year at Ananda. People began gathering at the Expanding Light center hours before the usual 11 A.M. Sunday service for a "purification" ceremony. There was also the community banquet to prepare. Meanwhile, families with small children were gathering at the Crystal Hermitage, for a special children's service. I drove over, arriving just as the last families were removing their shoes and entering the long, low building. I quickly slipped off my shoes and followed them inside to yet another temple, a geodesic dome, about thirty feet high and perhaps fifty feet in diameter.

So many families filled the dome that I couldn't move more than three or four feet past the door. The floor of the white-walled chapel was really a series of thickly carpeted steps, like bleachers, which led down to an altar decorated with dozens of pictures of Yogananda, the same ones I had seen at the Expanding Light temple. There was a Christmas tree on one side of the room and a wreath was hanging in one window. Parents and children crowded every square inch of the place. All were focused intently on a white-robed couple—the ministers—who stood in the well of the floor, in front of the many pictures.

The service began with a call to meditation. Even the toddlers in the room immediately closed their eyes and became still. "Focus on the point between your eyebrows and call to God in the language of your heart," said the woman minister. Outside the door I heard a mother scold her son with a whisper: "Isaiah, we're late, come on!" Inside, all eyes remained closed, all bodies were still.

In a moment the man who was also conducting the service began to tell a story about a little boy who was constructing a tiny village of sticks and stones in the dirt of his backyard. "There's this big rock in the yard, which is blocking the development of his village in the West," he said, winking to the adults in the room. Yogananda had sought development in the West, too. "The boy pushes it. He pulls it. He gets a long stick and tries to pry it. It still won't move."

Eventually the boy's father wanders into the yard and sees his son exhausted in failure. "He says, 'Son, have you done everything in your power to move that rock?' " continued the storyteller.

" 'Yes, I have,' answers the boy.

" 'No, you haven't, because you haven't asked me. I can move it for you, easily.' "

The father moved the rock and the little boy expanded his village westward, just as Yogananda expanded the reach of yoga westward. The moral of the story, said the minister, is that there is a heavenly father who will help us move life's stubborn rocks, if only we ask. "Every one of us has Master for a big, strong spiritual father. All we have to do is ask, and he will help us."

The story was followed by others, all illustrating Yogananda's paternal presence. As the congregation entered a meditation that would end the service, I quietly let myself out of the chapel and went to find my shoes in the jumble of boots, clogs, Batman sneakers, and Mary Janes that lay outside the door. Inside I could hear the ministers saying good-bye to the children and their parents. "Make a spiritual birthday wish to Master, for yourself, today," I heard the woman minister say. "Wish for something Master can help you with. What is the rock he can help you move?"

Back at the Expanding Light, I again took off my shoes and went inside, taking one of the few empty chairs left in a back row of the larger temple. There were six ministers in front of the altar this time. I recognized four from the night before: Jyotish and Devi Novak and Vidura and Durga Smallen. Again, everyone was chanting.

If the family service at the Crystal Palace was childishly simple, the Sunday meeting for adults was remarkably complex. The service reeled from theme to theme, from chant to sermon to prayer. And here again was the particular admixture of religious thought that made Yogananda's Hindu teaching so much more palatable to the West. The ministers quoted the Gospels of John, Matthew, and Luke. They also read from the Bhagavad-Gita and from the works of Kryananda. "Parmahansa Yogananda showed us that the reports of all the great saints coincided," said one minister. And they coincided in one important aspect. They all reported mystical encounters, "direct inner communion, with God." This is because, in all holy works, there is the "vibration of His intelligence," he said. "The word of God is the creative vibration of his intelligence. The word proceeds from God. It is God."

This belief, that Holy Scripture is the product of "God's vibrations," is no mere metaphor. It is central to the Ananda villagers and to the faith of perhaps a majority of New Agers who believe that subatomic vibrations—the tiny movements of the particles that make up all matter—are what connect the human body, mind, and soul to the totality of the universe. If these vibrations can be found everywhere, they reason, then mankind is part of everything: heaven, Earth, even God. And just as the meditators at MIU believed that through meditation they entered a Unified Field where they could manipulate reality, the villagers at Ananda believed they could, through meditation, touch a "vibrational" level of existence, where God resides.

Minister Devi Novak returned the service to a more Christian-like tone. She talked of Yogananda's birthday in the way a Christian preacher might speak of Christmas. The conclusion she suggested, of course, is that Yogananda and Christ are equals.

"In the birth of our great Master," she said, "the word was made flesh. What does it mean to you that the word was made flesh? How can we use this great miracle?" A moment later she said, "We may look at ourselves and see all sorts of flaws. But it doesn't matter. It's not our power that transforms us, it's Master's power that transforms us."

As an exercise, it was illuminating to reconsider what Devi Novak had said, substituting the name "Jesus" for "Master." The result was statements such as "In the birth of Jesus, the word was made flesh" and "It's Jesus' power that transforms us"—a fairly direct paraphrase of the opening of the Gospel of St. John. Devi's preaching was in a classically Christian, classically American style. Once I started looking for these parallels in the language of Christianity and the New Age Anandans, they seemed to be everywhere. The ministers at the Sunday service, for example, urged believers to act according to "Guru's will" in the same that the fundamentalist preachers admonish their flocks to follow "Jesus' will."

Finally, Devi offered solace and a direction for devotees to follow as the news of the Gulf war filled the new year with a sense of foreboding. "Whatever lies ahead for the United States and the world at large, let's look forward to the year as warriors. We will be warriors for God, and joy will be our gun. Though death and despair may be all around, rest in the joy that our guru is all around us."

With the end of the service, the hundreds of worshipers moved from the temple to the brightly decorated dining room for the birthday banquet. I was seated at a small table with just one other person, a woman in her forties named Virginia Helin or, in Hindu, Sadhana Devi. As we ate sweet fried bread, curried vegetables, and fried tofu with chutney, she told me she had been among the original settlers, who first came to live on the land permanently in 1969. She was just twenty-four years old.

"I sewed twelve tepees that summer," she recalled. "We cut the poles ourselves in the forest and put them up. I lived in one myself for four years. It wasn't so bad, especially when we got woodstoves. Of course, one person's tepee did burn down. And once we had a heavy rain and it froze, so I couldn't get out," she added, laughing. "Aside from the porcupines and the raccoons, that's the only problem I ever had with it."

Helin had come to Ananda from San Francisco, where she had been a social worker. "I was a middle-class kid who was looking to leave the world behind," she explained. At that time there were, no doubt, millions of middle-class kids who, frightened by the Vietnam War and the protest movement, may have felt similarly disillusioned by the world.

"One of my friends was going to Tibet. Other people were living in communes. I thought this would be incredibly unique. And I knew it was going to work. I had confidence in Kryananda. He was a level-headed person with vision. He was very good at involving people. You feel comfortable with him." Virginia Helin felt so comfortable that she never left. She studied Yogananda's works and became a devotee. She changed her name to Sadhana Devi and eventually married and had a child, a daughter now finishing high school. "She's in the first group of Ananda kids to go to public high school. From what I can tell, they have been less susceptible to peer pressure than other kids. They just don't cave in."

Though she is convinced that her tiny village is the best place to live and raise children, Helin admitted that Ananda had its drawbacks. "There's not much diversity here, and I miss that. I hope my daughter goes to a college where the student body is very diverse, so she learns about people. But we're part of the diversity of life, too. We're not separate from American society. We are a part of it."

Except for the isolation, Helin found life at Ananda to be nearly perfect. "Relationships are deeper, more meaningful here," she said. "I mean, I love my relatives outside Ananda, but those relationships seem like duty. Because we don't meditate together, we don't have any deep bonds. When we're together, all we do is go shopping. It's sad."

As Helin paused for a moment, the crowd around us began singing "Happy Birthday" and a large cake adorned with a single candle was brought out from the kitchen. A little girl from one of the banquet tables came forth to blow out the candle and she received the kind of polite applause that relatives offer at a family party. Jyotish and Devi Novak cut the cake and helped distribute pieces to the devotees. There were a few songs, but no speeches or sermons. Master's birthday was a low-key affair. Soon all were leaving, wishing one another "Happy Birthday." Many carried paper plates full of edible souvenirs.

After saying good-bye to Virginia Helin, I found Bill LoCicero, to thank him for helping to arrange my visit and several interviews. He told me I had one more place to visit at Ananda before driving to San Francisco and my flight home. He had arranged for me to spend some time with a family that had only recently moved to Ananda. They were part of a new wave of devotees, mature adults with families who were remarkably different from the back-to-the-land radicals who began Ananda in the 1960s. These were, instead, stable middle-class people purposefully seeking a life that was a few steps off the beaten path.

The Crams, Jeffrey and Sandra and their daughters Heidi and Shannon, lived with the other novices on seventy thickly wooded acres about seven miles from the main village. The land was at the end of a long, dirt fire road, which was quite difficult to follow in the darkness that was quickly falling. After several wrong turns, I found a cluster of old, weather-worn geodesic domes next to a leaky, home-made water tower. I parked my car near the water tank and started to wander through a grove of manzanilla trees, to the domes. There I met Jeff Cram, a man of medium build with a round face, dark hair, a beard, and glasses. He showed me around the domes, which were used for dining, classes, and group meditation. We then took his car, an expensive late-model Peugeot, down the winding road to his cabin.

Perched on the side of a hill, the Crams' all-wood cabin looked like a ski chalet or a well-maintained hunters' lodge. In the front yard was an elaborate wooden swing set. Snow sleds were propped against the side of the house. Near the door was a piece of wood, cut in the shape of a whale, with THE CRAMS written on it. The swing set, the sleds, and the nameplate were the first signs of middle-class domesticity I had seen in my entire visit to Ananda.

Inside I met Sandra Cram and her daughters, Shannon and Heidi, who were both sick with the flu. Shannon was collapsed in her mother's arms on a sofa that was pushed against one wall of the large room that took up almost all of the first floor of the house. Opposite the sofa was a small kitchen. In the center of the room was a dining table, and off to one side was an alcove where Heidi was lying in her parents' bed. There were only two other real rooms in the house, a small meditation room that was once a walk-in closet, and a sleeping loft for the girls, which was suspended over the kitchen area.

I accepted a cup of herbal tea and sat down to chat with Jeff and Sandy in the dim light provided by a small kerosene lantern. The Crams said they lived in relative luxury, compared with the others who were in their first year at Ananda. They had running water, an indoor toilet, a stove for cooking, and a radio, which they used to listen to Garrison Keillor's "Prairie Home Companion" every Sunday night.

The Crams were part of a class of more than a dozen newcomers. They started each day together with two hours of meditation in one of the geodesic domes back by the water tank. They all attended daily courses and shared breakfast and dinner together in the dining-domes. The Crams were in the sixth month of the year-long "novitiate" period, after which they would be allowed to occupy a home they were building on property in the main village. Like all houses built at Ananda, theirs would eventually become community property if they decided to move back into the regular world or if they died.

There was a time when the Crams would have considered such an arrangement ridiculous. Back in 1985, before they knew about Ananda, Jeff was a thirty-seven-year-old psychologist in a large group practice in Seattle, and Sandy, then thirty-four, owned and ran a Montessori nursery school. A former Mormon, Jeff's interest in religion had died when he married and broke away from the Church of Jesus Christ and Latter Day Saints. Sandy had been raised in the Episcopal Church, but she was hardly devout. Still, when their children started to grow up, the Crams decided to get involved in the local Episcopal church, to provide them with a minimal religious background.

"Then one night we were attending a course the priest was giving," said Jeffrey. "We thought it was going to be about what the Episcopal Church stands for. Instead, it was about all sorts of religious trends." The priest, who had attended a month-long retreat at Ananda, gave a positively glowing description of the place. Intrigued, the Crams sought out the small Ananda meditation group that was meeting in their area.

"The first time we went, we thought it was way out," recalled Sandy. "But the people were very nice and we went back." Soon they were swept into what she called "beginners' bliss." Meditation became a part of their daily lives. Sandy grew close to several people in the group. Jeff became enchanted with the drumming and chanting that the group practiced. "I was the kind of person who was all brain," he said. "I just did an awful lot of mental work. The guttural pleasure I felt with the chanting was exciting. I had never felt something like that before."

As he said this, Jeff leaned forward in his chair and began smiling like a man who had sampled forbidden fruit and was reporting that he liked the taste. No doubt he had been the kind of controlled, intellectually oriented man he described. But he must have also felt that something important was missing from his life. The way he described it, he fell very quickly into Kriya Yoga and embraced it wholeheartedly, like an atheist who has had a dramatic conversion.

Obviously Sandy had shared Jeff's immediate enthusiasm because within about a year's time the Crams were fully immersed in the study of Yogananda's work. In August of 1986 they spent one week of their vacation at Ananda. It was then that they met Kryananda for the first time. "We also saw the Ananda eyes for the first time," Jeff said. "People look contented here, and when you talk to them, they don't look away or act as if they have to be somewhere else right away. I felt *satsang*, fellowship."

"I felt it, too," Sandy added. "I would call it a sense of community. I had always sought community. Here I felt it."

The Crams returned to Seattle and spent a couple of years trying to establish a new Ananda community in rural Washington State with other devotees. By 1989, it was clear that their dream was not coming true. That spring Sandy went on a pilgrimage to Los Angeles, where there are several temples founded by Yogananda and his followers. She so enjoyed being among other believers that she telephoned Jeffrey to insist that they move to Ananda to live.

"There I was looking into the eyes of people who shared what I felt. I said, 'I want this all the time.' I called Jeffrey and said, 'We've got to move to Ananda.'"

That summer the Crams spent a month in the "Postulant Program." They were interviewed and allowed to explore the community. "I never meditated as much as I did that month," said Jeff. "Sometime during the second week I just started crying. Big, huge tears would roll down my cheeks when I meditated. It wasn't sadness I felt, but an inner peace, a calmness, a joy that I had never experienced before. I think my body was trying to tell me something: that this was the place."

By the end of the month, the Crams had decided they wanted to live in the village. Those who screened applicants had also determined that the Crams would be accepted. They went back to Seattle, sold the Montessori school, and put their house on the market. Their friends were surprised but not shocked. They knew that Jeffrey and Sandra had been interested in living in Ananda and encouraged them to follow their hearts. Sandy's mother and father were another story.

"My parents thought Ananda was a hippie commune, a Communist front, or another Jonestown," said Sandy. "Really to convince them that we were keeping the option of going back, we decided to lease the house rather than sell it." In the summer of 1990 Jeffrey quit his job. By August 1990, the Crams had put most of their belongings in storage and settled into the little house on the side of the hill.

In Ananda, Jeffrey expanded a side business he had always run, making and selling "biofeedback" equipment. With a fax machine and a telephone, he could run his business and support his family from anywhere. Sandy chose not to work in her first year so she could help her children adjust to the new community. When the girls were in school, she said, she took care of the house and did the shopping and laundry. Those tasks brought her frequently to Master's Store, where she spent many hours.

"In Seattle I lived impersonally," said Sandy. "I went to the same grocery store all the time, but no one there knew me. I would get in my car, drive on the freeway, then come home. Here, the layers of protection and guardedness you need to survive in the world come off. After a few months, I wasn't so wary, so frightened."

"I like two things a lot," added Jeffrey. "One is the renunciate life-style, because it takes a lot of pressure off you. When no one cares who has what house or goes where on vacation, you don't have to compete anymore. There's no greed here. And now I know that I'm not the provider for my family. God's the provider. What a relief. I also like it that the girls can walk safely, anywhere in town. Here, they don't have the heavy influence of TV and video and all that. It's wholesome, safe. I really appreciate that."

Both Sandy and Jeff said that at Ananda they had heightened their search for God. Freed from high-pressure jobs, they had more time for meditation. "There is support for that here, because everyone is seeking God," said Sandy. "Swami recommends three hours of meditation per day. I am not there yet, but I know I want to increase my meditation because I want to go deeper."

In almost every way, said the Crams, they were happier than they had been in the Seattle suburbs. Of course, their daughters missed the friends and pets they had left behind, but even young Shannon said she liked her new home, her little school, and the village. "I like it that I can walk anywhere I want," she said, "and I like the deer." When I asked about what the future held for the family, Shannon whispered in her mother's ear, "God will take care of us."

A strong sense of God's providence has inspired most Americans for centuries, and lives still in the hearts of many. But in this age of science, and reason, and doubt, and materialism, millions do not share in this reassurance. They do not have faith in a benevolent God. They do not have the sense that life is unfolding as it should, according to some sacred plan.

In coming to Ananda, the Crams chose to live by this kind of faith. They sought security in a community where they were told they were "warriors of light." Susan Dermond had sought security as well, moving to a town "where you don't lock your doors and the kids walk to school through apple orchards." Others had, no doubt, found a father figure in Kryananda and a surrogate family among the believers.

Still, with all its security, there was something unsettling about Ananda, as there had been at Maharishi International University in Iowa. The villagers had to give up a great deal—claims to property, careers, old friends—in order to live in a place where there was enormous pressure to behave like everyone else. Personalities seemed muted. Individuality seemed squelched. I didn't see any distinctive works of art created by Ananda villagers. And none of the people I had met had expressed many interesting ideas of their own. They talked, instead, about Yogananda's ideas and Kryananda's ideas. Though he does not live like a millionaire and rule by fiat, as Maharishi does, there's a kind of creeping deification taking place with J. Donald Walters. Considering all this, I couldn't declare Ananda a Jim Jones–style cult. But I left wondering what fears motivated those who escaped to Ananda, if the villagers understood the price they had paid—the risk they were taking—to live in utopia.

# Coda · THE ALL-AMERICAN NEW AGE

*Equality suggests to the Americans the idea of the infinite perfectability of man.*

Alexis de Tocqueville

DEMOCRACY IN AMERICA

FOR MONTHS THE IMAGE OF THE CRAM FAMILY NESTLING in their rustic cottage remained fresh in my mind. It was not the kind of final scene I'd expected to take with me after a one-year journey in an American subculture that promised a New Age of exotic spiritual practices and counterculture values. Curled against her mother in the solitary cabin, the lantern bathing her in soft, natural light, blond-haired Shannon looked like a little girl in another time—a nineteenth-century pioneer or perhaps a Pilgrim child. And her statement—"God will take care of us"—reflected the kind of direct religious faith that was the foundation of early American culture.

Surely, in the midst of famine and cruel weather, the first Americans often comforted themselves with a similar faith in God. Those settlers, who embodied traditional American character, had faced real dangers. In their homelands they had encountered religious persecution, poverty, and social isolation. Like today's New Agers, they were reformers who rejected the traditional customs and beliefs of their time as empty and irrelevant. In the wilderness of the New World they envisioned a Christian utopia. They believed that America would be God's "New Zion," and they sought to create the "shining city on a hill" of John Winthrop's sermon. They were certain God would take care of them.

As outcasts from the mainstream—even if by choice—the Anandans had encountered their own hardships. Though she looked back on it with some nostalgia, Virginia Helin had suffered through blizzards and floods and subzero nights during the four years she lived in a tepee. As a group, the Ananda community had faced larger crises that could have ended their utopian dream. Much of the village had been destroyed by a fire in 1978. It has been continually menaced by financial shortfalls and battles with local zoning authorities. These challenges do not equal the dangers early Americans had met, but they have threatened the survival of the community. As they overcame these obstacles, the villagers turned their victories into stories, legends really, which they cite as proof that God is on their side, that He will take care of them, too. Their story is consistent with a romantic American tradition—from Thoreau's Walden to John Wayne Westerns—that finds heroic renegades creating a new life in the wilderness. In this romantic tradition, the hero rejects the religious order, without rejecting God. Truth is found both in the unspoiled, incorruptible perfection of nature, and within, whether the seeker is a nineteenth-century transcendentalist or a twentieth-century Sedona vortex pilgrim.

In other ways, too, the Ananda villagers, and New Agers in general, parallel the early Americans. Like the Puritans who lived in persecution in Europe, New Agers know that their spiritual view, their religion, is disdained by the dominant culture of their era. Many, like Sandy Cram, even endure the criticism of family members who cannot understand their spiritual commitment. Yet like Sandy, they hold fast to their faith, convinced that it promises spiritual renewal and comfort.

As he discusses the new way of living that Ananda exemplifies, J. Donald Walters often refers to it as a "city of light," a description not so different from Winthrop's "shining city" of the New World. In fact, the title of Walters's book about New Age communities is *Cities of Light*. In it, he often sounds like a pious Pilgrim delivering a sermon. For example, after painting a bleak picture of modern life, a panorama of evil, banality, and despair, he writes that all modern cities will become unlivable because they are based on material, economic values. "What will work," he continues, "is people banding together to live for God, and in adherence to Godly principle."

This way of thinking does not point to the creation of a "new" age. Rather, it implies a return to an idealized version of an old New England village, a community of believers striving to live in relative simplicity, with God not far from their minds. Ananda suggests self-sufficiency, modesty, plainness, and rectitude—the bedrock Protestant values of early America. It may be difficult for those who regard the New Age as flaky, avant garde, or irresponsible to consider, but after my experience at Ananda, I became intrigued by the notion that the New Age is as much a revival of old American values as it is an embrace of the counterculture. Indeed, the villagers seemed to reflect perfectly the Protestant ethic described by the great historian and sociologist Max Weber. They were industrious, Godly, communal, and ascetic—all qualities Weber identified in his analysis of the utilitarian successes of Protestant societies. Ananda has survived, and thrived, because of its old-fashioned work ethic, and a piety that discourages materialism, competitiveness, and jealousies.

As a community, Ananda is the inheritor of another American tradition: utopianism. Settlers brought the dream of "perfect" communities to the New World from Europe. The term was invented and developed by Thomas More, who published *Utopia* in 1517. *Utopia* reflected the monastic ideal of More's time as well as the resurgent interest in democracy. Over the next two centuries a host of European writers suggested refinements, but it was in America that the dream of utopia would be pursued in earnest by nearly every generation. Among the first deliberate attempts to create an ideal community was Ephrata, Pennsylvania, a village founded by German pietists in 1732. Not unlike New Agers, the Ephratans believed they possessed an "inward light" of sacred knowledge. Ephrata collapsed in the 1760s, after the death of its founder. But a more prominent utopian movement of the time, the Shakers, survives to this day. In the nineteenth century serious attempts were made to create utopian communities at Oneida and Seneca, New York, at Fruitlands and Brookfarm in Massachusetts, and elsewhere. These efforts to create the perfect community, and the perfect citizen, reflect the idealism discovered by Tocqueville and revealed in *Democracy in America*. One experiment of that time, the Amana colonies of Iowa, are thriving communities today. More recent utopian experiments include the thousands of communes begun in the 1960s.

On a spiritual level, New Agers are only the latest participants in an unbroken tradition of folk religion. Americans have always shown a strong interest in the unseen world of spirits, magic, ghosts, and supernatural powers. In his 1989 book, *Worlds of Wonder, Days of Enchantment*, historian David Hall shows that even New England's Puritans were fascinated by astrology, prophetic dreams, ritual, and magic. Hall describes a Puritan society in which phantoms, dancing staffs, and witchcraft were commonplace. He notes that in 1684 Harvard College postponed commencement because of an eclipse.

The eighteenth-century Deists, who sought to make religion rational, must also be seen as ancestors of the New Age. Like the New Agers, the Deists were eager to fuse scientific thinking with religion. And like the New Agers, they saw God, or a God-force, in all of creation. Likewise, Emerson's Transcendentalism provided further inspiration for the New Age movement. Emerson rebelled against tradition and in *Nature* asked, "Why should we not have a poetry and philosophy of insight and not of tradition, and a religion by revelation to us, and not the history of theirs?" Modern spiritualism was born in Emerson's time, and it bequeathed to the New Age the practices of channeling and healing, as well as a pseudoscientific approach to metaphysics that is carried on today at Maharishi International University.

Most surprisingly, the New Age can also be seen as the mirror image of the charismatic churches that are part of contemporary conservative Christianity. Though these Christians and New Agers vehemently reject each other, they have much in common. "Right" living, a personal connection to God, an apocalyptic sense of the future, metaphysical healing, spiritual renewal—they share all of these. Both groups focus intently on spiritual renewal. For the Christians this involves the core, religious experience of being "born again" in Jesus. For the New Agers it means finding the spiritual path that will allow them to start life over. In both cases, a sober life-style is usually considered a visible sign of inner spiritual grace. For this reason Ananda is as dry and drug-free as any Christian family campground. And like conservative Christians, most New Agers believe that every person should have a direct, personal relationship with God. They might visit a channel, guru, or shaman in the way that a Christian consults with a pastor or speaks in tongues. But in the end, most New Agers have a solitary spiritual practice which they control and direct, in order to heal their bodies, their minds, and their souls.

This interest in healing is shared by the 20 to 30 million Americans who are called Charismatic or Pentecostal. Pentecostal Christians have a profound faith in everyday miracles. They hold regular conversations with Christ, they believe in communication from the spirit world, they expect God to bring them wealth, and they count on the Holy Spirit to heal everything from cancer to the common cold. Charismatics even have their own version of the laws of karma, believing that a sinful life brings the wrath of God through disease, while repentance and right-living can bring a miracle cure. Like New Agers, they may use modern medicine, but they are mindful of its limitations. And they often equate good health and prosperity with high spiritual development. In Sedona, John Paul Weber argued that spiritual practice and medical practice went hand in hand. Before it closed for financial reasons, doctors and nurses at Oral Roberts's City of Faith Hospital prayed with their patients before operating on them.

The New Age and Christian America are also connected by their fascination with apocalyptic prophecy. Many in the New Age believe that a spiritual battle between good and evil will soon erupt on Earth with catastrophic results. Marlene Myhre had mentioned this as we sat together on the porch of the New Age center in Sedona, watching the white cottonwood spores float on the evening breeze. I had heard it, too, at MIU, and on my final excursion in the movement, at Ananda. In all of these places, New Agers told me that a cataclysm would soon destroy nearly all of the Earth. It would be followed by the "New Age" of idyllic peace and prosperity. The destruction is necessary to cleanse and preserve a sinful planet. The utopia that would follow would be assured by the high spiritual development of those who survived and the benevolence of God.

These beliefs mimic the Biblically based apocalyptic scenario predicted by countless conservative Christian preachers and subscribed to by millions of their followers. In fact, in early 1991 TV preacher Pat Robertson, a stalwart leader of conservative Christian America, said that the war in the Persian Gulf marked the fulfillment of the Armageddon prophecies in the Scriptures. "We are moving into the days of prophecy," Robertson said on TV as the war was heating up. "We're not that far away, it seems to me. Our nation and our world is running pell-mell into chaos." On another broadcast Robertson simply declared, "The world is going to explode."

Of course, any comparison of New Age belief and conservative Christianity would draw heated objections from both sides. For their part, New Agers consider conservative Christianity to be authoritarian, dogmatic, stultifying, and, in the end, spiritually damaging. They consider orthodox Western faiths useful only as historical references or sources of certain general mystical and philosophical ideas. On the other side, conservative Christians attack New Agers as atheistic, occultist, evil. They would consider TM and Ananda to be cults, and the followers of Lazaris and Louise Hay as deluded or deliberate victims of the devil. Exposés on the New Age fill the shelves of Christian bookstores, and cult "deprogrammers" make a good living "rescuing" the children of devout Christian families from New Age groups. Even the Pope has criticized New Agers, warning against their many forms of meditation.

For the most part, the two groups—New Agers and conservative Christians—fight each other like distant armies. They lob criticisms like mortar shells, firing them from a safe distance and avoiding direct conflict. The only face-to-face confrontation I even heard of took place in Sedona a few weeks before I visited. Local Christian pastors had sponsored a debate between a spokesman for the New Age community and a born-again layperson who crusaded against the New Age. When I arrived, both sides were claiming victory and it was impossible to tell what had taken place. But church leaders had been so chastened by what they learned that they had organized a campaign to rescue the souls of the New Agers who accounted for perhaps half the city's population.

"We view people in the New Age as prisoners of war in Satan's camp," explained Rob Kirkpatrick, an assistant pastor I met at Sedona Community Church. A young Oklahoman who wore cowboy boots to Sunday service, Kirkpatrick was certain about his assessment of the New Age. "The devil is at work in that movement," he said, and to prove it, he quoted a passage from Genesis: "The devil said to Eve, 'You are not going to die and you shall be as God.'

That's the same as the New Age message. I'd like to go with it, I have to admit. It's very appealing. But it's false. False, but powerful," added Kirkpatrick. "I have seen evidence of physical healings performed by New Agers, healings of backaches and other things. But that's Satan masquerading as an angel. I used to laugh at the New Age, but miracles like that are part of Satan's deception. The healings are happening, but they are not of the Lord."

To fight the New Agers, Kirkpatrick and other Sedona pastors offer seminars on the purported evils of the movement and counseling for the spiritually troubled. They also monitor the local schools, hoping to root out New Age influences. This is a difficult job, Kirkpatrick said, "because it's everywhere and it's very subtle." New Age themes can be found in pop music, children's stories, even in computer games that feature wizards and dragons. "I didn't believe the New Age was big and real and serious until I got involved," Kirkpatrick told me. "Now I think it's bigger than most people know."

After a one-year survey of the New Age movement, I couldn't be certain of its size. Though various demographers and sociologists estimate that the movement includes 20 million devotees, it remains amorphous, splintered, leaderless. There is even evidence that the term "New Age" is falling out of use. The label has been used derisively by critics, in the same way that "fundamentalist" was used by opponents of conservative Christians to connote fanaticism. Because of this, many in the movement have begun to avoid the term, preferring instead to talk of "new consciousness" or "a spiritual renewal."

But if the language of the New Age movement is changing, there was no evidence to suggest that its ideas, practices, and philosophies are any less appealing. To the contrary, New Age ideas seem to be leeching into the larger society, where they are being adopted by people who would never identify themselves as part of the movement.

The most light-hearted examples of this could be found

in the television industry, where so-called documentaries on the occult and psychic phenomena enjoy increasing support from networks and local stations. The 1990 television series "Twin Peaks," for example, featured an FBI agent protagonist who spouted Eastern philosophy and had countless paranormal experiences in his efforts to solve a series of murders. In a series called "Beauty and the Beast" two different heroes used psychic powers to solve and prevent crimes. Visualization and support groups were so much a part of the mainstream culture that when a character on the popular TV show "Thirtysomething" was diagnosed with cancer, she soon began wearing a crystal and using meditations. Even "Saturday Night Live" jumped on the bandwagon with parodies of affirmation teachers and twelve-step groups.

More important evidence of New Age influence could be found in the real-life medical world. During the roughly twenty-year lifetime of the New Age, mainstream medicine has moved from an outright rejection of the body-mind connection to a cautious acceptance. A substantial amount of research had been done to support the notion that people in the best state of mental health suffer fewer illnesses and recover from disease more quickly. (The journal article on "postponement of death" cited by Bernie Siegel comes to mind.) The findings of such studies are so persuasive that hospitals in every part of the country now steer cancer patients and others toward therapists and support groups that use New Age–style meditation and visualization techniques. In Texas, TM-style relaxation techniques are used to help asthma patients. In Cleveland, patients at Children's Hospital are taught to use visualization and biofeedback to help their bodies heal. In Boston, a health maintenance organization prescribes "wellness" courses for its healthy members, and claims it saves each one hundreds of dollars in medical bills each year.

New Age influence can also be seen in the tenor of relationships between health professionals—doctors, nurses, therapists—and patients. Books by Bernie Siegel, Norman Cousins, and others have ushered in an era of new respect for individual patients. People are more aggressive in seeking information and taking control of their treatment today. In turn, many doctors have became more sensitive to the overall well-being of their patients. At the University of Massachusetts, medical students in a course titled "Death, Dying, and Dissection" are taught to consider the emotional life of surgical patients. At a California medical school, all students are admitted to the hospital for a day, to experience the medical bureaucracy as a patient. While the change in doctor-patient relations would be difficult to quantify, it is fair to suggest that today's patients are far more active on their own behalf and doctors are more responsive to the "holistic" needs of body, mind, and spirit.

The influence of the New Age can also be seen in the environmental movement. Environmentalism is practically a national religion today, and the language of this faith is infused with New Age concepts. Believers seek to "heal the Earth" and develop an environmental "consciousness." Those who campaign against pollution do so with the spirit of religious crusaders. Part and parcel of the environmental movement is a surge of interest in vegetarianism, natural foods, and animal rights, all part of the New Age.

Even American business has been affected by the New Age. Many of today's popular management consultants advise companies to restructure their organizations to allow for group decision-making and improved communication. The Owens-Corning Corporation has adopted these ideas, as has Johnson and Johnson. Peter Bloch, consultant to many Fortune 500 firms, predicts that "community" will be the catchphrase of the Nineties in business management. Ben and Jerry remain the subject of intense interest in the business press, and big advertisers promote everything from cars to cosmetics for "a New Age."

But by far the most remarkable evidence of the impact of the New Age can be seen in certain segments of organized

Christianity. Liberal Catholics, Episcopalians, and others are cautiously embracing New Age ideas about the feminine God, healing, and the sanctity of the environment. Reverend Jim, the Mennonite I met at the Earth First! protest, was the clearest example of how New Age spiritual ideas are accepted and modified for use by Christians. But I also saw this process at work at St. Margaret's, a small Episcopal church I visited in Washington, D.C., in early 1990. The church is led by a woman priest who sometimes refers to God as "she" and who often includes in her sermons a pitch for environmentalism. When I visited, a small group of parishioners had just finished a study of M. Scott Peck's *The Road Less Traveled*. Peck quotes the Bible, but he also argues that psychic phenomena are real and that the marriage of science and religion envisioned by Maharishi and Yogananda is inevitable. The Washington church is also home to many New Age–style support groups, including various twelve-step programs, that use spiritual practices to treat addictions and compulsions.

With this evidence of New Age influence in mainstream society, the movement must be seen as neither radically new nor counterculture. It is part of the culture. What is useful in the New Age—meditation, environmentalism, the mind-body connection, humane business practices, spirituality—is being swallowed up by the larger society. What is not useful—UFOs, channels, crystals—remains on the fringe. This process of assimilation and rejection is quite obvious and specific. It also points to the larger social ferment that produced the New Age movement and permitted it to grow and flower. The New Age is part of a long-term historic process in which Americans have continually revised the religious order, assimilating ideas and attitudes from groups once considered radical or even occult. The Transcendentalists, the Mormons, the Christian Scientists, and the Jehovah's Witnesses, to name a few, have added to the national religious consciousness even as they have existed on the social fringe. Such is the case with the New Age movement.

In *New Age Almanac*, scholar J. Gordon Melton traces the term "New Age" to counterculture groups that arose in the late 1800s. A number of mystics, preachers, and teachers made national speaking tours then, offering exotic new spiritual ideas. Among the more influential were Helena Petronova Blavatsky and Henry Olcutt, founders of Theosophy, a mystical practice that introduced Hinduism to much of America and Europe. Melton credits the Theosophical Society with popularizing many of the ideas now central to the New Age, including channeling, reincarnation, astrology, and yoga.

"Madame" Blavatsky was obviously influenced by earlier mystical movements, such as Swedenborgianism, and by her travels and studies in India. Inevitably an Indian guru, Swami Vivekananda, came to the United States in 1894 to offer direct, authentic teaching. He was greeted warmly, and his Vedanta Society quickly spread to most major cities. During this period others made efforts to connect science and religion, to reconcile the apparent contradictions of faith and reason. The turn-of-the-century also saw the development of chiropractic, osteopathy, and other forms of alternative medicine.

The various disciplines that would one day be known as the New Age movement continued to develop through the twentieth century. Foundations and institutes were created to promote everything from astrology and paganism to Hatha Yoga and vegetarianism. Edgar Cayce popularized channeling in the 1930s. UFOs were first described in the 1940s. The 1950s saw earnest research into psychic phenomenon and the beginnings of the holistic health movement. But it was not until the 1960s that interest in the counterculture became widespread and that the New Age could be discerned as a substantial movement.

No thinking adult has escaped exposure to the many theories about the origins of the Sixties turmoil and its legacy. We all know that the Vietnam War, a sexual revolution created by the Pill, Cold War anxiety, and the astounding pace of technological change combined to create widespread unrest and dissatisfaction among the young and the old. Writers, filmmakers, politicians, and others challenged the assumption that 1950s American had, indeed, defined the nation and its ideals. What followed were countless challenges to authority and social norms. If any one catchphrase captured the mood of these challenges, it was probably the oft-shouted, "Up the establishment."

Though it has often been left out of the various studies of the times, religion was profoundly affected by the turmoil of the Sixties. Traditional religion was widely rejected by the educated young because it was part of the "establishment." But the churches also suffered because such a large proportion of the nation's young—indeed the largest proportion in history—had access to higher education. In this century, at least, colleges and universities have been places where religious orthodoxy is challenged and young people's faith is eroded. As millions of young people entered college, many rejected the old faith and experiment with the New Age.

Experiment was possible because of the tradition of spiritual seeking in American culture, and because the failures of traditional religion were becoming starkly apparent. The churches had been part of the social structure that discriminated against minorities. Traditional religion enforced a code of behavior that was seen as outdated and morally corrupt, and it ensured the power of the white, male, establishment elite. Finally, traditional religion continued to suffer the long-term effects of its battles with both science and materialism. Awash in war-generated wealth and producing one technological marvel after another, America came to have a hollow kind of faith in the power of the economy. Preachers were hard-pressed to win the public's attention. Critics would argue, however, that churches failed to provide the moral leadership the country needed. Except for black preachers in the civil rights movement, the churches seemed to shrink from relevance in the din of the 1960s. In fact, the most profound theological development in 1960s

America was the rise of "Death of God" theology, which insisted that a traditional view of God no longer worked, and yet at the same time offered no alternative. The Death-of-God movement reached its conclusions after finding that modern people need real proof to support a belief in God, and that the Holocaust eliminated any notion that a benevolent deity exists. The Holocaust remains, for many, the ultimate challenge to the God of Judeo-Christian tradition.

Remarkably, none of this had a serious effect on superficial measures of religious life in America. Churchgoing apparently remains at a relatively constant rate, with about half the nation attending regularly, but a close examination of the statistics show a steep decline in church attendance among Roman Catholics and "mainline" Protestants. These more liberal denominations had served the American upper classes, the wealthy, and the intellectual elite. It was their college-age children, and many young Catholics and Jews, who abandoned the churches in the 1960s. These same groups—white, middle-class liberals—now make up the ranks of the New Age. This class distinction is important because it shows that economic security, exposure to new ideas, and a loosening of mainstream religion's hold all eased the seekers into the New Age. It is no accident that in my hundreds of contacts with the movement, I never encountered a New Ager who had left a black Baptist church or a Bible Belt country congregation. The New Age is for the more disaffected, the searching American hoping to recover a thread of belief.

By embracing the New Age, those who rejected mainstream religion in the Sixties proved that social turmoil, science, and higher education do not extinguish spiritual needs and religious impulses. In fact, one could argue that as modern life becomes more technological and more isolating, the need for a spiritual life deepens. Diseases such as AIDS, which defy medical science, force us to find philosophical, spiritual, or religious means for making sense of life. The men with AIDS who talked to me in the kitchen

of Hernandez House in Los Angeles described this phenomenon. They felt alienated from, or rejected by, mainstream religion. Nevertheless, they longed for the spiritual
experiences of deep meditation and relied on the comfort,
community, and hope provided by the New Age. They were
new American mystics who, like the charismatic Christians,
believed in supernatural healing, ongoing divine revelation,
and personal encounters with God.

The rank-and-file participants in the New Age movement
have the same basic human needs as the men with AIDS.
They understand what Thomas Merton meant when he
wrote, "Our real journey in life is interior." They want to
believe in a god, a higher power, or life-force. They want
to be part of a community. They want to participate in
rituals and be comforted by a spiritual healer. These basic
desires are evident everywhere in the New Age, and they
are proof that even in a highly intellectual, industrialized
society, spiritual hunger is essential to human experience.
They also confirm that the New Age is part of a larger
process, a certain segment of society's coming to terms with
the loss of traditional, religious certainty. Despite the erosion of dogma, doctrine, and structure, humankind must
still believe. As Wallace Stevens wrote, "We believe without
belief, beyond belief."

The search for new ways to believe is confirmed by a
sweeping study of American religious life done by sociologists Wade Clark Roof and William McKinney at the close
of the 1980s. Roof and McKinney found a 155 percent
increase among Americans who are no longer affiliated with
mainstream religion. This was by far the largest shift in
religious views they recorded, and it involved, for the most
part, adults in the twenty-five-to-fifty-five-year-old age
group who were among the nation's most educated and
moneyed citizens. Clark and Roof found that few of these
unchurched Americans were atheists. Instead, many held
fast to belief in the supernatural and the mystical. They
were more open to alternative life-styles and more inter-

ested in personal growth. In short, they seemed to be New Agers.

The New Age served the spiritual needs of millions of Americans who could no longer find a home in traditional religion but still yearned to believe. It gained momentum in the 1980s because the children of the 1960s were growing middle-aged, reaching the time in life when religion becomes a comfort. Certainly this is what Elizabeth Lesser of the Omega Institute was suggesting on the day we met. She had said that the postwar baby-boomers were, en masse, discovering their mortality. Those who were among the "unaffiliateds" in Roof and Clark's study didn't have traditional religion to fall back on for comfort, so they were making up their own. This process became a movement—the New Age movement—because there were so many baby-boomers engaged in this religious searching.

The many meetings and seminars of New Agers could be seen as services or rituals for these seekers and experimenters. Certainly the Bernie Siegel lecture I attended at the Whole Life Expo, with its spiritual-style singing, stories of healing, and inspirational tone, had the quality of a religious service. For that matter, so did the M. Scott Peck seminar, which included music, stories, and the participation of the congregation. At these events and many others, New Agers used many of the methods of regular religion: music, story, confession, sermons, even stagecraft. These presentations were intended to move the individual, to inspire, sustain, educate, and comfort. The New Age may be the free-lance religion, but it serves many traditional purposes and meets the basic spiritual needs of millions who believe they are outside the religious mainstream.

The New Age fits into the flow of American religious history more neatly than its Eastern mystical trappings and its name—New Age—would suggest. Historian Catherine Albanese places it squarely in the flow of "nature religion," a kind of secondary belief system that has always influenced Americans spiritually. Other academics have observed that the New Age is part of the constant, regular cycle of spiritual revival that marks American history. This recurring process of reexamination and recommitment to religion is one of the ways that the American people adapt to new social circumstances and make the romantic tradition of spiritual pioneering their own. University of Chicago scholar Martin Marty has referred to an American "countercovenant," a moral compact that calls a certain segment of society to ask the philosophical and spiritual questions that balance the high-achieving, manifest-destiny aspects of the American character. The keepers of this countercovenant "urge that we keep contracts only with nature, produce only what harmonizes with it, achieve without grim competition, and live with a natural and human universe."

Today's New Agers are the modern-day keepers of this "countercovenant," which was handed down to them by the Quakers and the Transcendentalists and the "social gospel" reformers of the turn of the century. Their movement has become popular because their message is needed to help many resolve their sense of identity. Today American economic and political supremacy are fading and with it goes the proof that we are God's special people. We may still fight many of the world's battles, as the Gulf war showed, but now we must ask the Arabs, the Japanese, and the Germans to pay for it. Likewise, simple self-reliance won't help us solve world hunger or a global environmental crisis. Those problems require different spiritual assumptions, different national beliefs.

In the tradition of American religion, millions have begun searching for new ways of thinking about themselves, their country, the Earth, God. At this point, the New Age is part of this bigger, stumbling attempt to find new beliefs to fit our times. In the late 1980s, this process was chaotic and undisciplined. "If anything, there's a kind of runaway, almost over-belief," observed Harvard theologian Harvey Cox. "We're getting to the point where people will believe anything." A brief study of the Maharishi's Unified Field

Theory, or a visit to Sedona's vortexes, would prove Cox's point. But the refinement of the New Age continues. And there are many in the movement—Bernie Siegel, Robert Bly, Sally Fisher, John Lee, Ben and Jerry, and countless others—who struggle to separate sense from nonsense.

What will be discovered at the end of this search for belief? William McLoughlin, a historian of religion at Brown University, suggests that this process will yield a new definition of God. Tomorrow's God will be more closely linked with nature, which will inspire us to make the expensive and difficult choices to ease the eco-crisis, he says. As we save the Earth, we will be saving God. Tomorrow's God may also be more feminine, to instill a sense of bounty and regeneration in our sense of God. Similarly, African, Asian, and Latin American spiritual notions will have more currency as our country becomes more diverse.

"Whatever we come up with, it will also draw heavily on our basic traditions," McLoughlin told me in an interview. "It may be a combination that includes aspects of the social gospel, a faith in miracles, and the concept of stewardship of the Earth. By the time it's over, the churches, the medical establishment, the law, education, all our institutions will be affected, as they were by previous awakenings."

I began my journey in the New Age as an outsider who had to struggle at times to remain open and receptive. Sometimes I failed. High atop a butte in Sedona, I felt silly pursuing the vortex energy. Inside the Philadelphia Holiday Inn, I felt psychologically manipulated as Lazaris led me on meditative adventures. And at MIU I was appalled by the authoritarian atmosphere.

These experiences confirmed for me the prevailing criticism of some aspects of the New Age movement as shallow, superstitious, cultish, and undisciplined. In too many cases, New Agers follow a set of beliefs that conveniently correspond to their needs and wishes. They practice a soothing, even hypnotic free-lance religion that isolates them from the rest of society and demands very little in the way of service, compassion, or sacrifice. For these devotees, the New Age is a spiritual therapy that makes them feel good temporarily, but does little to advance their intellectual or spiritual development—nor does it help feed hungry babies. The language of the New Age lacks the depth and the social conscience of Christianity and Judaism. Though efforts have been made to appropriate myths from other religions, the New Age has no distinct body of stories—like those in the Bible—that can be used to teach, inspire, enlighten, and unite. The stories I heard in my travels in the New Age were mostly the personal tales of individual seekers. Most lacked a transcendent theme or message. Few contained any moral or lesson that could be related to anything other than self-interests. Nowhere in my tour of the New Age did I see evidence of a serious commitment to service to the community at large. Perhaps this is because the New Age offers few models for this kind of commitment, few stories to explain why it is important.

But if the New Age has often failed to provide real answers to human problems, it has succeeded in raising a host of important questions. In this subculture I encountered earnest, intelligent people who were not satisfied with the alienated, sanitized, disconnected way of life endured by so many modern Americans. They longed for community, healing, a sense of the sacred. As I discovered, so did I.

While I was not drawn to the mystical experiences of meditation and dizzying sweat lodge rituals, I was moved by many of the other rites, activities, and practices of the New Age. With Irene Siegel, the suburban shaman, I felt the primal excitement produced by something as simple as drumming and a fire ceremony. Among the neo-pagans in the Sierras, I came to a deeper appreciation of nature's sacredness and the responsibility of stewardship. I was impressed by the sensuality of pagan ritual, especially when contrasted with highly intellectualized mainstream religion. I felt the same among the mystic baseball players. They found in their games a way to be more humanly alive. They overcame fear, mastered competitiveness, reveled in movement. They appropriated an American icon, turning it into a vehicle for healing.

Healing, as I learned in my New Age excursions, means more than physical recovery. Considered in a narrow way, many of the New Age healers are charlatans, because they cannot cure disease. They pose a real danger to the gullible and the innocent. But others, such as Sally Fisher and Sandy Scott, earnestly try to heal the spirits of New Age believers. Here, despite their mistakes and failings, they are attempting important, meaningful work. Critically ill people need, most of all, a healing of the heart, a reconciliation with themselves, their families, their friends. Those in the New Age who try to help this process sometimes work miracles.

With their constant references to healing, the New Agers also showed me that every person has wounds that must be attended. John Lee, the men's movement leader who spoke at the Whole Life Expo, was describing the universal losses suffered by American men. He was calling us to recognize the emotional toll exacted by a society that demands men to be fearless, competitive, stoic, and lonely. He also suggested ways that men can free themselves to live a life that is more open, honest, and loving. I, too, have struggled with the John Wayne model of maleness, and I have often been isolated by my tendency to "go it alone." If the New Age teaches trust, cooperation, and compassion, it teaches valuable lessons.

All of the major New Age interests—healing, community, mysticism, ritual, moral action, the search for the sacred— came together in the village life at Ananda. Here was a community where problems and achievements were shared and citizens were directly involved in civic activities such as the education of the young and the development of roads or playgrounds. None of the negative stereotypes associated with back-to-the-Earth, hippie culture remained at Ananda.

Instead I found responsible adults trying to lead reasonable
lives. If Kryananda and his closest disciples exercised some
power and authority in the village, it was no more than that
wielded by the mayor and the village council in any other
small community.

I found the Ananda way of life appealing. I, too, am
nostalgic for the kind of simple, small-town way of life
many Americans associate with a golden past. I have, perhaps, more reason to feel that longing because I was born
and raised in a village of eight hundred on an island off
the New England coast where some families have lived since
the seventeenth century. As a child I breathed in the Protestant ethic along with the salt air. With its constrictions and
severity, this way of looking at life also gave me an abiding
respect for the value of work, a healthy resistance to materialism, and an interest in the common good. The Ananda
villagers lived by these same values.

In the end I could not accept Yogananda as my master
and immerse myself in the mystical pursuit of God. Ananda
was too disconnected from the delights and problems of the
wider world. But I did take some inspiration from Ananda
and many other New Age sources. The men with AIDS
and those who served them demonstrated the value of each
waking moment and the power of love in the face of tragedy. A number of people showed me the value of meditation, even if it is simply the practice of quieting the mind.
I found new joy in play at the Omega Institute, and I developed a deeper sense of concern about the environment with
the Earth First! activists. Even the ice cream makers at Ben
and Jerry's taught me something: that capitalism can be
made more humane and still retain its dynamism.

Much like a middle-aged surgeon who has slowly come
to respect the body-mind connection, I slowly came to respect some of the ideas, methods, and people of the New
Age. The crystals and channels are part of the movement,
just as angels and demons remain part of Christianity. But
they do not make up the substance of the New Age any

more than the spirit world comprises what is important and true about the Church. Religion has true value when it enriches individual and community life, when it makes sense of suffering and makes death bearable, even meaningful. When I consider whether the New Age ever meets this test, I think of the men with AIDS, whom I met in Los Angeles. I am reminded, especially, of Billy Caine-Gonzales, who through the New Age has come to see himself as an instrument of God. Sometimes, at least, the New Age can make us instruments of the spirit.

# INDEX